HISTORIC ARKANSAS

★ ★

By

John L. Ferguson

J. H. Atkinson

Arkansas History Commission
Little Rock, Arkansas
1966

Library of Congress Catalogue Card Number 67-63022

Printed in the United States of America

FOREWORD

We sometimes have a tendency to look at history as something that only happened a long time ago. Remember, the men and women in this and any other history book did not realize that they were making history when they were going about their business, and in that way were creating a part of what we call history. With hallowed tones, we speak of the men and women in the early days of this country as the only ones who helped build our heritage. The pioneers of covered wagon days, the river boatmen and trappers, even earlier peoples such as Indians, Spaniards and Frenchmen, left some culture and craft that touches our lives today. Yet the story of history is a continuous one. Each of us is helping to write the next chapter of this continuous history. We all have an obligation to do our share in first learning, then working to help write the next and succeeding chronicles of this continuous process. A hundred years from now another generation will find that we have left tracks in the sands of life; will our deeds be worth recording so others later may know that we have built a better place for man?

Winston G. Chandler, Chairman
Arkansas History Commission

ABOUT THE AUTHORS

JOHN L. FERGUSON

was born near Nashville, Arkansas in 1926. His elementary and secondary education was in the public schools of York's Chapel and Nashville. He received the Bachelor of Arts degree from Henderson State Teachers College in 1950, the Master of Arts degree from the University of Arkansas in 1952, and the degree of Doctor of Philosophy from Tulane University, New Orleans, in 1960.

Dr. Ferguson has taught history and political science at Central College, Conway, Arkansas; at Little Rock University; and at Arkansas Polytechnic College, Russellville. Since 1960 he has been State Historian and Executive Secretary of the Arkansas History Commission, Little Rock. He has edited two books, *Arkansas and the Civil War* and *Arkansas Lives: The Opportunity Land Who's Who.*

J. H. ATKINSON

was born in Columbia County, Arkansas in 1888. He attended rural grade and high schools in that area, was graduated from the University of Arkansas with the Bachelor of Arts degree, and earned the Master of Arts degree at the University of Chicago. He taught and served as an administrator at several schools in Arkansas before becoming head of the history department at Little Rock Senior High School in 1923. He was Chairman of the Department of History and Economics at Little Rock Junior College (now Little Rock University) from 1927 until his retirement in 1957, after fifty consecutive years of teaching.

Mr. Atkinson is a founder and past president of both the Arkansas Historical Association and the Pulaski County Historical Society. He is a former member and chairman of the Arkansas History Commission. Since 1958 he has been editor of the *Pulaski County Historical Review.*

INTRODUCTION

The General Assemblies of 1963 and 1965 authorized the Arkansas History Commission to prepare and publish a textbook of Arkansas history suitable for use in the eighth, ninth, and tenth grades. The resulting product, which is here presented to the teachers and students of the schools of this state, is not a revision of older textbooks. It is a new work throughout, researched whenever possible from original sources, and entirely the work of the authors.

The book has been designed to give to the student a wealth of information about Arkansas, and to arouse in him a deeper attachment to the state and a more abiding interest in its future. To this end, many illustrations, maps and study aids have been included and an effort has been made to tell a good story.

The teacher, before beginning to teach the course should become thoroughly acquainted with the text. He should note the ten units, the chapter divisions of each unit, the study aids, the maps and the illustrations. He should also search his school library and his public library for material to which he can refer his students. A list of useful books may be found near the end of this volume. For statistical data, such as lists of officials with their terms of service, the teacher should consult the *Historical Report of the Secretary of State 1958*, made available to all schools free of charge, or the current edition of the *Arkansas Almanac*.

To know history one must know geography. Constant reference to an adequate map of the state is necessary. A large map should be provided for classroom use, and each student should be required to have a map of his own. Smaller maps can be secured free of charge from most service stations or from the Arkansas Publicity and Parks Commission at the state capitol in Little Rock.

For the convenience of the teacher, each chapter is designed to be the basis of one assignment. With supplementary material, it may be used for one or more class periods. How fully the topic is developed will depend on the material at hand, the class interest and the aims of the teacher. Student participation in the form of reports, comments and discussion should be encouraged.

It is suggested that the teacher use the study aids with each chapter, especially those headed "To test your reading." He may wish to omit some helps and use others of his own making. Reports and special assignments relating to the local community should be used whenever possible, since these help to increase student interest. A brief introduction at the beginning of each unit and a brief summary at the close, together with an occasional review of the material already covered, will help to give unity and continuity to the course.

Active members of the Arkansas History Commission while this work was in preparation included Mr. Winston G. Chandler, Chairman; Mr. Charles Martin, Vice-Chairman; Dr. Robert E. L. Bearden, Mr. J. L. Erwin, Mr. Gean P. Houston and Mr. J. L. Shaver. The Commission has accorded us the widest possible freedom and the most cordial cooperation. Mrs. Guy E. Williams, who first suggested that this project be undertaken, has offered frequent encouragement. We are indebted to Dr. Arch W. Ford, State Commissioner of Education, and to members of his staff for several valuable suggestions. Dr. J. E. Griner assisted with some of the preliminary planning. Mrs. Pearl Rinehart typed the manuscript, Mrs. Lois E. Jones prepared the index, and Mrs. Clare Speer helped with arrangement and other details. To the many other persons who have made helpful suggestions or have expressed their interest in other ways, we offer our thanks.

John L. Ferguson

J. H. Atkinson

ACKNOWLEDGMENTS

We are indebted to the following for permission to use photographs (numbers refer to pages):

Arkansas College—356.

Arkansas Gazette—18, 60, 79 (bottom), 130 (top), 135, 169, 218 (top), 312, 332, 349, 353 (top), 354 (top).

Arkansas Library Commission—352 (bottom), 353 (bottom).

Arkansas Power and Light Company—248 (top).

Arkansas Publicity and Parks Commission—12, 43, 46, 53 (bottom), 97 (bottom), 106, 132 (bottom), 138, 196 (bottom), 205, 210 (bottom), 245 (bottom), 260, 298 (bottom), 307 (bottom), 310, 311, 313, 315, 317, 337 (bottom), 338, 352 (top).

J. H. Atkinson—279, 285 (top).

Conway Chamber of Commerce—354 (bottom).

I. Wilmer Counts—322, 323, 324, 325, 326.

Paul Faris—47, 48, 51 (top), 97 (top), 195, 196 (top), 240, 278.

Mrs. Clarence W. Ferguson—194 (bottom), 226 (bottom), 269, 285 (bottom).

Mrs. Dewey Ferguson—94.

Mrs. Nancy J. Hall—330, 331, 333 (top), 339, 340.

Mrs. Lady Elizabeth Luker—175 (bottom).

David Pile—98.

Pine Bluff Public Library—181 (bottom), 188, 243, 253.

Winthrop Rockefeller—333 (bottom).

Sparks and Blackwood, Architects—348.

University of Arkansas Museum—3, 5.

Mrs. W. A. G. Woodward—87 (bottom).

All other photographs, illustrations, and maps are from the files of the Arkansas History Commission.

The state capitol, seat of Arkansas government since 1911.

The Old State House in Little Rock, the state capitol from 1836 until 1911.

Apple trees in bloom near Rogers. The General Assembly of 1901 chose the apple blossom as the state flower.

The state flag, adopted in 1913, was designed by Miss Willie K. Hocker of Wabbaseka.

The Medical Center of the University of Arkansas, Little Rock.

The Indian monument at Caddo Gap, erected in 1937, marks the farthest westward point believed to have been reached by DeSoto and his men.

Monument at Helena to Jacques Marquette, French priest-explorer who visited the Arkansas region in 1673.

The first Fort Smith was established in 1817 on a rocky bluff at Belle Point, where the Poteau River flows into the Arkansas.

Log house at Norfork, built by Jacob Wolf about the year 1825. It was used as a courthouse and post office as well as a residence.

"The Arkansas Traveler," a reproduction of the famous painting by Edward Payson Washburn. From 1949 until 1963 the tune of "The Arkansas Traveler" was the state song. "Arkansas," by Mrs. Eva Ware Barnett, is now (1966) the official song, as it was from 1917 until 1949.

The Territorial Restoration, opened in 1941, is a group of buildings in downtown Little Rock which date back to the pioneer period of Arkansas history.

Elkhorn Tavern on the battlefield of Pea Ridge. This building is a reconstruction of the original tavern which was destroyed during the Civil War period.

Entrance to Prairie Grove Battlefield Park. The tall structure in the center background is a stone chimney which was placed in the park in 1956.

Mechanical cotton picker in action. In agriculture as well as in industry, machines now do the work of many men.

Beef cattle now graze on many fields once planted to cotton and corn.

Logging trucks move in a steady stream from the great pine forests of southern Arkansas. In 1939 the General Assembly designated the pine as the official state tree.

The Markham Street interchange, a section of Interstate Highway 30, leads to downtown Little Rock.

Old Main at the University of Arkansas in Fayetteville.

Bridge across Beaver Reservoir east of Rogers.

A class at the Arkansas Arts Center, Little Rock, 1964.

An oil refinery at El Dorado.

CONTENTS

Chapter

MAPS

Unit One

Earliest Arkansas

The Chapters

1. Prehistoric Arkansas

2. The First Europeans

3. French Arkansas, 1673-1762

4. Spanish Arkansas, 1762-1803

DID YOU EVER WONDER how long people have been living in the region that is now Arkansas? That is a question that no one can answer, but from the evidence left in mounds, bluffs, pottery and stone implements, we know that it has been a long time. The ancestors of the Indians, as we know them, were first to inhabit the region.

After the discovery of America in 1492, Europeans became anxious to explore the interior. Numerous expeditions were fitted out for this purpose. One of these, under the leadership of Hernando de Soto, arrived on the eastern bank of the Mississippi River in May, 1541. The group, consisting of some 400 men, crossed over and spent about a year exploring much of the land now included in our state. They were from Spain and were the first Europeans to arrive.

A hundred and thirty-two years passed before other Europeans came. Then, beginning in 1673, the French, for the next ninety years, explored and settled the lower Mississippi Valley, including the region that is now Arkansas. They founded New Orleans, Biloxi, Natchez, Arkansas Post and other settlements. In 1762 they transferred to Spain the lands west of the Mississippi River. Thus the land now included in Arkansas came to be under the control of Spain from that time until it became a part of the United States. This first unit tells the story from the earliest time to the year 1803.

1   Prehistoric Arkansas

The recorded history of Arkansas began with the arrival of the Spanish explorer De Soto in 1541. But the land of Arkansas has existed for uncounted ages, and people have lived and died on this land for thousands of years. This chapter outlines the story of Arkansas in the shadowy centuries before history began.

Traces of early man. The prehistoric period of Arkansas reaches far back into the past—just how far no one knows. The written history begins in the spring of 1541 when De Soto and his men crossed the Mississippi River into Arkansas. Three men who were with De Soto left brief accounts, and from these we can learn something about the people here at that time. The earlier story must be learned from other sources.

Many people lived in Arkansas when De Soto arrived. No one knows exactly how long they had been living here, or where they came from originally. Those who have studied the question believe that they were descended from ancestors who crossed into Alaska from Asia in remote times. Over a long period they spread throughout North and South America and the neighboring islands.

The story of the early inhabitants of Arkansas is recorded in hundreds of earthen mounds, walls and terraces widely scattered over much of the present state, and in bluff-shelters or rock-shelters and caves in which they sometimes lived. It is also recorded in thousands of pieces of pottery, stone tools, and weapons found in many different places.

Indian mounds are still numerous in the eastern counties and along the Arkansas, Ouachita, Red and other rivers. The mounds and other earthworks are much less prominent than they were seventy-five or a hundred years ago. They have been plowed down, washed away by rains and flooding streams, and cut through by road builders. Some mounds are lost in the woods and forgotten, while others can no longer be recognized except by experts.

One of the most outstanding groups of mounds in Arkansas was the Knapp or "Toltec" group, located near the Arkansas River about sixteen miles southeast of Little Rock. In 1882 the mounds numbered fifteen and were enclosed by an earthen embankment five feet high and a mile long. The largest mound was estimated to be fifty-eight feet high and about 700 feet around its base. In 1965 only three mounds remained.

Natural cave-like shelters in the bluffs of northwestern Arkansas have also yielded traces of early man. Archeologists have excavated mounds, dug into bluff shelters, and explored village and camp sites. Their findings have enriched museum collections in Arkansas and elsewhere, and because of their work we are learning more and more about the land and people of the prehistoric past.

2

The Folsom people. Among the earliest inhabitants of Arkansas were the Folsom people, so called because evidence of their existence was first discovered near Folsom, New Mexico. Folsom man lived here when the last of the great glacial ice sheets was melting off the northern part of what is now the United States. The climate of Arkansas was damp and rainy, causing lush vegetation and dense forests. In the forests and over the face of the land roamed such animals as the bison, mastodon, the musk-ox, the giant ground sloth, and the saber-tooth tiger, along with camels and small horses no bigger than ponies.

The prehistoric Indians whom we call the Folsom people had no bows and arrows, but used a dart-thrower, a grooved stick with which the dart was hurled. They clothed themselves with skins and built simple shelters of branches and sticks. No one knows what became of them or why they finally disappeared.

People of the ancient Ozarks. The Bluff Dwellers, who lived in the dry shelters beneath rock ledges on the bluffs of White River and other Ozark streams, came long after the Folsom people had vanished. During the period of the Bluff Dwellers, from about 500 B. C. to 1300 A. D., the Ozark country was much the same as it is today. The woods were probably less dense and grass prairies more extensive.

Like the Folsom people, the Bluff Dwellers were hunters and used the dart-thrower. Their rock shelters first attracted the attention of local residents almost a century ago when they began to find bones and other articles there. In time scientific expeditions began to be made to the area. These expeditions recovered not only human mummies but also numerous articles such as baskets, woven bags, deerskin moccasins, woven sandals, grass overshoes, corn and acorns. These had been preserved because it had always remained dry in the parts of the shelters in which they were found. In recent years numerous shelters have been discovered and explored.

The Bluff Dwellers were followed by another people called the Top Layer people, because their remains are found in the shelters above those of the Bluff Dwellers. The Top Layer people, who lived in the Ozarks from 1300 A. D. to about 1700 A. D., had bows and arrows, pottery, and tobacco. They may have been related to the Osages, who also used the bluff shelters to some extent.

The Osages, who came from the north in search of buffalo, were already in

An Indian mound in Hot Spring County, 1961

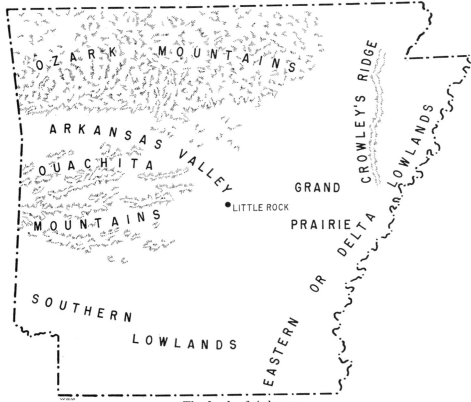

The land of Arkansas

the Ozarks when the first white settlers began to arrive. They hunted in the upper valleys of the Arkansas River, and their warlike nature caused them to be greatly feared. The Osages built houses of bent poles covered with woven grass and leaves, with a door in one side and a hole in the top to allow smoke to escape.

The mound people. The Marksville people, whose culture was first discovered at Marksville in Louisiana, lived in the lower Mississippi Valley about a thousand years ago. The Marksville people built mounds, made pottery, and worked in stone. Near Hot Springs they quarried novaculite, a hard, fine-grained rock, to make dart points and tools.

The Coles Creek Indians followed the Marksville Indians, and lived in the same general area from about 1100 A. D. to 1400 A. D. Their tribal life was more highly developed than the Marksville, and they excelled at work in pottery and stone. The Coles Creek people built great mounds in southwestern Arkansas near Red River.

Prehistoric Arkansans built such mounds without machinery, metal tools, or work animals. The dirt had to be dug with crude implements and carried in baskets, and the labor of building some mounds must have consumed many years. Temples and houses of chieftains stood on the flat tops of the mounds. They were centers of village and community life.

4

The Coles Creek people may have built mounds in eastern Arkansas also, and some of them lived in the Ouachita Mountains. Mound - building Indians lived in the region between Crowley's Ridge and the Mississippi River when De Soto entered Arkansas in 1541. Ornaments, tools and weapons from some mounds prove that the Indians of the sixteenth and seventeenth centuries traded and traveled over a wide area.

The Caddo of the southwest. The Caddo Indians, who lived in southwestern Arkansas and neighboring regions from about 1400 until late in the eighteenth century, probably came from Mexico or the Western plains. They conquered the Coles Creek people and occupied their mounds and villages. Few streams in southwest Arkansas were without at least one Caddo settlement.

Some of the Caddo towns were built around mounds. Caddo houses were walled with sedge grass or cane covered with clay plaster, and their conical roofs were also covered with sedge. Several related families occupied one house, with hanging mats of cane serving as partitions. Cane benches were used as beds, with buffalo robes for covering.

Excavating an Indian village site near the White River in Baxter County

5

The Caddo cultivated fields of corn, squash, beans, pumpkins and sunflowers, using stone hoes, sticks and buffalo bones as implements. The women ground corn in hollowed stone mortars and cooked in large pots. The Caddo made fine pottery, stone chisels, tomahawks, and ornaments of stone, shell, and feathers.

Buffalo hunts on the plains above Red River brought the Caddo into conflict with the Osages, who sometimes raided Caddo villages. The tribe declined after about 1760 and moved briefly to the Little Missouri River. Before Arkansas became a state the remnants of the Caddo were living west of Red River in Louisiana and Texas.

The Downstream People. The Quapaws or "downstream people," who lived in villages along the Mississippi and lower Arkansas rivers when the white men came, were called the Akansa or Arkansas by the Illinois Indians. The name may have been derived from a Quapaw social or tribal group of some kind.

Quapaw hunters stalked buffalo on Grand Prairie between the Arkansas and White rivers, harpooned fish, and decoyed and captured wild ducks and geese. Quapaw women raised tobacco as well as corn, beans, squash and pumpkins. From the forests they gathered pecans, wild plums, and persimmons. Mashed persimmons were used to make a kind of bread.

The Quapaws were not mound builders, though they sometimes established villages near old mounds. Their houses were rectangular, with poles for framework and cypress bark for covering. Large houses were divided into apartments and several related families lived under one roof. The oldest woman ruled each big household. Unmarried young men and guests stayed in houses with platforms for beds at each end. Some Quapaws lived in small houses covered with bark or cane and plastered with clay.

Like many Indian tribes, the Quapaws worshipped the sun and other gods and believed in spirits. Witch doctors with their spells and charms had great influence among them. When a Quapaw died, a period of mourning and wailing followed, with fires lighted on the grave and offerings of food placed there for the spirit. Quapaw men tattooed themselves, and ornaments were made of stone and shell. The warriors prized stone tomahawks as weapons, even after the white man made guns available.

STUDY AIDS

Vocabulary

Be sure that you understand the meaning of these words and phrases:

archeologist	glacial ice sheets
prehistoric	mummies
ledges	stalked
ancestors	mortars
terrace	implements
expedition	tattooed
dart-thrower	excavated

Location

Find the following on a map:

Grand Prairie	Mississippi River
Crowley's Ridge	Little Missouri
Red River	River
Ouachita	Ozark Mountains
Mountains	Arkansas River

To test your reading

On other paper, list 1-6. Opposite each number, write the word or words which complete each sentence.

1. The written history of Arkansas begins in the year ___.

2. The early people of Arkansas are thought to have descended from ancestors who crossed into ___ from ___.

3. Indian mounds are most numerous in the ___ and ___ parts of the state.

4. Material for the mounds is thought to have been carried in ___.

5. The Caddo Indians probably came from ___ or ___.

6. The Bluff Dwellers lived in northwest Arkansas in the period from about ___ B.C. to ___ A.D.

Things to do

1. Obtain two or three good maps of Arkansas, preferably new road maps. Keep them, or some like them, throughout the course. Use colored pencils or crayons to mark locations on the maps.

2. Start a class scrapbook. Arrange for members of the class to bring in newspaper clippings during the whole time that you are studying Historic Arkansas. Choose clippings about people and events that are important to the state or to your county and town.

3. Try to find out if there are any Indian mounds, bluff shelters or village sites near where you live.

4. Visit a museum which has displays of pottery, arrowheads and other articles relating to Indian life.

5. Write a story about an Arkansas Indian village as you think it might have been before the white men came.

6. Plan a meal using only foods that were known to the prehistoric people who lived in Arkansas.

2   The First Europeans

Less than fifty years after Columbus discovered the Americas, a ragged band of Spanish adventurers pushed into unknown Arkansas from the east. This chapter recounts the almost legendary story of De Soto and his men.

De Soto in Florida. The first white men to visit Arkansas belonged to a Spanish expedition commanded by Hernando de Soto. Less than fifty years had passed since Columbus had crossed the Atlantic Ocean and opened the Americas to Spanish conquest. In these years many Spanish soldiers and settlers had come to the New World. Settlements in the islands of the West Indies had been followed by the conquest of Indian empires in Mexico and Peru.

The gold and silver found in Mexico and Peru caused Spanish leaders to begin looking for other rich regions. Hernando de Soto, the governor of Cuba, was authorized to explore the interior of Florida, an area which at that time included what is now the southern part of the United States. In the spring of 1539 De Soto landed on the west coast of the Florida peninsula and began his march northward. His force included about 600 men, over 200 horses, a drove of hogs for meat, and a quantity of supplies and equipment.

For two years the expedition made its way through the area later known as Florida, Georgia, the Carolinas, Tennessee, Alabama, and Mississippi. Progress through the wilderness was slow and difficult, and probably a third of the men and horses fell before Indian attacks. Many of the survivors became discouraged, but De Soto was determined to push on into the wilderness in search of the riches he had set out to discover.

De Soto enters Arkansas. On May 21, 1541 the De Soto expedition reached the east bank of the Mississippi River. The men wore tattered garments and animal skins. Their weapons and armor were rusty and their horses poor. The Spaniards spent almost a month in building four great barges for use in crossing the river. Repeatedly the Indians in large numbers approached in canoes, but their arrows did little damage.

By June 18 all was ready for the crossing. In the darkness of early morning the Spaniards launched their barges and began moving across the river. Before noon the entire expedition was ashore in eastern Arkansas.

De Soto in eastern Arkansas. The story of De Soto's expedition was related by three survivors. Each of the three accounts is brief, with dates, distances and directions either given sparingly or guessed. Some natural landmarks are mentioned, and the names of Indian villages were recorded, but the villages disappeared during the century

DeSoto arrives at the Mississippi. From a painting which appeared
in the "St. Louis Globe-Democrat," 1902

and longer which passed before white men came again to Arkansas. The true route of De Soto may never be known, but historians have studied the accounts and tried to guess where he went as accurately as possible.

According to the most complete of these studies, the Spaniards crossed the Mississippi River at Sunflower Landing, in southern Phillips County below the present city of Helena. A few miles from the crossing they came to a large Indian town which had been abandoned by its inhabitants. Other towns in the area were also deserted at the approach of the invaders. The Spanish crossed a small river on a bridge, and waded northward through swamps waist-deep in water.

On Crowley's Ridge De Soto entered a fertile and heavily-populated Indian province. The land was high and dry, and the Spaniards saw mulberry, persimmon and walnut trees. The fields near Big Creek and the L'Anguille River were so thickly set with villages that two or three were sometimes visible at one time. The Spaniards erected a cross made of two pine trees on top of a large artificial mound, and tried to instruct the Indians in the Christian religion.

After crossing a stream on a bridge of timbers and poles built by Indians, De Soto and his men occupied a town near the Mississippi and just above the mouth of the St. Francis River. Like other towns in the region, this

9

settlement was surrounded by a timber stockade, with towers for defensive purposes. Outside the stockade was a lake, and a ditch fed by a canal from the Mississippi River. Large fields of corn could be seen nearby.

The Spaniards remained near the mouth of the St. Francis for a month or longer. They used nets to catch fish from the ditch, made clothing of deer and bear skins, and found buffalo hides from which they made protective coverings for their horses. The Indian chiefs gave them presents of fish, shawls and skins in great quantity.

De Soto sent a group of his men northwest to look for gold, provisions, and for possible information about a route to the sea. After penetrating the prairies between the St. Francis and White rivers, the men returned almost starved and reported n o t h i n g but "pondy swamps," wide plains covered with tall grass, and Indians who lived in movable tents. De Soto then decided to push to the southwest where there were reported to be large villages and plenty of corn.

In August 1541 the Spaniards crossed White River near the present town of St. Charles with the help of a fleet of Indian canoes. In the region of Arkansas Post they came to the largest town they had seen in Florida. The land was level and fertile, and along the river the Indians cultivated extensive fields.

Journey through the west. De Soto turned northwest from the Arkansas Post area because he heard of mountains lying in that direction, and he thought that mountains might yield gold and silver. The expedition made its way through swamps where the men killed fish with clubs and had to

sleep in ponds and puddles. Eventually the swamplands gave way to broken hills, until at last the Spaniards came upon a town located at the foot of a mountain with a river nearby.

This town, which was probably on the site of present-day North Little Rock, was populous and wealthy. There the invaders took slaves, clothing, salt, and a vast amount of provisions. The soil was rich, yielding corn in such abundance that the old was thrown away to make room for new. Beans and pumpkins were not only plentiful but better than those of Spain. The Spaniards hunted "wild cows," or buffalo, which roamed the area in great numbers.

From this point the explorers crossed the Arkansas River and moved southwest past present-day Benton, followed the Saline River a short distance to the south, and then turned west. They reached the Ouachita River between Malvern and Arkadelphia and started upstream.

De Soto was now in the Ouachita Mountains, a "very rough country of hills," where Indian dwellings were scattered and towns few. He spent a month in the area, much of it near Hot Springs, where the horses fattened on an abundance of corn and drank from a "very warm and brackish lake." The Spaniards made salt as the Indians did, by gathering baskets of dry sand from the river's edge, straining w a t e r through it, and then boiling the brine until the water evaporated and the salt hardened.

Near the site of the present town of Caddo Gap the Spanish soldiers encountered fierce resistance from the Indians, whom they described as the best fighting men they had met. By this time winter was coming on, and

De Soto decided to turn to the southeast, where he had heard there were great towns, provisions, and perhaps an outlet to the seacoast.

Down the Ouachita. On leaving Caddo Gap, the Spanish probably followed Antoine Creek and the Little Missouri River until they reached the Ouachita, or they may have kept near the Caddo River to Arkadelphia. Descending the banks of the Ouachita, the expedition spent the winter of 1541-42 near Calion, not far from El Dorado.

The Spanish went into winter quarters at an Indian town situated in a level and very populous country. The winter was bitterly cold, and for a month the snow was so deep the Spaniards did not leave the town except for firewood. The Indians provided plenty of corn, beans, walnuts, and dried persimmons, and taught the Spanish how to set traps for rabbits.

In the spring of 1542 De Soto moved on down the Ouachita River into Louisiana, hoping to find a way to reach the sea. His force had been reduced to some 300 men and forty horses, some of which were lame. Near the present town of Ferriday, in Louisiana, De Soto died, knowing that his expedition had been a tragic failure. The survivors built ships and the next year reached Mexico.

Probable route of the DeSoto expedition

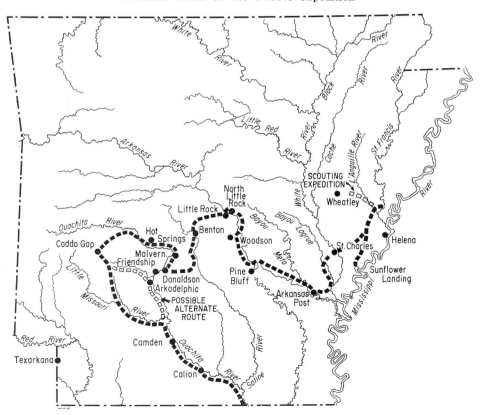

The Indians as seen by De Soto. The Spanish accounts indicate that the native population in De Soto's time was much greater than at any later date of which we have record. Most of the Indians lived in fixed homes and permanent villages, though some dwelt in movable tents or wigwams. Houses were often built on artificial mounds, and in villages surrounded by stockades.

The Indians lived by fishing and hunting primarily, but they also raised corn, beans, pumpkins and possibly other crops. They made baskets, pottery, stone implements and fiber cloth. To the Spaniards the Indians appeared tall and handsome. Politically, they were organized under chiefs and subordinate leaders. The Arkansas natives had no domestic animals except the dog, no wheeled vehicles, and no roads except trails through the forests.

The significance of the De Soto expedition. The Indians of Arkansas were undoubtedly relieved when De Soto and his men disappeared. The Spaniards robbed, murdered, enslaved and mutilated the Indians, and left the ashes of burned towns behind them as they moved across the land. The Spanish priests made no real progress in converting the Indians to Christianity.

De Soto's failure to find gold or jewels caused the Spanish Empire to lose interest in the Mississippi Valley. The Spaniards learned something about Arkansas geography and people, but since no treasure was found they made no use of this knowledge. Spain and all Europe promptly forgot about Arkansas for another 131 years.

Scale model of a Mound Builders Indian village excavated near
Wilson, Mississippi County

STUDY AIDS

Vocabulary

Be sure that you understand the meaning of these words:

barges
landmarks
artificial
stockade
invaders

brackish
mutilated
launched
region
cultivated

Location

Find the following on a map:

Sunflower
  Landing
Big Creek
L'Anguille River
St. Francis River

White River
St. Charles
Arkansas Post
Caddo Gap
Calion

To test your reading

On other paper, list 1-6. Opposite each number write the word or words which complete each sentence.

1. De Soto is thought to have crossed the Mississippi River about twenty miles below the present city of ___.

2. It was ___ years after the Spanish left Arkansas before other Europeans came.

3. De Soto's force originally included about ___ men.

4. The Spaniards remained for a month or more near the mouth of the ___ River.

5. The Spaniards spent the winter of 1541-1542 not far from ___.

6. De Soto died near the town of ___ in Louisiana.

Things to do

1. Find out if there is a De Soto historical marker or tablet in your community or county. If so, learn who placed it there and when it was erected.

2. Was the visit of De Soto really important to the history of Arkansas, or is it just an interesting story? Arrange a panel discussion or classroom debate.

3. Write a story about the De Soto expedition from the Indians' point of view.

4. Choose a committee to visit your school library and your public library and see what books and other materials are available on the history of Arkansas. Have them make a list and report to the class. Plan a series of reports based on the books and materials.

3 French Arkansas, 1673-1762

The history of white settlement in Arkansas begins with the foothold established by the French in 1686 at Arkansas Post. The French explored Arkansas, developed the fur trade and planted a few small settlements, but they could not hold the Mississippi Valley. In 1762 Arkansas passed into the hands of Spain.

Marquette and Joliet visit Arkansas.
After the departure of De Soto 131 years passed before white men came again to the Arkansas region. In the year 1673 seven Frenchmen from Canada, in two canoes, floated down the Mississippi. Led by Jacques Marquette, a Catholic priest, and Louis Joliet, a fur trader, the little expedition had been sent by the French government to explore the course of the river and find out where it emptied into the sea.

In Arkansas, Marquette and Joliet first stopped at an Indian village on the western bank of the Mississippi near the site of Helena. Again descending the river, they visited the Quapaw village of Arkansas, near the mouth of the Arkansas River. From the Indians, who were courteous and friendly, the French were able to learn much about the region.

At length Marquette and Joliet decided that the Mississippi flowed into the Gulf of Mexico, and that farther travel southward might lead to their capture by the Spaniards. On July 17, 1673 the expedition left the village of Arkansas and began the long return journey to Canada.

La Salle claims Arkansas for France.
In the spring of 1682 La Salle, in command of a much larger French force, came down the Mississippi. After building a small fort near where Memphis now stands, he stopped at a Quapaw town near the mouth of the Arkansas. Here a cross was raised bearing the arms of France, and La Salle took formal possession of the country. Then at the mouth of the Mississippi on April 9, 1682 La Salle claimed all the Mississippi Valley for France, naming it "Louisiana" in honor of King Louis XIV.

La Salle proposed to establish a colony at the mouth of the Mississippi River, and returned to France to prepare an expedition. Sailing from France in 1684, his four vessels missed the mouth of the river and landed on the coast of Texas. Here two of his ships deserted and the others were lost. The stranded Frenchmen built a fort and some of them managed to survive for two years. Early in 1687 La Salle set out on foot with some twenty survivors to try to reach the Mississippi. On the banks of the Trinity River La Salle was assassinated by two of his companions. Henri Joutel, with six men, pushed on to the northeast.

The first settlement. Henri de Tonty, an Italian officer in the service of France, accompanied La Salle on his descent of the Mississippi in 1682. Then in 1686 De Tonty, whose original Italian name was "Tonti," set out from Fort St. Louis on the Illinois River to meet La Salle at the mouth of the Mississippi. When he failed to locate La Salle, De Tonty and his men returned to the Quapaw villages near the mouth of the Arkansas.

La Salle had already given De Tonty a tract of land on the lower Arkansas, and De Tonty left six of his men there to establish a trading post. This "Post of Arkansas" or "Arkansas Post," founded in June 1686, was the first white settlement in Arkansas and the entire lower Mississippi Valley.

When Joutel and his men, making their way from the coast of Texas, arrived at Arkansas Post on July 24, 1687 they found a small log cabin with a tall wooden cross nearby. Two of De Tonty's men, Couture and De Launay, were still there. They were the original white settlers of Arkansas.

John Law's colony. Soon after the death of La Salle, France became involved in a European war and for more than ten years gave little attention to the Mississippi Valley. In 1699 the French returned to develop the region. They established several settlements south of Arkansas Post, including Natchez and New Orleans.

In 1717 John Law, a Scottish financier living in France, organized the

Settlement of Arkansas Post, 1686. From a painting which appeared in the "St. Louis Globe-Democrat," 1902

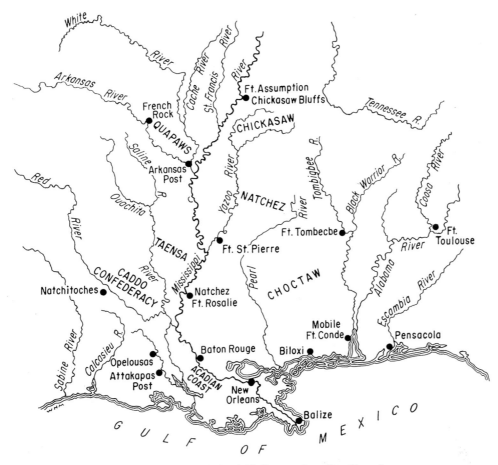

The lower Mississippi Valley under the French

Western or Mississippi Company to develop Louisiana. Law himself secured a large grant of land on the north bank of the Arkansas River near Arkansas Post. He planned to bring in Germans to settle his colony, and some settlers actually came and began to build cabins and clear the land.

The news that Law had become bankrupt caused the collapse of the colony on the Arkansas. Most of the people left, and some of the settlement's cabins and storehouses were deserted. The Mississippi Company sent a director and a few soldiers to Arkansas Post, which was continued as a small trading station.

Exploring the Red and the Arkansas. The Mississippi Company sent out several exploring expeditions. In 1719 Benard de la Harpe advanced up the Red River into parts of what is now southwestern Arkansas. La Harpe and his men found the stream choked by a vast entanglement of fallen trees and vegetation, later called the Great Raft.

In 1721-22 La Harpe undertook an expedition up the Arkansas River. The explorer and his sixteen men pushed upstream from Arkansas Post to a point probably fifty miles above Little Rock. La Harpe's expedition accomplished little except the discovery of Big Rock, which he named "French Rock," and the slaughter of numbers of buffalo, bear, deer and wild turkeys.

Government in French Arkansas. The Mississippi Company gave up its right to govern Louisiana in 1731, and the area became a royal colony. As early as 1722 Louisiana had been divided into nine districts or commands, each with a military commander and a judge. Arkansas was the eighth district, with the administrative center at Arkansas Post.

Until 1762 French laws were in force in Arkansas. A special set of laws known as the Black Code regulated s l a v e r y and the Negro population throughout Louisiana. During the en-

tire period of French control Louisiana had thirteen governors, the greatest of whom was Bienville. He served at three different times for a total of twenty-six years.

After the breakup of John Law's colony the Arkansas district was neglected by the French. Military garrisons at Arkansas Post were never large, and another fort at the mouth of the St. Francis River was soon abandoned. During some periods no troops were stationed at Arkansas Post, and the place was almost deserted.

The Church in French Arkansas. Catholic Christianity came to Arkansas with Marquette, who was a missionary as well as an explorer. De Tonty gave land at Arkansas Post to the Jesuits, a

Big Rock on the Arkansas River, as it appeared in the early days

Catholic religious order, for a house and chapel but nothing was done for several years. Not until 1727 was a priest stationed at the Post, and he remained but two years. Though the Jesuits maintained missionaries in Arkansas only a part of the time, priests traveling up or down the Mississippi sometimes stopped to perform marriages and baptisms.

The Arkansas country was the most sparsely settled part of Louisiana. The few settlers were hunters, traders, and explorers. Some of them were outlaws seeking refuge in the forests. Whites as well as half-breeds and Indians showed so little respect for religion and morals that the last Jesuit missionary finally gave up and left.

Wars with the Indians and English. While the French were settling parts of Canada and the Mississippi Valley, the English were planting a string of colonies along the eastern seacoast of North America. Beginning in 1689 the French and English fought a series of great wars in which the Indian nations took sides.

The Quapaws of Arkansas sided with the French against the powerful Chickasaw Indians who lived east of the Mississippi. French expeditions based in Arkansas failed to defeat the Chickasaws, and in 1748 or 1749 the Chickasaws attacked and almost captured Arkansas Post. Later the French erected a new post at a different location and increased the garrison.

The Seven Years' War, called in America the French and Indian War, ended with the decisive defeat of France by England. In 1762 France ceded New Orleans and all of Louisiana west of the Mississippi River to her ally Spain. The Spanish did not really want the area, but took it hoping to use it as a shield to protect Texas and Mexico from

the English. By the Peace of Paris in 1763 the English acquired Canada and the former French territory east of the Mississippi.

French influence in Arkansas. Except for a brief period in 1803, Arkansas was never again under French rule after the first Spanish governor landed in New Orleans in 1766. The French had developed a flourishing trade in deerskins and other articles with the Indians, but few French settlers ever came to the Arkansas region to make their homes.

Some French names of Arkansas streams

French hunters and traders ascended the many streams of Arkansas and followed dim Indian trails far into the interior. From their reports, as well as from those of official exploring parties, came the first maps of the region. Several of the early French maps of Arkansas are surprisingly accurate.

The French left behind a liberal sprinkling of place names. Dozens of Arkansas rivers, creeks, mountains, prairies, towns, townships and streets have French names. Many Indian names, such as "Arkansas" and "Mississippi," have come down to us in French form.

☆ ☆ ☆ ☆

STUDY AIDS

Vocabulary

Be sure that you understand the meaning of these words and phrases:

stranded	ceded
Great Raft	financier
garrison	French Rock
Black Code	royal colony
half-breeds	Jesuits

Identification

Tell what part each of the following had in the story:

Marquette	De Tonty
Joliet	Couture
La Salle	De Launay
King Louis XIV	Seven Years' War
Chickasaws	John Law
Joutel	La Harpe
	Bienville

To test your reading

On other paper, list 1-7. Opposite each number, write the word or words which complete each sentence.

1. The first settlement to be made in the Louisiana Territory was at ___ in the year ___.

2. Marquette and Joliet came to Arkansas in the year ___.

3. La Salle came down the Mississippi in the year ___.

4. The leader of the expedition up the Arkansas River in 1722 was ___.

5. As early as 1722 Louisiana was divided into ___ districts. The eighth was the District of Arkansas.

6. The John Law Colony was located near ___.

7. The greatest of the Spanish governors was ___.

Things to do

1. Make a list of rivers, towns, streets and mountains in Arkansas that have French names.

2. Search for the story of Petit Jean Mountain and report to the class.

3. Arrange a visit to Arkansas Post National Monument and to Arkansas Post County Museum.

4. If you live in or near Little Rock, visit the actual "little rock" on the bank of the Arkansas River from which the city takes its name.

5. Obtain a copy of the *Arkansas Historical Quarterly* and bring it to class. Do you think that having copies of this magazine available would help you in your study of Arkansas history?

4   Spanish Arkansas, 1762-1803

During forty years of Spanish rule, Arkansas began to grow a little. A few American settlers came from Kentucky and Tennessee, and Spanish officials handed out liberal gifts of land. New European wars caused Spain to return Louisiana to France in 1800, but the French did not take control until shortly before Arkansas became American in 1803.

Spanish rule in Arkansas. The Spanish were in no hurry to take control of Louisiana, and when they did they had to put down a rebellion by the French people of New Orleans who objected to being given to Spain. Not until 1769 was Spanish authority firmly established.

Arkansas played no part in the troubles which attended the transfer of Louisiana, and Spanish control was established quietly at Arkansas Post. Under the Spanish system, Louisiana was ruled by a governor appointed by the king, with headquarters in New Orleans. Arkansas lay within the area supervised by a lieutenant governor at St. Louis, and each local district had its commandant. Spanish officials were generally mild and tactful in their dealings with the colonists. Frenchmen were appointed to many governmental positions.

Arkansas Post remained the center of administration of the District of Arkansas. The District itself was a vaguely-defined but huge area which took in the whole of present-day Arkansas, Oklahoma, and perhaps other territories. Its eastern boundary extended southward along the Mississippi River from about the present Missouri-Arkansas line to a point near the present Arkansas-Louisiana border. From these two points on the great river, the northern and southern boundaries of Spanish Arkansas extended westward to include all of the waters tributary to the Mississippi.

Arkansas Post under the Spanish. Arkansas Post failed to grow much in size and importance under the Spanish. In 1768 the population numbered only 138 persons, including thirty Negroes and mulattoes and a few Indians. The Spanish commandants at the Post struggled with a variety of problems. The Indians, who were constantly being influenced by English agents across the Mississippi, had to be kept loyal with liquor and other gifts. Though some respectable French families lived in the Post area, many of the people were outlaws, gamblers, and vagabonds. Floods, food shortages, and fevers added to the problems of Arkansas Post.

About 1770 the Spanish moved their military garrison downstream from Arkansas Post to Fort Charles III, named for the Spanish king, near the mouth of the Arkansas River. Ten years later, floods caused the abandonment of the fort and another move upstream to a site above the old De Tonty location. For a few years about 1800 the Span-

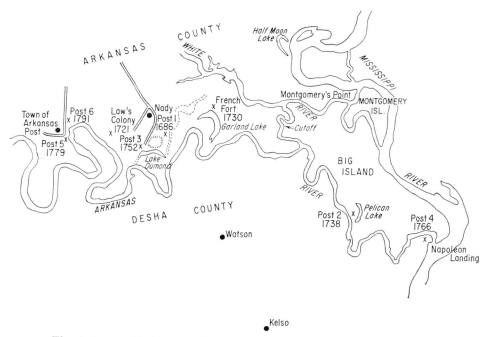

The Arkansas Post area. The Post itself has been located in at least six different places since 1686

iards maintained a garrison at Fort Esperanza, later called Hopefield, near present-day West Memphis.

The Spanish generally took their Catholic religion more seriously than did the French, but even they failed to keep priests at the Post regularly. A new chapel was built, and the commandants tried to have marriages legally performed and children baptized. The last priest to live at Arkansas Post during the Spanish period performed seventy - two baptisms, conducted twenty-six funerals and assisted at twenty-one marriages in 1796-99.

Arkansas and the American Revolution. In 1775, only a few years after Spain took over Louisiana, the American Revolution broke out. From the beginning the Spanish were sympathetic with any plan to drive the English from the Mississippi Valley. In 1779 Spain entered the war on the side of the Americans, and Spanish forces soon captured Baton Rouge, Natchez, Mobile and Pensacola.

Across the Mississippi from the District of Arkansas, the English and their Indian allies were a constant threat. Late in 1780 the commandant at Arkansas Post claimed control of the east bank of the Mississippi in the name of the king of Spain. In 1783 a force of over a hundred Englishmen and Chickasaws led by James Colbert crossed the Mississippi and attacked Arkansas Post. The invaders seized the village but were beaten off when they tried to storm the fort. When the Spanish and Quapaws counterattacked, the English withdrew down the Arkansas.

By the treaty of peace which ended the American Revolution in 1783, Spain not only kept Louisiana but regained Florida, which she had lost to

21

England twenty years before. Yet the Spanish victory was an empty one, for the Americans soon proved more troublesome than the English had been.

The settlement of Spanish Arkansas. Arkansas Post was by no means the only settled place in Spanish Arkansas. As early as 1766 a trading post was set up at the mouth of White River on a site known later as Montgomery's Point. Spanish restrictions on immigration and travel discouraged settlement until after the American Revolution, and probably slowed immigration later. Few Spaniards ever came to the Arkansas district to live.

Land grants to Americans increased in number after about 1792. Americans and French planted new settlements on the rich lands along the rivers of eastern and southern Arkansas. Before 1803 French settlers had appeared on the banks of the Black, White, and Little Red rivers, and along the Arkansas as far upstream as Dardanelle. As late as 1830 many of the old French houses, with their tall chimneys, high pointed roofs, and gables were still standing.

Most of the American settlers came from Kentucky and Tennessee. In 1800 three Kentuckians started a settlement at Big Prairie, near the mouth of the St. Francis River. In the same year William Patterson, a Methodist local preacher, built a warehouse where Helena now stands. Sylvanus Phillips settled at the mouth of the St. Francis as early as 1797.

Despite the increasing rate of settlement, the population of Arkansas was still small when Spanish rule came to an end. A census of 1785 placed the white and Negro inhabitants of the district at 196, and another census taken fourteen years later showed only 368. The people were scattered so widely that these figures were probably too low, but even then it is unlikely that more than 600 people, excluding Indians, lived in Arkansas in 1803.

Agriculture made little progress during the wilderness years when Arkansas was ruled by France and Spain. The people lived by hunting and trading with the Indians. The clumsy river boats floated down to New Orleans loaded with bear oil, tallow, salted buffalo meat, pecans, and skins. They came back, making slow and laborious headway against the current, with the tools, weapons, cloth and other supplies required by the earliest of the pioneers.

Spanish land grants. Apart from a few place names, the principal Spanish contribution to Arkansas was a tangle of land titles which troubled the United States government for over forty years after the purchase of Louisiana. Apparently the only Arkansas land grants under French authority were those made to De Tonty and John Law. Under Spanish rule hundreds of grants were made, especially as the cession to the United States drew near. The king of Spain made several huge grants of lands in Arkansas.

For both French and Spanish the unit of land measurement was the arpent or arpen, slightly more than four-fifths of an acre. Grants to heads of households usually totaled 800 arpents or about 680 acres, with fifty arpents or about forty-two acres additional for each child. The Spanish land system was loose and indefinite, and many officials and landholders failed to comply with the law. Often lands were not even surveyed, and sometimes the governor's signature was forged when a grant was made. A very high percentage of the Spanish land grants proved to be fraudulent.

Arkansas becomes American. After 1790 the position of Spain in the lower Mississippi region grew steadily weaker. In Europe the Spanish became involved in the wars resulting from the French Revolution. In America the power of the United States was growing. The Spanish had trouble with the Americans over the navigation of the Mississippi River, and finally had to give in. The warlike Osage Indians became a problem in Arkansas.

By 1800 Louisiana had become such a burden to Spain that she was ready to give it up. By a secret treaty signed on October 1 of that year, Louisiana was returned to France. Napoleon, the French dictator, planned to build a great colonial empire in the New World but he delayed taking actual control of Louisiana until 1803.

President Thomas Jefferson and other American leaders were afraid that Napoleon might close the Mississippi River to American commerce, and they decided to try to buy a small area near the mouth of the river to make sure that it would remain open. By this time Napoleon's plans had changed, and the French offered to sell all of Louisiana to the Americans. In a short time the transaction was closed. The American government agreed to pay $15,000,000 for Louisiana in the treaty signed on April 30, 1803.

The Spanish, whose officials still governed Louisiana when the French signed it away, were unhappy about the Louisiana Purchase but there was nothing they could do. The people of Louisiana had not been consulted about the transfer, just as they had not been consulted in 1800 or in 1762. The handful of settlers, traders, hunters and outlaws who lived in Arkansas probably did not care very much, since earlier changes had made little difference to them.

STUDY AIDS

Vocabulary

Be sure that you understand the meaning of these words and phrases:

commandant   restrictions
site   tallow
constant   gables
chapel   arpent
immigration   land grants
commerce   forged

Identification

Tell what part each of the following had in the story:

Napoleon   Thomas Jefferson
William Patterson   James Colbert
Sylvanus Phillips   Louisiana Purchase

Location

Find or locate the following on a map:

Fort Esperanza   Big Prairie
Black River   Montgomery's
Little Red River   Point

To test your reading

On other paper, list 1-7. Opposite each number, write the word or words which complete each sentence.

1. Montgomery's Point was at the mouth of the ___ River.

2. In 1768 the population of Arkansas Post was only ___.

3. In 1799 the population of the District of Arkansas was ___.

4. A trading post was set up at the mouth of the White River in the year ___.

5. Most of the American settlers in Arkansas came from the states of ___ and ___.

6. The Spanish moved their military garrison downstream from Arkansas Post to ___, named for the Spanish king.

7. For both French and Spanish the unit of land measurement was the ___ or ___, slightly more than ___ of an acre.

Things to do

1. Go to your courthouse and ask if there were Spanish land grants in your county.

2. Begin a collection of post cards showing scenic, historic, and otherwise interesting places in Arkansas.

3. Make a list of the family names represented in your class. With the help of your parents, the school librarian, or someone else, try to classify the national origin of each name, such as English, Scottish, Irish, and so on. Are there any members of the class who have French or Spanish names?

4. Pretend that you are a priest at Arkansas Post during the Spanish period. Write a letter in which you describe your problems and difficulties.

Reviewing the Unit

1. Who were the various peoples who lived in Arkansas in prehistoric times? Since they left no written records, how do we know anything about them?

2. Why did the Spaniards lose interest in Arkansas after De Soto's visit?

3. What was the first permanent white settlement in Arkansas? Where, when, and by whom was it established?

4. How did the French influence the development of Arkansas?

5. What part did Arkansas have in the American Revolution?

6. Why did Spain decide to return Louisiana to France?

7. What did the French and Spanish mean by the term "Louisiana"?

Unit Two

Pioneer Arkansas, 1803-1836

PIONEER ARKANSAS was on the path to statehood for a period of thirty-three years. During the first half of this time it was a part of either Louisiana Territory, or Missouri Territory. During the last half, it had its own government.

The region of which Arkansas is a part had been explored and settled, to some extent, by the Spanish and the French before it came to be incorporated in the United States. Most of it, however, was still known to but few besides the Indians. In the period 1803 to 1836 thousands came up its rivers and over its Indian trails seeking adventure or seeking homes.

At first the rivers and the Indian trails were difficult and hazardous as routes of travel, but as the channels of rivers were cleared and trails became roads, access became less difficult. New settlements developed, postal routes and post offices were established and newspapers came to be a part of the life of the territory.

To divide up the land and to enable the people to secure titles to their homes, a system of land survey was necessary. This was begun in 1815 and continued for many years. It involved much expense and the work of many men. It is the system now in use. In addition Indian claims were settled and the Indians were removed farther west. Arkansas became a possession of the United States in 1803, a territory in 1819 and a state in 1836.

1   The Path to Statehood

A third of a century went by after the Louisiana Purchase before Arkansas became a state. Politically, pioneer Arkansas was first a district, then a county, and finally a territory. This chapter traces the development of early Arkansas to the threshold of statehood.

Arkansas under American control. The French flag flew over Louisiana for only twenty days before Napoleon's commissioner handed the region over to the Americans late in 1803. In the spring of 1804 an American officer took over at Arkansas Post from the last Spanish commandant.

Under American control, Arkansas at first became a part of the District of Louisiana. After Louisiana became a territory Arkansas was made a district, with its seat of justice at Arkansas Post. In 1812 the name of Louisiana Territory was changed to Missouri Territory.

On the last day of the year 1813 the Missouri legislature changed the District of Arkansas into Arkansas County. It included all the present state of Arkansas except the northeast and extreme north. Henry Cassidy was elected the first representative from Arkansas County to the Missouri lower house.

According to the census of 1810 Arkansas had 1,062 people. By 1819, immigration had boosted the population to about 14,000, leading to the creation of four new counties. In 1815 the Missouri legislature established Lawrence County to include what is now northern Arkansas, with Davidsonville as the county seat. Pulaski, Clark and Hemp-stead counties, taken from part of Arkansas County, were formed late in 1818 just before Arkansas was separated from Missouri.

Creation of Arkansas Territory. When the people of Missouri Territory began seeking admission to the Union as a state, they proposed to leave Arkansas outside. The Missourians believed that to include Arkansas would make their new state too large.

A movement at once got under way in the Arkansas region to make Arkansas a separate territory. In 1818 and 1819 a number of petitions were presented to Congress asking creation of Arkansas Territory. The petitioners complained that Arkansas and Lawrence counties were not allowed enough representation in the Missouri legislature, and that Missouri officials had failed to provide law enforcement and courts for Arkansas.

Late in 1818 a bill to make Arkansas a territory was introduced in Congress. Members of Congress from some of the Northern states delayed the bill by trying to eliminate or restrict Negro slavery in Arkansas, but all such efforts failed. President James Monroe signed the act creating the Territory of Arkansas on March 2, 1819.

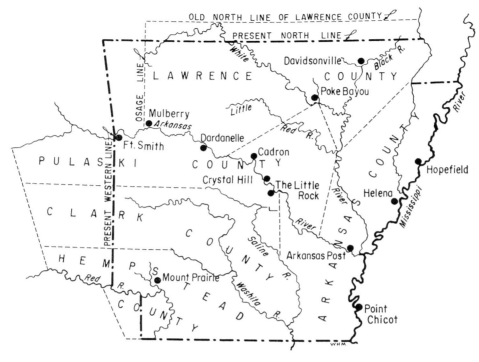

OLD NORTH LINE OF LAWRENCE COUNTY

PRESENT NORTH LINE

L A W R E N C E   C O U N T Y

Davidsonville

Black R.

Poke Bayou

OSAGE LINE

White

Little

Red R.

River

Mulberry
Arkansas

Dardanelle

Cadron

PRESENT WESTERN LINE

Ft. Smith

P U L A S K I

C O U N T Y

Crystal Hill

The Little Rock

River

River

Helena

Hopefield

Mississippi

A R K A N S A S

C L A R K   C O U N T Y

Saline R.

Arkansas Post

H E M P S T E A D

Red R.

Mount Prairie

Washita R.

C O U N T Y

Point Chicot

WHM

Arkansas in 1819

Beginning the territorial government.
The new government of Arkansas Territory was to begin operation at Arkansas Post on July 4, 1819. President Monroe appointed James Miller of New Hampshire as governor, and Robert Crittenden of Kentucky as secretary. When Governor Miller failed to arrive in time, Crittenden and the three judges of the Superior Court acted as a legislature and organized the territorial government.

In the first election, held November 20, 1819, almost 1,300 votes were cast. James Woodson Bates, for whom Batesville was later named, was elected delegate to Congress. Voters in each of the five counties chose one member of the Legislative Council, or upper house of the General Assembly. The House of Representatives was made up of one member from Clark County and two members from each of the other four counties.

Arkansas Post remained the capital of Arkansas for only two years. In 1821 the capital was moved to Little Rock, though a long dispute over who owned the land there caused considerable trouble at first.

The rise of political parties. Robert Crittenden, secretary of the territory, was the leading figure in Arkansas politics for ten years. The first two governors, James Miller and George Izard, were away much of their terms and Crittenden acted as governor. A strong faction of officeholders and other supporters formed around Crittenden.

A faction opposing Crittenden appeared in the campaign of 1827, when the Secretary backed another candidate for Congress against Henry W. Conway.

Conway won the election, but was later killed by Crittenden in a duel. Ambrose H. Sevier succeeded Conway and became leader of the group opposing Crittenden.

In 1829 President Andrew Jackson removed Crittenden as secretary and appointed William S. Fulton of Alabama in his place. John Pope of Kentucky, another Jackson supporter, became governor. The Crittenden party then started a newspaper called the **Arkansas Advocate** to compete with the pro-Sevier **Arkansas Gazette,** and opened all-out political warfare on Sevier, Pope, and Fulton.

rooms, and churches. In 1831 Congress granted Arkansas ten sections or 6,400 acres of public land, which was to be sold and the money used to build a state house.

The General Assembly voted to exchange the ten sections for a brick residence in Little Rock belonging to Robert Crittenden, planning to use Crittenden's house as a capitol building. Governor Pope vetoed the plan, and was then authorized by Congress to sell the ten sections and build a state house. Construction began in 1833, and three years later the first General Assembly

Ambrose H. Sevier

Robert Crittenden

In the 1831 elections the Crittenden faction failed to defeat Sevier but took over the General Assembly. By this time the Crittenden supporters were becoming known as Whigs, while the Sevier people backed President Jackson and the Democrats.

The new state house. Arkansas had no adequate territorial capitol building, and the General Assembly and Superior Court had to meet in cabins, rented

of the new State of Arkansas met in the building now known as the "Old State House."

Triumph of the Democrats. Crittenden's attempt to exchange his house for the ten sections of land weakened his party. In 1833 Sevier defeated Crittenden in the race for Congress, and Sevier men gained a majority in the General Assembly. From this time onward the Sevier people, or Democrats, were secure in their control of the territorial government. In 1835 William S. Fulton succeeded John Pope as governor.

Party politics from 1819 to 1836 was based largely on personalities rather than issues. Except for the delegate to Congress, all the leading public officials were appointed by the president rather than elected by the voters. Until 1829 the governor appointed county officials, but after that date they were elected.

As a territory Arkansas depended on the Federal government for many things. The General Assemblies spent a great deal of time addressing memorials to Congress asking for new roads, new post offices and postal routes, new army posts, land surveys, river improvement and the removal of the Indians. New counties were created until by the close of 1835 the number stood at thirty-four. Territorial legislatures

John Pope

The Robert Crittenden home, as it appeared in 1890

also passed numerous laws relating to taxes, land, appropriations, debt, slaves, and the militia.

The fight for statehood. In 1833 Delegate Ambrose Sevier asked Congress to permit Arkansas to form a state constitution. Sevier and his friends felt that statehood would bring new settlers and many other benefits to Arkansas, and they were afraid that the future might produce more trouble over slavery.

Congress was slow to act, and during 1835 the supporters of statehood stirred up a popular campaign in Arkansas. Public meetings were held at several places over the territory and almost all of them adopted resolutions urging immediate statehood. At the August election some precincts conducted an informal vote on the question, and the results favored the admission of Arkansas to the Union. A special census taken in 1835 showed that Arkansas now had sufficient population to become a state.

The opponents of statehood were fairly strong, and Governor William S. Fulton refused to go along with a plan to frame a state constitution and then ask Congress to approve it later. When the General Assembly in 1835 proceeded to authorize the holding of a constitutional convention, Fulton allowed the bill to become law without his signature.

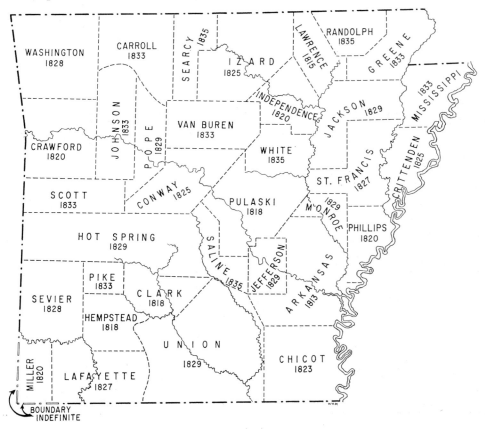

The counties of Arkansas in 1836, with date each county was created

William S. Fulton

Statehood achieved. The constitutional convention, made up of delegates elected by the voters, met in Little Rock in January 1836. The only important issue which caused trouble in the convention was how the members of the new state General Assembly should be apportioned among the counties. Delegates from the northern and western counties, where most of the white people lived, wanted only white men to be counted in the apportionment. Southern and eastern delegates wanted slaves counted in the apportionment, since this would give their section more senators and representatives in the new legislature. A compromise settlement was finally reached.

The new state constitution was adopted on January 30, and a copy sent to Washington for approval. Opposition in Congress to the admission of Arkansas delayed statehood for several weeks. Antislavery members objected to the admission of another slave state, and some Whigs opposed Arkansas because it would be Democratic in politics. Congressional action was not completed until June. President Jackson signed the bill admitting Arkansas to the Union on June 15, 1836.

Little Rock held a great celebration on the Fourth of July. After an election in August, the first state General Assembly met on September 12. On the following day James S. Conway became the first governor of the State of Arkansas.

STUDY AIDS

Vocabulary

Be sure that you understand the meaning of these words and phrases:

eliminate	petitions
faction	precinct
adequate	proceeded
seat of justice	celebration
resolutions	restrict
representation	duel
apportioned	memorials

Identification

Tell what part each of the following had in the story:

Henry Cassidy   Henry W. Conway
Robert Crittenden   Ambrose H. Sevier

To test your reading

On another paper, list 1-8. Opposite each number, write the word or words which complete each sentence.

1. In 1812 the name of Louisiana Territory was changed to ___.

2. Arkansas County was created out of the ___ in 1813.

3. According to the census of 1810 Arkansas had ___ people; in 1819 it had about ___.

4. Four counties created before Arkansas Territory was organized were: ___, ___, ___, ___.

5. The four governors of Arkansas Territory, in order, were ___, ___, ___, ___.

6. The Crittenden party established a newspaper called the ___.

7. Henry W. Conway was killed in a duel by ___.

8. The Crittenden supporters became known as ___; the Sevier supporters as ___.

Things to do

1. Form a historical club or society to study your own local history. If there is already an active historical society in your county, get in touch with the president or secretary and arrange to attend meetings and help with society projects.

2. Do you think that Little Rock is the best place for the state capital today? Arrange a panel discussion or debate.

3. Visit the Territorial Restoration and the Old State House in Little Rock.

4. Write a report on Andrew Jackson as president. Consult books in your library for information.

5. Find out how your town or city received its name. Has the name been changed at any time in the past?

6. Has anyone ever written a history of your county or city? Inquire at your school and public libraries.

2 Early Exploration and Settlement

Arkansas was an unknown land in 1803, but American explorers were soon moving up and down the rivers and overland as well. Behind the explorers, or even ahead of them, came the first wave of American settlers. This chapter discusses some of the earliest Arkansas travelers and their accounts of the pioneers and their land.

Explorers on the rivers. In the fall of 1804, President Thomas Jefferson sent William Dunbar to explore the Ouachita or "Washita" River. Accompanied by Dr. George Hunter, Dunbar went up the river to Hot Springs, where he found nothing but a log cabin and a few huts of split boards. The shoals at Rockport, near present-day Malvern, gave the expedition difficulty. Dunbar and Hunter found few people living along the Ouachita.

In 1806 Thomas Freeman explored Red River and described the Great Raft, a tangled mass of timbers and vegetation which the Frenchman La Harpe had seen almost a century before. James B. Wilkinson, who came down the Arkansas in 1806 - 07, saw two bands of French hunters but no white settlements except at Arkansas Post. The land was a vast wilderness inhabited only by buffalo, elk, deer and other game.

Fortesque Cuming, traveling down the Mississippi River in 1807, found settlers below the mouth of the St. Francis River. Sylvanus Phillips, who founded Helena later, lived in a two-story house, and a dozen families made their homes on Big Prairie and along the river for a few miles to the south. The people, mostly Kentuckians, raised cattle but little cotton or grain except for themselves.

Southwestern Arkansas in 1816. David Musick and William Parker, sent by the governor of Missouri Territory, traveled on horseback from Arkansas Post to Mount (or Mound) Prairie near Red River in the summer of 1816. The two men estimated that they covered nearly 200 miles before reaching the first settlement, which consisted of thirteen families living on the Ouachita River about ten miles from Hot Springs. Since there was no settlement at the springs, those who visited the hot waters for their health stayed on the Ouachita.

Thirty miles downstream Musick and Parker came to a settlement on the Caddo River, probably the one established by Jacob Barkman a few years earlier. South of the Caddo they passed through a "delightful farming country abundantly watered by clear healthy streams." Another fifty miles brought them to the Ozan settlement in what is now Hempstead County. Mount Prairie was fifteen miles from Ozan.

On their return journey the travelers stopped at the Wolf Creek settlement

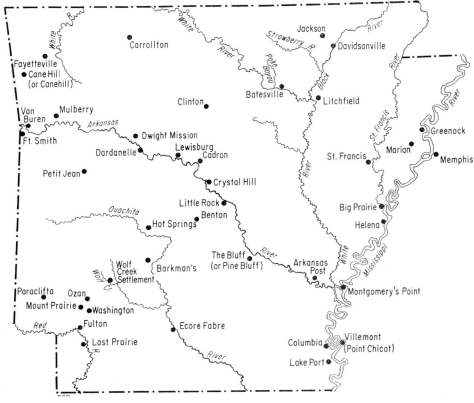

Some settlements of 1835-36 and earlier

near the present towns of Antoine and Delight. From there they returned to Hot Springs and later made their way back to Missouri. The report of Musick and Parker placed the population of southwest Arkansas at about 213 families, and praised the fine farms, corn crops and livestock there.

Schoolcraft in the Ozarks. Late in 1818 Henry Rowe Schoolcraft traveled south from Potosi, Missouri and entered what was soon to become Arkansas Territory at Mammoth Spring. He passed down the Spring River Valley, across to White River and up that stream into Missouri again. Later Schoolcraft descended White River to Poke Bayou, a village of a dozen houses where Batesville

would later be located. From there he returned to Missouri along the road which connected Arkansas Post and St. Louis.

Schoolcraft and his one companion saw the mountains of northern Arkansas as they had been in Indian times. The forested hills and valleys harbored innumerable flocks of turkey as well as uncounted deer, elk, beaver, squirrels, and other game. Bears hid in the dense canebrakes along the streams. Packs of wolves were in evidence, along with the dreaded panther. Overhead wheeled great flights of the passenger or wild pigeon, as well as ducks and geese going south.

The explorers ventured into unknown caves and passed deserted Osage hunt-

34

Cadron settlement, as seen by Thomas Nuttall in 1819

ing camps. Occasionally they came on the primitive log cabins of white hunters whose families wore skins and lived on meat, corn bread, wild honey, butter, and milk. These isolated people knew little about the outside world and were interested primarily in hunting. Disputes were sometimes resolved by shooting rather than by lawyers and courts. There were no schools or churches, and many of the people were very superstitious and believed in witchcraft.

Settled places in the Ozarks of 1818-19 were widely separated and small, as was the case all over Arkansas. Schoolcraft noted that a village near Strawberry River had a small gristmill run by water power, a whiskey distillery, a tavern, and a blacksmith shop.

Nuttall on the Arkansas. Thomas Nuttall, a scientist who made a trip up and down the Arkansas River in 1819-20, reported that Arkansas Post had only thirty or forty houses. The houses, usually surrounded by open galleries,

had many doors but no glass windows. Three business firms, supplied from New Orleans and Pittsburgh by way of the rivers, dominated the trade of the Arkansas and White River settlements. Prices of goods were high.

Agriculture was beginning in the Post area in 1819. Cotton sold for six and one-half cents a pound in the seed, and two gins had been established. Rice growing on a small scale had been successfully attempted. Figs, grapes,

Dardanelle Rock, from an early drawing

The old tavern at Washington, Hempstead County, as it appeared in 1936

plums and peaches were being produced. Cattle ranged on the prairies and in the canebrakes.

On first entering Arkansas Nuttall was impressed by the "vast trackless wilderness of trees," but as he moved up the river from Arkansas Post he found settlements never more than thirty miles apart. A few French settlers lived at the Bluff, a low ridge covered with pine which later became the site of Pine Bluff. A road from the vicinity of the Little Rock led to Mount Prairie and into Louisiana on the south, and to St. Louis in the opposite direction.

Nuttall saw several houses on both sides of the river near the Little Rock. At Crystal Hill, a few miles upstream, was a settlement begun by Jacob Pyeatt and his brother James as early as 1812. Five or six families lived at Cadron, at the mouth of Cadron Creek. A new sawmill was in operation near Cadron, but the Arkansas region lacked a grist mill for grinding corn.

Along the river between Cadron and Fort Smith, Nuttall saw white and Cherokee settlements. The explorer climbed Dardanelle Rock for a view of the river and mountains. Fort Smith consisted of two blockhouses and lines of cabins designed to house the seventy soldiers stationed there.

Early in 1820 Nuttall returned to Arkansas Post, which had just become the capital of the new Territory of Arkansas. On his way to New Orleans he visited Point Chicot, a settlement on the Mississippi below the mouth of the Arkansas.

An Englishman crosses the territory. About fifteen years later, an interesting glimpse of life and travel in Arkansas was provided by an Englishman named George William Featherstonhaugh. He and his son crossed Arkansas in a small wagon in 1834. Entering the territory from Missouri, they followed the military road through Little Rock to the Red River near Fulton. The road was often blocked by fallen trees, deep in mud and water, or filled with stumps and rocks.

In Washington, Hempstead County, the travelers heard that Sam Houston was staying at the tavern while hatching plots to free Texas from Mexican control. Featherstonhaugh crossed Red River and visited Lost Prairie, one of the earliest settlements in Miller County, before returning to Little Rock in December. The Englishman reported a story about a Christmas party at one of the taverns or hotels in Little Rock which was attended by about a hundred men but only three women. The men "soon got amazingly drunk" and danced armed to the teeth, but there were "only a few shots fired in fun."

Featherstonhaugh took a boat down the river from Little Rock as soon as the water rose enough to travel. The boat stopped at plantation landings to load cotton until it was piled high with bales. At Arkansas Post the traveler met Frederick Notrebe, a trader and planter reported to be the richest man in Arkansas.

From the Post the boat passed down the Arkansas River and through the cutoff, or connecting channel, into White River. At the hotel of William Montgomery, which stood on Montgomery's Point on the north side of White River where it enters the Mississippi, Featherstonhaugh completed his Arkansas journey.

STUDY AIDS

Vocabulary

Be sure that you understand the meaning of these words and phrases:

harbored	canebrakes
isolated	vegetation
gristmill	blockhouses
gin	estimated
galleries	shoals
vicinity	primitive
cutoff	witchcraft

Identification

Tell what part each of the following had in the story:

William Montgomery	William Dunbar
	Thomas Freeman
Frederick Notrebe	David Musick
	Jacob Pyeatt

Location

Find these places on a map:

Rockport	Strawberry River
Mount Prairie	Cadron
Ozan	Mammoth Spring
	Crystal Hill

To test your reading

On other paper, list 1-5. Opposite each number, write the word or words which complete each sentence.

1. The traveler who explored north Arkansas in 1818 was ___.

2. The traveler who explored the Arkansas River in 1819 was ___.

3. The traveler who crossed Arkansas in a small wagon in 1834 was ___.

4. In 1806 Thomas Freeman explored Red River and described the ___.

5. The planter reported to be the richest man in Arkansas was ___.

Things to do

1. Ask your local newspaper to consider beginning a series of articles on local history. Perhaps your class or historical club can help find material for such a series.

2. Do you think that people who come to the United States from foreign countries today face as many problems as the early settlers did? Why or why not?

3. Imagine yourself a traveler in pioneer Arkansas. Tell of some of your experiences.

4. Draw an outline map of Arkansas showing the principal rivers, and the routes traveled by the explorers mentioned in this chapter.

3   Rivers, Roads, and Communication

In our era of automobiles, paved highways, railroads and airplanes, we can scarcely imagine the difficulties of transportation and communication that confronted the pioneers. Rivers were more important than roads as means of travel, the mails were uncertain and slow, and newspapers were few. This chapter will help you to understand how stream channels were cleared, roads opened, and newspapers and post offices established.

The river highways. Those who came to Arkansas in the early days found the rivers the easiest routes of travel into the interior. During much of the year canoes, rafts, and even larger craft could go up and down streams such as the St. Francis, the White, the Arkansas, the Ouachita and the Red. Moving a large boat upstream against the current was difficult, but it was far easier than trying to penetrate the swamps and mountains by land.

The coming of the steamboat made river traffic easier and faster. The first steamboat to enter the Arkansas River was the **Comet,** which docked at Arkansas Post early in 1820. Two years later the **Eagle** stopped at Little Rock on its way to Dwight Mission, and in the same year the **Robert Thompson** reached Fort Smith. By the end of 1836 steamboats had ascended the White, Black, Red and St. Francis rivers.

Commercial activity on all the rivers increased greatly after 1830. In 1834 nine steamboats were operating on the Arkansas at one time. The boats delivered supplies to merchants and to army garrisons, and carried cotton, hides, furs, pelts, bear oil, pecans and other products back to New Orleans. As steamboats improved in size and speed, cargoes became larger and more valuable. Passengers were chiefly immigrants to the territory and visitors to Hot Springs. In 1834 the usual passenger fare from Little Rock to New Orleans was twenty-five dollars.

River hazards and Captain Shreve. River navigation was hazardous for boats of all kinds. Steamboats sometimes exploded, broke down, or became stranded because of low water. The steamboat pilot had to avoid sandbars, logs, boulders, shoals, and trees. Snags and sawyers, as logs and branches embedded in sand bars or stream banks were called, were a major danger.

Henry M. Shreve, a steamboat captain, invented the snagboat and in 1833 began clearing the Great Raft of Red River. By the close of the 1835 season his four boats had reduced the hundred-mile log jam to twenty-three miles, though a permanent opening was not made for another three years. Afterward new rafts kept forming at the head of the old, and the channel of Red River was not entirely navigable for many years.

Early in 1834 Shreve cleared the Arkansas River channel as far upstream as Little Rock. The people crowded the landing to see the two snagboats, and a party of Little Rock citizens was taken aboard one of them to watch her operations. As a demonstration the snagboat removed a huge cottonwood tree from the muddy bank opposite the town. The tree was raised, the root sawed off and dropped into deep water, and the trunk cut up in three pieces and set adrift. The entire task took about an hour.

Difficulties of land travel. The land traveler in early Arkansas had to walk or ride horseback along dim Indian trails too narrow for carts or wagons.

Often the trail itself could be followed only by blaze marks cut into trees. No bridges crossed the streams. Even after the trail or "trace" had been widened by cutting trees so wagons could pass, progress was slowed by stumps, mud and water.

Like those who used the rivers, the traveler by land met danger at every turn. Becoming lost in the woods was possible, if not probable. If he camped at night under the trees, fires had to be lighted to keep away wolves and panthers. At a settler's cabin the traveler might be charged dearly for a hard bed and a bad-tasting meal of corn bread and greasy bacon. Many of the inns or taverns which served as hotels were dirty and frequented by gamblers and

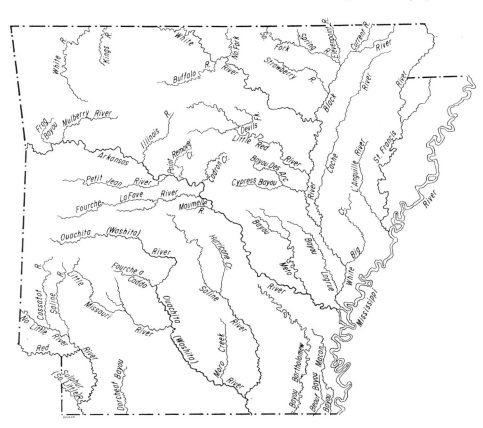

The rivers of Arkansas

A snagboat at work on the Great Raft of Red River

cutthroats. Such conditions were common throughout the Western frontier regions in early days.

Early roads and traces. The first roads were built and improved by settlers or the Federal government. Arkansas delegates to Congress worked constantly to secure appropriations to build roads. Such roads were usually constructed by the army for use in protecting the frontier, and became known as "military roads."

One of the earliest permanent roads connected Arkansas Post with Crystal Hill and Cadron along the north side of the Arkansas River. Another was the Southwest Trail, which ran from Mis-

Stage line and steamboat advertisements. From the "Arkansas Gazette," March 4, 1834

souri through northeastern Arkansas to Little Rock and on through Washington to Fulton on Red River. Thousands of settlers followed this route into Arkansas, and many others passed along it on their way to Texas. From time to time Congress appropriated money to improve the Southwest Trail, which was known also as the National Road and the Military Road.

Construction of a road from Memphis to Little Rock began in 1826, but years passed before it was an easy route to travel. Miles of swamps and numerous streams made the road hard to build and maintain. Several years after it was opened the trip from Memphis to Little Rock sometimes required twenty days by wagon.

By 1836 several other important roads had been built. One extended from Little Rock along the north side of the Arkansas River to Fort Smith. Another reached from Hopefield near

Memphis to Batesville, Fayetteville and Van Buren. A third east-west trace led from Villemont on the Mississippi to Camden, and then into the Choctaw Nation by way of Washington and Mount Prairie. Roads southward from Hot Springs ran to Monroe and Natchitoches in Louisiana. A road connected Arkansas Post with Davidsonville and St. Louis to the north and Monroe on the south. Shorter roads were blazed into sections where pioneers wished to establish homes. Poor as they were, such early roads made it possible for settlers and travelers to enter regions away from the main rivers.

Late in 1826 the first stage line began carrying mail and passengers between Little Rock and Arkansas Post. At first the stage ran only once in two weeks, and the fare one way was eight dollars. Stage lines were soon established to Hot Springs and other places, but travel by stage continued to be rough and dangerous for a long time.

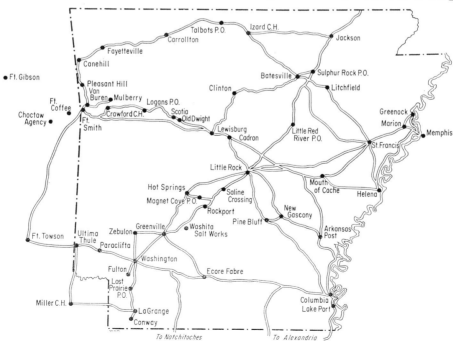

Some early roads and traces

A trip to Little Rock in 1832. The route from Montgomery's Point to Little Rock was frequently traveled in territorial days. In 1832 William F. Pope accompanied his uncle, Governor John Pope, on a return trip from the east. Forty persons made up the party. On Sunday, October 14, they went by boat from Montgomery's Point up White River and through the cutoff to Arkansas Post. In the house of Frederick Notrebe, where the group was entertained at dinner, some of the travelers were surprised to see silver, china, cut glass and other fine furnishings. Except for Notrebe's house, Arkansas Post was in a run-down condition.

The river was too low for the boat to ascend farther, so Notrebe furnished the travelers with two light wagons drawn by small ponies. The baggage filled one of the wagons. Governor Pope and his servant, both large men, rode in the other. The remaining members of the party, except one man who rode on horseback, set out and walked the entire distance of over a hundred miles.

The route lay across Grand Prairie north of the Arkansas River. The first afternoon they covered about thirteen miles before reaching a farmhouse where they spent the night. In the next two days the Pope party traveled about eighty miles. They stayed one night at a two-story plantation home with well-kept grounds and a large number of outbuildings and Negro quarters. Another night was passed at a house within twelve miles of Little Rock. The next day about noon they arrived at a point across the river from Little Rock and that afternoon crossed by ferry to the town.

Newspapers and the mails. Late in 1819 William E. Woodruff, a native of New York who came to Arkansas from Tennessee, began publishing the weekly **Arkansas Gazette** at Arkansas Post. Two years later the newspaper was moved to Little Rock. Until 1830, when Charles P. Bertrand began the **Arkansas Advocate** at Little Rock, Woodruff's paper was the only one in the territory.

Early newspapers contained much literary material as well as news and advertisements. Editors competed with one another for government contracts to print the laws, and took sides on political questions. In 1826 Woodruff started the first circulating library in Arkansas.

William E. Woodruff

Printers had to secure paper from New Orleans or elsewhere, and when rivers were low the supply sometimes failed. For news, editors depended on other papers or took the word of travelers who happened to pass. Mail service was so slow and uncertain that settlers sometimes asked travelers to deliver letters for them. Postal rates were high, and postage stamps did not come into use until 1847.

In 1816 Congress provided for a post road from St. Louis to Davidsonville in Lawrence County and from there to Arkansas Post. A post office was established at Davidsonville in June 1817, and another at Arkansas Post a short time later. Down this route a mail rider came once each month, bound for Monroe in Louisiana. According to some accounts he often carried all the Arkansas mail in his shirt pocket.

As settlement increased so did the number of post offices and postal routes. Mail service improved gradually, but flooded streams, robbers and other hindrances rendered the mails unreliable for years. Many of the pioneers who came to Arkansas never heard from their relatives in the Eastern states again.

Pioneer print shop of the "Arkansas Gazette," as exhibited in the Territorial Restoration, Little Rock

STUDY AIDS

Vocabulary

Be sure that you understand the meaning of these words and phrases:

rafts	military roads
pelts	sandbars
route	blaze marks
channel	boulders
trace	demonstration
log jam	sawyers
penetrate	snagboat
cargoes	cut glass

Identification

Tell what part each of the following had in the story:

William E. Woodruff	Henry M. Shreve
Charles P. Bertrand	William F. Pope
	Southwest Trail

To test your reading

On other paper, list 1-8. Opposite each number, write the word or words which complete each sentence.

1. In 1820 the first steamboat, the ___, reached Arkansas Post.

2. In 1822 the first steamboat, the ___, reached Little Rock.

3. The Great Raft was on ___ River.

4. Construction of a road from Memphis to Little Rock began in ___.

5. William E. Woodruff began publishing the *Arkansas Gazette* at ___ in the year ___.

6. The first post office was established at ___ in the year ___.

7. In 1826 the first circulating library in Arkansas was established by ___.

8. The first stage line began in 1826 and operated between Little Rock and ___.

Things to do

1. Imagine yourself one of Governor Pope's party in 1832. Write a story of your trip to Little Rock.

2. If you live near a large river, find out about commercial activity on the stream at the present time. Is the river navigable, or will it be made navigable soon?

3. Try to determine the routes of early roads in your county and make a map.

4. Look for pictures of early steamboats and other river craft used by American pioneers.

5. Try to find someone who has a collection of early American stamps. Perhaps the owner can arrange to show his collection to the class.

4 Pioneer Society and Life

In 1820 Governor James Miller described Arkansas as a country "very new, and society very uncultivated." This story will help you to understand the meaning of his statement.

The Indian trade at Arkansas Post. From 1803 until after the removal of the capital to Little Rock, life in Arkansas centered largely around Arkansas Post. For more than a hundred years Indians from a wide area had come to the Post to trade with the white men. In 1805-06 ten to fifteen firms there were engaged in the Indian trade.

In order to win the good will of the Indians and protect them from dishonest traders, the United States government decided to set up a trading house or "factory" at Arkansas Post. In the fall of 1805 John B. Treat, the government agent or "factor," arrived with a supply of goods. The following year he erected a building, fifty by forty feet in size and one and a half stories high, with a room beneath for curing skins and hides. He also provided a house in which the Indians lived when they came to trade at the Post.

The Arkansas Trading House kept a large variety of goods. The Indians wanted articles such as guns, gunpowder, scarlet cloth, blankets, saddles, bridles, brass kettles, mirrors, knives, red calico shirts, and silver ornaments. In exchange they offered deer, bear, and beaver skins, and bear oil and tallow. With a number of traders competing for the Indian market, business was brisk at Arkansas Post. In 1810 the government "factory" was closed, but the Indian trade continued to be the main business carried on there.

Despite the removal of the territorial capital to Little Rock, Arkansas Post remained a town of considerable importance until the Civil War. Several wealthy and cultured families continued to live there, and it was the center of trade and shipping for a large area.

The people and living conditions. In the early years of American control, most of the people who lived at Arkansas Post and along the Arkansas River were of French descent. American settlers appeared in increasing numbers after about 1815. Though mixed with the population were some adventurers and outlaws, the majority of the new settlers were people of worth, character, and intelligence.

Amusements were popular among the pioneers, possibly because of French influence. At Arkansas Post parties and balls were all-night affairs every weekend. Both men and women appeared at the gambling tables. Timothy Flint, a Protestant missionary who preached in French at the Post in the summer of 1819, found the people polite but disinterested. Some would come dressed for a ball and go directly from the serv-

The Stagecoach House near Little Rock, built in 1836 or earlier, was an inn on
the Southwest Trail

ice to the dance. Others would come in, listen for awhile and then go next door to a billiard room.

Money was scarce and supplies often short. In 1825 Governor George Izard asked the government for an iron chest in which to keep the public funds, since the merchants in Little Rock were rarely able to cash the bills sent by the United States treasury. A special agent had to be sent to New Orleans to cash checks. When the rivers became too low for large boats, flour and coffee were often in short supply and prices rose sharply.

According to Governor James Miller in 1820, many of the people lived in houses that were little better than squares of rail fence. In 1834 George W. Featherstonhaugh noticed that the pioneers were often indifferent to per-

sonal comforts. Accustomed to hardships, they endured poor food and housing but seemed cheerful and contented. Bread, meat and coffee were the staple foods.

Illness was widespread among the people of early Arkansas and the death rate was high, especially among children. Fevers were common during the warm months. Arkansas had no regular public health work, and there were no hospitals and few good doctors. Patent medicines were widely used. Since most doctors also performed dental work, dentists were slow to appear.

Hunting and fishing. Pioneer Arkansas was already widely known as a sportsman's country. Early French explorers described the abundance of game in the

46

valleys of the Arkansas, the White, and the St. Francis rivers. The first inhabitants of Arkansas seen by Thomas Nuttall in 1819 were hunters, and he thought it natural that the Quapaw Indians should believe the future life was in happy hunting grounds. Henry Rowe Schoolcraft and his companion, both inexperienced hunters, lived almost entirely on wild life during several months of tramping over south Missouri and north Arkansas. In two months of travel in the Arkansas Ozarks, Schoolcraft recorded twenty different species of game, ranging from quail to buffalo. The lakes and streams of early Arkansas abounded in fish.

To the pioneer, hunting and fishing were not only recreation but often his principal means of providing food and clothing for his family. Many hunters kept packs of bear dogs and sometimes went on bear hunts that lasted for several days. In pioneer homes bear meat and venison were often chief articles of diet. Bear skins served as rugs and bed coverings, while deer hides were used to make clothing. Barbecues and fish fries were popular social occasions.

Crime and punishment. Every new country or region has its problems of crime and law enforcement, and pioneer Arkansas was no exception. Judges were reluctant to come to the new territory. Criminals often escaped into the woods and were never captured. Occasionally bands of armed bandits charged into Little Rock and other places and released their friends from jail. Arkansas had no penitentiary until after statehood. The first criminal to be executed was a soldier who was hanged in Little Rock in 1828.

Prominent men of pioneer Arkansas sometimes challenged one another to duels over personal differences. The General Assembly began passing laws against dueling as early as 1820, but participants simply went beyond the bounds of Arkansas. Though duels were never frequent, the practice did not disappear entirely until the Civil War.

Pioneer Arkansans took their politics so seriously that campaigns sometimes resulted in street fights and even murders. During the campaign of 1827 conditions in Little Rock became so tense that people avoided sitting near open windows, even in broad daylight. In election years newspapers were filled with threats and slanderous letters.

A pioneer fireplace, with cooking utensils and other items used by early settlers. How many objects can you identify?

When the law failed to punish criminals, respectable citizens sometimes took the law into their own hands. In 1834-35 vigilance committees took action against the John A. Murrell gang of outlaws. Suspicious characters were examined and whipped. In 1835 a citizens' association ran most of the gamblers out of Little Rock.

Little Rock in pioneer days. When the territorial government moved to Little Rock in 1821 the place contained fewer than a dozen houses and no regularly laid off streets. The town grew so slowly that in 1822 there was talk that the capital might be moved again unless the developers took more interest in its improvement. At one time an attempt was made to rename Little Rock, and "Arkopolis" appears on some early maps.

Little Rock experienced its first period of growth in 1824. By the month of July about forty families lived there instead of the five or six of a year earlier, and a building boom was under way. In 1827 the town contained about sixty buildings, six of them brick, eight of them frame, and the others log cabins. With the growth of Little Rock, life in the territory came to center more and more around the new location, but contact with Arkansas Post continued both by boats on the river and by the road across Grand Prairie.

Like other frontier towns, the capital of Arkansas Territory had its unattractive aspects. In 1827 Little Rock was still covered with trees and the streets were no more than trails from house to house. After the trees were cut down the stumps were left, and as late as 1835 the streets were deeply gullied and covered with stumps and

"Square" nails, such as these from a building at Dover, Pope County, were used in the construction of many pioneer houses

rubbish. Little Rock had no system of fire protection for many years. The "Town Branch" overflowed with every hard rain. Drinking and gambling were common.

Despite such hindrances, Little Rock made progress. Moral conditions improved after churches began to be established. Washington Irving, who stopped at Little Rock in 1832, noted in his journal that the place was a flourishing village with two rival newspapers and three hotels. Horse races and theatrical performances began in 1834. In the five years after 1830 the population increased from 450 to over 700. The Texas Revolution and the approach of statehood gave a great boost to the capital. In the spring of 1836 taverns and houses were occupied, business was increasing, and the future of Little Rock and Arkansas looked bright.

By the end of the territorial period several other settlements were coming to be important shipping points and centers of trade and community life.

This was true of Batesville, Fort Smith, Helena, Pine Bluff, and Camden, as well as Washington and Fayetteville which were not located on waterways.

STUDY AIDS

Vocabulary

Be sure that you understand the meaning of these words and phrases:

calico	tavern
variety	venison
descent	reluctant
patent medicines	campaign
	vigilance committee

Identification

Tell what part each of the following had in the story:

Thomas Nuttall	John A. Murrell
Timothy Flint	Washington Irving
	James Miller

To test your reading

On other paper, list 1-9. Opposite each number, write the word or words which complete each sentence.

1. Arkansas Post was the center of trade and shipping for a large area until the ⸺.

2. The government "factor" at Arkansas Post was ⸺.

3. The government store at Arkansas Post was called a ⸺.

4. A Protestant missionary who preached at Arkansas Post in 1819 was ⸺.

5. A name for Little Rock that appears on some early maps is ⸺.

6. A noted author who visited Little Rock in 1832 was ⸺.

7. In 1830 the population of Little Rock was ⸺; in 1835 it was ⸺.

8. By 1836 these towns were becoming important: ⸺, ⸺, ⸺, ⸺, ⸺, ⸺, ⸺.

9. In 1827 Little Rock contained about ⸺ buildings, ⸺ of them brick, ⸺ of them frame, and the others ⸺.

Things to do

1. When was your town or county seat first settled? Draw a simple map showing principal streets, public buildings and parks as they are today. Which part of town is the oldest, or has the oldest buildings?

2. Using other books in your library, prepare a report on the practice of dueling. What were the rules governing the conduct of duels?

3. Draw a picture of Little Rock as you imagine that it appeared in 1827.

4. Construct a model of a pioneer home or building. Use an authentic picture, and consult other books for more information.

5. Write a story about a bear hunt in pioneer Arkansas.

5 Surveying the Land

The land of Arkansas first belonged to the Indians. From the Indian tribes title passed to the United States government, and from the government to private owners. This chapter tells the story of the earliest land surveys and land claims.

The Indian land system. Among the Indians of early Arkansas, land belonged to the tribe rather than to individuals. At the time of the Louisiana Purchase, the Quapaws claimed the land south of the Arkansas River for a distance of about a hundred miles, and extending westward for an indefinite distance. The Osages claimed a large area north of the Arkansas.

Whenever the people of an Indian village decided to move, they could choose any location on tribal lands so long as they did not interfere with others. A family or a single individual could do the same. Among the Indians land was never bought or sold. Since they lived principally by hunting, individual Indians had little reason to claim large areas. The land which one occupied was his own until he decided to leave, or until someone drove him away.

The Spanish land claims. Soon after the purchase of Louisiana, President Thomas Jefferson appointed a commission of three members to investigate the Spanish land grants and decide which of these grants should be honored under American law. The commission reported that only about a fourth of the Spanish titles were valid under the laws of Spain, and that only these should be honored under the laws of the United States.

Many of the claimants whose titles were declared invalid appealed to Congress and the courts, where disputes continued for years. A number of counterfeit land grants made the situation more complicated. In Arkansas the Bowie land frauds of 1829 were based on the pretended claims of John J. Bowie of Helena to Spanish lands. Numerous grants were forged in New Orleans and distributed among influential people in Arkansas. Prosecution was difficult, but a special court finally ruled against most of the Bowie claims.

Legal trouble over Spanish claims confused Arkansas land titles for many years. The United States courts finally recognized 160 of these claims totaling almost 75,000 acres. A third of the acreage was in Arkansas County, while the rest was scattered over a dozen other eastern and northeastern counties. The United States government surveyed all the old Spanish grants during the period 1816-25.

The pioneers claim the land. The United States acquired title to the land of Arkansas by the purchase of Louisiana from France, and by making treaties with Indian tribes in which the Indians agreed to give up or exchange their lands. Except for the relatively few Spanish grants which were honored by the American government, practical-

Square-hewing a log with a broadaxe, Newton County

ly all land in Arkansas was once the property of the United States.

The government allowed settlers to acquire lands according to fixed rules. The governmental policy was to survey lands into tracts of convenient size and offer them for sale. When a settler paid for his land, the government gave him a deed called a "land warrant" or "land patent." Sometimes lands were given to former soldiers.

The earliest of American pioneers who came to Arkansas were mostly hunters and trappers who had little intention of settling down and buying land. They built log cabins where they pleased, cleared small garden plots, and moved on when game became scarce. When the farmers began to arrive, they were often so eager to obtain the best lands that they refused to wait for surveyors and sales. They entered the country by river boat or covered wagon, selected land near a spring, and began clearing away the forest. Such settlers on public lands were known as "squatters."

Landholdings near Arkansas Post in 1829. The arpent, about four-fifths of an acre, was the unit of land measurement used by the French and Spanish

The "Sunk Lands" of northeastern Arkansas, from an early drawing

Since these squatters were helping to develop the country, Congress in 1814 passed a preemption law for their benefit. This law gave the squatter the first chance to buy the land he had settled when it should be offered for sale by the government. The first settler therefore had a "preemption right" or "squatter's right" to the land he had begun to improve.

Land speculators often tried to use the preemption law for their own advantage. Such speculators searched for hunters and others who had lived briefly on choice lands, purchased their preemption rights for a few dollars, and filed claims. Such claims resulted in a large number of new regulations, decisions, and laws.

The New Madrid earthquake. On December 16, 1811 the New Madrid area, embracing what is now northeastern Arkansas and southeastern Missouri,

experienced a severe earthquake. A series of earth tremors and shocks continued for about a year, and the earthquake was felt throughout much of Arkansas and the Mississippi Valley.

The New Madrid earthquake changed the face of the land over a wide region. The tremors formed new lakes and bayous, and altered the courses of the St. Francis and the Mississippi rivers. Large areas were submerged and became the "Sunk Lands" of northeastern Arkansas. Entire forests were swallowed up by the earth, and some of the damaged land could not be surveyed for many years.

Many settlers in the New Madrid region lost their lands because of the earthquake. In 1815 Congress passed a law granting them certificates entitling them to select other unoccupied lands in the territory. Holders of these "New Madrid certificates" often sold them, and many fell into the hands of speculators. One group of speculators tried to locate one such claim on the site of Little Rock, and an attempt was made to get control of Hot Springs in the same way.

Land surveying begins. In the War of 1812 the United States government offered a bounty of 160 acres to every soldier who would enlist. Beginning in 1815 two million acres of the best lands located between the Arkansas and St. Francis rivers were surveyed and set apart for military bounties. Each veteran was given a warrant and the land department located it by a lottery process.

To begin the survey, a group of surveyors went to the mouth of the St. Francis River and measured off a "base

A "witness tree" in Newton County, said to have been marked by a surveying party in 1839. The large hole in the trunk was made so that the figures, carved when the tree was much smaller, could be seen

Stone marking the intersection of the base line and the principal meridian, located at the border of Monroe, Lee and Phillips counties

line" straight west to the Arkansas River. Another group began at the mouth of the Arkansas and surveyed another line called the "fifth principal meridian" or "prime meridian" due north to the Missouri River.

After the base line and the principal meridian had been established, the surveyors laid off subordinate base lines called "standard lines" and subordinate meridians called "guide meridians." Township lines parallel to the base line were surveyed at intervals of six miles, and range lines parallel to the principal meridian were marked out at similar intervals. In this way the land was divided into townships six miles square.

Townships were numbered north and south of the base line and east and west of the principal meridian. Each township included thirty-six sections of land. A section contained 640 acres and was further subdivided into quarter sections

53

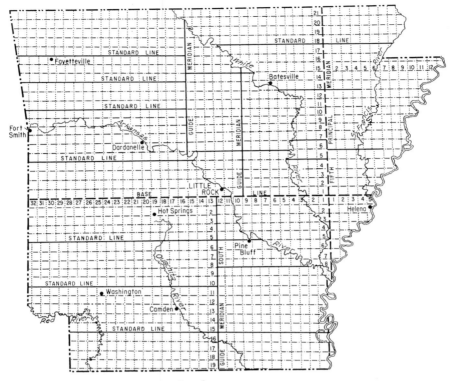

Land survey map

of 160 acres each. Quarter sections included four forty-acre tracts of land.

Land surveying required the keeping of careful records and plats, and all lines had to be marked. In wooded regions surveying parties marked corners by driving stakes into the ground, and by carving figures on "witness trees." Where there were no trees the surveyors heaped up mounds of varying size, with larger mounds marking township corners. Within each mound the surveyor was required to deposit a rock, a small cylinder of charcoal, or a quantity of glass or cinders from a blacksmith's shop.

Slow progress of the survey. Surveying all the lands of Arkansas required many years, much money and the services of many men. Begun in 1815, the survey was still going on when Arkansas became a state in 1836. The base line was completed to the western border of Arkansas in 1841. Lands in areas most in demand were surveyed first. Often several groups of surveyors were at work in different parts of Arkansas at the same time.

Surveyors usually contracted to survey a certain number of townships at a fixed sum per mile. At first the contract price for surveying uplands was three dollars a mile and for bottom lands four dollars a mile. Later the rate of payment was increased to four dollars and six dollars. Surveying bottom lands was especially difficult because of thickets, canebrakes, and marshes. A complete survey of sixty townships at three dollars a mile would have cost over $50,000, so surveying was always expensive.

In 1818 the General Land Office ordered the survey of sixty townships for sale. The work was finished the following year, but none of the land was sold until 1821. Land offices which opened at Arkansas Post and Davidsonville in 1820 were soon moved to Little Rock and Batesville, as more convenient locations. In 1832 Congress divided Arkansas into four land districts and established new offices at Fayetteville and Washington.

Prior to 1820 the government tried to sell 160-acre tracts of land for two dollars an acre, payable in four years, but too many settlers failed to pay and the plan was abandoned. The Arkansas land offices at first sold tracts as small as eighty acres for $1.25 an acre, requiring full payment at the time of purchase. In 1832 a new regulation permitted sale of forty-acre tracts.

STUDY AIDS

Vocabulary

Be sure that you understand the meaning of these words and phrases:

survey	warrant
investigate	lottery
honored	standard lines
situation	guide meridians
squatter	fifth principal
preemption	meridian
range lines	base line
invalid	military bounties

To test your reading

On other paper, list 1-10. Opposite each number write the word or words which complete each sentence.

1. Each township is divided into __ sections.

2. Each section contains __ acres.

3. Settlers who lived on government land without a __ were called __.

4. The United States survey of Arkansas began in the year __.

5. In prairie regions corners were marked by __.

6. At first the price for surveying upland was __ a mile.

7. A law made in 1832 permitted the sale of __ acre tracts.

8. In wooded regions surveyors marked corners by __.

9. The number of Spanish claims finally recognized was __.

10. The Osages claimed a large area of land north of the __ River.

Things to do

1. Find out the number of the section, township and range in which your school is located; also your home.

2. Try to locate a section line or a township line near your school.

3. Inquire about the location of "land corners" and "witness trees" in your area.

4. See if you can find someone who owns an original land warrant or land patent. Such warrants were usually large documents made of parchment, and signed by the President of the United States or by his secretary.

5. If you live on a farm, determine how much the land would have cost if it had been purchased from the United States government in 1819 or 1821.

6   The Indians Depart

Four principal Indian tribes lived in Arkansas during the pioneer period, but before 1836 all of them were gone. The whites were never content until they secured all the Indian lands, and the Indian nations lacked the strength or the will to resist. This chapter tells the story of the disappearance of the Indians from pioneer Arkansas.

The Osage treaties. In the period 1803 to 1836 four principal Indian tribes, the Osages, Quapaws, Choctaws, and Cherokees, lived in the Arkansas region. The Osages and Quapaws had been in Arkansas for a long time. The Cherokees and Choctaws first drifted in from east of the Mississippi and later received grants of land from the Federal government. Small groups of Delawares, Shawnees, Caddo and others also lived in Arkansas.

In 1803 the Osages, a roving tribe of buffalo hunters, lived in the region north of the Arkansas River and extending to the west. Increasing trouble with the whites led to a treaty in 1808 between the Osages and the United States. By the terms of this treaty the Osages gave up all their lands in what is now northern Arkansas except the extreme western part. In 1816 Major William L. Lovely, a government agent, persuaded the Osage chiefs to cede another tract north of the Arkansas River and west of the line of 1808.

The small area remaining to the Osages in northwestern Arkansas disappeared entirely after new treaties were signed in 1818 and 1825. These treaties eliminated Osage claims to present-day Washington and Benton counties, and located the tribe in what is now Oklahoma.

The Quapaw cessions. Though they continued to claim the region south of the Arkansas River, the Quapaw tribe had declined seriously in numbers before Arkansas became a territory. Three villages, with a total population of about 600 persons, lay south of the river between Arkansas Post and the Pine Bluff area. A few scattered families lived outside the villages.

As white settlement increased, pressure began to be placed on the government to restrict the Quapaw claims. In 1818 the Quapaws ceded to the United States all their lands except a reservation located south of the Arkansas and extending from Arkansas Post to Little Rock.

Soon the whites were clamoring for the reservation lands also, and in 1824 Acting Governor Robert Crittenden negotiated a new treaty with the Quapaws. The Indians agreed to give up all their lands, move to Red River, and join the Caddo.

The Quapaws did not prosper on Red River. The Caddo were unfriendly, the crops failed, government agents defrauded the Indians, and diseases and starvation carried away one fourth of their number. The remaining Quapaws made their way back to their old homes on the Arkansas, but white settlers had already taken their former lands. In

Lands once claimed by the Osages and Quapaws
in the present states of Arkansas, Missouri,
Kansas, Oklahoma and Louisiana

1833 the government gave the Quapaws new lands in what is now extreme northeastern Oklahoma, where many of their descendants still live.

The Choctaw reservation. The original home of the Choctaw Indians was in the central and southern parts of Alabama and Mississippi. They were friends of the French, and when England took over the land east of the Mississippi River in 1763 some of the Choctaws began moving west into Arkansas. In 1819 there was at least one Choctaw village on the Arkansas River and individual families were scattered over the southern part of the territory.

A treaty signed in 1820 provided for the removal of the main body of the Choctaw tribe from Mississippi and Alabama to a reservation in Arkansas. The eastern line of the new reservation was to run from Point Remove Creek, on the Arkansas River near the present city of Morrilton, to the Red River near Fulton. West of this line, territory including about a dozen present-day Arkansas counties was to be turned over to the Choctaws.

The treaty caused a storm of protest in Arkansas. At least 3,000 white settlers lived in the part of southwestern Arkansas which was to be occupied again by Indians. Some of the settlers prepared to move to Texas while others threatened to make war on the Choctaws. The Arkansas General Assembly petitioned Congress for help.

The Choctaws accepted a compromise settlement in 1825. A new treaty gave them lands between the Arkansas and Red rivers but located west of a line from Fort Smith due south to the Red. Only those white settlers living west of the new line had to move elsewhere. The new Choctaw line became the southern part of the permanent western boundary of Arkansas.

The Arkansas Cherokees. The original home of the Cherokees was in Tennessee, Georgia, and the Carolinas. Soon after the American Revolution, trouble with white traders and settlers caused some of the Cherokees to move west. Most of them settled along the St. Francis and White rivers, where in 1805 their number was estimated at more than 1,000. Beginning in 1812 the Indians moved still farther west and settled along the north side of the Arkansas River between the present cities of Morrilton and Fort Smith.

By a treaty made in 1817, many Cherokees in the east exchanged their lands for new holdings between the Arkansas and White rivers. During 1818 and 1819 Cherokees came to Arkansas in such numbers that the "Cherokee Nation West" soon made up a third of the entire tribe. The eastern boundary of their reservation was a line extending from the vicinity of the present Morrilton to a point near Batesville.

The Arkansas Cherokees were a civilized, agricultural people. For many years they had intermarried with the whites and many of them now resembled white people more than Indians. Industrious Cherokee farmers acquired extensive property holdings, including land, slaves, and livestock. Their farms were often well-cultivated and their families generally enjoyed decent food, clothing, and housing. Cherokee government and law enforcement compared favorably with that among the whites. Sequoya, who invented the Cherokee alphabet, lived in Arkansas for several years.

Cherokee and Choctaw lands and boundaries

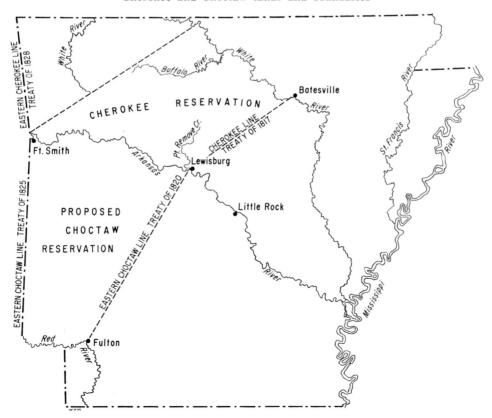

Dwight Mission. In 1818 one of the chiefs of the western Cherokees invited a Protestant mission board to send missionaries to his people. As a result, Cephas Washburn and Alfred Finney, accompanied by their families, established Dwight Mission in the spring of 1820. The mission was located on Illinois Bayou near the present city of Russellville, and included the first school to be established in Arkansas Territory.

Within two years Washburn had an enrollment of about seventy-five or eighty Cherokee boys and girls in the mission school. In 1828 there were eight families attached to the mission, all from New England, and the entire

Cephas Washburn

Dwight Mission, from a drawing made in 1824

establishment included thirty buildings. The school at Dwight acquired a wide reputation for a high quality of instruction. When the Cherokees left Arkansas the mission moved with them into what is now Oklahoma.

The Cherokee-Osage wars. Trouble between the Cherokees and Osages began almost as soon as the first Cherokees settled in Arkansas. As the number of Cherokee immigrants continued to increase the Osages took the warpath.

59

In 1817 the Federal government sent Major Stephen H. Long to establish an army post at Belle Point, near where the Poteau River enters the Arkansas. Named "Fort Smith" for General Thomas A. Smith, the new post was intended to help keep peace among the Indians. Another military post, called Cantonment Gibson or Fort Gibson, was later established on Grand River in present-day Oklahoma.

At a council in St. Louis in 1818 the Cherokees and Osages agreed to a treaty of peace, but its terms were soon broken. Governor James Miller of Arkansas, who was also superintendent of Indian affairs, secured a temporary peace in 1820, but war broke out again the next year. Most of the fighting was carried on by raiding parties. The United States government compelled the conclusion of peace in 1822, but trouble between the two Indian tribes continued for years.

Removal of the western Cherokees. In 1823 Acting Governor Robert Crittenden established the western boundary of the Cherokee reservation and ordered all the Indians living south of

the Arkansas River to move to the north bank. Cherokee leaders were dissatisfied with the boundary and persuaded the Federal government to order a new survey. The result added almost a million acres to the Cherokee holdings.

The boundary settlement failed to prevent increasing friction between whites and Cherokees. In 1828 the Indians agreed to a treaty by which they exchanged their Arkansas reservation for other lands in what is now northeastern Oklahoma. Arkansas was henceforth free of Indians except for the later passage of the eastern Cherokees and other tribes on their way to Oklahoma.

The new boundary between the Territory of Arkansas and the Cherokee Nation was run in 1828-29. It extended north from the Arkansas River, at the head of the Choctaw line in the vicinity of Fort Smith, to the southwest corner of Missouri. The western boundary of Arkansas was now permanently established, except for the corner adjoining Texas which was not surveyed until after Texas won its independence from Mexico in 1836.

Fort Smith in 1821

STUDY AIDS

Vocabulary

Be sure that you understand the meaning of these words:

negotiated
reservation
invented
mission

bayou
reputation
friction
treaty
cantonment

Identification

Tell what part each of the following had in the story:

Cephas Washburn
Thomas A. Smith
Point Remove
  Creek

Robert Crittenden
Sequoya
William L. Lovely
Alfred Finney

To test your reading

On another paper, list 1-10. Opposite each number, write the word or words which complete each sentence.

1. The four principal Indian tribes that lived in Arkansas in territorial days were —, —, —, —.

2. Four other tribes of lesser importance that lived in Arkansas were —, —, —, —.

3. The Osages lived north of the — River.

4. The Quapaws lived south of the — River.

5. The Quapaws first moved to — River and united with the —.

6. In 1820 the — Indians were granted land in southwestern Arkansas.

7. The original home of the Choctaws was in the states of — and —.

8. Dwight Mission was established in the year — on — Bayou, near the present city of —.

9. In Arkansas in 1820 the superintendent of Indian affairs was —.

10. The Indian who invented the Cherokee alphabet was —.

Things to do

1. Make a report on some of the crafts and skills which the American Indians taught the white men. Boy Scout and Girl Scout handbooks tell about Indian crafts and skills that are still useful today.

2. Find out if anyone in your community has a collection of Indian arrowheads, pottery or other articles. If so, try to arrange a visit to the collection, or perhaps a classroom display.

3. Determine the treaty and date at which the last Indian title to land on which you now live was extinguished.

4. Do any rivers, creeks, mountains, towns or other places in your county have Indian names?

Reviewing the Unit

1. Why was Arkansas detached from Missouri and made a separate territory?

2. What were newspapers like in the early days?

3. Why was the work of Captain Shreve so important to pioneer Arkansas?

4. Why was pioneer Arkansas known widely as a sportsman's country?

5. Who were some of the explorers and travelers during the pioneer period, and which parts of Arkansas did each visit?

6. How could pioneer settlers secure title to land?

7. Why did the Choctaw treaty of 1820 arouse such a storm of protest in Arkansas?

Mount Magazine, in western Arkansas, from a drawing made in 1859

Unit Three

Frontier Arkansas, 1836-1861

The Chapters

THE FIRST quarter century after Arkansas became a state was an era of vigorous growth and rapid development. Young Arkansas was a frontier state, but frontier conditions were changing rapidly.

Attracted by the abundance of cheap land, immigrants by the thousands poured into Arkansas. Year by year great acreages of forest disappeared before the axes of the newcomers. Farms multiplied in the uplands, and extensive cotton plantations spread over the delta and river valleys. The slavery system became more and more important to the Arkansas economy.

Increasing settlement brought social institutions such as schools and churches. Political parties wrangled over public issues, and Arkansans learned by experience that wildcat banking was no road to easy prosperity. Some Arkansans sought gold or glory in California, Texas or Mexico, while at home a talented crop of writers and travelers gave Arkansas a reputation as a permanent frontier.

1   Democrats, Whigs, and Know-Nothings

Political rivalry was keen during the years of early statehood. Democrats, Whigs and Know-Nothings struggled for position and power. Frontier politics was generally serious business, but sometimes campaigns resembled a kind of sport.

The Constitution of 1836. The first constitution of Arkansas was similar to constitutions drawn up during the same period in some of the other Southern states. The governor was to serve for a term of four years, but was forbidden to serve more than eight years in any twelve. Other state officials such as the secretary of state, auditor, and treasurer were to be chosen by the General Assembly, as were the Supreme Court judges and circuit judges.

The General Assembly was a legislative body of two chambers, the Senate and House of Representatives. Regular meetings were to be held once every two years. Senators served four-year terms, representatives only two. Voters in the counties and townships chose local officials. The county court, composed of justices of the peace, was important in local government, since it levied taxes and built roads, bridges, and public buildings.

Like other states, Arkansas was entitled to two United States senators and at least one representative in the lower house of Congress. After 1850 Arkansas had sufficient population to elect two representatives. The General Assembly chose United States senators for six-year terms, while representatives were popularly elected for terms of two years.

Democratic-Whig rivalry. National political parties as we know them today appeared while Arkansas was still a territory. Supporters of President Andrew Jackson called themselves Democrats, while Jackson's opponents were known as Whigs. In Arkansas the supporters of Congressional Delegate Ambrose H. Sevier, Governor John Pope, and Governor William S. Fulton became Democrats. Many of the supporters of Robert Crittenden became Whigs.

The Democratic party was the majority party in Arkansas until the Civil War. In every presidential election the state's electoral votes were cast for the Democratic national ticket. The Democrats controlled the state government, and all the governors and United States senators were Democrats. Only one Whig, Thomas W. Newton, was ever elected to Congress from Arkansas, and he served for only part of a term.

Despite the fact that its candidates usually lost, the Whig party possessed considerable strength. It was strong in the north and northwest, where slaves were few, though some lowland planters also were Whigs. In the General Assembly of 1842 the Senate had fourteen Democrats and seven Whigs, while the House numbered forty-two Democrats and twenty Whigs. In 1844

CONSTITUTION

OF THE

STATE OF ARKANSAS.

WE, the People of the Territory of Arkansas, by our Representatives in Convention assembled, at Little Rock, on Monday, the 4th day of January, A. D. 1836, and of the Independence of the United States the sixtieth year, having the right of admission into the Union as one of the United States of America, consistent with the Federal Constitution, and by virtue of the Treaty of Cession, by France to the United States, of the Province of Louisiana, in order to secure to ourselves and our posterity the enjoyment of all the rights of life, liberty, and property, and the free pursuit of happiness, do mutually agree with each other to form ourselves into a free and independent State, by the name and style of " *The State of Arkansas,*" and do ordain and establish the following Constitution for the government thereof.

The preamble to the Constitution of 1836

there were twenty-one Democrats and four Whigs in the Senate, and sixty Democrats and fourteen Whigs in the House. Some historians believe that the Whigs had more popular support than such figures reveal, and that the method of districting the state did not give them representation according to their numbers.

Popular interest in politics. Campaigns and elections were matters of great interest to many people in Arkansas. Newspapers displayed emblems and slogans, and editors reported the news in ways designed to favor the party of their choice. Campaigns featured stump speakings, torchlight parades, rallies, fist fights, and occasional stab-

bings. Liquor flowed freely, especially at election time.

The "log cabin and hard cider" campaign of 1840 was especially colorful. The Whigs advertised their presidential candidate, William Henry Harrison, as a plain man who would be content to live in a log cabin and drink hard cider

Emblem from a Whig campaign banner, 1840

like the common people. According to the Whigs, Democratic President Martin Van Buren was an aristocrat who had to have a palace and the best wines. Both parties held rallies all over Arkansas, including one Whig parade in Little Rock which turned out 4,000 or more marchers. The Whigs used canoes, log cabins, cider barrels, live raccoons, and humorous songs to stir up enthusiasm. Harrison failed to carry Arkansas but won the presidency.

Marion County, deep in the Arkansas Ozarks, became the scene of a civil war which resulted in part from political rivalry. There two leading families, the Tutts and the Everetts, each desired to control county offices. The Tutts were Whigs and the Everetts were Democrats. Quarrels on election days led to fights and eventually to murders. The people of the county took sides, and between 1844 and 1849 conditions in Marion County were very bad. Governor John S. Roane finally sent the state militia into the area to restore order.

A ballot box used in the elections of 1860, Phillips County

Nominations and voting. Party candidates for office were chosen by conventions rather than by primaries. Party members in the townships first selected delegates to county conventions. County conventions chose candidates for

The courthouse of Clark County at Arkadelphia, built in 1844

county offices and appointed delegates to the party's state convention. The state convention made nominations for governor and other high offices, after which the candidates carried their campaigns to the voters.

The convention system made "machine" rule, or control of the party by a few leaders, fairly easy. Conventions often did little more than approve the candidates who had been selected already by political leaders, and adopt a platform of principles prepared in advance.

For voting there was no poll tax requirement and no registration system. The voter entered the polling place, told the clerks how he wished to vote, and they entered his vote in a public poll book. In 1846 the General Assembly provided for a secret ballot, but returned to the voice method in 1850 because so many voters could not read and write. Ballot voting was revived again in 1854. The state Constitution of 1864 went back to voice voting, and not until the adoption of the Constitution of 1874 did the use of ballots come to stay.

James S. Conway

Elias N. Conway

During the early territorial period, the right to vote was limited to white men over twenty-one years old who had lived in Arkansas for a year and paid a territorial or county tax. Later the tax requirement was abolished and the residence requirement reduced to six months, and the Constitution of 1836 continued this arrangement.

The Conway - Johnson Dynasty. The Democratic party, which ruled Arkansas from statehood until the Civil War, was itself controlled by a powerful family machine which historians have called the Conway-Johnson Dynasty. The Conways, the Johnsons and their friends became politically dominant while Arkansas was still a territory. Henry W. Conway served as delegate to Congress from 1823 until his death in 1827. Henry's brother, James S. Conway, became the first governor of the state in 1836 and served four years. Another brother, Elias N. Conway, served two terms as governor from 1852 until 1860.

Ambrose H. Sevier, delegate to Congress from 1827 until 1836, was a cousin of Henry W. Conway and son-in-law of Superior Court Judge Benjamin Johnson. When Arkansas achieved statehood Sevier became a United States senator and served until 1848. Benjamin Johnson was Federal district judge from 1836 until his death thirteen years later. His son Robert W. Johnson was in the lower house of Congress from 1847 until 1853, and then in the Senate until the Civil War.

The Rector family was also a part of the combination. William Rector, who was surveyor general of Missouri, Illinois and Arkansas, may have caused his nephew Henry W. Conway to come to Arkansas in 1820. Elias Rector, a cousin of Henry W. Conway, served as Federal marshal for Arkansas. Another cousin, Wharton Rector, was prominent in Arkansas public life.

The Conway-Johnson-Rector machine had to contend with occasional challenges to its control of the Democratic party. In 1844 the Democrats held two state conventions before they could agree on a slate of candidates, and their second candidate for the governorship withdrew before the election. Yet the compromise Democratic candidate, Thomas S. Drew, still managed to defeat the Whig and independent Democratic contenders for the office. In 1852 the machine choice for governor, Elias N. Conway, defeated an independent candidate who had the support of many Whigs.

The Know-Nothing party. By 1854 the Whig party was dead nationally because of trouble over the slavery issue. Some Arkansas Whig leaders like Albert Pike and Absalom Fowler joined the new American or Know - Nothing party, which tried to take the place of the Whigs.

The American party operated through a system of secret lodges which Pike organized in Arkansas. Members were pledged to secrecy, and when asked about the party usually professed to "know nothing" about it. The Know-Nothing party wanted to keep foreigners out of the United States and was hostile to the Catholic Church.

For a time the Know - Nothings seemed about to become a strong party. They made a determined campaign in 1856, but the decisive defeat of their candidates for governor and for Congress was a blow from which the American party never recovered.

Trouble increased among the Democrats after the opposition parties disappeared. The two congressmen elected in 1858, Thomas C. Hindman and Albert Rust, came out openly against the Conway-Johnson Dynasty. In 1860 Henry M. Rector, an independent Democrat, defeated the Conway-Johnson candidate and for the first time overturned machine rule of the state house.

STUDY AIDS

Vocabulary

Be sure that you understand the meaning of these words and phrases:

levied	slate
featured	dynasty
militia	secret lodges
electoral votes	professed
aristocrat	decisive
delegate	machine rule
cast	slogans

Identification

Tell what part each of the following had in the story:

Henry M. Rector	Albert Pike
Albert Rust	Elias N. Conway
Marion County war	Robert W. Johnson
	Absalom Fowler
Thomas C. Hindman	

To test your reading

On other paper, list 1-9. Opposite each number, write the word or words which complete each sentence.

1. The only Whig ever to be elected to Congress from Arkansas was ___.

2. The first two United States senators from Arkansas were ___ and ___.

3. Supporters of Ambrose H. Sevier became ___.

4. Supporters of Robert Crittenden became ___.

5. The first governor to overturn machine rule in the state was ___.

6. Albert Pike and Absalom Fowler were leaders of the ___ party.

7. The term of the governor, according to the Constitution of 1836, was ___ years.

8. The majority party in Arkansas until the Civil War was the ___ party.

9. The Know-Nothing party was also known as the ___ party.

Things to do

1. Imagine yourself at a Whig or Democratic rally in Little Rock in 1840. Tell of some of the things that you saw and mention some of the men present.

2. Go to your courthouse or city hall and find out how voting is carried on today. If possible, secure a blank ballot for the latest election and bring it to class. How do voting practices today compare with those described in this chapter?

3. Draw a chart showing leading members of the Conway, Johnson and Rector families and public offices they held.

4. Visit Mount Holly Cemetery in Little Rock and notice the many graves of prominent Arkansas people. How many can you find whose names are mentioned in this book? (Consult the index.)

5. Draw a cartoon such as the Whigs might have used in the 1840 campaign.

2 The First Banks

Today banks are usually ranked among the most reliable and respectable institutions in any community. Things were different in frontier Arkansas, as this chapter will tell you.

The problem of money. While Arkansas was on the road to statehood, in the years 1803 to 1836, the population increased from a few hundred to about 52,000. With this increase in population came the need of better roads and river transportation, new mercantile establishments, sawmills, gristmills, schools, churches and all other things necessary to a new and rapidly developing section of the country.

Money was scarce and sufficient funds were not available to provide the needed improvements. Some thought that this problem could be solved by setting up banks and authorizing them to make loans and to issue bank notes. Others opposed this idea because they thought that it would lead to financial disaster for both Arkansas and the individuals who might become involved.

Efforts to establish banks failed in the General Assemblies of 1833 and 1835, but the bank advocates did not give up. In the constitutional convention of 1836, over strong opposition, they secured the adoption of a provision in the new constitution authorizing the state legislature to set up two banks. One was to be known as the state bank, while the other was to be established for the special purpose of aiding and promoting the agricultural interests of Arkansas. The General Assembly was given full authority to pledge the faith and credit of the state to raise the funds necessary to start the banks in operation.

Financing the new banks. The first General Assembly of the State of Arkansas, which met in 1836, lost no time in passing laws establishing the two banks authorized in the constitution. The State Bank was to have a capital of $1,000,000 and was to be managed by a board of directors chosen by the General Assembly. The other bank, known as the Real Estate Bank, would have a capital of $2,000,000 and be under the direction of a board elected by the stockholders.

The capital for each of the banks was to be secured by the sale of bonds. Payment of both the interest and the principal of these bonds was guaranteed by the State of Arkansas. For the State Bank a bond issue of $1,000,000, paying five per cent interest, was authorized and offered for sale but only $169,000 was raised. Partly because of a nationwide panic and depression, the remainder of the bonds could not be sold and were finally cancelled. Later another bond issue of $1,000,000, this time paying six per cent interest, was authorized and sold. Thus the State Bank had $1,169,000, plus about $100,000 turned over to it by the state, on which to operate.

The State Bank was expected to lend money to borrowers at eight per cent interest, giving the state a profit on its investment. Some advocates of the bank claimed that profits to the state would be so great that taxes could be abolished.

The Real Estate Bank was to be owned by individual stockholders who would become responsible for its operation. To provide the $2,000,000 for the capital of this bank the state issued 2,000 bonds, each with a face value of $1,000 and bearing six per cent interest. The stockholders were to mortgage to the state land of sufficient value to guarantee the state against loss. The bank would then make loans, repay its indebtedness to the state, and in time provide an ample return for each stockholder.

The Real Estate Bank succeeded in disposing of more than three-fourths of its bonds at face value, bringing in $1,530,000. The rest of the bonds could not be sold and were cancelled. An additional bond issue of $500,000 was used as security for a loan of a little over $121,000 from a New York bonding company. For its operation, the Real Estate Bank had this money plus whatever was paid in by the stockholders.

The banks in operation. The plan of organization adopted for each of the two banks was the same as that which had been used by the First and Second Banks of the United States. A central bank was established in Little Rock, with branch banks in other important centers of population over the state.

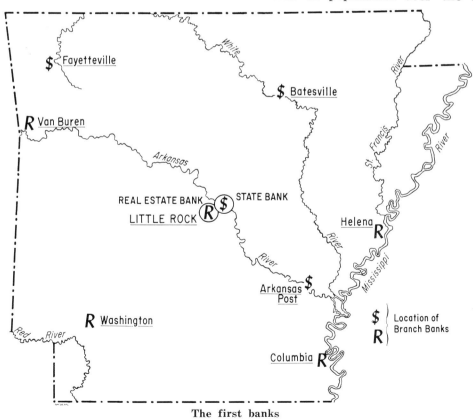

The first banks

State Bank branches were located at Batesville, Fayetteville, and later at Arkansas Post. The Real Estate Bank began with branches at Washington, Helena, and Columbia in Chicot County, adding another at Van Buren a little later. Supporters of the bank system argued that branch banks were needed because of poor transportation facilities, and that they would help in developing the areas in which they were located.

The State Bank at Little Rock was the first to open for business. It was housed in a handsome two-story brick

The State Bank of Arkansas, Little Rock

A five dollar bill issued by the branch bank of Arkansas Post, 1839

building, erected at a cost of $28,000, on the southeast corner of Markham and Center streets. When the bank began its operations on August 8, 1837 the nation was in the midst of a financial panic. People flocked in to borrow money, and in the first week many loans were made. The branch banks, which opened later, were also provided with expensive new buildings.

The Real Estate Bank did not begin operation until December 12, 1838, more than a year after the State Bank

had opened its doors. The delay was caused principally by the difficulty in getting people to subscribe for stock. Many were afraid to become involved in the new enterprise. Stock was sold in only sixteen counties, with Chicot County the leader. Since no branch bank was allowed to open until it had a paid in capital of at least $50,000, several months passed before all the Real Estate branch banks were in operation. In all the banks the demand for loans was great.

72

The bankers usually tried to accommodate those who wanted to borrow and who could give what appeared to be adequate security, but neither the bankers nor the borrowers were experienced in banking. Mistakes were frequent, and sometimes dishonesty entered the picture. The banks often lent too liberally, and many people borrowed more than they could ever repay.

The failure of the banks. It soon became evident that the people had little confidence in the enduring value of the paper money or notes issued by the State and Real Estate banks. So many people cashed in their paper notes for gold and silver that it became difficult for the banks to keep a supply of coins. Late in 1839 both banks stopped paying out gold and silver, an action which further shook the confidence of the public in the bank notes.

The banks continued to issue new paper currency and to make additional loans. The bank notes declined rapidly in value and prices rose in proportion,

Archibald Yell

since such notes had become the money in general use throughout Arkansas. Gradually the people realized that the banks were in serious trouble, and many borrowers woke up to the fact that they were in trouble too since they could not repay their loans.

"Waxhaws," the home of Archibald Yell in Fayetteville

Nothing was done about the banking situation until Archibald Yell, who had opposed the banks from the beginning, succeeded James S. Conway as governor in 1840. At Yell's urgent request, the General Assembly investigated the banks and uncovered evidence of fraud and dishonesty on the part of some of the bank officials. The financial condition of the two banks and their branches continued to grow worse until in the period 1842-44 all were closed.

The aftermath of financial failure. The collapse of the State Bank and Real Estate Bank left Arkansas in a tragic financial plight. The bank notes became worthless. Hundreds of people suffered financial ruin. During the long period that was necessary to close out the business of the banks, the expensive bank buildings had to be sold at a small fraction of their original cost. Mortgaged lands that had been taken over by the banks brought little if anything to pay off bank loans. In 1836 Arkansas had a debt of only a few thousand dollars, but seven years later the state owed more than $3,000,000 and had little to show for it.

Problems arising from the banking failures continued to trouble Arkansas for many years. Some of the Real Estate Bank bonds passed into the hands of the Holford banking house in London. The state claimed that the Holford firm secured the bonds illegally, and finally in 1884 refused to pay them. Arkansas had made such a failure of her first experiment in banking that state securities sold below par for many years. The banks may have brought some temporary advantages to the state, but in the long run they hampered rather than helped the development of Arkansas.

The people of Arkansas decided that no such disaster should overtake them again. In 1844 the General Assembly authorized an amendment to the constitution providing that "no bank or banking institution shall be hereafter incorporated or established in this state." Two years later the amendment was ratified. There were no more banks in Arkansas until after the Civil War.

Calico Rock on White River, 1858

STUDY AIDS

Vocabulary

Be sure that you understand the meaning of these words and phrases:

funds	stockholders
mercantile	face value
operation	financial panic
capital	depression
"faith and credit"	subscribe
board	adequate
bonds	notes
	hampered

Identification

Tell what part each of the following had in the story:

Archibald Yell   James S. Conway

To test your reading

On other paper, list 1-7. Opposite each number, write the word or words which complete each sentence.

1. The number of branch banks connected with the Real Estate Bank was ___.

2. The number of branch banks connected with the State Bank was ___.

3. In 1836 the population of Arkansas was about ___.

4. The State Bank was to have a capital of ___.

5. The Real Estate Bank was to have a capital of ___.

6. The State Bank building in Little Rock cost ___.

7. In 1846 an amendment to the state constitution was ratified providing that ___.

Things to do

1. Make a study of the banks in your community. Find out when each was established.

2. Visit a bank and ask the banker to explain how a bank makes loans.

3. Ask a coin collector or dealer to show the class some examples of coins and currency that were used during this period.

4. Pretend that you are Governor Archibald Yell and that your classmates are members of the General Assembly. Address the class on the subject, "Why the State Bank and the Real Estate Bank Should Be Investigated."

3   The Frontier Moves West

Though life may have been monotonous for many people, the frontier years were crowded with exciting events. Thousands of Indians crossed Arkansas on their way to the west. Arkansans stood guard on the Indian border, fought in Texas and Mexico, and followed the lure of gold to California. America was expanding, and Arkansans moved with the frontier.

Indian removal through Arkansas. Each year from about 1832 to 1839 several thousand Indians passed through Arkansas on their way to what is now Oklahoma. These were the Choctaws, Chickasaws, Creeks, Cherokees and Seminoles, who had been forced to give up their ancestral lands in the Southern states east of the Mississippi River. The Indians usually traveled in groups of 500 or more persons.

In passing through Arkansas the Indians followed several routes. Most of them came up the Arkansas River by boat to Fort Smith, but frequently low water made travel by land necessary. Some parties assembled at Memphis, traveled by land to Rock Roe near Clarendon on White River, and then overland to Little Rock. From Little Rock they went by land or by water to Fort Smith.

Other Indians came up the Ouachita River to Camden and went west by way of Washington in Hempstead County. Some passed through southern Missouri and crossed the northwestern corner of Arkansas. Still others proceeded west by way of Batesville.

The removal of the Indians was attended with great suffering. The contractors whom the government placed in charge of transportation often failed to provide food and clothing. Thousands of men, women and children died, and the contractors sometimes refused to allow time to bury the dead properly. Late in 1832 when about 2,000 Choctaws were camped near Little Rock, from ten to twenty died each day from cholera.

The passage of such large numbers of Indians caused some uneasiness in Arkansas, and the Federal government built an arsenal in Little Rock and a new fort at Fort Smith. Occasionally trouble resulted when whites sold whiskey to Indians, or when starving Indians tried to steal food. Arkansas farmers and merchants profited by selling corn, beef and other supplies when the Indians had money or the contractors were willing to buy.

The Indian border. The national policy of forcing the Southern Indians into the area bordering Arkansas on the west created several new problems. The Five Civilized Tribes, as the Choctaws, Cherokees, Creeks, Chickasaws and Seminoles were called, needed protection against the plains Indians who resented their coming. At one time a battalion of Arkansas cavalry was stationed at Fort Towson, in the Choctaw Nation, to

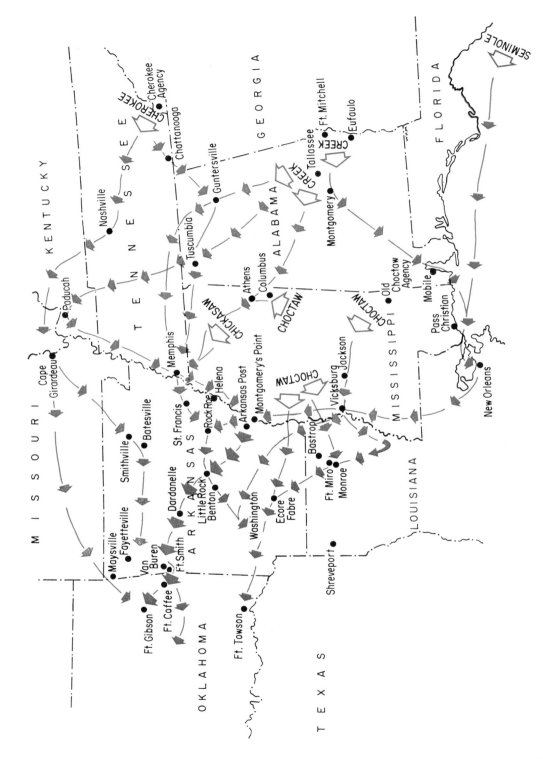

Indian removal routes

protect the Choctaws and Chickasaws from the Comanches and Pawnees.

The presence of the Indians attracted lawless elements to the Arkansas border, especially in the northwest. The Cherokee line became a gathering place for sellers of whiskey, traders, gamblers, and undesirables of every description. Outlaws took refuge in the Indian country. Murders and robberies became frequent. Civil strife among the Cherokees made it possible for white desperadoes to blame the Indians for many crimes. Law enforcement officers and courts could not cope with the situation.

In 1839 a citizens' committee in Washington County raised a body of cavalry which hunted down, captured and hanged several suspected murderers. Conditions improved to some degree after this action, but the western border was still untamed when the Civil War came. Occasionally hostile parties of Indians caused trouble, as in 1846 when the Benton County militia was called out to remove some Cherokees.

Trade with Mexico. In the spring of 1839 a caravan of about forty men and fifteen wagons, led by Josiah Gregg, left Van Buren for Chihuahua in Mexico. The wagons carried an assorted stock of merchandise, principally dry goods. The caravan had to pass through Santa Fe, as a port of entry into Mexico, and reached Chihuahua in October after a journey of over 1,100 miles. In April 1840 the traders returned to Van Buren.

Also in 1839 a Mexican trading expedition of about a hundred men, eighty

Indian lands west of Arkansas in 1836. The Chickasaws later received the western part of the Choctaw territory

wagons and 500 mules passed along Red River on its way to and from New Orleans. On their return journey the Mexicans carried cloth goods valued at $300,000. Though Arkansas merchants hoped for a new supply of much-needed gold and silver from the Mexican trade, distances and dangers were so great that little was ever realized.

The Texas revolution. When the Texas settlers revolted against Mexico in 1835-36, Arkansas people were greatly interested in their cause. General Sam Houston, the Texas leader, was well-known in Arkansas, and the revolution had been planned in a small tavern in Washington. Several former residents of Arkansas were among the signers of the Texas declaration of independence.

Governor William S. Fulton sent six companies of volunteers to the southwest border area, but fear of a Mexican or Indian attack on Arkansas proved groundless. Texas offers of free land attracted volunteers from Arkansas. Enlistment in the Texas army was par-

Arkansas, Texas and the Mexican War

ticularly heavy in Miller and Lafayette counties, where the boundary line had never been surveyed and the people were not sure whether they lived in Arkansas or Texas.

As the fighting continued, citizens of Little Rock and other places held public rallies and barbecues to raise money and men for General Houston. A stream of volunteers from the Eastern states, including David Crockett of Tennessee, passed through Arkansas headed southwest. Crockett was killed at the Alamo, as was James Bowie who made the bowie knife famous. Arkansas people rejoiced when Texas succeeded in winning its independence from Mexico.

Arkansas troops in Mexico. Following the Texas revolution, many people from Arkansas and other states moved into Texas. In 1845 Texas became a part of the United States, and the next year a dispute over the boundary between Tex-

Mexican monument on the battlefield of Buena Vista

79

as and Mexico caused the United States to become involved in a war with Mexico. Arkansas men responded quickly when Governor Thomas S. Drew called for volunteers. Ten companies of men assembled at Washington, Arkansas where they were formed into the First Regiment of Arkansas Cavalry. Archibald Yell, a former governor, left his seat in Congress and became colonel of the regiment. Yell's unit, composed of about 800 men, marched overland to Mexico by way of Shreveport and San Antonio.

A battalion of infantry, made up of five companies with over 400 men in all, assembled at Fort Smith for duty on the Indian frontier. These troops were stationed at Fort Smith, Fort Gibson and Fort Towson while the regular army forces were in Mexico. Two or three other companies enlisted from Arkansas and were attached to army organizations.

Yell's cavalry engaged in only one major battle, at Buena Vista in northern Mexico early in 1847. The Arkansas troops were undisciplined, poorly trained, and overconfident. Though the Americans won the battle, the Arkansas men were routed by Mexican lancers and Colonel Yell was killed.

Some of the Arkansas troops who fought in the Mexican War were little better than frontier outlaws, and caused trouble for American authorities. Because of atrocities against civilians Yell's unit was at one time almost ordered out of action. But many Arkansas soldiers fought bravely, at Buena Vista and in the drive on Mexico City which ended the war, and at least seventy-five lost their lives. Ambrose H. Sevier resigned his seat in the United States Senate to help negotiate the final treaty of peace with Mexico in 1848.

The California gold rush. About the time the war with Mexico ended, gold was discovered in California. Notices of the discovery began to appear in newspapers late in 1848, and by the following spring thousands were on their way to California. The excitement extended to Arkansas and companies of emigrants were organized in several places. At Little Rock and perhaps elsewhere, returning soldiers from the Mexican War set out for the West.

Some of the Arkansas emigrants went to New Orleans, and from there to California by boat around the southern tip of South America. Others traveled by water to Central America and then across the isthmus to the Pacific side, where they took passage on vessels going north to California.

Most of the Arkansas companies, as well as many others, set out overland from Fort Smith. Westward the route lay to Santa Fe in New Mexico, and then down the Rio Grande to a point from which they could turn west to the headwaters of the Gila River. The emigrants followed the course of the Gila to the Colorado River, and from there went to the coast or elsewhere in California.

The rush to California caused concern in Arkansas and other states because so many people were leaving for the West. Every day during the autumn months of 1850 an average of twenty covered wagons and other vehicles bearing a hundred people passed Bayou Meto toll bridge, on the Memphis to Little Rock road. The human tide to California slackened in 1851, but year by year people continued to move westward. In 1860 more than 11,000 natives of Arkansas lived in Texas and another 2,000 in California.

Arkansas and the great West, 1849-1860

Arkansas cattlemen occasionally drove herds all the way to California, where the cattle might bring fifty dollars a head as compared with five or ten dollars in Arkansas. Usually several owners combined their cattle for the drive. In 1857 several herds, at least two of which included 500 to 700 head, started on the journey. Three herds that left Dover in Pope County apparently reached California. A cattle herd sometimes averaged fifteen to twenty miles a day on the long westward journey.

The Mountain Meadows massacre. In the spring of 1857 a caravan of about seventy men, women and children set out from Carroll County to go to California. They were led by Alexander Fancher, who had made the trip twice before. The party included forty wagons and a drove of about 700 cattle. On the way westward some Missourians and other emigrants joined the Fancher caravan, making a total of about 137 persons.

The route to California taken by the emigrants led them through Utah, which had been settled by Mormons, or members of the Church of Jesus Christ of Latter-Day Saints. At that time the Mormons were having trouble with the United States government, and believed that they were about to be attacked by the army. They had also heard of the recent murder of Parley P. Pratt, a Mormon apostle, near Van Buren, Arkansas.

The Fancher caravan passed through Salt Lake City and headed southwest. The Mormons were reluctant to sell them supplies, and friction increased. In September 1857 while encamped at Mountain Meadows in southwestern Utah the emigrants were attacked by a large party of Indians and Mormons disguised as Indians. Behind their wagon barricades the emigrants fought off the attackers for three days. Promised safe passage by John D. Lee, a Mormon leader, they were persuaded to surrender and then were murdered. Only seventeen small children were spared, and they were taken into Mormon homes until returned to relatives in Arkansas by the United States army. The property of the emigrants was divided among the attackers.

Investigations of the massacre at Mountain Meadows went on for many years, and John D. Lee was finally executed for his part in the crime. The names of Arkansas victims who lost their lives are engraved on a tall granite monument standing on the grounds of the courthouse at Harrison, near the place from which the Fancher caravan set out.

Fort Smith in 1851, drawn by Edward Payson Washburn

STUDY AIDS

Vocabulary

Be sure that you understand the meaning of each of these words:

ancestral
barricades
battalion
caravan
engraved

cavalry
isthmus
arsenal
atrocities
emigrants
cholera

Location

Find these places on a map:

Chihuahua
Van Buren
Rio Grande River
Fort Towson
Shreveport

San Antonio
Gila River
Santa Fe
Dover
Mountain Meadows
Bayou Meto

Identification

Tell what part each of the following had in the story:

Alexander Fancher
John D. Lee
Josiah Gregg
Sam Houston

David Crockett
James Bowie
Archibald Yell
Ambrose H. Sevier

To test your reading

On other paper, list 1-5. Opposite each number, write the word or words which complete each sentence.

1. In traveling to Oklahoma most of the Indians went by boat up the ___ River.

2. In 1857 herds of cattle were driven from Arkansas to ___.

3. The Fancher caravan was destroyed in the ___ massacre.

4. Colonel Yell was killed in the Mexican War at the Battle of ___.

5. Texas became a part of the United States in the year ___.

Things to do

1. On a map of the United States, trace the overland route of the "Forty-Niners" from Fort Smith to San Francisco.

2. Visit pioneer Washington, near Hope in Hempstead County.

3. Make a list of historic sites in your area. Tell why each site is important.

4. If you live in the vicinity of Harrison, visit the Mountain Meadows monument near the courthouse. Make a list of the victims and survivors. Is your family related to any of those listed?

5. Have you ever visited the Alamo, the San Jacinto battlefield, or any of the other historic places connected with the Texas Revolution? If so, tell the class about it.

6. Write an "eye-witness" account of one of the following:

   (a) Yell's cavalry regiment in Mexico.
   (b) A cattle drive to California.
   (c) A trading caravan to Mexico.
   (d) Indian removal through Arkansas.

4   Twenty-Five Years of Growth

The population of Arkansas in 1860 was more than eight times as large as it had been in 1835. Immigrants from the Eastern states cleared the land and established farms and plantations. Negro slaves became more numerous in the lowlands. Manufacturing was still in its infancy, but by 1861 the first railroad and telegraph lines had appeared.

Immigration to frontier Arkansas. The population of Arkansas increased rapidly after statehood had come. From 1803 to 1835 the number of people grew from less than a thousand to around 52,000, or an average annual increase of about 1,600 people. During the next twenty-five years, from 1835 until 1860, the population expanded at an average rate of 15,000 a year. The population of Arkansas was 97,000 in 1840, 209,000 in 1850, and 435,000 in 1860. Some of the gain represented an increase of births over deaths, but much of it resulted from immigration.

Most of the new settlers came from states east of the Mississippi River, with Tennessee far in the lead. Next in order were Alabama, Georgia, North Carolina, Mississippi, Kentucky, and South Carolina, with smaller numbers from Missouri, Virginia, Illinois, and other states. People of foreign birth living in Arkansas in 1860 numbered fewer than 4,000, mainly Irish and German.

Many of the earliest settlers preferred to live in the northern and northwestern parts of Arkansas. In 1860 Washington, Independence, Carroll, Benton, and Lawrence counties led in white population. Large slaveowners usually avoided the hill country and established plantations in fertile bottomlands such as lay along Red River in the southwest. After 1850 settlement of the southern and eastern parts of the state proceeded rapidly.

Towns, farms and plantations. The principal occupation in frontier Arkansas was farming. In 1860 about 65,000 people were classified as farmers, farm laborers, laborers and overseers. In the same year carpenters numbered 1,613, merchants 1,296, physicians 1,222, blacksmiths 1,094 and teachers 933. Clergymen, lawyers, wheelwrights and shoemakers each numbered less than 500, and other occupations were represented by still smaller numbers.

Since most of the people were farmers and travel was difficult, towns grew slowly. In 1860 Little Rock with a population of 3,727 was the largest town in the state. Next came Camden with 2,219 people, and Fort Smith with 1,530 was third in size. Van Buren, Fayetteville, Arkadelphia, Batesville and Searcy each had between 500 and 1,000. No other town in the state had a population of more than 500. The total population of the ten largest towns in Arkansas was less than 13,000.

Emigrant wagons bound for Arkansas

Much of the rich new land in Arkansas was planted to cotton, especially after 1850. Arkansas climbed to sixth place among cotton-growing states as production rose from 65,000 bales in 1850 to 367,000 bales in 1860. Plantations grew in number and size as new land was cleared or "deadened" by girdling the trees. Arkansas cotton moved downriver to New Orleans and then to mills in the Northeast and in Europe.

In the hill regions, small farmers raised corn, wheat, tobacco, and live-stock. Usually the farmer raised his own potatoes, fruit, and vegetables, which with his grain, hogs and cattle assured his family a living. Members of farm families made their own clothing from wool or cotton produced on the farm. Some farmers found it unnecessary to buy sugar, since honey could be taken from "bee trees" in the woods and sorghum molasses made from home-grown cane.

Since there were no railroads or good roads, raising farm commodities for market was generally unprofitable unless the farm was located near a river. The small farmer sometimes sold his surplus produce and bought salt, coffee, iron implements, and perhaps a pendulum clock for his fireplace mantel. He made plows from the forks of trees, tanned his own leather to make shoes and harness, and even built his own wagon.

Even large cotton plantations were often nearly self-sufficient. Food for the planter's family and his slaves was raised on the plantation, and much of the clothing was made at home. Food,

Farmer plowing with ox

An Ozark cabin, with "mud" chimney and rail fence

counties in flax production. Fibers of the flax plant were used in making linen thread, and flaxseed in making linseed oil.

Negro slavery. Negro slavery became more important in Arkansas as plantation owners developed the rich cotton lowlands near the larger rivers. The slave population, only 1,617 in 1820, grew to almost 20,000 by 1840. In 1860 there were 111,115 slaves in Arkansas, about a fourth of the total population of the state.

The slave population in 1860 was concentrated in the southern and eastern counties, though there were at least a few slaves in every county. The average slaveholder owned nine or ten Negroes, though in south Arkansas and along the Mississippi River a few planters had a hundred or more. Usually one white family owned one slave family, and more than half the slaveholders owned four slaves or less. Four out of five white families in Arkansas owned no slaves at all.

White owners brought their slaves with them when they moved to Arkansas, or purchased them at the large slave markets in New Orleans or Memphis. No organized slave trade developed in Arkansas, but owners often advertised slaves for sale or for hire. Slave sales sometimes separated Negro families, though many owners tried to sell mothers and small children together.

Arkansas slaveholders usually lived in plain frame houses or log cabins. Slave cabins were grouped in an area called the "quarters" near the house of the owner. The slaves ate pork, corn bread, molasses, wild game, and vegetables in season, and wore clothing which was coarse but adequate. Negroes and whites often worked together in homes and fields.

feed and livestock were grown in all the counties of Arkansas.

In 1860 Arkansas had about half as many horses and mules as there were people, and work oxen averaged 1,500 per county. Hot Spring County had the largest number of cows, while Washington and Benton counties led in numbers of sheep. As early as 1841 thoroughbred horses were being raised in Arkansas, and Durham cattle and Berkshire hogs appeared before the Civil War.

Corn, grown in every county, was used for meal and livestock feed. Northwestern counties led in wheat production. Tobacco was grown mostly for home consumption, and southeastern counties produced a little rice. In 1860 Madison County led eighteen other

A slave sale in the Old South

"Frog Level," a plantation home built in 1852 near Magnolia, Columbia County

Masters generally treated slaves well, since they were valuable property. In 1860 a good field hand might be worth as much as $1,500. Medical care was provided whenever possible. The master could whip an unruly slave, but brutal mistreatment and overwork were condemned by public opinion and by state law. Township patrols kept Negroes from holding unlawful meetings or wandering about the countryside without permission.

Occasionally slaves ran away from their masters, and a few escaped to Indian Territory or to the North. Outlaw bands sometimes stole Negroes and resold them. In 1834-35 rumors spread that the John A. Murrell gang, which had hideouts in the White River swamps, planned a slave rebellion, but no such revolt ever came.

The Constitution of 1836 prohibited any general emancipation, but after 1839 individual owners could free their slaves under certain conditions. Arkansas whites were suspicious of free Negroes, who numbered about 600 in 1850. In 1843 a state law provided that no

An advertisement for runaway slaves. From the "Arkansas Gazette," October 2, 1833

more free Negroes could come to Arkansas. Another law passed by the General Assembly in 1859 required all free Negroes to leave the state, but it was repealed the next year.

The "Old Brick House," near Center Point, Howard County, built by John Russey about the year 1851

The effect of slavery on Arkansas.
Slavery was profitable in Arkansas, or at least the owners thought so. The institution of slavery was still growing when the Civil War put an end to it. Slaves were increasing in number, especially in the southern and eastern counties, and slave prices were rising. New plantations were established as rapidly as the land could be cleared for cotton. Within a few years lowland Arkansas would have been as heavily Negro as parts of Mississippi and Louisiana.

Slavery provided a stable, secure way of life in which people of both white and black races knew where they belonged, but it hindered the development of Arkansas in many ways. Money was invested in land and slaves, while mineral resources remained undeveloped and manufacturing made little progress. The slavery system contributed to the neglect of schools, roads and railways. The growing of cotton on the same land year after year exhausted the soil. Above all, the institution of slavery left Arkansas with a race problem which has not yet been solved.

Early manufacturing. Though the ten years after 1850 witnessed some growth, manufacturing in Arkansas was still in its infancy when the Civil War began. Most of the 518 factories in operation in 1860 were small, and a total of fewer than 1,900 workers were employed. Washington County, which had numerous water power sites, was far in the lead as a manufacturing area.

Lumber mills were the most important of the early factories. Before 1826 the mills were run by water power. With the introduction of steam power, sawmills could be moved deeper into the forests away from streams. In 1860 the state's 117 lumber mills included establishments operated by water, steam,

Water mill wheel. Cane Hill, Washington County

horses, mules, and oxen, and lumber was often sawed by hand. Most of the timber cut before the Civil War was in the southern and eastern parts of the state. In 1860 Jefferson County had twelve sawmills, Crittenden County nine, and Ashley and Bradley counties eight each.

Salt manufacturing was important to the early settlers. According to some accounts, John Hemphill established a salt works on the Ouachita River near Arkadelphia as early as 1811. Another Clark County pioneer, Jacob Barkman, opened trade with New Orleans in 1812 and later built a cotton factory on the Caddo River. About 1857 a factory at Royston, on the Little Missouri River near Murfreesboro, began producing cotton and woolen yarn and thread.

Water mill in the Arkansas Ozarks, built in 1854

Among manufactured products in 1860, flour and meal ranked next to lumber in value, with ninety-seven mills in operation. Tanyards produced leather, some of it of good quality. The blacksmith shop, where horses were shod and wagon irons fitted, was an important establishment in every frontier community. In Little Rock, a factory began making hats and caps about 1842, and three years later a brewery began operation. Gunsmiths, cabinetmakers, and saddlemakers opened shops here and there.

Except for soil and timber, the natural resources of Arkansas were barely touched before 1860. Whetstones were quarried in Garland County for the New Orleans market as early as 1818. Two blast furnaces in the northern Ozarks

manufactured iron after 1850. In 1857 a zinc smelter was established in what is now Sharp County. Lead deposits were exploited in the Boone County region and two smelters operated near Lead Hill. Manganese mining began in the Batesville area in 1850-52. Coal was mined near Spadra, in Johnson County, soon after 1840, though it remained commercially unimportant. In 1857 the first geological survey of Arkansas, directed by David Dale Owen, began and was still in progress when Owen died three years later.

The first railroad and telegraph lines. The California gold rush of 1849 led to an increase of interest in railroads. Several leading citizens of Arkansas hoped that the proposed transcontinental line might be built through the state. Interest in railroad construction was high among the people of the north and northwest, but the big planters remained content with river transportation. Governor Elias N. Conway opposed levying taxes or issuing bonds to aid railroad companies.

In 1853 the General Assembly chartered the Cairo and Fulton and the Memphis and Little Rock railway companies. The Cairo and Fulton, which proposed to build a railroad across Arkansas from Missouri to Texas, made little progress until after the Civil War. Late in 1858 the Memphis and Little Rock line began operating trains from Hopefield on the Mississippi to Madison on the St. Francis River, a distance of about thirty-eight miles. A railroad bridge, which included a drawbridge to permit the passage of steamboats, was completed across the St. Francis in 1861. The early railroad engines were wood-burners, and floods often endangered the flimsy track.

A telegraph line connecting Fayetteville with St. Louis began operation in 1860. Later the same year the line was extended to Van Buren and Fort Smith. Early in 1861 Little Rock and Memphis were connected by a telegraph line.

Rockport on the Ouachita River, Hot Spring County, 1859

STUDY AIDS

Vocabulary

Be sure that you understand the meaning of each of these words and phrases:

drawbridge	brewery
smelter	girdling
wheelwright	blast furnaces
blacksmith	tanned
whetstone	bee tree
stable	emancipation
	geology

Location

On a map locate these counties:

Washington	Madison
Jefferson	Crittenden
Benton	Clark
	Boone

Identification

Tell what part each of the following had in the story:

John Hemphill	Elias N. Conway
Jacob Barkman	Royston
Cairo and Fulton	Spadra

To test your reading

On other paper, list 1-9. Opposite each number write the word or words which complete each sentence.

1. In the twenty-five years following 1835 the population of Arkansas increased from ___ to ___.

2. In 1860 in Arkansas the largest town was ___. It had a population of ___. The second largest was ___, which had a population of ___.

3. In 1860 the leading county in manufacturing was ___.

4. In 1860 the leading money crop in Arkansas was ___.

5. The first railroad in Arkansas began operation in the year ___.

6. The first railway drawbridge was over the ___ River.

7. The man who directed the first geological survey was ___.

8. The number of slaves in Arkansas in 1860 was ___.

9. The average number of oxen in each county in 1860 was ___.

Things to do

1. From what state or states did your ancestors come to Arkansas, and when did they arrive? Discuss this with your parents or other relatives, and report to the class.

2. Are there any buildings or houses in your community that were erected before 1860? Find out about them and make a report. You may wish to illustrate your report with pictures, drawings and floor plans.

3. Make a list of the ways by which people in your community earn a living and compare this list with ways given in this chapter. Which are the oldest and newest occupations now present in your community?

4. Visit cemeteries in your community and look for burials made earlier than 1860. Make a list of those you find.

5. Have an exhibition of old tools and household implements.

6. Look for slave bills of sale or other documents having to do with slavery.

7. Is there a blacksmith shop anywhere near where you live? If so, arrange a visit.

5   Schools and Churches on the Frontier

Pioneer educators and preachers had a hard struggle in the American West. Life was difficult, and some people found little time for either formal schooling or organized religion. Yet the zeal of many pioneers for book learning and their love of the Bible brought growing numbers of schools and churches to the frontier.

Early private schools. The hardships of frontier life left the people little time to think of setting up schools. There was almost no money to establish and maintain schools, and much of Arkansas was so sparsely settled that few children lived within reach of a possible school site. In the early days there was little need for colleges, and no colleges were established until the decade preceding the Civil War.

The earliest schools were privately owned and operated. Sometimes parents put up a building and hired a teacher, or a teacher came into a community and persuaded parents to pay him a few dollars a month for instructing their children. The teacher often accepted room and board in some private home as part pay, and received farm produce for most of the remainder due him. Preachers often served as teachers in these frontier schools.

Reading, writing, and arithmetic constituted the usual course of study. Webster's "Blue-back Speller," which served as a reader also, and the McGuffey Readers were widely used as textbooks. The first Little Rock school, opened in 1823 by Jesse Brown, offered reading, writing, arithmetic, English grammar and geography. The annual tuition was $24, payable quarterly, a sum which Brown often found difficult to collect. The school at Little Rock, like many others on the frontier, was open to both boys and girls.

The typical frontier school was conducted in a log house which often served also as a church and courthouse. The interior usually consisted of one room, with a door at one side or end and a fireplace at the other. The window was a large hole cut in the wall and covered by a board shutter. The furnishings were crude and on dark days light came from candles, the fireplace or a bear oil lamp. A well or nearby spring provided water. Pupils often rode horseback or walked several miles to school.

Public schools before the Civil War. The Federal government tried to encourage the establishment of public schools in Arkansas and other newly settled areas by reserving the sixteenth section of land in each township for the support of education. In 1829 the General Assembly authorized the leasing of these lands, but land was so abundant elsewhere that little money came in for the use of schools. After Arkansas became a state, Congress gave the state government permission to sell the school

MOVE, SÓN, WOLF, FOOT, MOON, ÓR; RULE, PULL; EXIST; ϲ=K; ġ=J; ş=Z; ϲн=sн.

The waves of the sea beat upon the beach.
Bleachers bleach linen and thus make it white.
The miller grinds corn into meal.
The flesh of calves is called veal.
Apples are more plentiful than peaches.
The preacher is to preach the gospel.
Teachers teach their pupils, and pupils learn.
A roach is a short, thick, flat fish.
Men get their growth before they are thirty.
The beak of a bird is its bill, or the end of its bill.
Greenland is a bleak, cold place.

No. 54.—LIV.

WORDS OF THREE SYLLABLES, ACCENTED ON THE FIRST, AND
LEFT UNMARKED AS AN EXERCISE IN NOTATION.

bot a ny	fel' o ny	sor' cer y
el e gy	col o ny	im age ry
prod i gy	har mo ny	witch er y
ef fi gy	cot ton y	butch er y
eb o ny	glut ton y	fish er y
en er gy	can o py	quack er y
lit ur gy	oc cu py	crock er y
in fa my	quan ti ty	mock er y
big a my	sal a ry	cook er y
blas phe my	reg is try	cut ler y
en e my	beg gar y	gal ler y
am i ty	bur gla ry	rar i ty
vil lain y	gran a ry	em er y
com pa ny	gloss a ry	nun ner y
lit a ny	lac ta ry	frip per y
lar ce ny	her ald ry	fop per y
des ti ny	hus band ry	or re ry
cal um ny	rob ber y	ar ter y
tyr an ny	chan ce ry	mas ter y

Page from a "Blue-back Speller"

lands, invest the money and use the interest to set up public schools.

In 1843 Governor Archibald Yell persuaded the General Assembly to enact a general school law. Under its provisions, the people of any township could elect a commissioner to sell the school lands and three trustees to supervise the schools. The trustees were to build school houses, employ teachers, and keep the schools open four months in each year. Private donations and tuition payments were expected to help with expenses. The township was to pay the tuition and furnish the books of pupils whose parents could not afford the cost.

The General Assembly in 1849 provided for the sale of seventy-two sections of land which Congress had once set aside for a state university, and also for the sale of lands containing salt springs which the Federal government had donated to the state. The revenue from sales of these lands was to help support the public schools.

The income from land sales and private sources was never great enough to finance a public school system. In the Little Rock district for example, the sale of 480 acres of school lands in 1843 brought little more than $1,800. Another 160 acres could not be sold, and ten years passed before a public school was established there. Arkansas had 727 public schools in 1860, but most of them were supported principally by tuition fees and other private funds. On an average each school received less than $200 a year from public sources. Washington, Johnson, and Saline counties led in the number of public schools.

The failure to establish a good system of public education before the Civil War was due partly to the unwillingness of the people to pay taxes to support schools. Many early settlers had little appreciation of education. During most of the year the children were needed to work on the farms, and Arkansas had no law making school attendance compulsory. The census of 1860 showed that more than 23,000 white Arkansans over twenty years of age could not read or write.

Academies and high schools. Private schools called academies, of which there were 109 in 1860, made up to some degree for the lack of public schools. In

These books are designed for *schools organized under the common school law of this State approved 3rd February* 1843, *and such as will be governed by that law;* of which you are no doubt fully aware. The kinds of books &c. procured and the prices at which they will be sold are as follows:

KINDS OF BOOKS &C.

	PRICE OF EACH BOOK.
	DOL. CTS.
United States Primer,	05
Webster's Spelling book,	06¼
Sequel to Webster's spelling book,	25
Goodrich's Reader No. 1,	10
Goodrich's Reader No. 2,	15
Goodrich's Reader No. 3,	25
Willard's History of the United States,	30
Gallaudet's Dictionary	30
Morse's Geography,	50
Davie's Arithmetic, first lessons, No. 1,	15
Davies' Arithmetic, No. 2,	25
Slates 7 by 11 inches; each to be sold for	15
Slate pencils at ½ of a cent each, or per dozen	06
Bullion's English Grammar, per copy	15
Root's copies, for the whole series No. 1, No. 2, No. 3 and No. 4	30

For future reference to the prices of these books, it would perhaps be well to have this communication recorded in the journal of the Board of School Commissioners or in the Clerk's office of your county.

A statement of the prices of school books and supplies, addressed to county school commissioners by the state auditor in 1846. Six and one-quarter cents was a monetary unit called "one-half bit"

1854 a fourth of the white children of Arkansas were enrolled in public schools, and about another fourth in academies. These academies were somewhat similar to modern high schools, though all were supported by tuition fees and consisted largely of boarding students. Most were organized by groups of citizens, and a few by churches. The earliest academies were usually operated for either boys or girls but not for both. The average course of study included the basic subjects plus Latin, Greek, and advanced mathematics.

The first incorporated academy was established at Batesville in 1836. Within four years others were in operation at Fayetteville, Lewisburg, Little Rock, Napoleon, Rocky Comfort, Pocahontas, and perhaps elsewhere. After 1840 the number of chartered academies multiplied, and many others were established but never incorporated. By 1860 a number of towns including Batesville, Cane Hill, Fayetteville, Fort Smith, Little Rock, Princeton, Rocky Comfort, Spring Hill, and Tulip had become well known as educational centers. Tulip, located in a wealthy plantation section of Dallas County, became the site of the Arkansas Military Institute.

The term "high school" came into use in 1848 with the appearance of the "Little Rock High School for Young Ladies." Similar high schools were organized before 1860 at Helena and Pine Bluff, among other places. Jefferson High School at Pine Bluff was the first such institution to admit both boys and girls.

The Fayetteville Female Seminary, 1852. Drawn by William Quesenbury, better known as "Bill Cush." Miss Sophia Sawyer was principal of the school

The high schools were community enterprises rather than privately owned academies.

Colleges and special education. A number of private schools were called colleges, but most of them were little more than academies. Several of the most important colleges were supported by churches or religious denominations. The Catholic College of St. Andrew opened in Fort Smith in 1851 and lasted until 1858. Cane Hill College in Washington County, a Cumberland Presbyterian school, was set up in 1852. Arkansas College at Fayetteville, which also began in 1852, was connected with the Christian Church and at one time

Dormitory of Cane Hill College, as it appeared after the Civil War. The other college buildings were destroyed during the conflict

had 200 students. In Little Rock the Masonic order opened St. John's College as a military school in 1859. Soulesbury College, a Methodist institution established at Batesville in 1850, was the only one of the leading colleges that accepted both boys and girls as students.

Education of the blind and deaf was just beginning when the Civil War came. Private schools for these groups had opened briefly in Clarksville as early as 1850. The "Arkansas Institute for the Education of the Blind," which began at Arkadelphia in 1859, received state support and was moved to Little Rock after the war. A state school for the deaf at Fort Smith was incorporated just in time to be ruined by the war.

Arkansas established no state university before the Civil War, though in 1827 Congress donated seventy-two sections of land for the purpose. Efforts to sell the land brought in little money, and the General Assembly finally authorized its sale for the benefit of the public schools.

Pioneer families often recorded births, marriages and deaths in large Bibles. This one belonged to a family near Lead Hill, Boone County

Religion on the frontier. Before the Louisiana Purchase only the Catholic Church had been allowed to conduct organized religious work in Arkansas. Protestant activities probably began before 1810. William Patterson, a Methodist local preacher who settled in the Helena area about 1800, may have preached along the Mississippi. A Cumberland Presbyterian minister, John P. Carnahan, held services at Arkansas Post in 1811.

Methodists and Baptists established regular congregations before Arkansas became a territory. Eli Lindsey began a Methodist circuit in the Strawberry River area of northeast Arkansas in 1815. John Henry organized Henry's Chapel, a Methodist church at Mount Prairie, about 1818. By the year 1820 the Methodists had six circuits and over 500 members in Arkansas.

Baptists organized Salem Church in what is now Randolph County in 1818.

Restored pioneer church near Lynn, Lawrence County

LEBANON CHURCH
Organized 1852

Six years later Silas T. Toncray led in beginning a Baptist church in Little Rock, and in 1828 the congregation put up a log meeting house. The first Baptist association of churches had its origin in Little Rock in 1824.

Presbyterians were active in Arkansas during the territorial period. John P. Carnahan conducted Cumberland Presbyterian camp meetings near Little Rock. A Presbyterian church was organized in Little Rock in 1828 by James Wilson Moore, and Benjamin F. Hall began a Christian church there four years later. Episcopal church work commenced in 1839 when Bishop Leonidas Polk organized Christ Church Parish in Little Rock.

The Catholic Church had a slight foothold among people of French descent, but early Arkansas remained a mission field for Catholics as well as Protestants. Catholic missionaries visited several Arkansas settlements about 1824. St. Mary's mission near Pine Bluff, begun in 1833 or earlier, was a center of Catholic influence. The Catholic faith had reached Little Rock and Fort Smith by 1840.

The growth of religious influence. The frontier was a difficult field for ministers and priests, but the influence of the churches increased steadily. Camp meetings attracted settlers from wide areas. Church membership kept pace with the development of the state. The number of Methodists increased from fewer than a hundred in 1815 to about 30,000 in 1860. Between 1850 and 1860 the number of church buildings of all faiths rose from 362 to 1,008. In 1860 half the church houses of Arkansas

Pioneer Methodist camp ground near Center Point, Howard County. Services are conducted under the shed at the left. The structure in the background provides living quarters for campers

were Methodist and another fourth Baptist. Others represented were Cumberland Presbyterians, regular Presbyterians, Christians, Catholics, Episcopalians and union churches. Log meeting houses were gradually replaced by frame structures. Brick churches remained few, and church furniture was often crude.

Before the Civil War Methodists, Baptists and Presbyterians divided into Northern and Southern denominations over the slavery question, and the Arkansas churches went with the Southern branches. The Baptists organized a state convention at Tulip in 1848, and by 1860 had a dozen district associations of churches in various parts of the state. The Methodists in 1860 had two annual conferences, each made up of five district conferences. Presbyteries and synods of the Presbyterian churches were well established before the Civil War. Catholic authorities created the Diocese of Little Rock in 1843 and placed Bishop Andrew Byrne in charge. Except for some scattering German and Irish immigrants who settled mostly at Fort Smith and Little Rock, the Catholics made few gains before 1860.

Many Negro slaves belonged to white churches and attended services regularly. Some churches had slave galleries in the rear of the building, or some other seating section set apart for slaves, and allowed them to attend services with the whites. Other churches held separate services for whites and blacks. Slaves sometimes became ministers and preached to groups of other slaves. Only about one slave out of six held church membership, but the proportion of white people who were members was probably no greater.

Christian Church, Little Rock, erected in 1845. Because of the clock tower, which was added later, the structure was known as the "Town Clock Church"

Many of the early churches opposed drinking, dancing, card-playing and similar practices. Members who failed to attend church services regularly were excluded, as were those found guilty of improper or immoral conduct. In 1856 the General Assembly passed the first of the "three-mile" laws, which prohibited or restricted the sale of liquor within three miles of a designated point, usually a church or school. Before the Civil War several similar laws were enacted.

STUDY AIDS

Vocabulary

Be sure that you understand the meaning of these words and phrases:

maintain	faith
community	diocese
circuit	institute
three-mile laws	course
source	leasing
	incorporated

Identification

Tell what part each of the following had in the story:

Jesse Brown	William Patterson
John Henry	Silas T. Toncray
Blue-back Speller	John P. Carnahan
Christ Church	Benjamin F. Hall
Parish	Soulesbury College

Location

On a map locate the following places:

Napoleon	Princeton
Lewisburg	Tulip
Rocky Comfort	Pocahontas
Cane Hill	Spring Hill

To test your reading

On other paper, list 1-8. Opposite each number, write the word or words which complete each sentence.

1. The first incorporated academy was established at __ in the year __.

2. The first general public school law was enacted in the year __.

3. The first high school was __.

4. The denomination owning half of the church buildings in Arkansas in 1860 was the __.

5. St. John's College at Little Rock, sponsored by the __ was opened in the year __.

6. Education for the blind and deaf began at __ as early as __.

7. The first Baptist association of churches had its origin in __ in the year __.

8. A Presbyterian church was organized in Little Rock in the year __ by __.

Things to do

1. Make a list of the religious groups or churches represented in your community and compare it with those listed in this chapter. Which churches in your community are oldest?

2. From what sources are funds obtained for financing schools in your community? Compare these sources with ways in which schools were financed before the Civil War.

3. Imagine that you are a student in the first school in Little Rock in 1823. Write a letter to a friend in which you describe the school, your studies, and the town. (Review the section called "Little Rock in pioneer days", in Unit 2, Chapter 4.)

4. Set up a model interior of a typical frontier school.

5. Did your community or city have one or more academies during the early days? Find out all you can about them.

100

6   Disposing of the Public Lands

Throughout the frontier period the process of land disposal continued. The Federal government gave great tracts of Arkansas soil to the state government for various purposes. From government ownership the land passed to speculators, former soldiers, railroad companies, and settlers.

Federal land grants to Arkansas. The United States government, which owned almost all the land in Arkansas after the Louisiana Purchase and the removal of the Indians, made large donations of land to the state. About one third of all the land in Arkansas was given to the state to be used in providing for education and for public improvements such as building levees, draining swamps, and erecting public buildings.

The sixteenth section in each township, a total of almost a million acres, was donated for public schools. Another 500,000 acres was given in 1841 for internal improvements such as levees and drainage ditches. A grant of two townships, 46,080 acres, was supposed to be used to establish a state university. About the same amount was given to the state because the selected areas contained springs from which salt could be made. Fifteen sections, or 9,600 acres were donated for the erection of what is now the Old State House, and there were other minor grants.

The government of Arkansas was expected to rent or sell all these lands and use the money for the benefit of the people of the state. In addition to the outright donation of land, Congress continued the sale of public lands in Arkansas and allowed the state government five per cent of the net proceeds.

The swamp land grants. The largest gifts of land from the United States to Arkansas were made under the Swamp Land Acts, the first of which was passed by Congress in 1849. These acts provided for transferring the ownership of about 8,600,000 acres of "swamp and overflowed" lands from the United States to the State of Arkansas. The Arkansas government was expected to sell this vast acreage, which amounted to more than a fourth of all the land in the state, and use the money to build levees and drain swamps.

The swamp land grants resulted from the increasing need of flood control along the rivers, and the widespread desire for more agricultural land. The river valleys were becoming filled with farms, plantations, and towns, and levees were needed to control flood waters. If swamps could be drained and made productive, great new areas might be opened for cotton and other crops. Individuals and local groups had attempted some levee and drainage work, but such projects were too large to be handled in this way.

In 1850 the General Assembly set up a Board of Swamp Land Commissioners, composed of three members appointed by the governor, to take over the lands which had been donated by the Federal government. The board was to fix land prices, plan levees and drainage canals, and let contracts for having them built. Employees, contractors and others were to be paid either in land or in land certificates called "swamp land scrip." The scrip could be sold, or used to purchase tracts of the swamp and overflowed lands.

The commissioners met at Helena early in 1851 and divided the state into three swamp land districts, each to be managed by a commissioner and his staff of agents and engineers. By the fall of 1852 the board was able to report the construction of more than a hundred miles of levees. Most of the new levees lay along the Mississippi River, and the cost had averaged $3,000 a mile. Since most of the swamp land was valued at fifty cents an acre, 6,000 acres had to be sold to pay for the construction of each mile of levee. Levee building continued for several years.

Levee and drainage projects, by providing work for thousands of men and hundreds of teams of mules, horses, and oxen, helped Arkansas to recover from a severe depression caused by the failure of the State and Real Estate banks. Unfortunately many of the levees prov-

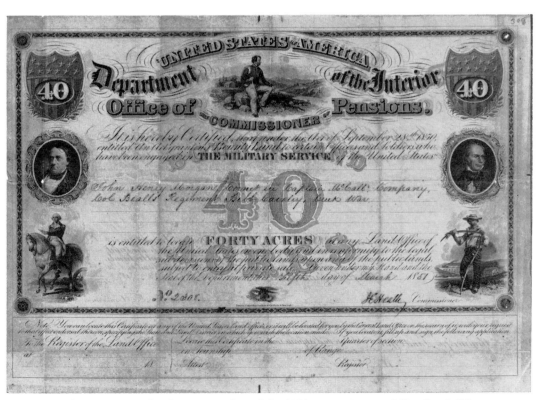

Military bounty land warrant, issued in 1851 to a veteran of the Creek War

Document authorizing payment for levee work, signed by Governor Conway in 1860

ed to be poorly located. Great floods in 1858 and 1859 not only overflowed the bottom lands of the St. Francis River but washed miles of the new levees into the Mississippi.

Federal land grants to railroads. As early as 1853 the United States government began making land grants to Arkansas for the benefit of proposed railroads, and the policy was continued after the Civil War. The Cairo and Fulton, Memphis and Little Rock, and Little Rock and Fort Smith railroads eventually received ten sections of land for each mile of track laid. These lines thus came into possession of 2,600,000 acres of Arkansas land, or about one twelfth of the entire area of the state. After the Civil War most of the railroad lands were sold in small tracts to individual owners. The railroad companies retained a considerable acreage for their own use.

Free land in Arkansas. The Federal government gave vast tracts of public land in Arkansas to former soldiers. Veterans of the War of 1812 and the Mexican War were entitled to 160 acres each. Later Congress granted bonuses of 160 acres to veterans of all United States wars and to their heirs. By 1859 about 1,500,000 acres had been taken up by soldiers' bonuses. Much of this land the former soldiers themselves never occupied, but sold their claims to someone else.

By the year 1840 Arkansas had come into possession of a considerable amount of land through the failure of owners to pay their taxes. Under the Donation Law of 1840 settlers could obtain title to this land in return for the payment of taxes in the future. The law, as amended later, permitted a family to acquire 160 acres for each member of the immediate family, regardless of age or sex. The Arkansas donation act attracted widespread attention, with inquiries coming from as far away as New York and Massachusetts. The demand for free land under provisions of the law soon exceeded the supply.

The ease with which land could be acquired in Arkansas was doubtless the main cause of the coming of thousands of new settlers who arrived in the two decades preceding the Civil War. People living in states east of the Mississippi River frequently sold their farms at attractive prices, moved to Arkansas and acquired even larger holdings for little or no cost. Most of the individual owners received title to their lands, either directly or indirectly, from the State of Arkansas as a result of Federal grants to the state. But it should be remembered that some acquired their lands from the Federal government either by purchase or as donations for military service. Many others bought land from the railroad companies or the levee and drainage districts. Yet in spite of donations and sales, at the outbreak of the Civil War the United States government still held title to almost one third of the land in Arkansas. After 1862 settlers were able to acquire land under the Federal Homestead Act.

STUDY AIDS

Vocabulary

Be sure that you understand the meaning of these words:

donation   levees
scrip   township
tract   bonuses
heirs   decade
                  homestead

To test your reading

On other paper, list 1-6. Opposite each number, write the word or words which complete each sentence.

1. The sixteenth section in each township was given for __.

2. The largest gifts of land to Arkansas were made under the __ Acts.

3. More than a hundred miles of levees had been built by the fall of __.

4. The U. S. began to make railroad land grants as early as __.

5. The Donation Law of 1840, as amended, permitted a family to secure __ acres of free land for each person in the family.

6. In 1861 the U. S. still held title to about __ of the land in Arkansas.

Things to do

1. What kind of title or deed to land do most Arkansas property owners hold today? Secure from the courthouse or from some lawyer a blank deed form and study it carefully.

2. Examine an abstract of title to a piece of real estate. Notice all of the different owners. How long has some member of your family owned the land or lot where you now live?

3. Ask an abstract man to talk to your class about tracing land titles.

4. Suppose that your ancestors came to Arkansas about 1850. Tell some of the different ways in which they may have come to be landowners.

5. If there are levees near your home or school, when were they built? Find out and report to the class.

7   Literature and Legend

Many early accounts of the Arkansas region were mixtures of truth and tall tales. Partly because of such writings Arkansas acquired a bad reputation, but they also helped to give the state a rich tradition of homespun humor. This chapter discusses some of the authors and the stories they told.

The early reputation of Arkansas. Tall tales became associated with the Arkansas region very early in its history. A French writer named Dumont who accompanied La Harpe on his exploration of the Arkansas River in 1722 tried to amuse his readers with stories about giant bullfrogs and swamps crowded with turtles. After the Louisiana Purchase explorers and travelers produced accounts which often combined truth with attempts to entertain the reader. Even some reliable writers tended to emphasize the bad aspects of life in early Arkansas.

In 1820 the editor of the **Arkansas Gazette** complained that prejudiced travelers were spreading unfavorable reports about Arkansas. Albert Pike wrote in 1834 that Eastern newspaper editors seemed to think that Arkansas was "entirely out of the world." One such editor referred to Little Rock as a place "somewhat west of sunset." Many people thought of Arkansas as a place of swamps, hills, and backwoods, inhabited by ignorant and ill-mannered people. But then, as now, there were all types of people here.

"Fent" Noland, Arkansas humorist. A few Arkansas writers themselves contributed to the developing reputation of the territory and state. The most outstanding of these was Charles Fenton Mercer Noland of Batesville. Noland was a lawyer, politician, journalist, and sportsman who was intensely interested in the popular Arkansas recreations of fishing, hunting and horse racing.

In 1836 Noland began writing for the **Spirit of the Times,** a weekly newspaper for sportsmen published in New York. Over a period of nearly twenty

C. F. M. Noland

years he contributed some 225 articles to this publication. Signing himself "N of Arkansas" or "Pete Whetstone of Devil's Fork," Noland wrote about horse racing, hunting, fishing, society, politics and other aspects of frontier life. Some of his work was true to life and some was exaggerated, but all was written in humorous style.

"Fent" Noland's articles were reprinted widely in the United States and England. The author, who died in 1858, became widely known and acquainted with many of the most prominent men of his time. He spent the last few years of his life in Little Rock writing for the **Arkansas Gazette.** The Noland house in the Territorial Restoration in Little Rock is a well-deserved tribute to his memory.

The Big Bear of Arkansas. Another writer who helped make Arkansas famous was Thomas Bangs Thorpe of Louisiana. His stories, like those of Noland,

were published in the New York **Spirit of the Times** and then reprinted in many other newspapers and magazines.

Thorpe's finest story, "The Big Bear of Arkansas," appeared in 1841 and became the most celebrated of all stories about the state. Through translations it came to be known to readers in Germany, France, Italy, and even in India. Later Thorpe wrote "A Piano in Arkansas," "The Devil's Summer Retreat, in Arkansas," and other productions of similar style.

The stories of Thorpe and Noland helped to establish the reputation of the Arkansas native as a teller of tall tales through which there ran a rich vein of earthy humor. Arkansas became known as the "Bear State," the home of the backwoodsman who was always as ready with a joke as with his rifle.

Arrington on desperadoes and dueling. Alfred W. Arrington of Little Rock and

Private office of C. F. M. Noland, Territorial Restoration, Little Rock

'I throw'd back my gun to gin it to her, as she come; the lick I aimed at her head struck across the shoulders and back, without doing any harm, *and she had me!*"—*Page* 137.

"Why, much as I tell you; we had it round and round, about and about, over and under."—*Page* 38.

Illustrations from "Big Bear's Adventures and Travels," a collection of stories about Arkansas and other frontier regions, published in 1858

"He jumped into the lake and tried to mount the log."—*Page* 28.

"While he turned up his eyes as if to holla louder, the big bear give him a dig with her paw in the seat of his pantaloons, and carried away drawers and all."—*Page* 46.

Illustrations from Gerstaecker's "Wild Sports in the Far West," edition of 1861

Fayetteville was a preacher, lecturer, lawyer, and writer who was widely known as a speaker of outstanding ability. His special field as a writer was the lack of law and order in Arkansas and neighboring areas. Arrington's books, **Duelling and Duellists of the South-West** and **The Desperadoes of the South-West,** were first published separately in New York in 1847 and later issued in a single volume. His stories often appeared in New York newspapers and were widely reprinted.

Through his books and stories, Arrington pictured Arkansas as a place where tavern brawls and duels were common, where outlaws operated freely and where lawlessness prevailed. His stories were interesting and entertaining, but they gave to many readers the false impression that Arkansas was largely a land of ruffians and criminals.

A German traveler in Arkansas. Frederick Gerstaecker of Germany, a world

traveler, hunter, and writer, came to Arkansas in 1838. He traveled from Memphis through the eastern part of the state, reached Fourche la Fave River, and visited Danville and Perryville. The next year he returned and spent several months in hunting and observing the mode of life of the backwoodsmen. In 1841 Gerstaecker came for a third visit. This time he traveled to the upper reaches of White River, again passing the time in hunting and learning the ways of the pioneers.

Gerstaecker came to Arkansas to gather material for writing. He was a careful observer, and his books, which were first published in German, are excellent sources of information. Among them are **The Regulators in Arkansas, The River Pirates of the Mississippi,** and **Wild Sports in the Far West.**

The works of Gerstaecker helped to further develop the image of Arkansas outlined by Noland, Thorpe, and Arrington. As a writer Gerstaecker was superior to any of these, and presented a better balanced picture of frontier Arkansas and its people. His books became well known in Europe but probably reached few readers in America before the Civil War. Noland, Thorpe and Arrington are almost forgotten but Frederick Gerstaecker is still remembered as a writer of international reputation.

Other writers. Albert Pike, a Little Rock lawyer, editor and politician, enjoyed a high local reputation as a poet. In 1839 his "Hymns to the Gods" was published in a leading British magazine. Other literary productions by Pike included "Prose Sketches and Poems,"

Albert Pike, in Masonic regalia. Through his work with Freemasonry, Pike became one of the most famous Arkansans of the nineteenth century

"Ariel," and "Ode to the Mocking Bird," as well as a few humorous poems and stories. After the Civil War Pike moved to Washington, D. C. and devoted himself to Masonic writings and Hindu philosophy.

William Quesenbury, who pronounced his name "Cushenberry," was a Fayetteville editor better known as "Bill Cush." He was a painter, humorist, and poet, as well as probably the first cartoonist in Arkansas. Sanford C. "Sandy" Faulkner is usually considered to be the author of the humorous dialogue and fiddle tune called "The Arkansas Traveler." The piece attained wide popularity and helped to preserve the idea that Arkansas was a remote backwoods region. Other storytellers have given "The Arkansas Traveler" dialogue many different forms since the original appeared in print about 1858 or earlier.

Growth of the press. Starting a newspaper in the early days was easy. An editor might borrow money to buy a small press and then gather his own news, solicit the advertisements, set the type, and even deliver the paper locally. Little weekly papers appeared in many Arkansas communities, but few of them lasted long.

In 1850 there were fourteen newspapers in Arkansas. All of them were weeklies except one, which was published bi-weekly, and the total circulation of the thirteen weekly papers was 7,250 copies. Five newspapers were Democratic in politics, three were Whig, and the remaining six were devoted to literature, religion, and other subjects.

The next ten years saw an increase in the number of Arkansas newspapers to thirty-seven. The total circulation of all these papers in 1860 came to almost 40,000. The first daily newspapers, the **True Democrat** of Little Rock and the **Times and Herald** of Fort Smith, appeared on the eve of the Civil War when telegraph lines penetrated the state for the first time.

Pioneer painters. Traveling artists appeared in some Arkansas towns as early as 1834, offering to paint portraits for a fee. John Henry Byrd, who came to Little Rock about 1840, was the first resident artist of any real importance. He did portraits of wealthy planters and their families, and later exercised his skill with the Confederate army.

One of Byrd's students was responsible for the most famous of all Arkansas paintings, the **Arkansas Traveler.** Edward Payson Washburn, son of the pioneer missionary Cephas Washburn, painted the **Traveler** in 1858 at Norristown, near present-day Russellville. He then began a companion picture called the **Turn of the Tune,** but died before it was finished. Innumerable copies have been made of both paintings, and for many years they were favorites all over the Southwest. The original of the **Arkansas Traveler** is in the Old State House in Little Rock.

STUDY AIDS

Vocabulary

Be sure that you understand the meaning of these words and phrases:

tall tales	dialogue
mode	observer
reaches	impression

Identification

Tell what part each of the following had in the story:

C. F. M. Noland	William
Frederick	Quesenbury
Gerstaecker	Sanford C.
Alfred W.	Faulkner
Arrington	John Henry Byrd
Thomas Bangs	Edward Payson
Thorpe	Washburn
	Albert Pike

Location

Locate the following on a map:

Danville	Devil's Fork
Perryville	Fourche la Fave

To test your reading

On other paper, list 1-9. Opposite each number, write the word or words which complete each sentence.

1. The number of newspapers in Arkansas in 1850 was ___.

2. The author of "The Big Bear of Arkansas" was ___.

3. The author of *Duelling and Duellists of the South-West* was ___.

4. Pete Whetstone was an assumed name used by ___.

5. The author of *Wild Sports in the Far West* was ___.

6. The first daily paper in Little Rock was ___.

7. Arkansas' first cartoonist was ___.

8. A leading writer on Masonry was ___. He also enjoyed a reputation as a ___ and a ___.

9. The leading sportsman's magazine of the day was ___.

Things to do

1. Organize a television panel in which Fent Noland, Thomas Bangs Thorpe, Alfred W. Arrington and Frederick Gerstaecker discuss their books and articles and why they wrote them.

2. Visit the Noland house in the Territorial Restoration in Little Rock.

3. Find a copy of "The Arkansas Traveler" dialogue and present it as a classroom play. Perhaps you can find someone who can play the fiddle tune of the same name.

4. Visit the Albert Pike house in Little Rock.

5. Read and report on one of the books, articles or poems mentioned in this chapter.

6. Why was Arkansas called the "Bear State"? What are some of the other nicknames by which Arkansas has been called? Make a report to the class.

Reviewing the Unit

1. During the period of early statehood, how were candidates chosen and elections conducted?

2. Why did the people decide in 1846 that no more banks should be allowed to operate in the state?

3. How did slavery affect the development of Arkansas?

4. Why did Arkansas come to be known as a wild, lawless region?

5. Why did the Federal government give so much land to the state? What did the state government do with the land?

6. Why did Arkansas fail to develop a good system of public schools before the Civil War?

7. Where did most of the new settlers come from? Why did Arkansas towns grow so slowly?

Unit Four

Confederate Arkansas

The Chapters

1. Secession and War
2. The First Two Years of the War
3. The Last Two Years of the War
4. Life in Confederate Arkansas

IN 1861 ARKANSAS joined an attempt by eleven Southern states to establish an independent republic called the Confederate States of America. For four trying years most of the white people of Arkansas worked, fought, suffered and died for the cause of Southern independence. Southerners believed that they were fighting for their homes, their property and their way of life against those who would ruin and destroy them.

Arkansas itself became a battleground in the great Civil War. Armies marched and campaigned in the northwest, along the rivers, in the south and in other areas. Bandits took advantage of wartime conditions to loot and ravish. Arkansans suffered as never before or since.

In the end the Confederacy lost the struggle because of internal disunity as well as superior Northern military strength. The war left a heritage of destruction and bitterness, and all its effects have not yet disappeared.

1   Secession and War

Arkansas was an unwilling participant in the Civil War. She was one of the last four of the eleven Southern states to secede, and did not do so until the outbreak of war forced her to take a stand. But when the choice was made most Arkansans immediately rallied to do their part for Southern independence.

Arkansas faces a crisis. In 1860 Arkansas was enjoying a period of progress and prosperity. In the last ten years the population had doubled and now was about 435,000. The future seemed bright, but in the background were bitter disputes between the Northern and Southern states which threatened to reach a climax. If war should come, Arkansas would be involved.

With slavery, the most outstanding of the issues between North and South, the majority of people in Arkansas were not greatly concerned. Four fifths of the white families in the state owned no slaves. Few of those who did own slaves believed that the system was in danger. For many years the slavery question had caused trouble, but somehow compromises had always been reached.

The presidential election of 1860 brought on a crisis. Arkansas was caught up in the rush of events. The new Republican party with its candidate Abraham Lincoln was making its second bid for the presidency. The Democrats, long in control of national affairs, were unable to agree on a candidate. The party split into Northern and Southern wings and each division nominated a candidate. This practically insured the election of Lincoln. Since the Republican party opposed the extension of slavery, some Southern leaders declared that if Lincoln were elected the South should secede and become an independent nation.

Formation of the Southern Confederacy. The presidential campaign of 1860 caused no great excitement in Arkansas, but many people eagerly awaited the outcome of the election. Lincoln's name did not appear on the Arkansas ballot, and the Southern Democratic candidate received a majority of the votes cast in the state. As soon as it was certain that Lincoln had been elected, South Carolina called a convention and passed an ordinance of secession declaring that the state was no longer a part of the United States. She sent delegates to the other Southern states urging them to follow the same course. The Arkansas General Assembly, which was in session at the time, listened to the South Carolina delegates but took no action.

While Arkansas hesitated, other Southern states were busy passing ordinances of secession. South Carolina was soon joined by Mississippi, Florida, Alabama, Georgia, Louisiana, and Texas. In February 1861 representatives of the seceding states met in Montgomery, Alabama, and organized the Confederate States of America. Jefferson Davis of Mississippi was elected president. Other Southern states, including Arkansas, watched and waited.

Arkansas refuses to secede. As the secession movement grew, people in Arkansas became greatly concerned. In January 1861 Governor Henry M. Rector, at the direction of the General Assembly, called an election for the people to vote on whether Arkansas should hold a convention to consider secession. At the same time the voters were to elect delegates to the convention in case the vote should be favorable. At the election on February 18 the vote was favorable and delegates were chosen.

Companies of troops were already being organized in different parts of Arkansas, and demands were raised that the United States arsenal in Little Rock be surrendered to the state government. Early in February troops from Helena and several other places moved into Little Rock and declared that they would take the arsenal by force if necessary. Alarmed by the possibility of bloodshed, Governor Rector persuaded the Federal commander to surrender the arsenal and evacuate his troops. The governor then took charge in the name of the state.

The secession convention met in the Old State House in Little Rock on March

The United States arsenal at Little Rock, 1861. The site is now MacArthur Park

4, 1861. David Walker, who opposed secession, was elected president. The convention continued in session for two and a half weeks. Feeling ran high and many fiery speeches were made, but it soon became evident that a majority of the members did not think that the situation at that time called for secession. The convention voted down a resolution condemning Lincoln's inaugural address, and defeated a conditional ordinance of secession.

The opinion seemed to prevail that Arkansas should secede if the Federal government made war on the Confederate States. Still hoping for a compromise settlement that would avoid war, the delegates agreed to go home until after the people had voted on the secession question at a special election to be held in August.

War brings secession. The Civil War began on April 12, 1861 when Confederate guns opened fire on Fort Sumter, in the harbor at Charleston, South Carolina. When President Lincoln asked Arkansas to provide a regiment of troops to force the seceded states back into the Union Governor Rector refused. The governor sent a force to take the Fort Smith arsenal, and Arkansas regiments began organizing to fight for the South.

The secession convention, recalled in special session, met again in the Old State House in Little Rock on May 6. Before a packed house, a secession ordinance was introduced and passed by vote of sixty-five to five. When the chairman asked that the decision be made unanimous, Isaac Murphy of Huntsville was the only delegate who refused to change his vote. On May 20 Arkansas was admitted to the Confederacy. She had seceded only when the coming of war forced her to take a stand with the South. Virginia, Tennessee and North Carolina also seceded after the war had actually begun.

Organizing for war. After passing the ordinance of secession, the convention remained in session for almost a month longer attempting to prepare the state for war. It provided for raising "The Army of Arkansas," chose military officers and gave them instructions and set up a military board to manage the war in Arkansas after the convention had adjourned.

The military board consisted of the governor as chairman and two advisers elected by the convention. This board was given full military power subject to the order of the convention and subsequent acts of the legislature. A war loan of $2,000,000 was appropriated for its use and it was authorized to call out 30,000 men and more if necessary.

The secession convention adjourned on June 3 and the military board took over the management of the war effort. It issued a call for 10,000 volunteers for a year in the state service and set about finding provisions and equipment. The response to the call was quite satisfactory. In a short time the recruiting stations over the state were rushing men into Little Rock to be trained on the arsenal grounds. For the board, securing arms was a problem. Some men brought their own guns but many had no arms of any kind.

Throughout the summer months of 1861 the problems facing the military

Henry M. Rector

board increased in number, especially after the battle of Oak Hills or Wilson's Creek on August 10. Governor Rector, as chairman of the board, was anxious to save the state the expense of keeping the troops in the field and for that reason favored transferring them to the Confederacy. But he also feared that if this were done they would be taken out of the state and the state would have no one to defend it. For that reason he opposed transfer. In 1862 the transfer was finally completed and the work of the military board came to an end.

STUDY AIDS

Vocabulary

Be sure that you understand the meaning of these words and phrases:

crisis   evacuate
secession   conditional
inaugural address   compromise
regiment   ordinance

Identification

Tell what part each of the following had in the story:

David Walker   military board
Henry M. Rector   Little Rock arsenal
                Isaac Murphy

To test your reading

On other paper, list 1-7. Opposite each number write the word or words which complete each sentence.

1. Until the war began most of the people of Arkansas favored the ___.

2. The number of states that formed the Confederacy was ___.

3. The number that joined later was ___.

4. The only member of the convention to vote against secession was ___.

5. The first state to secede was ___.

6. The secession convention met in the building now called the ___ in Little Rock.

7. The secession convention met on ___ and adjourned on ___.

Things to do

1. Have a TV program in which Governor Henry M. Rector faces a panel of interviewers. Let them ask him questions about Arkansas' secession and about his efforts to organize the state for war.

2. Make a list of the states that joined the Confederacy, with dates when each state seceded. Consult an encyclopedia or United States history book.

3. Had you lived in Arkansas in 1861, which side would you have favored? Why? Plan a classroom debate or discussion.

4. Visit the old arsenal building in Little Rock. It is now a museum.

2   The First Two Years of the War

Confederate Arkansas entered the great struggle with high hopes, but the story of the fighting soon became a depressing account of frustration, defeat and failure. At the end of two years northwest Arkansas and the White River region had been lost, and central Arkansas lay open to Federal invasion.

The war spirit. The late spring and summer of 1861 was a time of great excitement in Confederate Arkansas. Recruiting offices were open in almost every county. At picnics and barbecues, accompanied by rousing speeches, young men were urged to enlist. Even men who could see little reason for going to war were caught up in the tide of popular enthusiasm.

Arkansas men flocked to the colors, but supplies were a problem. Soldiers had to bring their own clothing and weapons, or hope to secure guns on the battlefield. Patriotic local people equipped home companies whenever they could. Young women made flags, and staged theater parties or strawberry suppers to raise money for military equipment.

The story of a company raised at Mount Ida in Montgomery County is typical of most of the 200 others that mustered in 1861. Two men began organizing the Mount Ida company on July 4, and enlisted a hundred men in two weeks. Weapons included old flintlock rifles and double-barrel shotguns. A homemade drum and a fife made of cane provided martial music. The home folks contributed enough food to supply the company until it reached Fort Smith and government rations. Two ox wagons hauled the company's bed quilts, pots, skillets, and pans. Not a man in the company knew anything about military tactics, and most of them would never come back.

A carnival air prevailed in that fateful summer of 1861. The boys marched away to stirring music and the fond farewells of mothers and sweethearts. The war was to be a glorious adventure, and since Yankees could not fight they would soon be home again. Ahead of them lay four years of blood, death, and final defeat.

The strategic importance of Arkansas. The region west of the Mississippi River, including Arkansas, was a secondary theater of action during the Civil War. The great battles were fought in Virginia, Georgia and other states east of the river, and there the outcome of the war was actually decided. But even though Arkansas was not a major battleground the state played a role of considerable importance, partly because of its location.

The Mississippi River formed the eastern boundary of Arkansas, and this fact brought the war into the state.

Arkansas Confederate soldiers

A major Union military objective was to get control of the great river and cut the Confederacy in two. For the first two years of the war the Union troops and ships were fighting their way down the river from the north and up from New Orleans in order to achieve this objective.

Arkansas was also a part of the struggle for Missouri and the western frontier. Missouri was a divided state, torn between the Union and the Confederacy, and it became one of the first battlefields. If the Confederates could hold or retake Missouri they could outflank the Union push down the Mississippi, and Arkansas became the Confederate base of operations. Arkansas also bordered the Cherokees, Choctaws and the other Indian nations, and both sides wanted to win the allegiance of the Indians.

The loss of the northwest. Among the first companies to enlist were ten from Ashley, Drew, Union, Dallas and Hot Spring counties. These companies, each composed of about a hundred men, were taken to Memphis by boat and then moved by rail to Virginia. There they became the Third Arkansas Infantry, one of the most famous regiments in Lee's Army of Northern Virginia. The First Arkansas Infantry also reached Virginia early in the war.

Arkansas troops in much greater numbers moved to the Missouri border. By midsummer in 1861 several thousand men had assembled north of Pocahontas, and more thousands in Washington and Benton counties. The first battle came on August 10 at Oak Hills, or

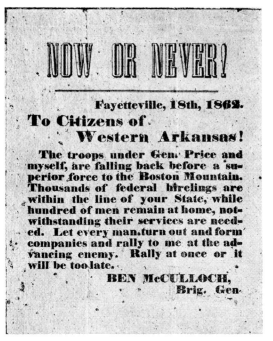

NOW OR NEVER!

Fayetteville, 18th, 1862.
To Citizens of
Western Arkansas!

The troops under Gen. Price and myself, are falling back before a superior force to the Boston Mountain. Thousands of federal hirelings are within the line of your State, while hundred of men remain at home, notwithstanding their services are needed. Let every man turn out and form companies and rally to me at the advancing enemy. Rally at once or it will be too late.

BEN McCULLOCH,
Brig. Gen.

Leaflet issued by Confederate General Mc-Culloch, who was killed soon afterward at the Battle of Pea Ridge

The Battle of Pea Ridge, from a sketch by a Northern officer

Wilson's Creek, near Springfield, Missouri. At Wilson's Creek, Southern troops from Arkansas and Missouri defeated a Union force and sent it retreating northward, but the Confederates were too poorly-equipped and led to follow up their advantage.

Early in 1862 a new Union army commanded by General Samuel A. Curtis moved into northwest Arkansas. Confederate General Earl Van Dorn planned to defeat the Federals, win Missouri and outflank the army led by U. S. Grant then moving into Tennessee. On March 6, 1862 the Confederate forces attacked Curtis at Pea Ridge or Elkhorn Tavern in Benton County. The battle was contested hotly for three days. The Con-

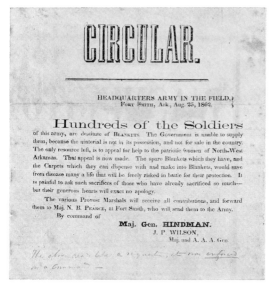

Thomas C. Hindman

A Confederate appeal for blankets, 1862

federates outnumbered the Union army, but were defeated by poor generalship and left the field in possession of the Federals. The Confederate Cherokees led by Albert Pike gave a poor account of themselves at Pea Ridge.

Pea Ridge was the largest and most important Civil War battle west of the Mississippi River. Over 26,000 men were engaged, and at least 2,500 were killed and wounded. The failure of the Confederate drive northward meant the final loss of Missouri, and perhaps Tennessee and the Mississippi River

also. The discouraged Confederate troops retreating southward after the battle began to desert, and some even joined the other side.

Arkansas left unprotected. After the defeat at Pea Ridge, Confederate authorities ordered Generals Van Dorn and Sterling Price to transfer their troops east of the Mississippi where Union armies were attacking in great strength. The move left Arkansas open to invasion. Governor Henry M. Rector and the Arkansas senators and repre-

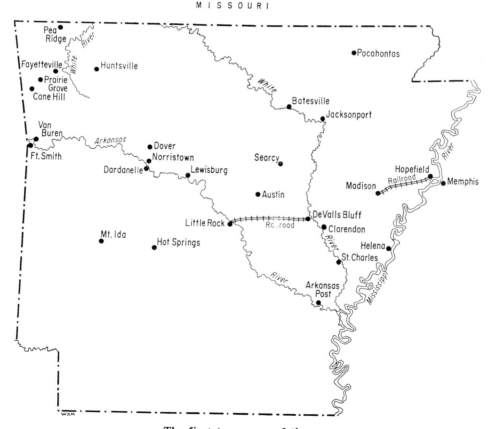

The first two years of the war

sentatives in Richmond complained that the Confederate government had deserted the state. Rector even threatened that Arkansas and the other Southern states west of the Mississippi might secede from the Confederacy. To relieve the situation Southern leaders placed General Thomas C. Hindman of Helena in command in Arkansas.

Hindman at once began to raise and equip a new army. He placed the state under martial law, drafted men into the army, set up price controls, and burned thousands of bales of cotton to keep them out of enemy hands. Lead mines, factories, and a chemical laboratory to provide medicines went into operation. Military officers seized foodstuffs and other supplies needed by the army, and personal travel was restricted.

Governor Rector and the General Assembly protested to the Confederate government that Hindman was trampling on the rights of the state. Finally General Theophilus H. Holmes was sent to replace Hindman, but Holmes seized all the salt works and continued many of Hindman's policies.

The Federals on White River. In 1862 the Little Rock to Memphis line was the only railroad in Arkansas, and it had a gap from DeValls Bluff to Madison. Troops had to be moved overland or by boat, and this made control of the rivers especially important. The Confederates began to fortify Arkansas Post to defend the Arkansas, and defenses were erected at St. Charles to stop any Union advance up White River.

Union General Curtis made no attempt to pursue the retreating Confederates after Pea Ridge because he considered the Ozark country too rough and

Hot Springs as it appeared during the Civil War

difficult. Instead he moved back into Missouri, marched a hundred miles or more to the east, and then south again into Arkansas. Early in May with about 20,000 troops Curtis occupied Batesville and the region along the White River as far as Jacksonport. He planned to advance on Little Rock, where he had been ordered to install himself as military governor of Arkansas. Expecting such a move, Governor Rector left Little Rock and for a short time set up the state capital at Hot Springs.

The Federals moved as far south as the vicinity of Searcy, but Curtis had to postpone his plan for capturing Little Rock. Not only was Confederate strength increasing, but about half of his army was ordered to the aid of Union forces east of the Mississippi River. In addition Curtis was hampered by lack of supplies and by difficulties in transportation.

While General Curtis was still in the Batesville area, Union authorities sent a fleet of gunboats up White River to reduce St. Charles and take support to his army. St. Charles was captured on June 17, 1862, but not until a lucky shot from a Confederate shore gun had disabled the gunboat **Mound City** with heavy loss of life. Because of shallow water the gunboat fleet returned to Memphis, but White River had been opened to the Federals. In July Curtis and his troops moved down the river, crossed over to Helena and joined other Federal forces stationed there.

Prairie Grove and Arkansas Post. Late in 1862 Confederate General Hindman, still in command in western Arkansas, moved his force of 11,000 men northward to attack Federal armies threatening Fort Smith. The battle at Prairie Grove, near Fayetteville on December 7, was a Confederate success in the field, but Hindman could not hold his ground and had to retreat. The Federals pursued him to Van Buren and there scored another victory. Hindman's army was practically destroyed by the campaign, and now the upper Arkansas River area was defenseless.

Confederate Gunboat No. 51, a converted passenger steamer, on White River

Only a month after the Battle of Prairie Grove, Arkansas Confederates suffered another disaster. Early in January 1863, a large Federal fleet with some 32,000 men attacked Arkansas Post, where the Confederates had built Fort Hindman. The Confederate garrison of about 5,000 men, commanded by General Thomas J. Churchill, put up a spirited defense and surrendered only when one regiment raised the white flag without orders from the commander. The town of Arkansas Post was destroyed and never rebuilt. The Union army at Arkansas Post was the largest ever assembled at any battle in Arkansas, and the number of Confederate prisoners taken there exceeded the entire number captured in all of the other engagements in the state during the four years of the war.

Political rivalry continues. The coming of war did not put an end to political rivalry in Arkansas. The opponents of Governor Henry M. Rector, who had defeated Richard H. Johnson in 1860, were very influential. Johnson was editor of the **True Democrat,** a widely-read Little Rock newspaper. His brother Robert W. Johnson became one of the two Confederate States senators representing Arkansas in Richmond.

Harris Flanagin

In addition to its other activities, the secession convention of 1861 drew up a new state constitution which reduced the term of office of the governor from four years to two years. Rector assumed that the change did not apply to his own term, but in 1862 opposition leaders began calling for an election and the Supreme Court supported their demand. In the election Governor Rector was defeated by Harris Flanagin of Arkadelphia, then on active duty with the Confederate army. The embittered Rector resigned before his term ended.

Casemates or gun emplacements at Fort Hindman, Arkansas Post, after the battle

THE APPEARANCE OF THE CASEMATES BEFORE THE ATTACK.

CASEMATE No 1 DESTROYED BY GUN-BOAT DE-KALB

CASEMATE No 2 DESTROYED BY U.S. GUN-BOAT LOUISVILLE

REAR VIEW OF CASEMATE No 2.

STUDY AIDS

Vocabulary

Be sure that you understand the meaning of these words and phrases:

recruiting
outflank
mustered
fleet
spirited
fife

flintlock rifles
martial law
skillets
allegiance
protested
embittered

Location

Locate each of these on a map:

DeValls Bluff
Madison (town)
Pea Ridge
Jacksonport

Searcy
St. Charles
Prairie Grove
Arkansas Post

Identification

Tell what part each of the following had in the story:

Samuel A. Curtis
Wilson's Creek
Henry M. Rector
Mound City
Thomas C.
  Hindman

Harris Flanagin
Thomas J.
  Churchill
Elkhorn Tavern

To test your reading

On other paper, list 1-7. Opposite each number, write the word or words which complete each sentence.

1. Two Arkansas regiments t h a t reached Virginia early were the ___ and the ___.

2. The Confederate commander at Pea Ridge was ___.

3. The Union commander at Pea Ridge was ___.

4. The general sent to replace Hindman was ___.

5. In 1862 the only railroad in Arkansas was the ___.

6. Hindman's forces suffered heavy losses both at ___ and ___.

7. The largest number of Confederates ever to be captured in a battle in Arkansas was captured at ___.

Things to do

1. Imagine yourself a volunteer in a Confederate company organized in the summer of 1861. Write a letter home telling of your experiences.

2. Draw a sketch map of Arkansas and locate the battles mentioned in this chapter.

3. Plan a class visit to Pea Ridge and Prairie Grove. Both battlefields have been developed as parks.

4. Visit the Flag Gallery in the Old State House, Little Rock, and look especially at the Confederate regimental flags.

3   The Last Two Years of the War

After the summer of 1863 the Federals controlled the Mississippi River and most of Arkansas except the southwest. The Red River campaign and Price's raid into Missouri ended the major fighting, and the Arkansas Confederate government disintegrated as the war came to an end.

The summer of disaster. Vicksburg, the great Confederate stronghold on the east bank of the Mississippi River, was the major Union objective in the West in 1863. Vicksburg was the principal obstacle to Federal control of the river. Union commanders had considered Arkansas Post a threat to their plans, and with it destroyed the advance on Vicksburg was resumed. As the Confederate position became more desperate at Vicksburg and elsewhere, many Southern troops were moved out of Arkansas to provide reinforcements. The people of Arkansas became deeply discouraged, and some began to fear that the Confederate cause was lost.

In an attempt to restore Confederate confidence and to help relieve the pressure on Vicksburg, Generals Holmes and Sterling Price decided to attack the Union garrison at Helena. From several points in the state Southern troops converged on the city. The attack, made on July 4, 1863, was a tragic failure, and the Confederates were thrown back with heavy losses. On the same day Grant captured Vicksburg and the Federals gained control of the Mississippi. At about the same time General Robert E. Lee lost the great Battle of Gettysburg in Pennsylvania.

With the Mississippi under their control, the Federals again turned their attention to the Arkansas. In August an army commanded by General Frederick Steele set out from Helena and advanced by way of DeValls Bluff and Brownsville, near the present city of Lonoke, toward Little Rock. Instead of attacking the prepared Confederate defenses north of the Arkansas opposite Little Rock, Steele built a pontoon bridge across the river below the town and advanced up both sides of the stream. After skirmishing at Bayou Fourche, the Confederates withdrew in the direction of Benton. Union forces occupied Little Rock on September 10, 1863. The state government fled to Washington in Hempstead County where it remained until the close of the war.

A few days after the fall of Little Rock, Steele sent a detachment of troops under Powell Clayton to seize Pine Bluff. Later Benton and other nearby points were occupied. Before the end of 1863 the area controlled by Confederates had been reduced to little more than the extreme southwest. Confederate forces were still strong enough to annoy the Federals with raids and hit-and-run attacks, but there was little chance that they could ever drive the

Union boats and supplies at Des Arc, 1863

Union armies out of Arkansas. Confederate plans to recapture Little Rock were abandoned after the failure of an attack on Pine Bluff in October.

Arkansas and the Red River campaign. For the spring of 1864 Federal leaders planned a campaign which they hoped would complete the conquest of the Southwest. General Nathaniel P. Banks was to lead a joint military and naval expedition up Red River to Shreveport in Louisiana. General Frederick Steele would move south from Little Rock and join forces with Banks. After completing the occupation of Louisiana and Arkansas, the Federals would invade Texas and bring the war in the West to an end. The Confederate armies of General Edmund Kirby Smith, commander of the Trans-Mississippi Department, would be crushed and forced to surrender. In Texas the Union leaders expected to secure large stores of cotton, which was much in demand by New England textile mills.

Steele's army left Little Rock for the south on March 23, 1864. After crossing the Ouachita River at Rockport, near

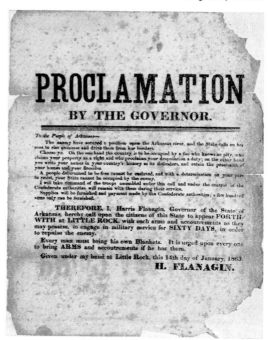

Emergency proclamation by Governor Harris Flanagin, January 14, 1863

Little Rock's Main Street in 1863

present-day Malvern, on a pontoon bridge, the Federals moved to Arkadelphia and toward Washington. On April 9 a Union army from Fort Smith joined Steele, giving him a total force of 13,000 men, 30 cannons, 800 wagons, and 12,000 horses and mules.

On Prairie De Ann, near the present city of Prescott, Steele came up against a Confederate force and for three days skirmishing continued. The state government prepared to leave Washington, and the archives were moved to Rondo near the Texas border. But the Union forces suddenly turned eastward and occupied Camden, one of the most important Confederate strongholds in south Arkansas.

The Federal stay of eleven days in Camden proved uncomfortable because of a shortage of supplies. On April 18 a Union wagon train loaded with corn and other food supplies was captured by Confederates at Poison Spring, a few miles west of Camden, and the escorting force of about 1,100 men was scattered. On April 25 an empty wagon train headed for Pine Bluff was taken by Confederates at Marks' Mills, along with most of the guard accompanying it.

News of the rout at Marks' Mills, where the Southerners captured more prisoners and military equipment than at any other battle in Arkansas, caused Steele to decide to return to Little Rock. Banks had been defeated in Louisiana, and Confederate reinforcements were beginning to arrive from Red River. At Jenkins' Ferry on April 30 the Federals fought off a Confederate attack with difficulty, and made good their escape across the Saline River to Little Rock. Steele's Camden expedition had cost the Union forces dearly in men and supplies, and had accomplished nothing.

The closing scenes. Though the war dragged on for another year, Union armies mounted no more offensives in

Arkansas after the Red River campaign. Most of Steele's troops were ordered east of the Mississippi to help General William T. Sherman batter his way into Atlanta and across Georgia to the sea. Steele held his line along the Arkansas River by keeping strong garrisons at Little Rock, Fort Smith and Pine Bluff with patrols working between those posts.

In the fall of 1864 the Confederates left their stronghold in southwest Arkansas to launch their last offensive. Kirby Smith believed that an invasion of Missouri might lead to the recovery of Arkansas and divert troops from Sherman. With an army that grew to almost 12,000 mounted men General Sterling Price forded the Arkansas River at Dardanelle and moved across north Arkansas. The raiders pushed deep into Missouri but met only defeat and disaster. In the long retreat down the Missouri-Kansas-Arkansas line to Texas, Price's army melted away.

Throughout the last year of the war there were dozens of skirmishes all over Arkansas. Guerrillas were active everywhere except near strong Union or Confederate posts. Many Southern

The last two years of the war

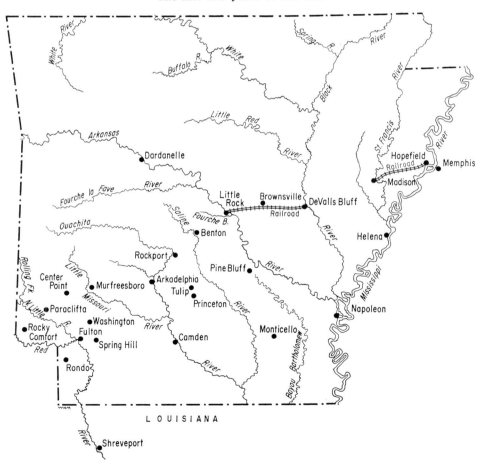

Federal troops entering Little Rock, 1863. From a painting by Stanley M. Arthurs

soldiers simply walked away before the end came. After the Confederate armies of the east surrendered in April 1865, Kirby Smith tried to make an alliance with Maximilian, the French-backed emperor of Mexico. Smith was deposed by his own officers and the Trans-Mississippi armies surrendered on May 26, 1865.

Some of the Confederate generals fled to Mexico for awhile, but most of the Southern soldiers returned to their homes and began trying again to make a living. The last military action of the Civil War in Arkansas was a skirmish at Monticello on May 24, 1865.

Wartime lawmaking. At several sessions during the Civil War members of the General Assembly of Arkansas wrestled with the new and difficult problems created by the conflict. The secession convention had seized the

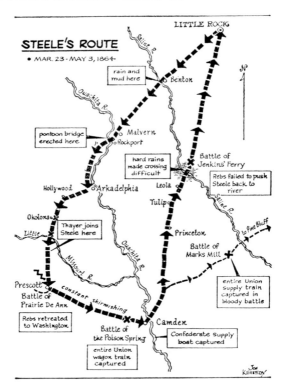

STEELE'S ROUTE
● MAR. 23 - MAY 3, 1864
LITTLE ROCK

rain and mud here
Benton
Ouachita R.
Saline R.

pontoon bridge erected here
Malvern
Rockport
Battle of Jenkins' Ferry

hard rains made crossing difficult
Leola
Rebs failed to push Steele back to river

Hollywood
Arkadelphia
Tulip
Saline R.

Okolona
Thayer joins Steele here
Little
Princeton
to Pine Bluff

Missouri R.
Ouachita R.
Battle of Marks Mill

Prescott
Battle of Prairie De Ann
constant skirmishing
entire Union supply train captured in bloody battle

Rebs retreated to Washington
Battle of the Poison Spring
Camden
Confederate supply boat captured

entire Union wagon train captured

Joe Kennedy

130

public lands and other property owned by the Federal government, but the state still faced severe shortages of manpower, money and supplies. Confederate Arkansas was a frontier state and had little of the means needed to fight a great war.

Successive legislative sessions in 1861-64 tried to deal with the flood of paper money which circulated everywhere, help with the support of soldiers' families, and provide food for the armies and the civilian population. The use of grain to make whiskey was banned because the grain was needed for food. A limit was placed on cotton acreage with the hope that farmers would raise more corn and wheat.

The last session of the Confederate General Assembly met in Washington in the autumn of 1864. So much of Arkansas was under Federal occupation that many districts and counties were not represented. A number of acts were passed, including one establishing soldiers' homes at Washington, Camden,

and Monticello. By this time final defeat was so near at hand that it was too late for lawmaking to be effective.

The Confederate government disintegrates. The adjournment of the General Assembly on October 2, 1864 ended political activity in Confederate Arkansas. A Unionist state government under Isaac Murphy had already been formed in Little Rock, and as the war drew to an end Governor Murphy appealed for reconciliation. In an address to the people in May 1865 Murphy proclaimed that the fighting was over and asked that the Confederates work with him to rebuild Arkansas.

Confederate Governor Harris Flanagin urged that citizens and returning soldiers band together to preserve the peace in the different communities, and sent Augustus H. Garland to Little Rock to negotiate with the Federal commander. When Union authorities refused to treat with or recognize any act of his government, Flanagin delivered the

The Confederate state capitol, Washington, as it appeared after the war

Patrick R. Cleburne

archives and went home to Arkadelphia. The Confederate government of Arkansas, like the Confederacy itself, did not surrender but simply ceased to exist.

The war record of Arkansas. From the Confederate point of view, the war record of Arkansas was a proud one. With a white population of only 324,000 in 1860, the state sent 60,000 men into the Southern armies. Arkansas regiments fought valiantly in Virginia as well as in Tennessee, Mississippi, Georgia and other states. Most of the Arkansas troops served in the Army of Tennessee, which campaigned in the middle South.

Patrick R. Cleburne of Helena emerged as the most distinguished of Arkansas military leaders. During the course of the war Cleburne rose in rank from private to major-general, and was one of the first to advocate freeing the slaves and enlisting Negroes in the Con-

federate army. After saving the Army of Tennessee at Ringgold Gap and Missionary Ridge, Cleburne was killed at the Battle of Franklin in late 1864.

Arkansas produced other heroes. Joseph Fry, a naval captain, almost stopped the Federal ironclads at St. Charles on White River in 1862. David O. Dodd, a youth of seventeen, became the "Boy Martyr of the Confederacy" when he was hanged for spying by Union authorities in Little Rock on January 8, 1864. But the real heroes and heroines were the people of Arkansas, who sacrificed and fought the war with little help from anybody.

Flags of Arkansas Confederate regiments preserved in the Old State House, Little Rock

STUDY AIDS

Vocabulary

Be sure that you understand the meaning of these words and phrases:

garrison   rout
skirmish   patrol
wagon train   archives
objective   pontoon bridge

Identification

Tell what part each of the following had in the story:

Patrick R.   Vicksburg
   Cleburne   David O. Dodd
Joseph Fry   Frederick Steele
Prairie De Ann   Edmund Kirby
                        Smith

To test your reading

On other paper, list 1-7. Opposite each number, write the word or words which complete each sentence.

1. The three main battles connected with General Steele's expedition were the battles of ___,___ and ___.

2. The number of days spent in Camden by the Federals was ___.

3. The largest number of Federal prisoners captured in any battle in Arkansas was taken at ___.

4. In the fall of 1864 an Arkansas army of about ___ men commanded by General ___ invaded Missouri.

5. The attack on Helena was made on ___ 1863.

6. Union forces occupied Little Rock on ___ 1863.

7. On his southern campaign Steele had a force of ___ men, ___ cannons and ___ horses and mules.

Things to do

1. Visit local cemeteries and see if you can find graves of Confederate or Union soldiers. Is there a Confederate monument in your town or county seat? Who erected it, and when? Copy the inscriptions and read them to the class.

2. Visit the Confederate capitol building in Washington, Arkansas.

3. Did one or more of your ancestors serve in the Confederate or Union army? What was his rank, company, and regiment? Look for old letters, diaries and other papers written or printed during the war.

4. Arrange a trip to one of the state parks at Poison Spring, Marks' Mills, or Jenkins' Ferry, or visit the Chidester House in Camden.

5. Search for the story of David O. Dodd and report to the class.

4   Life in Confederate Arkansas

War always brings sacrifice, suffering and sorrow. The courage and faith of Arkansas people as they saw their cause lost in defeat is one of the brightest pages in the history of a bitter period.

Wartime conditions and problems. Conditions in Confederate Arkansas varied greatly with the time and location. In 1861 no hostile forces entered the state. Troops were mustered and war preparations went on, but many people went about their business as usual. In most of the state outside some areas of the Ozarks the people supported the war with enthusiasm.

In the second year of the war Federal forces began to occupy northwest Arkansas and parts of the eastern lowlands. In the last two years of the struggle they dominated most of the state north of the Arkansas River and some areas to the south. In no section was Federal control ever complete. Federal garrisons held the larger towns but the Confederates usually ruled the countryside. Many Arkansas people saw no battles and no Federal soldiers.

War brought new problems to the ordinary people of Arkansas, and as the years passed such problems grew more serious. Like the soldiers in the field, families at home suffered increasing hardships. These bore especially heavily on those who lived in enemy-occupied sections.

The food problem. Food was the most crucial problem of the war years. Farmers were urged to grow wheat and corn instead of cotton. Soldiers received furloughs in order to help with the crops. Sugar, coffee, tea and other foods not produced in Arkansas became scarce. As the war went on, gristmills and flour mills broke down, were destroyed or were taken over by occupying forces and it became harder for people to secure meal and flour. Confederate soldiers in the field sometimes suffered from hunger because no food was available and sometimes because supply wagons failed to keep up with them.

In areas not occupied by the Federals the food supply was generally adequate throughout the war. In other sections the people sometimes faced starvation and had to take refuge in south Arkansas, Texas, or Missouri. A wagon train of 1,500 persons left Fort Smith in August 1864, headed for the northwestern states. The Union army gave food to many refugee families.

The northwestern counties of Arkansas suffered especially heavily as a result of the war. Farms lay in ruin. Houses and rail fences were burned, and uncultivated fields grew up in bushes. Lone chimneys stood out against the sky where homes once had stood. Many of the people never returned.

Refugees driven from their homes during the fighting in southern Missouri and northwestern Arkansas

Guerrillas, jayhawkers and bushwhackers. Federal and Confederate armies brought destruction to Arkansas, and the irregular bands of armed men that infested the state caused untold suffering. The Ozark counties in particular were overrun for most of the war by guerrillas, jayhawkers and bushwhackers. Guerrillas were well-organized large groups which claimed to be fighting for either the United States or the Confederacy. Southern officers encouraged enlistment of "partisan rangers," or guerrilla units, in order to annoy the enemy.

Jayhawkers and bushwhackers usually operated singly or in small bands of two, three or a dozen men. They belonged to no army but hid out and struck at one side or the other when they saw the chance. Pro-Union irregulars were called jayhawkers by the Confederates, while Union troops referred to pro-Southern irregulars as bushwhackers.

Guerrilla warfare as conducted by these outlaw bands was merciless. Murder, arson, robbery, rape, pillage and ambush characterized their operations. Some irregulars attacked only those who sympathized with the other side in the war, but others raided wherever loot could be found. Regular army troops of both sides hunted down and killed the outlaws. For years after the war bandits continued to roam the hills, and killings continued as returning soldiers took revenge for wrongs done their families and kinsmen.

Social institutions. In the early years of the war, churches and schools carried on much as usual. Some churches were deprived of their ministers when they joined the army. A Confederate regiment raised at Pine Bluff included forty-two preachers in its ranks. At Fayetteville in the second year of the war only one church still had a minister and regular services.

All of the colleges closed. Cane Hill College and Arkansas College at Fayetteville suspended operations when the war began. Students and faculty members joined the army. The buildings of Arkansas College housed Confederate troops and were burned early in 1862. St. John's College at Little Rock became a military hospital.

Common schools and academies continued to operate for awhile, but before the end of the war most of those in enemy-occupied areas had closed. Behind the Confederate lines some schools continued in operation until the war ended.

Wartime amusements. Throughout the war years social affairs continued. Dances, parties and picnics were held for boys who were going away to the army. Around the army camps social activities flourished. In the spring of 1861 it was reported from a camp in eastern Arkansas that many ladies visited the troops every day, and music and dancing occupied almost every evening. An officer in Little Rock in 1863 wrote of picnics, fishing parties on the river, and a military ball at the Anthony House, the town's leading hotel. At army camps in south Arkansas late in the war "backwoods frolics" were popular.

The soldiers engaged in sports, games and athletic contests. Cavalry units held tournaments in which riders attempted to catch a small ring on the end of a long lance. Army bands entertained with concerts featuring songs such as

Hubbert's Hotel, the only building left standing in Berryville at the close of the Civil War

136

"Lorena," "Dixie," "The Bonnie Blue Flag," and other Southern favorites. Ladies gave programs and concerts with proceeds going to a hospital, soldiers' aid society, or some military unit. Even the Negroes gave balls and benefits for the Confederate cause. But away from the towns and army camps there was little merrymaking.

Mining and manufacturing. During the first two years of the war the Confederates mined niter or saltpeter, used for making gunpowder, in caves near the upper White River. The Federals sent expeditions to wreck the mines and in 1863 operations practically ceased. The Southerners took small quantities of lead from mines in Newton and Johnson counties before Union forces overran the area.

Cloth mills at Cane Hill, Murfreesboro, Van Buren and Norristown proved too small to supply the need for cotton and woolen cloth. With outside supplies cut off, the home spinning wheel and loom had to be brought into service. Home clothmaking was hampered by a shortage of cards, or instruments used for arranging the fibers of cotton and wool before spinning them into thread. Clothing was made in the home, and shoes were produced by local shoemakers when they could secure leather. Shops at Camden and Fulton made shoes for the soldiers.

Salt was sometimes dug from beneath smokehouses, as well as produced at salt works. The works on the Rolling Fork River in Sevier County had three large furnaces and seventy-nine cast iron kettles, each holding from fifty to 150 gallons. Salt water from wells was boiled in these kettles until the water evaporated, leaving the salt.

Confederate Arkansas had few facilities for making weapons. Blacksmiths

GRAND BALL!

IN HONOR OF
GEN'S BLUNT & McNEIL.

Your Company is respectfully solicited at a Grand Ball to be given in Fort Smith on
MONDAY EVENING, NOV. 16th, 1863.

HONORARY MANAGERS:

Maj. Gen. BLUNT,	Lieut. Col. BASSETT,
Brig. Gen. McNEIL,	Major SULLIVAN,
Col. CLOUD,	" WOODWORTH,
Col. BOWEN,	" SCHROELING,
Col. EDWARDS,	" WARD,
Col. WILLIAMS,	" SMITH,
Capt. WM. THOLEN,	" ANDERSON,
Capt. H. G. LORING,	" CALKINS,
Capt. HASKELL,	Lieut. TAPPAN.

COMMITTEE OF INVITATION:
Dr. BOMFORD, Col. GRIFFITH, J. S. BOSTICK, G. J. LEWIS.

FLOOR MANAGERS:
Capt. KINTER, Capt. NEWMAN, Lieut. TATUM, Lieut. WHICHER.

Supper will be prepared by Dickerson of the Cosmopolitan.

An invitation to a ball in honor of Union Generals Blunt and McNeil, Fort Smith, November 16, 1863

pounded farm tools into swords and knives. A railroad machine shop at Hopefield near Memphis served as an armory for repairing guns until the Federals destroyed it. The Little Rock arsenal repaired guns and cannons and manufactured cartridges, and the state penitentiary became a factory for making military goods. After Little Rock fell to the Federals, Camden, Arkadelphia and Washington became manufacturing centers for army supplies.

As the war continued, shortages of goods and commodities caused prices to rise. Confederate paper currency declined in value and many people lost confidence in its worth. Near the close of the war chewing tobacco was $6 a plug, butter cost $5 a pound, chickens $2.50 each, coffee $18 a pound when it could be found, and a good saddle horse was worth $2,000. Confederate money finally became practically worthless and trade was carried on by barter.

Caring for the sick and wounded. Illness was an ever-present problem both at home and in the army. Even ordinary medicines such as quinine and castor oil were in very short supply, and the people at home had to find substitutes. There were no hospitals and most of the doctors were away in the army. In army camps, measles and other diseases often took a heavy toll. At a Confederate camp near Austin in 1862 some 1,500 men were reported to have died of illnesses partly caused by drinking impure water.

Army hospitals were set up in churches, schoolhouses, and private residences. After a battle every building in the vicinity was usually transformed into a temporary hospital. Since surgeons were few and their methods crude, the sufferings of the wounded were severe. Ladies organized hospital associations to try to help. Appeals were made in Little Rock for stoves to heat hospitals and for other supplies of all sorts. Carpets were cut up and used as blankets.

Travel and communications. When the war began, Arkansas had only thirty-eight miles of operating railroad line. It extended from Hopefield, across the Mississippi from Memphis, to Madison on the St. Francis River. Early in 1862 trains began to run on a new section of track reaching from Little Rock eastward to DeValls Bluff on White River. Throughout the rest of the war the gap of forty-five miles between DeValls Bluff and Madison remained unclosed. Passengers going from Little Rock to Memphis had to take a steamer from

Confederate monument and Patrick R. Cleburne tombstone, Helena

DeValls Bluff to Clarendon, ride a stage from Clarendon to Madison, take the train to Hopefield, and then ferry the Mississippi. The trip required at least thirty hours.

Steamboats afforded the most important means of travel except when streams became too low for boats to operate. Land travel was slow and difficult. One army unit required five days in going from Pine Bluff to Little

Rock, and another took six days in moving from Little Rock to Arkadelphia. Roads that were rough and dusty in dry weather became pools of deep mud and water when it rained. There were few bridges, and armies sometimes had to crossway roads with poles in order to get through swamps. Civilian travelers as well as soldiers often slept on the ground.

The Butterfield Overland Mail line, which ran coaches from St. Louis to Fayetteville and Fort Smith on their way to San Francisco, ended its operations in Arkansas soon after the state seceded. As the war dragged on, stage lines connecting Arkansas towns went out of business because of worn-out equipment or the danger from bushwhackers. Mail service was slow and uncertain, and newspapers had to stop publication because of paper shortages and other difficulties. The **Washington Telegraph** was the only Arkansas Confederate newspaper which managed to survive throughout the war.

Depot at Huntersville, at the western terminus of the Memphis and Little Rock railroad. Huntersville was located on the north bank of the Arkansas River opposite Little Rock

STUDY AIDS

Vocabulary

Be sure that you understand the meaning of these words or phrases:

bushwhacker
jayhawker
guerrillas
refugees
loom

furlough
ambush
tournaments
loot
rail fences

smokehouse
crucial

proceeds
kettles
niter

Location

Find these places on a map:

Norristown
Hopefield

Austin
Sevier County
Clarendon

To test your reading

On other paper, list 1-9. Opposite each number write the word or words which complete each sentence.

1. The only Arkansas newspaper to survive throughout the war was the ___.

2. Trains began to run from Little Rock to DeValls Bluff early in the year ___.

3. One Confederate regiment had ___ preachers.

4. Pro-Union irregulars were called ___.

5. Pro-Southern irregulars were called ___.

6. St. John's College at Little Rock became ___.

7. Shoes for soldiers were made in shops at ___ and ___.

8. Near the close of the war a good saddle horse was worth ___ dollars.

9. When the war began Arkansas had only ___ miles of operating railroad.

Things to do

1. Find out all you can about what happened in your area during the Civil War. Talk to older residents who may remember stories about the war. Remember that what a person recalls is not always accurate!

2. Pretend that you are living in northwest Arkansas in 1865. Write a story about conditions there.

3. Visit the Currency Room in the Old State House, Little Rock. The display of Confederate and Southern States money there is one of the most complete in existence.

4. Arrange a musical program using songs that were popular during the Civil War.

5. Organize a temporary "Civil War Museum." Try to find spinning wheels, cards, salt kettles, bullet molds, tools, photographs, musical instruments, kitchen utensils, saddles, bridles, clothing, books, and anything else that might have been used during the war.

Reviewing the Unit

1. Why is Arkansas called an "unwilling participant" in the Civil War?

2. How did the geographical location of Arkansas affect its role in the war?

3. How did the Arkansas Confederates attempt to meet the need for food? For manufactured goods?

4. Why is the summer of 1863 cal'ed the "summer of disaster" for the South?

5. What part did Arkansas play in the Red River campaign?

6. What finally happened to the Confederate government of Arkansas?

7. Which one of the battles fought in Arkansas would you consider most important? Why?

Unit Five

Radical Arkansas

THE CIVIL WAR brought disorganization and disintegration to the entire social system of Arkansas. As the war came to a close, people began to realize the immense task of rebuilding that confronted them. The slaves had been freed, many farms had been ruined, the political system had been disrupted and poverty and want faced the people of the state.

Efforts toward political reorganization began before the war ended. The road to recovery might have been smoother if the Reconstruction Acts had not delivered Arkansas to the Radicals. The Clayton regime took over in 1868, drafted and put into effect a new constitution and placed the government into the hands of new and inexperienced officials. Confusion and corruption followed.

In the years following the close of the war, constructive measures were taken to establish an educational system. Efforts were made to build railroads, to bring immigrants to the state and to develop new industries. One of the most difficult problems was the adjustment of the Negroes to freedom. The state was handicapped by the ravages of the war, by the lack of money, and by political corruption. In some ways reconstruction left deeper scars than had the war itself.

1   The Union Again

Though Arkansas was a Confederate state, many Arkansans preferred the old Union. Some of them fought for the Stars and Stripes. A year before the Civil War ended, loyal Arkansans formed a Unionist state government which by 1867 had made great progress in bringing all the people together again under the old flag.

Union sentiment in Arkansas. When Arkansas seceded in 1861 most of those who had opposed secession went over to the Confederacy, but some refused. Many of the hill people of the Ozarks and Ouachitas owned no slaves and were not interested in fighting for the Confederacy. The same was true of many Arkansas people of German and Irish descent.

The first secret peace society in the entire Confederacy came to light in Van Buren, Searcy, Newton and Izard counties in November 1861. More than a hundred members of the Peace and Constitutional Society were marched to Little Rock, some of them in chains, and forced to join the Confederate army. The Society was pro-Union, but many of the members wanted only to protect their homes and families and be left alone.

Some Confederate war measures were highly unpopular. The conscription law of 1862 exempted one overseer or slave owner for every twenty slaves. Many Arkansas people thought this made the conflict look like a "rich man's war, but a poor man's fight." Shortages, profiteering, inflation, and seizures of private property by the Southern army angered many people. The failure of the Confederacy to defend Arkansas successfully against invasion aroused resentment.

As Federal armies overran Arkansas and hardships increased, some wives appealed to their husbands to leave the Confederate army and come home to provide for their families. As it became clear that the war could not be won, numbers of Confederate soldiers quit the struggle and some joined the Union forces.

Fighting for the Union. Arkansas men who preferred the Union side often made their way to Missouri and enlisted in the Federal army. Colonel M. LaRue Harrison, for whom the city of Harrison was later named, organized a cavalry regiment of Arkansas troops as early as August 1862. Recruiting for Union service picked up rapidly after central Arkansas was occupied. By the end of 1863 eight regiments had entered Federal service, and the number had risen to fourteen before the war ended.

Negro troops made up more than a third of the 15,000 Arkansas men who wore the Union blue. Early in the war the slaves generally stayed on the farms and plantations, even when the white master went away to the Confederate

Union troops on dress parade in front of the Old State House during the Civil War

army. When Federal troops invaded Arkansas the situation began to change. Refugee slaveowners took some slaves to south Arkansas and Texas. With many plantations abandoned, thousands of other Negroes swarmed to Federal army camps and many of them enlisted. Before the end of the war seven Arkansas Negro infantry regiments and one artillery battery, a total of over 5,500 men, were in the service of the United States. Negro troops fought at Poison Spring, Jenkins' Ferry, and possibly at other battles in Arkansas.

Lincoln and Arkansas. Early in the war differences began to develop between President Abraham Lincoln and Republican leaders in Congress over the proper policy toward the seceded states. Lincoln was a moderate who wished to re-

store the Union as rapidly and with as little bitterness as possible. Some of the leaders of the president's own party in Congress were radicals who wished to punish the South for secession, and use the Negroes to transform the South into a Republican rather than a Democratic section. The Radicals thought that since the Republicans had won the election of 1860 only because the Democratic party was divided, they would lose later elections unless the South could be made Republican.

Lincoln was encouraged by reports of Unionist sentiment in Arkansas, and regarded Arkansas as a Southern state that could be speedily returned to the Union. Senator William K. Sebastian of Helena had refused to resign his seat in the United States Senate in 1861. Lincoln, along with some Arkansas

Unionists, hoped that Sebastian would return to Washington and claim his seat, but Sebastian never tried.

After General Curtis occupied Helena in the summer of 1862, Lincoln appointed John S. Phelps of Missouri as military governor of Arkansas. The arrangement was unsuccessful because Phelps became ill, the Union conquest of Arkansas was delayed, and there was friction with military commanders. In July 1863 Lincoln removed Phelps as governor.

Lincoln's Emancipation Proclamation of September 22, 1862 encouraged Unionists everywhere. The proclamation declared that on and after January 1, 1863 all slaves in the rebel states would be free. Early in 1863 Union meetings were held in several places in Arkansas, but the Confederates were still strong enough to restrain pro-Union elements until the fall of Little Rock.

The Unionist state government. Union sentiment increased greatly after the Federals took control of the Mississippi and Arkansas rivers and occupied Little Rock in 1863. Prominent Confederates like William M. Fishback and General Edward W. Gantt switched sides and began urging Arkansans to support the Union cause. Encouraged by Lincoln, General Steele followed such mild and conciliatory policies that many Arkansas people decided that the Yankees were not so bad after all.

"Mustered out" Union Negro volunteers at Little Rock in 1866

In late 1863 Unionist meetings were held at Fort Smith, Benton, Waldron, Dardanelle, Helena, and Little Rock. "Union clubs" were organized. In December President Lincoln issued a proclamation offering pardons to nearly all secessionists who would take an oath of allegiance to the United States. When ten per cent of the qualified voters had taken the oath in any state, this group could form a Union government, which would be recognized by Lincoln. The president and other moderate Republicans hoped that this program would attract the support of many people in Arkansas and the South.

Delegates were immediately chosen by Union clubs and local gatherings to meet in Little Rock on January 4, 1864 and organize a state government. The three to four dozen delegates who attended claimed to represent twenty-two of the fifty-four counties. Presided over by John McCoy of Newton County, the convention spent three weeks drawing up a new constitution and setting up a provisional government.

The new Constitution of 1864 renounced slavery and secession, and declared that the Confederate state debt would not be paid. At an election in March more than 12,000 voters approved the constitution and elected Isaac Murphy as governor. With the blessing of President Lincoln and General Steele, Murphy took office on April 18, 1864.

The Murphy government and the Conservatives. The Murphy administration faced determined opposition from two directions. The Confederates, who had their own state government at Washington until the war ended, regarded Murphy as a traitor. On the other hand, the Radical Republicans who controlled Congress disliked the Constitution of 1864 because Negroes were not given

Isaac Murphy

the right to vote and hold office. Congress refused to restore Arkansas to the Union, and denied seats to the senators and representatives sent by the Murphy government.

The new General Assembly held three sessions in 1864-65. Governor Murphy kept down expenditures, set up a militia to control bushwhackers, and by the fall of 1865 had county governments and the courts operating again. The General Assembly ratified the Thirteenth Amendment to the Federal Constitution, which permanently abolished slavery.

With the war ended, the former Confederates set out to regain political control of the state. By 1866 they had organized as the Conservative Democrats or Conservatives, and in the elections of that year they won control of the General Assembly. In the session of 1866-67 the Conservatives voted pensions for Confederate soldiers and seriously considered a vote of thanks to Jefferson Davis for his services as Confederate president. Two former secessionists were elected to the United

States Senate. The General Assembly refused to ratify the proposed Fourteenth Amendment to the Federal Constitution, a Radical measure designed to guarantee all citizens equal protection of the laws. Negro labor was strictly regulated, and Negroes were denied the right to sit on juries, serve in the militia, and attend white public schools. Acts were passed providing for the establishment of a state university and a tax-supported system of public schools, and railroad construction was encouraged.

Some of the supporters of Governor Murphy began protesting to Congress against some of the measures passed by the General Assembly. To them it appeared that the Conservatives were trying to restore prewar conditions wherever possible. For its part, the General Assembly thanked President Andrew Johnson for his moderate policy toward the South and sent a delegation to Washington to receive his approval.

Public opinion in 1867. Two years after the war, Arkansas seemed again on the road to peace and stability. Most of the people accepted the results of the war and were now working hard to rebuild the state. They had little respect for Isaac Murphy, but they could look forward to replacing him with a Democrat when his term expired the next year.

Only a small Radical Republican minority wanted revolutionary changes in Arkansas life. Many Northerners had moved to Arkansas during and after the war, usually to make money by taking advantage of unsettled conditions. The Conservatives called them "carpetbaggers," because some of them were said to have brought all their belongings in a small satchel made of carpet material. Allied with them were the "scalawags," or Southern men who advocated Radicalism, and Negro leaders who wanted equality as well as freedom for their people.

ELECTION NOTICE

By authority and direction of a County Mass Meeting, held at Van Buren on the 31st October last, the undersigned, Commissioner for Crawford County, hereby gives notice that an Election will be holden at the Court House in the City of Van Buren,

On Monday, the 23d Day of Nov'r instant,

for the election of a Representative to Congress, and for four Delegates to a proposed State Convention.

The Poll will be open at 9 A. M., closing at sunset. Unconditional Union Men will be legal voters.

L. C. WHITE, Commissioner.

Van Buren, Nov. 10, 1863.

A Unionist election notice of 1863

STUDY AIDS

Vocabulary

Be sure that you understand the meaning of these words and phrases:

battery   carpetbaggers
resign   scalawags
conscription   renounced
ratify   inflation
Emancipation
    Proclamation

Identification

Tell what part each of the following had in the story:

William K.   Edward W. Gantt
   Sebastian   Union clubs
Peace and Consti-   Isaac Murphy
   tutional Society   John McCoy
William M.   John S. Phelps
   Fishback

To test your reading

On another paper, list 1-9. Opposite each number write the word or words which complete each sentence.

1. The city of Harrison is named for ___ who organized a ___ regiment of ___ as early as ___.

2. By the end of 1863 ___ Arkansas regiments had been enrolled for the ___ army and by the end of the war the number had risen to ___.

3. More than ___ Arkansas Negroes were in the Union army.

4. Negro troops fought on the Union side at the battles of ___ and ___.

5. The Arkansas senator who refused to resign his seat in the United States Senate in 1861 was ___ of ___.

6. The Emancipation Proclamation declared that ___.

7. A loyal state government was organized in ___ on January 4, ___.

8. Isaac Murphy took office as governor on April 18, ___.

9. The General Assembly of 1866-67 was controlled by ___.

Things to do

1. Write a newspaper account of the General Assembly of 1866-67.

2. Pretend that you have just returned from a trip through Arkansas in 1867. Tell what you learned about public opinion in the state at that time.

3. Pretend that you are Governor Isaac Murphy in the year 1866. Address the class on the subject, "Problems and Progress in Arkansas Since 1863."

4. Obtain a copy of the Emancipation Proclamation and read it to the class.

5. Organize a "Union Club" and elect delegates to attend the constitutional convention of 1864. Instruct the delegates as to what provisions should be included in the new constitution.

2   The Radicals Take Over

The Radical Republicans tried to make Arkansas safe for Republicanism by giving the ballot to the Negroes and denying it to ex-Confederates. With the backing of Congress, in 1868 they wrote a new state constitution and took over the government of Arkansas.

The Radical plan of reconstruction. After President Lincoln was assassinated in 1865, leadership of the moderates passed to his successor Andrew Johnson. Like Lincoln, the new president wished to restore the Union speedily and had no desire to make things difficult for the South. In the North the Radicals, who opposed Johnson, won control of Congress and of the Republican party. They then proceeded to impose their own brand of reconstruction on the South.

The Reconstruction Acts passed by Congress in March 1867 declared illegal all existing state governments in ten Southern states, including Arkansas. The South was divided into five military districts, with Arkansas and Mississippi comprising the fourth. The general who headed each district was given complete control of civil authorities, and directed to set up military tribunals and start the process of reconstruction.

Under the Radical plan each of the "rebel" states had to hold a new convention and present to Congress a new constitution giving Negroes the right to vote and hold office. The new state government must ratify the Fourteenth Amendment before it could be readmitted to the Union. Voters had to be able to take the "Ironclad Oath," which

disfranchised most ex-Confederates. About the only people who could vote were Negroes, wartime Unionists, draft dodgers, Southerners too old or too young for military service in the war, and carpetbaggers.

The Radical plan in action. When General Edward O. C. Ord arrived in Arkansas in the spring of 1867 to take charge of his district, he found the state at peace and its finances in satisfactory condition. Murphy was allowed to remain as governor, but the Conservative-dominated General Assembly was not permitted to meet again and the Confederate pensions law was voided. At first the liberties of the people did not suffer greatly under military government.

Registration of voters soon got under way and continued for several weeks. The Radicals met at Little Rock and organized the Republican party of Arkansas, and General Ord turned the registration of voters over to them. Registration committees moved from place to place, signing up Negroes and excluding former Confederates. Many Negroes were reluctant to register, but Radical organizations like the Freedmen's Bureau and the Union League forced or persuaded most of them to do so.

In November 1867 delegates were chosen for the new constitutional convention, and the Radicals elected their candidates to sixty of the seventy-five positions. With the Radicals in control of the election machinery the Conservatives had no chance to win, and many of them stayed away from the polls.

The Radicals write a new constitution. The convention met in Little Rock on January 7, 1868 and remained in session until the middle of February. The carpetbaggers were in full control and elected Thomas M. Bowen president. Other leaders were Joseph Brooks, an Iowa Methodist preacher; James Hinds, a New York lawyer; John McClure from Ohio; and William H. Grey, a Negro preacher from Helena. The list of delegates included twenty-three carpetbaggers, thirty scalawags, eight Negroes, and a minority group of about a dozen Conservatives.

Conservative newspapers like the **Arkansas Gazette** ridiculed the convention, and Conservative delegates like J. N. Cypert and John M. Bradley tried to

ABSTRACT OF RETURNS OF REGISTRATION
IN THE
STATE OF ARKANSAS,
UNDER THE ACT OF CONGRESS OF MARCH 23D, 1867.*

COUNTIES.	Registered WHITES.	Registered COLORED.	TOTAL.	COUNTIES.	Registered WHITES.	Registered COLORED.	TOTAL.
ARKANSAS,	498	1030	1528	MARION,	...	...	391
ASHLEY,	706	608	1314	MISSISSIPPI,	292	193	485
BENTON,	...	...	1009	MONROE,	525	551	1076
BRADLEY,	908	368	1276	MONTGOMERY,	492	26	518
CALHOUN,	422	184	606	NEWTON,	424	1	425
CARROLL,	...	767	767	OUACHITA,	1084	870	1954
CHICOT,	268	894	1162	PERRY,	...	...	318
CLARK,	...	...	1576	PHILLIPS,	955	2681	3636
COLUMBIA,	1313	870	2183	PIKE,	...	...	565
CONWAY,	921	148	1069	POINSETT,	172	39	211
CRAIGHEAD,	522	41	563	POLK,	394	1	395
CRAWFORD,	704	147	851	POPE,	...	...	865
CRITTENDEN,	245	505	750	PRAIRIE,	...	...	1583
CROSS,	415	184	599	PULASKI,	1494	2402	3896
DALLAS,	668	337	1005	RANDOLPH,	848	59	907
DESHA,	231	592	823	ST. FRANCIS,	564	464	1028
DREW,	1081	576	1657	SALINE,	712	42	754
FRANKLIN,	741	102	843	SCOTT,	557	17	574
FULTON,	...	...	306	SEARCY,	574	1	575
GREENE,	921	5	926	SEBASTIAN,	1011	195	1206
HEMPSTEAD,	1307	1195	2502	SEVIER,	567	260	827
HOT SPRING,	...	...	825	UNION,	922	708	1630
INDEPENDENCE,	1458	142	1600	VAN BUREN,	...	...	896
IZARD,	762	31	793	WASHINGTON,	1813	81	1894
JACKSON,	849	283	1132	WHITE,	1278	156	1434
JEFFERSON,	1048	2733	3786†	WOODRUFF,	...	...	1027
JOHNSON,	664	72	736	YELL,	731	150	881
LAFAYETTE,	560	931	1491				
LAWRENCE,	...	...	753				
LITTLE RIVER,	426	327	753	Total,	33,047‡	21,969‡	65,751‡
MADISON,	...	...	716				

Arkansas voters registered under provisions of the Reconstruction Acts. In several counties Negro voters outnumbered whites, though this was not true of the state as a whole

obstruct the Radicals. Most of the delegates simply enjoyed the huge salaries and compensation which they voted themselves while the carpetbaggers wrote the constitution. Cypert's attempt to readopt the Constitution of 1864 failed, but the final vote on the new document was forty-six in favor to twenty against, showing that the Conservatives had gained some support. Fifteen members refused to sign the new constitution.

The Constitution of 1868 affirmed racial equality, and denied the vote to ex-Confederates except those who would support Radicalism. Free public schools and a state university were to be established. Representation in the General Assembly was weighed heavily in favor of counties where Negroes were numerous, and no change was to be allowed until after 1875. Under this document the Radicals hoped to make Arkansas into a Republican stronghold.

The Radicals organize their government. Voting on ratification of the constitution and the election of officials was scheduled to begin on March 13, 1868. The convention made Radical victory certain by placing the electoral machinery under the control of a commission dominated by Joseph Brooks. The Conservative Democrats declared for white supremacy, put up no candidates, and concentrated on defeating the constitution. The Republican state convention nominated Powell Clayton for governor and a full slate of candidates on a platform of freedom and human equality.

The campaign was partisan and bitter. The Democrats sent out such speakers as Augustus H. Garland, Uriah M. Rose, Thomas C. Hindman, and Albert Pike. Hinds, Brooks and Clayton campaigned for the Republicans. The Radicals accused the Democrats of plotting rebellion and intimidation. The Democrats denounced Republicans as carpetbaggers, crooks, ignoramuses, and "Negro equalizers." The propaganda and tactics of the Freedmen's Bureau and Union League were matched by the terroristic activities of a Southern secret organization called the Ku Klux Klan.

Federal military officers conducted the voting on ratification, and the new constitution carried by a small majority. The Democrats charged fraud and protested to Washington, but nothing came of it. The new General Assembly met on April 2 and hastily ratified the Fourteenth Amendment to the United States Constitution. On June 22 Congress readmitted Arkansas to the Union, and on July 2 Powell Clayton was inaugurated as governor.

STUDY AIDS

Vocabulary

Be sure that you understand the meaning of these words and phrases:

Radicals   intimidation
Moderates   Freedmen's Bureau
tribunals   Union League
disfranchised   Conservatives
                        Ku Klux Klan

Identification

Tell what part each of the following had in the story:

Edward O. C. Ord   John McClure
Thomas M. Bowen   Powell Clayton
Ironclad Oath   Augustus H.
Joseph Brooks   Garland

To test your reading

On another paper, list 1-7. Opposite each number write the word or words which complete each sentence.

1. After Lincoln's assassination leadership of the moderates passed to ___.

2. The Reconstruction Acts of March 1867 declared illegal ___.

3. In November 1867 delegates were chosen for ___.

4. Those in control of the constitutional convention of 1868 were the ___.

5. The president of the convention was ___.

6. The number of members refusing to sign the new constitution was ___.

7. Arkansas was readmitted to the Union on June ___ of the year ___.

Things to do

1. Secure a copy of the Constitution of the United States and read the Thirteenth, Fourteenth and Fifteenth Amendments to the class. Discuss the meaning and purpose of each amendment.

2. After consulting books in your library, write or give a report on the Ku Klux Klan.

3. Visit the office of your county clerk and find out how new voters are registered at the present time.

4. Hold a mock session of the constitutional convention of 1868. Different students may represent different viewpoints and make speeches advocating or defending their beliefs.

3   The Negro and Freedom

The victory of the North in the Civil War ended human slavery in Arkansas, but at first the Negro did not know what to do with his new freedom. The Federal government and various private organizations tried to help him, but in the end politics and economic necessity kept him tied to the old plantation system.

The Negroes as freedmen. In Arkansas one of the most serious postwar problems was the changed relationship between Negroes and whites. Before emancipation nearly all Negroes belonged to the whites, lived on the farm or plantation and were a part of the economic unit. The social organization was fixed, with each individual having a place where he belonged. There was no unemployment. The master provided the slave with housing, food, clothing and medical care.

After the war the Arkansas Negro became a "freedman" who had to provide for his own needs and those of his family. Not only was he poorly prepared to look out for himself, but the poverty of his surroundings gave him little opportunity. The outlook for the freedman in Arkansas and other Southern states was made darker by the fact that his former owners had been killed in the war or were now too poor to help him.

Work for Negro refugees. When Union armies moved into eastern Arkansas in 1862, multitudes of Negro slaves left the plantations and followed the troops. Many of them believed that the coming of the bluecoats heralded the "day of

jubilee," when there would be no more work and suffering.

After Curtis occupied Helena the Negro problem grew from day to day. Military authorities employed refugees at whatever work could be found around the camps, and two Negro regiments were enlisted at Helena. But refugee families still had to be supported, and Northern troops sometimes abused them.

Since the United States needed cotton and many plantations in Arkansas had been abandoned by their owners, Federal authorities decided to lease the plantations to men who would employ the freedmen in agriculture. Each leaseholder was to have as many Negroes as he could use. The freedmen were to be paid, housed, fed, clothed and humanely treated. The leaseholders were to pay the government two dollars for each 400 pounds of cotton produced and five cents for each bushel of corn.

Freedmen's camps were established near military posts, with superintendents to issue rations to Negroes and work them or hire them out. Every freedman was to be employed on a plantation or be sent to a camp. Federal agents also divided occupied Arkansas

"Blissville," a Negro refugee settlement in Little Rock, 1866

into districts and set up work colonies of freedmen under army supervision.

Despite Confederate raids and dishonest leaseholders, in 1864 more than 11,000 freedmen were at work on about a hundred Arkansas plantations. President Lincoln encouraged planters to return to their lands and employ the free Negroes. Charitable organizations in the North sent so many supplies to the freedmen that many of them were unwilling to work at all.

The Freedmen's Bureau. The Bureau of Refugees, Freedmen, and Abandoned Lands, known usually as the Freedmen's Bureau, was established in 1865 to help the Negroes adjust to freedom. The bureau could set aside abandoned or confiscated lands in the Southern states for freedmen and loyal white refugees. Each Negro or white refugee would be allowed to rent forty acres for three years, with the option of purchasing the land if he wished. The government would provide temporary relief for the needy.

At first the Freedmen's Bureau seemed on its way to real accomplishment. General John W. Sprague, who first headed bureau work in Arkansas, chose some civilians and even a few ex-Confederates as agents. Many of the best men in the state hoped that the bureau would find a solution to the Negro labor problem.

An application to lease abandoned lands, 1864

153

The plan to settle freedmen on small farms of their own failed because President Andrew Johnson pardoned practically all the former Confederate plantation owners and restored their lands to them. Since few planters had money to pay wages, the freedmen as early as 1865 began working for a share of the crop.

The Freedmen's Bureau fed thousands of white refugees and Negroes, and established special hospitals which were poorly managed but did help to prevent epidemics. The Arkansas state government under Murphy was either unable or unwilling to assist the suffering. Many Arkansas whites also opposed the efforts of the bureau to educate the Negroes, and the Conservative General Assembly of 1866-67 failed to provide for Negro schools.

Many Negroes ardently desired education for their children, a privilege which had been denied them under the old slavery system. Aided by the Quakers and other Northern religious and charitable groups, Freedmen's Bureau agents succeeded in establishing a few day schools, Sabbath schools, and night schools. In 1867-68 there were fifty-one such schools with almost 3,500 pupils. The masses of Negro and white refugee children were not reached by the program, but it was an important beginning in popular education.

Beginning in 1866 the Freedmen's Bureau encountered increasing opposition from the former Confederates in Arkansas. These Conservatives resented the attempts of the bureau to secure justice for Negroes in the courts. The bureau had its own courts for certain cases, and whites objected to what they regarded as preferential treatment for Negro laborers. After 1866 the Freedmen's Bureau became little more

Building in Arkadelphia which housed an office of the Freedmen's Bureau

than a political tool of the Radical Republicans, working with the Union League to keep the Negroes in line with the objectives of the carpetbaggers.

Survival of the plantation system. Arkansas leaders who served the Confederacy during the Civil War were willing to accept the fact that slavery was dead, but they did not want to give up the plantation system. They were at a loss to know how to enable the free Negro to fit into the community, but they did know that they still needed his labor on the plantations.

Some Radical leaders talked about breaking up the large plantations and giving the land to the Negroes and poor white farmers. But many Northerners wanted to buy plantations, lend money to Southern planters, or handle cotton transactions. The Republicans proved to be more interested in using the Negro for political purposes than they were in giving him land.

The plantation system not only survived, but expanded after the war as more cotton land was cleared. Many Negroes and poor whites became sharecroppers, who worked the land and divided the produce with the owner.

STUDY AIDS

Vocabulary

Be sure that you understand the meaning of these words and phrases:

leaseholder
rations
planters
"day of jubilee"
confiscated

epidemics
masses
option
encountered
postwar
freedman

Identification

Tell what part each of the following had in the story:

John W. Sprague   Andrew Johnson

To test your reading

On other paper, list 1-9. Opposite each number, write the word or words which complete each sentence.

1. Two Negro regiments were enlisted at ___.

2. The leaseholders were to pay the government ___.

3. Freedmen's camps were established near ___.

4. In 1864 more than ___ freedmen were at work on about ___ Arkansas plantations.

5. The official title of the Freedmen's Bureau was ___.

6. The Freedmen's Bureau was established in the year ___.

7. After 1866 the Freedmen's Bureau became little more than ___.

8. In setting up schools Freedmen's Bureau agents were aided by ___ and ___.

9. In 1867-68 there were ___ such schools with almost ___ pupils.

Things to do

1. Pretend that you are an official of the Freedmen's Bureau in Arkansas in 1866. Tell what the bureau has done to help the Negro people adjust to freedom.

2. Arrange a debate on the subject, "Resolved—That the large plantations should have been broken up after the Civil War and the land given to poor farmers."

3. Imagine that you have leased an abandoned cotton plantation from the Federal government, and have employed a number of freedmen to work it. Write a report to President Lincoln in which you describe the accomplishments and failures of the first year.

4   The Radical Government

The Radical Republicans set up a political machine which for a few years ruled Arkansas by fraud and by force, but their regime was not entirely bad. They tried to encourage education and promote economic progress, but most such efforts ended in failure.

Clayton organizes his machine. Governor Powell Clayton, who had come to Arkansas with a Kansas cavalry regiment during the Civil War, proved to be one of the ablest of the Republican leaders. The General Assembly of 1868, with only one Democrat in each house, was under Clayton's control. The Constitution of 1868 gave great appointive and financial powers to the governor, and the General Assembly increased such powers until Clayton was almost a dictator. For three years Powell Clayton dominated the government of Arkansas.

Under Clayton, state and local offices multiplied in number as the Radicals sought to build a strong political machine. Salaries increased, as did taxes. But despite his power, Clayton soon realized that his position was anything but secure. The choice of Clayton, a carpetbagger, as governor antagonized influential scalawags among the Republicans. In the late summer and fall of 1868 there were signs that the night-riding Ku Klux Klan was growing stronger and bolder. In Crittenden County an agent of the Freedmen's Bureau was assassinated. Thomas C. Hindman, who had shown some willingness to go along with the Radicals, was shot and killed at Helena. James Hinds was killed and Joseph Brooks wounded on their way to a rally near Clarendon, and the body of a Clayton agent was thrown into a well at Searcy.

Clayton delayed his counterattack against the KKK until the general election of 1868 was over. In order to carry the election for the Republicans, Clayton rejected the returns from several heavily Democratic counties. Republican congressmen were declared elected, and the electoral vote of the state was counted for Ulysses S. Grant, the Republican presidential candidate.

The militia. On the day after the election Clayton placed ten counties under martial law, and later added others to the list. The governor claimed that the KKK was planning a rebellion, and that lawless elements had taken over the counties placed under martial law.

The General Assembly had provided for raising a militia force, but the governor's attempt to arm his troops was hindered when the steamer **Hesper** was boarded below Memphis by masked men from the steam tug **Nettie Jones**. The mysterious raiders, who may have been Ku Kluxers, threw the cargo of 4,000 muskets and ammunition into the Mississippi River. Clayton collected enough weapons from other sources to arm

Powell Clayton

2,000 militiamen, and almost 5,500 men served before the militia disbanded in 1869.

For more than four months in 1868-69 parts of Arkansas were under martial law. Four military districts were established. The militia, poorly-disciplined and mostly Negro, moved through the state stealing, looting, and occasionally killing white men. Clayton hired secret agents who provided militia officers with lists of men to be arrested. Open warfare broke out at Center Point in Sevier County, which was stormed and captured by a militia force. In northeast Arkansas, the militia commander enlisted the aid of a Missouri outlaw named William Monks and terrorized the area. Lewisburg in Conway County was the scene of a great deal of trouble.

PROCLAMATION
By the Governor.

WHEREAS, the counties of Ashley, Bradley, Columbia, Lafayette, Mississippi, Woodruff, Craighead, Green, Sevier, and Little River, are now in a state of insurrection, and the civil authority within them is utterly powerless to preserve order and protect the lives of the citizens; unauthorized bodies of armed men (in most cases disguised) are engaged in acts of lawlessness and violence; the county officers have either been killed or driven away from their homes or intimidated from the performance of their duties; the quiet and law-abiding citizens, in many instances, have not been allowed an expression of their sentiments, or the exercise of their duties and privileges of citizenship, and, while hundreds of them have been murdered, in no instance known to the Executive have the assassins been brought to punishment by the civil authorities; the State is being invaded by bands of outlaws from Texas and Louisiana, who are committing murders and depredations upon the citizens; the registration laws could not be fairly executed, and were necessarily set aside; and in many of these counties a perfect reign of terror now exists,

The first paragraph of Governor Clayton's proclamation of martial law, November 4, 1868

Clayton's use of the militia aroused protests within his own party. The scalawag, or native Unionist Republicans began uniting with the ex-Confederates against the governor's policy. Actually the Ku Klux Klan was never as strong in Arkansas as the Radicals believed, but even after martial law ended the militia was called out again from time to time in different parts of the state. Trouble broke out at Dardanelle and in Chicot County, as well as in other places. Pope County, in turmoil throughout the period of reconstruction, was under military rule for three years.

Success and failure in education. In 1860 Arkansas had 727 common schools attended by almost 20,000 pupils. The common schools were usually supported by tuition fees and Federal land grants, but any white child might attend if his parents could not pay. Twenty-five schools were supported by public funds entirely. There were 113 schools teaching more advanced subjects, all supported by tuition fees.

The Civil War ruined most of the schools. Reconstruction began when the General Assembly of 1866-67 provided for a system of free public schools for white children. Support was to come from a property tax and from sales of state lands. The plan might have worked had not the Radicals taken over the government and instituted their own program.

The Radical educational program which began in 1868 was much more expensive and ambitious. A number of high-salaried officials was appointed by the governor. The new school system was to be supported by increased property taxes, and a poll tax of one dollar a year on each man over the age of twenty-one. Separate schools were provided for Negroes and whites, and the Freedmen's Bureau schools were taken into the state system.

Under Thomas Smith, the first state superintendent of public instruction, some progress was made. By the close of 1870, 657 new schoolhouses had been erected and over 100,000 white and Negro children were in school. After 1870 the system declined because of extravagance, corruption, and political influence. The public lost confidence in the people who were managing the schools and tax revenues decreased. The panic of 1873, which brought economic depression to the entire country, completed the ruin of the reconstruction experiment in public school education. By 1874 the schools were closed except where private funds supported them.

The Radicals succeeded in giving Arkansas a state university for the first time. Arkansas Industrial University, later called the University of Arkansas, which opened in Fayetteville in 1872, had 321 students before the end of reconstruction. Noah P. Gates was the first president. State officials also began planning to establish a branch college for Negroes at Pine Bluff. The state school for the blind, which had first opened as a private institution in 1859, was moved from Arkadelphia to Little Rock. The Arkansas Deaf Mute Institute, later the Arkansas School for the Deaf, was opened in Little Rock under the Clayton government.

The Radicals encourage immigration. The Republicans were eager to develop the natural resources of Arkansas, and they believed that the way to such development was open now that slavery had been destroyed. Free laborers of all races and nationalities should be

HAVE YOU A HOME OF YOUR OWN?

IF NOT

COME TO ARKANSAS.

Is there a spot on God's green earth that you own; that you, your wife, your children, can truly call home? is a question that interests more people to-day more than all others combined. This inquiry comes home to the heart of every true man and woman who feel that their children—penned up in tenement houses in large cities—do not and cannot breathe the pure air of heaven and feel the warm sunshine, so much enjoyed by those more fortunate. All cannot live in cities, nor all be mechanics. Then why not embrace the opportunity of securing a home for yourself and family, and give your children a chance to secure homes while young, and settle near you to be a help and comfort in your declining years. To-day the government has over 5,000,000 acres in the State of Arkansas, subject to be located for homesteads under the United States homestead law, one-fourth, or more, of which is believed to be unfit for cultivation; and to accurately ascertain which is good, tillable land, *is* one of the principal objects of the Homestead Company. The Homestead Company is a corporation chartered under the laws of the State of Arkansas, and has its principal place of business at Little Rock, Arkansas.

Opening paragraph of a circular advertising Arkansas lands available to immigrants

welcomed to the state, and the Republicans were confident that most such immigrants would vote for their party.

In 1868 Dr. James M. Lewis, a carpetbagger from Massachusetts, became the first commissioner of immigration and state lands. Lewis printed and distributed thousands of pamphlets in English and German setting forth the attractions of Arkansas. An attempt was made to induce Negroes to move to Arkansas from Georgia and other states, but the immigration bureau accomplished little. By 1871 when W. H. Grey succeeded Lewis the bureau had

become another Negro political organization.

Private immigration societies and companies had little success. Planters of the lower Arkansas Valley imported a few Chinese laborers. A few Germans and Negroes came to Arkansas, but the census of 1870 showed a gain of only 49,000 people in ten years and most of this was due to natural increase.

Levees and railroads. The Clayton regime launched an extensive program of public works and internal improvements, with major emphasis on flood control and railroad building. Levee construction began in 1869 with much publicity but made no real progress. By 1873 the state had issued $3,000,000 in levee bonds but most of the money had been wasted or stolen.

Bond issues to aid railroads added millions to the state debt. Some of the prewar railroad companies resumed work and applied for aid, but found that they must compete with dozens of new companies. By the end of 1871 the number of companies chartered had reached eighty-six, controlled by fewer than twenty politicians and their allies. Power to make or deny grants rested in the hands of the governor of the state.

For a bonded indebtedness of $6,900,-000 Arkansas finally got only 271 miles of railroad. The gap in the Memphis and Little Rock railway was closed in 1871, and progress was made on the Little Rock and Fort Smith track. The Cairo and Fulton, which completed its line in 1873, refused state aid and avoided political graft and slowdowns. The hard times of 1873 practically stopped railroad construction.

Debt and taxes. Governor Isaac Murphy left a surplus in the treasury when his term ended in 1868, but Arkansas still owed $3,363,000 on account of bonds issued to the Real Estate Bank and the State Bank chartered in 1836. Most of these bonds were held by the heirs of James Holford and Company, a British firm. In an attempt to restore the state's credit so that new bond issues could be sold, the Clayton administration in 1869 took up the old bonds and issued new ones for the amount of the principal and interest then due. The new bonds sold poorly and at a heavy discount on the New York stock exchange. Then in 1870 the state government had to begin borrowing money to make interest payments on the debt. The refunding plan, like other Radical financial schemes, created more problems than it solved. Many people regarded the Holford debt as unjust and illegal.

Taxes under Republican rule were heavy, though rates were somewhat modified in 1871. Assessments were high, and counties spent money as ex-

The first locomotive on the Cairo and Fulton railroad, 1872

travagantly as did the state. Scrip, or paper promises to pay, was issued in enormous quantities and speculators did a thriving business. While the government was in Radical hands the state debt increased by over $10,000,000.

County, municipal and school district debts probably exceeded that amount. For that outlay the state had public improvements worth about $100,000. Many of the counties had nothing to show for their indebtedness.

STUDY AIDS

Vocabulary

Be sure that you understand the meaning of these words and phrases:

dictator
exceeded
counterattack
bonded
    indebtedness

refunding plan
prewar
stock exchange
policy

Identification

Tell what part each of the following had in the story:

Thomas C.
    Hindman
James Hinds
Center Point
Hesper

Nettie Jones
Thomas Smith
Noah P. Gates
James M. Lewis
James Holford and
    Company

To test your reading

On other paper, list 1-7. Opposite each number, write the word or words which complete each sentence.

1. Pope County was under military rule for a period of __ years.

2. In 1860 Arkansas had __ common schools attended by almost __ pupils.

3. The first state superintendent of public instruction was __.

4. Arkansas Industrial University was opened in the year __.

5. Other state schools opened in reconstruction days were __, __, __, __.

6. The gap in the Memphis-Little Rock railway was closed in the year __.

7. Under Radical control the state debt increased by over __ dollars. For this outlay the state had public improvements worth about __ dollars.

Things to do

1. Write a paragraph on one of the following subjects:

    (a) martial law under Clayton
    (b) the Radicals and the schools
    (c) Republican financial policies
    (d) attempts to promote immigration

2. The General Assembly created a number of new counties during the reconstruction period. When was your county organized and for whom or what was it named?

3. Write a play that shows something about life in Arkansas during the reconstruction period.

5 The Breakup of the Republican Party

The Arkansas Republican party soon divided into two major factions called the "Minstrels" and the "Brindletails." In 1872 the Minstrel candidate, Elisha Baxter, defeated Joseph Brooks in the race for governor, but the Brindletails were by no means ready to accept the election results as final.

Republican opposition to Clayton. The Arkansas Republican party commenced to break apart almost as soon as the Radicals took power. The native Unionist or scalawag faction, led by James M. Johnson of Madison County, was displeased that the carpetbaggers had taken the most powerful offices. Johnson wanted to be governor, but had to be content with the post of lieutenant governor when Clayton maneuvered himself into top place.

A leading carpetbagger, Joseph Brooks, took offense when he was denied a seat in Congress. With a faction of carpetbaggers and Negroes behind him, Brooks came forward as an advocate of economy in government and began to attack Clayton's extravagance.

One of the earliest party quarrels arose over the contracts for public printing. The Radicals established a number of newspapers, headed by the **Daily Republican** of Little Rock, and competition was keen for the fat state contracts which Clayton handed out. Clayton's declaration of martial law, his refunding of the state debt, and his railroad policies caused many Republicans to break with him.

In 1869 the supporters of James M. Johnson and Joseph Brooks denounced Radicalism and organized the Liberal Republican party. The bolters appealed to the Democrats and prewar Whigs to join them on a platform favoring the restoration of the right to vote to all ex-Confederates. Lieutenant Governor Johnson made an unsuccessful effort to seize the office of governor while Clayton was out of the state.

Fearful of the influence of the Liberal Republicans, Clayton declared himself in favor of the right of ex-Confederates to vote, and promised to restore the ballot to all qualified white people. The strife among the Republicans became more bitter after word leaked out that Clayton intended to make himself United States senator. In 1870 the Democrats and Liberal Republicans won control of the Arkansas House of Representatives, though Clayton's supporters managed to hold the Senate.

The General Assembly of 1871 elected Clayton to the United States Senate, but Clayton refused to accept until some way could be found to keep Johnson from becoming governor. When the Clayton faction tried to remove Johnson as lieutenant governor, the House of Representatives struck back by impeaching Clayton. Popular criticism became so great that both sides agreed

_____ Precinct.

Carroll County, Arkansas,

October 5 1870.

"I, _____, do solemnly swear (or affirm) that I will support and maintain the Constitution and Laws of the United States, and the Constitution and Laws of the State of Arkansas; that I am not excluded from registering or voting by any of the clauses in the first, second, third and fourth sub-divisions of Article VIII of the Constitution of the State of Arkansas; that I will never countenance or aid in the secession of this State from the United States; that I accept the civil and political equality of all men, and agree not to attempt to deprive any person or persons, on account of race, color or previous condition, of any political or civil right, privilege or immunity, enjoyed by any other class of men; and, furthermore, that I will not in any way injure, countenance in others any attempt to injure, any person or persons on account of past or present support of the Government of the United States, the Laws of the United States, or the principle of the political and civil equality of all men, or for affiliation with any political party."

No.	NAMES.	NAMES BY REGISTRAR.
26	William M. McBrummer mark	William M. Brummer
27	George W. Wood mark	George W. Wood
28	George W. Jennings	George W. Jennings
29	James M. Hull	James M. Hull

Page from voter registration book, Carroll County, 1870. The oath was required of all prospective voters

163

to compromise. Clayton received his Senate seat, Johnson became secretary of state, and Clayton's supporter Ozra A. Hadley succeeded him as governor. The Clayton faction was still in control, but its position had become extremely shaky.

The election of 1872. By the year 1872 party lines had become much more distinct than was the case two years earlier. Political nicknames came into widespread use. The followers of Clayton were called "Minstrels," because one of the party leaders had once performed in a minstrel company. The supporters of Joseph Brooks, whose conduct on the platform caused someone to compare him to a brindle-tail bull, were known as the "Brindletails" or "Brindles."

In May 1872 the Brooks faction organized the Reform Republican party, named Brooks for governor, and called for "universal suffrage, universal amnesty, and honest men for office." Since

Bribery of voters was practiced widely during the reconstruction period, in other states as well as in Arkansas

many Democrats were still not allowed to vote, the Democratic convention put up no candidate but recommended support of Brooks. The Liberal Republicans, weakened by the withdrawal of the Brindles, also nominated no ticket but advocated the defeat of the Minstrels.

Clayton and his Minstrels realized that they would lose the election unless they offered a candidate and platform that would divide the opposition by attracting some of the Democrats and scalawags. The Minstrel convention therefore nominated Elisha Baxter, an Arkansas Unionist of excellent reputation, and adopted a platform promising reform, honesty, and voting rights for all the people.

The campaign was one of the most exciting in the state's history. Brooks, a Methodist preacher of the old style, stumped the state vigorously. The Democrats distrusted Brooks, but most of them voted for him because they feared that Clayton would control Baxter if he were elected. Nationally, the Democratic party endorsed Horace Greeley, a Liberal Republican, in an effort to defeat President U. S. Grant.

The Minstrels won the election of November 5, largely because they controlled the machinery for registering voters and conducting the vote. Election officials added and threw out ballots at will. Brooks supporters opened their own polling places in many precincts, and practiced fraud as zealously as did supporters of Baxter. Four counties and numerous precincts in other counties made no returns. According to the official count, Baxter defeated Brooks by 41,000 votes to 38,000. Other Minstrel candidates for state office were also declared elected, and the electoral vote of Arkansas went to Grant though Congress later refused to accept it.

The Baxter revolution. As soon as the election results were announced, the Brindletails began claiming that their candidate Brooks had been cheated out of the governorship. Appealing to the Democrats for support, the Brooks faction seemed determined to inaugurate its leader by force. With civil war a possibility, Baxter and Clayton hastened to repeat their campaign promises to the Democrats and Liberal Republicans. Democratic leaders decided to trust Baxter, whom they actually liked better than Brooks, and the Brindletails had to drop their revolutionary plans for the moment.

With the approval of Senator Powell Clayton, Governor Baxter first moved to make good his promise to do away with discrimination in voting. In March 1873 the voters ratified a constitutional amendment which restored full suffrage to former Confederates. The new governor made non-partisan appointments to public jobs, consulted Democrats as well as Republicans on state matters, and transferred the public printing to the Democratic **Arkansas Gazette.** At the same time Baxter stopped efforts by Republican legislators to pass measures which he regarded as corrupt and partisan. One of these was a railroad bill which proposed to release the railroad companies from their indebtedness to the state and to tax the people to pay the interest on the railroad bonds.

The independent course followed by Governor Baxter rapidly won the support of the Democrats, but alienated more and more leaders in his own party. When bribery failed, Baxter's enemies

Elisha Baxter

began to work with Brooks in an attempt to overthrow the governor in the courts. At first the plots got nowhere because Clayton still hoped he could control Baxter.

At a special election late in 1873 the Democrats won control of the General Assembly. Democratic leaders were already proposing a convention to draw up a new state constitution, and Baxter favored the idea. When Baxter also refused to issue any more railroad bonds, Clayton and United States Senator Stephen W. Dorsey decided to transfer their support to Brooks in an attempt to save the state for the Radicals. In less than two years Elisha Baxter had brought about a complete political realignment in Arkansas.

STUDY AIDS

Vocabulary

Be sure that you understand the meaning of these words and phrases:

Minstrels	Reform
Brindles	Republicans
discrimination	Liberal
polling places	Republicans
inaugurate	impeaching
alienated	full suffrage

Identification

Tell what part each of the following had in the story:

James M. Johnson	Stephen W. Dorsey
Ozra A. Hadley	Elisha Baxter
Horace Greeley	Joseph Brooks

To test your reading

On other paper, list 1-8. Opposite each number, write the word or words which complete each sentence.

1. In 1871 the General Assembly elected Clayton to ____.

2. Full suffrage was restored to Confederates in the year ____.

3. Brooks came forward as an advocate of ____.

4. Lieutenant Governor Johnson made an unsuccessful effort to seize ____.

5. The followers of Clayton were called ____.

6. The followers of Brooks were called ____.

7. The Liberal Republican party in Arkansas was organized by ____ and ____.

8. The Minstrels won the election of 1872 largely because ____.

Things to do

1. Make a chart showing how the Republican party of Arkansas broke up into rival factions.

2. Draw a cartoon representing Joseph Brooks making a speech during the campaign of 1872. Why were his followers called "Brindles"?

3. After consulting books in your library, make a report on the national presidential election of 1872.

6 The Downfall of Radicalism

When the Republican governor elected in 1872 began throwing the Radical program overboard, his Republican opponents tried to remove him from office by force. The resulting struggle returned Arkansas to the Democrats and ended reconstruction.

The Brooks-Baxter War. The Radical plan to oust Governor Baxter got under way on April 15, 1874 when the Pulaski circuit court ruled that Joseph Brooks had been legally elected governor in 1872 and was entitled to the office. Brooks immediately took the oath before Chief Justice John McClure. Aided by General Robert F. Catterson and some of the militia, the Brindle leader then removed Baxter from the governor's office, seized the state armory, and began fortifying the grounds around the Old State House.

Most of the Republican leaders at once deserted Baxter and rallied to Brooks. Only Secretary of State James M. Johnson and Congressman William W. Wilshire refused to go along with the plot. Brooks asked President Grant for arms, and received assurances from Clayton and Dorsey that Grant would support him.

Baxter first retreated to St. John's College in Little Rock, where he received the protection of the cadet corps, and then made his headquarters at the Anthony House. With the Democrats rallying to his support, Baxter declared martial law and began organizing a militia. Like his rival Brooks, the governor appealed to President Grant and to the people for support.

The Federal government at first refused to interfere, but United States troops from the arsenal were stationed along Main Street in Little Rock to keep the two factions apart. Excitement over the state was intense. In response to Democratic appeals over 2,000 Baxter men arrived in Little Rock, and probably half as many came to support Brooks. Many of the militiamen on both sides were Negroes.

Arkansas might have had a real civil war, but Brooks and Baxter feared to offend the Federal authorities or do anything that would bring U. S. troops into action. At Little Rock there were threatening demonstrations and some minor skirmishing, but no battles. At New Gascony in Jefferson County, King White's Baxter men inflicted a loss of ten or twelve on a Brooks force. The Baxter steamboat **Hallie** was captured at Palarm Creek, above Little Rock, by Brooks men firing from the banks of the Arkansas River. During the "war" probably 200 people lost their lives, but most of the casualties were due to accidents.

Supporters of both Brooks and Baxter were busy in Washington attempting to secure the support of the Grant administration. On April 22 Grant cautiously endorsed a proposal by Baxter that

Brooks troops at the Old State House during the Brooks-Baxter War

the General Assembly be convened to settle the dispute. Brooks maintained that the courts should decide the question, and secured a decision by the Arkansas Supreme Court in favor of his own claim.

When the Baxter members of the General Assembly convened in special session in Little Rock, President Grant suggested that the Brooks men be seated also. Baxter not only agreed, but offered to disband his forces if Brooks would do likewise. Scorning Clayton's advice, Brooks turned down the president's suggestion, refused to

disband his troops and accused Grant of encouraging bloodshed by his attitude.

The attitude of Brooks angered Republican politicians in Washington. On May 15, exactly a month after the trouble began, President Grant recognized Baxter as governor and commanded the Brooks forces to disperse. Within two days all the Brooks troops were out of Little Rock, and Governor Baxter and the General Assembly occupied the State House. The legislators refused to reconsider the results of the election of 1872, and by the end of May all the Brooks supporters in state offices had been replaced by Democrats and Baxter Republicans.

The Constitution of 1874. The Democrats, calling themselves the Democratic-Conservative party, moved immediately to solidify their power. The General Assembly passed an act calling a convention to meet at Little Rock on July 14, 1874 for the purpose of framing a new constitution. At the referendum on June 30 the voters approved the convention, 80,259 to 8,547. At least seventy of the ninety-one delegates elected were Democrats. Republican charges that ballot boxes had been stuffed and Negroes intimidated by militiamen were ignored.

Guarded by Baxter's state militia, the constitutional convention remained in session until early September. Presiding was Grandison D. Royston of Hempstead County, who had served in the constitutional convention of 1836. The scalawags controlled the Republican minority, and there were only four Negro delegates. The new constitution restored the ballot to all white men, prohibited any form of registration as a prerequisite for voting, and limited the power of the governor by making most offices elective. The number of state officers was reduced, and the General Assembly was restricted in its power to tax, borrow money, and pass special legislation.

The convention set October 13 as the date for an election ratifying the constitution and choosing a governor and other state officials. After Baxter declined their nomination for governor, the Democrats named Augustus H. Garland to head a full slate of candidates. Radical leaders advised Republican voters to ignore the election, with the hope that Congress would overturn

A clash in front of the Anthony House, Little Rock, following a speech by Governor Baxter

Democratic rule and return the state to the carpetbaggers.

The election resulted in the ratification of the constitution by a vote of 76,453 to 24,807. Numbers of Negroes voted for the constitution and for Garland after the Democrats assured them of full civil rights. The Garland government took office on November 12, 1874 and Arkansas was once again controlled by the Democrats.

The last gasp of Radicalism. Baxter's term as governor would have run two years longer had the convention of 1874 not produced a new constitution. A few Radicals encouraged Volney V. Smith, lieutenant governor under Baxter, to lay claim to the office of governor. Smith claimed that the Garland government was illegal, and that when Baxter left office the governorship

169

FRANK LESLIE'S ILLUSTRATED NEWSPAPER

Entered according to the Act of Congress, in the year 1875, by FRANK LESLIE, in the Office of the Librarian of Congress, at Washington.

No. 1,016—Vol. XL.]   NEW YORK, MARCH 20, 1875.   [Price 10 Cents. $4.00 Yearly.

HALT THERE, GENERAL BOUM!

JUDGE POLAND TO GEN. U. S. G. BOUM.—*"By the Constitution of the United States, and by your oath of office 'to preserve, protect and defend' it, you are estopped from going further in this direction. The existing State government in Arkansas should not be interfered with, either by Congress or by any department of the National Government, which has no more right to interfere with it than has England or France."*

President U. S. Grant ("General Boum") and the Radicals stopped on their way to Arkansas by the Poland committee of Congress and the Federal Constitution. From a cartoon in "Leslie's," a national newspaper, March 20, 1875

passed to himself as lieutenant governor.

Smith tried to set up a state government of his own, and hastened off to Washington to secure Federal support. Grant and his cabinet refused to intervene, since the Poland committee of Congress was then investigating the Arkansas situation. Governor Garland offered a reward for Smith's arrest, a group of Negro leaders repudiated Smith's claims, and the Radical scheme collapsed. President Grant appointed Smith consul to the Island of St. Thomas in the West Indies and got him out of the country.

Clayton and his associates placed their last hope in the Poland investigating committee, created by the United States House of Representatives shortly after the Brooks-Baxter War. Headed by Luke P. Poland, a Republican congressman from Vermont, the committee investigated affairs in Arkansas and finally recommended in 1875 that the Federal government leave the Garland government alone. Clayton persuaded President Grant to send a special message to Congress supporting Joseph Brooks as governor, but the House accepted the Poland report and took no action.

Why the Radicals lost. The Radicals failed completely in their effort to make Arkansas into a Republican state. There were many reasons for their failure. One was the fact that their organization was known as the party of the Union, while most white Arkansans had supported the Confederacy. Another was the low character and corruption of many carpetbagger and scalawag leaders. Still more important was the refusal of the small white farmers of Arkansas to join the Negroes in support of the Republicans.

Nationally, the Republican party by 1880 no longer needed Arkansas and the other Southern states to win elections. The Northern people grew tired of all the strife and trouble in the South. Northern capitalists found that they could work with Southern Democratic politicians in exploiting the timber and other natural resources of Southern states. At last Grant and the Republicans gave up the attempt to keep Arkansas Radical, and the state government passed into the hands of the Conservative Democrats.

☆   ☆   ☆   ☆

STUDY AIDS

Vocabulary

Be sure that you understand the meaning of these words and phrases:

cadet corps	ignore
ballot boxes	solidify
exploiting	Poland report
Democratic-Conservative party	capitalists
servative party	circuit court
disperse	armory

consul   casualties
           referendum

Identification

Tell what part each of the following had in the story:

Volney V. Smith	Augustus H.
Luke P. Poland	Garland
New Gascony	Robert F. Catterson
U. S. Grant	William W.
	Wilshire

To test your reading

On other paper, list 1-6. Opposite each number write the word or words which complete each sentence.

1. Baxter first retreated to ___ in Little Rock.

2. He later made his headquarters at the ___.

3. Many of the militiamen on both sides were ___.

4. The Baxter steamboat *Hallie* was captured at ___.

5. The president of the constitutional convention of 1874 was ___.

6. The Democratic nominee for governor in 1874 was ___.

Things to do

1. Pretend that you are a newspaper reporter and write a series of "eye-witness" accounts of important events in Arkansas during the year 1874. Illustrate your stories with cartoons and drawings. You may wish to make a bulletin board display and title it "You Were There."

2. Make a list of Arkansas newspaper headlines as they might have appeared during the month beginning April 15, 1874.

3. Which side would you have favored in the Brooks-Baxter War? Why? Discuss.

Reviewing the Unit

1. Why was there so much Union sentiment in Arkansas?

2. What policies did President Lincoln follow with respect to Arkansas?

3. Why did the Radicals draw up a new state constitution?

4. Was the Freedmen's Bureau a failure? Why or why not?

5. In what ways did Baxter disappoint those Radical leaders who had helped him to become governor? Why did they decide to transfer their support to Brooks?

6. What did the Republican state government accomplish in the field of public education?

7. Why did the Radicals fail in their effort to make Arkansas into a Republican state?

Unit Six

Conservative Arkansas, 1874-1898

The Chapters

WHEN THE Democrats returned to power in 1874 the people of Arkansas were exhausted by fourteen years of civil war and radical experiments at reconstruction.   They wanted peace, stability, and a chance to make a decent living.

The new Conservative leadership of Arkansas reflected the wishes of the white majority by avoiding political experiments and by trying to save the few tax dollars that came into the state treasury.   The Conservatives encouraged railroad companies, industries, and immigrants to come to Arkansas.

Trouble arose when many of the poverty-stricken farmers and some of the industrial workers tried to better their economic condition by political action.   The farmers' organizations blamed the Conservatives and their business allies for hard times, and almost won control of the state government.   In the end the popular protest caused the Democratic party to move away from some of the old Conservative policies.

Despite conservatism and poverty, Arkansas made some progress in public education and several other fields.   Changing ways of life invaded the cities.   On the western border and elsewhere the forces of law and order contended against violence and banditry.   But in the backwoods as well as in the joke-books, old Arkansas was still frontier.

1   The Conservatives in Power

With the adoption of the Constitution of 1874, the old Confederate element again took control of state affairs. But instead of trying to turn back the clock to prewar days, Conservative leaders attempted to bring railroads and industry into Arkansas to overcome the problems of poverty and defeat.

The political temper of 1874. When the Brooks-Baxter War ended reconstruction, the government of Arkansas was in bad condition. The state was deeply in debt and there was little money to operate the government. State properties had been neglected. Taxes were high, but little revenue came in because of poor economic conditions. The panic, or financial trouble, of 1873 caused a depression over the entire country.

Most white citizens were disgusted with Radical Republicanism. They wanted a permanent end to control of the state by carpetbaggers and their Negro allies. The Democratic party became the party of white supremacy and conservative principles. Many people who had been Whigs before the war now became Democrats.

Loyalty to the Democratic party became a fixed principle with many Arkansas people. They felt they could not desert the Democratic party without betraying the white race and the traditions of the South. This strong attachment to the Democratic party gave the leaders of that party a long lease on political power in Arkansas. The state became a part of the "Solid South."

The meaning of Conservatism. The Democratic party was led by Southern men who had served the Confederacy. They were determined to keep Arkansas safe for the white majority. Once in power they resisted political change and were suspicious of many new ideas. For this reason they were called Conservatives.

The Democrats knew that they could not restore things as they had been before the Civil War. Their leaders did not think as had most Arkansas leaders of prewar times. Earlier leaders had emphasized agriculture, especially cotton growing. The new Conservatives wanted to bring railroads and industry to Arkansas so that the state might grow in population and wealth. They talked a great deal about the glories of the Old South and the Confederacy, but in their zeal for new industry they resembled the Radical Republicans.

Conservative policies. The major policies of the Conservative Democrats grew out of their strong dislike of Radical reconstruction and their equally strong desire to promote the growth and prosperity of Arkansas. The Radicals had taxed the people heavily and

Augustus H. Garland

and property of the people. The Conservatives reacted strongly against these policies. The Constitution of 1874 limited the taxing and spending powers of government. The Conservatives stood for economy and retrenchment, which meant that they would spend no money unless absolutely necessary.

Even when tax money was available the Conservatives were slow to spend it on education and other social needs. Their 1874 constitution contained restrictions which made it hard for the state to regulate railroads and business firms.

In their eagerness to promote railroad building and industrial growth, Conservative politicians took jobs with railroad companies and businesses and accepted favors from them. When the General Assembly met, agents of businesses and railroads were in Little Rock and often got laws passed or rejected. Railroads and industries managed to

had spent money extravagantly. They had interfered with the lives, habits,

The old Jackson County courthouse at Jacksonport, as it appeared after restoration in 1966. The courthouse was begun in 1869 and turned over to the county in 1872

avoid paying their share of taxes, and the tax load fell on the farmers.

The Republicans who usually controlled the national government during this period were also interested in promoting railroads and industry. The Democrats of Arkansas found it easy to work with Republicans in Washington provided the latter did not interfere with race relations or try to put the Arkansas Republicans back into power.

Conservative policies in the years after reconstruction set the pattern of the future for Arkansas. In race relations, politics, law and economics Conservative ideas would still be alive in Arkansas ninety years after the Brooks-Baxter War.

The Conservative political system. The convention system of making party nominations for public office was used by the Democrats until near the end of the century. As long as candidates were named by county, district and state conventions it was easy for a few powerful politicians and their business allies to decide who should hold the offices. Struggles for power were settled by agreements made behind closed doors. Since the two United States senators from Arkansas were elected by the General Assembly until 1913, these important positions were filled in much the same way.

Campaign buttons, James K. Jones

Democratic leaders were neither better nor worse than those of other states and periods in history, and some were men of real ability. The most outstanding Conservative was Augustus H. Garland, who served one term as governor (1874-1877) and then went to the United States Senate. During the first term of President Grover Cleveland (1885-1889), Garland was attorney general of the United States. He was the first Arkansan to hold a cabinet position.

A former Arkansas congressman, Clifton R. Breckinridge of Pine Bluff, was United States Minister to Russia for three years beginning in 1894. In Russia he tried hard to help Jews who were being persecuted by the government. United States Senator James K. Jones of Arkansas was chairman of the Democratic National Committee in 1896 and 1900, when William Jennings Bryan was the party's candidate for president.

STUDY AIDS

Vocabulary

Be sure that you understand the meaning of these words and phrases:

stability   properties
social needs   retrenchment
Solid South   race relations
white supremacy   allies
                      traditions

Identification

Tell what part each of the following had in the story:

Clifton R.   James K. Jones
    Breckinridge   Augustus H.
                     Garland

To test your reading

On other paper, list 1-9. Opposite each number write the word or words which complete each sentence.

1. The Democratic party became the party of ___.

2. The Democratic party was led by Southern men who ___.

3. The major policies of the Conservative Democrats grew out of their ___.

4. The Constitution of 1874 limited the ___ of government.

5. Struggles for power were settled by ___.

6. The most outstanding Conservative was ___.

7. The chairman of the Democratic National Committee in 1896 was ___ of Arkansas.

8. Until 1913 the two United States senators from Arkansas were elected by ___.

9. With many Arkansas people ___ became a fixed principle.

Things to do

1. Secure a new copy of the Arkansas constitution and make a report on one of its sections. Notice the number of amendments that have been added since 1874.

2. Let each member of the class make a list of Conservative policies and ideas which he thinks are still influential in Arkansas today. Read and compare these lists.

2 Problems Confronting the Conservatives

The Conservative Democrats faced a number of political, economic and social problems following their return to power. Among them were the Negro vote, the state debt, convict leasing, and low wages.

Republicans and the Negro vote. Reconstruction had ended partly because the Republican party of Arkansas split into warring factions. Party strife continued, but Powell Clayton kept control until he went to Mexico in 1897 as American ambassador. Clayton and his friends usually decided who would get Federal jobs in Arkansas such as postmasterships.

The Negro vote was a problem for the Conservatives. The Democrats did not object to voting by the Negro as long as they could control his vote. At first they hoped to attract Negro support for their party by talking about the need of harmony between the races. Negroes were sometimes elected to minor offices. Some Negroes were so disappointed by the failure of reconstruction that they supported the Democrats, but most of them remained loyal to the Republicans or voted for one of the new farmer-labor parties.

Arkansas Republicans usually elected a few members of the General Assembly. More than a third of the Arkansas vote in most presidential elections went to the Republican candidate. Republican voters were numerous in Little Rock and the mountain counties of the north and northwest.

In some campaigns the Republicans tried unsuccessfully to defeat the Democrats by joining with farmer-labor groups in "fusion tickets." Since many Republican voters were Negro tenant farmers and wage earners, or white farmers in the Ozark hills, such combinations were natural enough.

The fusion tickets were a real threat to the Conservative Democrats. In 1892 they passed a poll tax amendment to the Arkansas constitution to discourage Negroes from voting. The poll tax and other measures taken by the Democrats seriously weakened the Republican party in Arkansas.

The state debt. The Democrats inherited a state debt of more than $13,600,000 when they came to power in 1874. The Radical Republicans were responsible for over $10,000,000 of this debt. During reconstruction the state had issued scrip, or paper notes, in large quantities as well as bonds for railroad and levee construction. The Radicals also floated new bonds to pay the old Holford debt which dated back to the Real Estate Bank of Arkansas.

Times were so hard that the Conservatives had to borrow more money just to keep the government going. A strong faction in the Democratic party maintained that the Holford, railroad and levee bonds should not be paid at all. They argued that the bonds were

Parade on Main Street, Little Rock, during the visit of former President U. S. Grant in 1880

unconstitutional, that they had been passed and sold by bribery and fraud, and that the state had received little or no benefit from them.

The "repudiation question" seriously divided the Conservatives. The faction that favored paying all the debt was strong enough to avoid repudiation for a few years. They argued that the state had to keep faith with the bondholders, and that Northern capitalists would not invest money in Arkansas if the state repudiated its debt. Some of those who advocated payment either held bonds themselves or were agents of bondholding companies. Democratic as well as Republican politicians had been involved in fraudulent issues of railroad and levee bonds.

The repudiationists gained ground after the Arkansas Supreme Court in 1877 declared the railroad and levee bonds unconstitutional. William M. Fishback led the fight for a constitutional amendment which would forbid payment of the Holford, railroad aid, and levee bonds. The amendment failed at the election of 1880 because of a legal technicality. Four years later it passed by a large vote and became the First Amendment to the Constitution of 1874. Three-fourths of the state debt was wiped out in one stroke.

In 1887 a state debt board was set up to find ways to pay the remaining $5,000,000. A special property tax was levied and earmarked for debt payment. The Federal government agreed to reduce its part of the debt. By 1897 the Arkansas debt was within manageable limits.

Trouble with state treasurers. The Conservative Democrats enjoyed a reputation for honesty in office. They claimed to be reformers, and the system of convention nominations protected them from public campaigns. Their Confederate war records caused many people to respect and trust them.

The public was surprised when three Arkansas treasurers in succession were accused of mishandling the state's money. Robert C. Newton, the first treasurer after reconstruction, was involved in a bank failure which caused a loss to the state of over $22,000. Governor Thomas J. Churchill, who had been treasurer before he became governor, was accused by a legislative committee of a shortage of almost $300,000. An attempt to impeach Churchill failed, but after he left the governorship the Supreme Court ordered him to repay $80,-522 to the state. Churchill claimed that the shortage was due to errors in bookkeeping.

William E. Woodruff Jr., treasurer from 1881 to 1891, left a shortage set by investigators at almost $150,000. Woodruff was acquitted on criminal charges but had to refund more than $90,000. A Little Rock newspaper called the Woodruff shortage the worst thing of its kind in the history of Arkansas.

The convict lease system. One of the worst abuses in Arkansas public life was the system of leasing convicts to private contractors. The contractors were entitled to the labor of the convicts for specified periods of time. Sometimes contractors subleased convicts to other individuals or companies.

The lease system had been used by the state government since the beginning of the Arkansas penitentiary in 1842. The Conservatives continued the practice because it saved money for the state and at the same time gave some of the politicians and their contractor friends a chance to make money.

For years the convict lease system was a source of scandal, rumor, popular protest, and unsuccessful attempts at reform. Investigations showed that prisoners were often neglected and mistreated. In the coal mines convicts were worked through the winter bare-

Penitentiary buildings, Little Rock, 1890. The present state capitol was later built on this site

Street view of Coal Hill, Johnson County, 1887

footed in icy water, and flogged if they failed to dig as much coal as the contractor wanted. A fourth of the Arkansas prisoners died every year.

In 1886 the convict miners at Coal Hill, in Johnson County, staged a sit-down strike, one of the earliest strikes of its kind in American history. The contractors and their political friends made promises, on this and other occasions. Several attempts were made to place contractors under stricter control by the state, but little improvement resulted. A law of 1888 extended the leasing system to the counties.

The farmer-labor parties attacked the lease system because of its injustice and because convict labor competed with free labor. The Populist platform of 1892 recommended establishment of a self-supporting penitentiary farm and a state reformatory for young offenders. The Democrats also went on record against the lease system, but the organized profiteers were so powerful that it was continued in changed form under a so-called reform act of 1893.

The wage earning class. Since Arkansas was an agricultural state, the in-

Workers employed by the Bluff City Lumber Company of Pine Bluff.
The oxen were used in logging operations

181

dustrial wage earning class was small. The average number of industrial workers was 4,500 in 1880, 14,000 in 1890, and 26,500 at the turn of the century. Negro workers provided the bulk of the state's labor supply.

Industrial workers received low pay and often suffered from poor living and working conditions. Arkansas had few laws of any importance to protect the wage earners from exploitation. A laborer's lien law, first enacted in 1868 and revised in 1883 and 1895, gave workers a legal claim on the value of goods and articles which they produced. Laws passed in 1893 and 1897 gave a preference to creditors of insolvent persons or corporations whose claims were for wages or salaries. The convict lease scandals led to a half-hearted legislative attempt to provide for state regulation and inspection of working conditions in coal mines.

Railroad workers were among the first to organize unions to represent their interests. Arkansas workers who belonged to the Knights of Labor helped bring the Jay Gould railroad system to terms in 1885. Another strike the following year resulted in violence at Little Rock and other places, and ruined the Knights of Labor in Arkansas. Governors Simon P. Hughes and William M. Fishback called out the state militia against striking railroad workers in 1886 and 1894.

Farm laborers in 1880 drew from eight to fifteen dollars a month for their work, including meals. Daily wages were fifty cents with board or seventy-five cents without board. Farm wages dropped even lower after 1890 as the price of cotton went down. Many wage earners supported the Union Laborites and Populists in Arkansas politics.

Interior, Bank of Little Rock, 1890

STUDY AIDS

Vocabulary

Be sure that you understand the meaning of these words and phrases:

fusion tickets
insolvent
farmer-labor
  groups
legal technicality
party strife
repudiation
contractor

ambassador
flogged
harmony
tenant farmer
reformatory
profiteers
laborer's lien law
property tax

Identification

Tell what part each of the following had in the story:

Simon P. Hughes
William M.
  Fishback
State Debt Board
First Amendment
William E.
  Woodruff, Jr.

Coal Hill
Knights of Labor
Robert C. Newton
Thomas J.
  Churchill

To test your reading

On other paper, list 1-9. Opposite each number write the word or words which complete each sentence.

1. The average number of industrial workers was __ in 1880 and __ at the turn of the century.

2. The fusion tickets were a real threat to the __.

3. The "repudiation question" seriously divided the __.

4. In 1877 the Arkansas Supreme Court declared the __ bonds unconstitutional.

5. One of the worst abuses in Arkansas public life was the __.

6. A law of 1888 extended the convict lease system to the __.

7. Many wage earners supported the __ and __ in politics.

8. Republican voters were numerous in __ and in the __ of the north and northwest.

9. Three state treasurers who had difficulties with state finances were __, __, and __.

Things to do

1. Have a debate on the question of repudiating the state debt, using this topic: "Resolved—that Arkansas should not pay the Holford, railroad and levee bonds."

2. Think of yourself as a newspaper reporter in 1886 or 1893 and write an article on the convict lease system.

3. If you live in an agricultural region, find out how much farm workers customarily receive for their labor and compare it with the wage rates of 1880. Remember that living expenses are much higher today.

3   The Railroad Era

The coming of railroads brought more changes to Arkansas than anything since the planting of the first white settlements. Railroads meant new towns, new industries, new people, and new patterns of political and economic control.

The coming of the railroads. Iron rails were already reaching across Arkansas when reconstruction ended. The St. Louis, Iron Mountain and Southern Railway Company, which laid its track along the Old Southwest Trail route from northeast to southwest, was the first railroad to cross the entire state. In 1874 a proposed railroad line from Little Rock to Fort Smith reached as far as Clarksville. Little Rock and Memphis were connected by a line completed three years before the Brooks-Baxter War.

After the end of the nationwide depression in 1879, Northern and English capitalists invested heavily in railroad construction in Arkansas and other Southern states. In 1880 there were 822 miles of railroad track in Arkansas. Ten years later Arkansas boasted over 2,200 miles of track, and by 1897 the total had grown to 2,750 miles.

In 1890 seventy-five per cent of the railway mileage in the state was owned by five companies. The largest of these companies was the St. Louis, Iron Mountain and Southern. The railroad companies did not belong to Arkansas people but to Northern capitalists like Jay Gould, the Wall Street financier. Gould secured control of a network of railroads in Arkansas and throughout much of the entire nation.

The passing of the steamboats. The golden age of steamboat traffic on Arkansas rivers had been the ten years before the Civil War, but in the period 1865-1880 the steamboat made a comeback. The river towns boomed again, as cotton and other produce was shipped downstream to New Orleans markets and up the Mississippi to Memphis and beyond.

The lengthening miles of railway track and the puffing steam locomotives spelled slow death for steamboat trade after 1880. Shipping by water was too expensive, uncertain and slow to compete with the railroads. As the forests were cut away and more land placed in cultivation the rivers became clogged with silt. The big, graceful steamboats disappeared from Arkansas streams and their place was taken by ugly barges hauling commodities such as coal.

As river traffic declined Arkansas people moved away from the river towns to new settlements along the railroads. Many of the older towns and villages vanished entirely, while others declined in population and wealth. Only towns located on railroads could look forward to growth and prosperity.

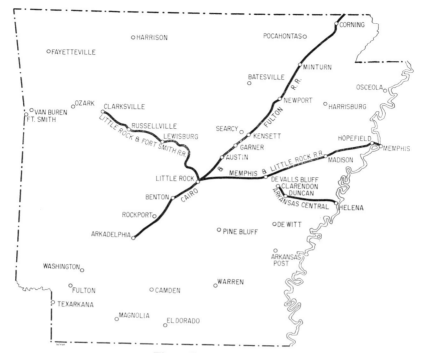

The railroads in 1873

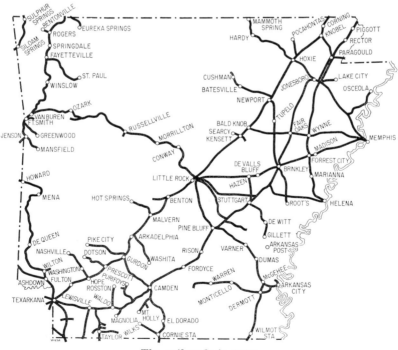

The railroads in 1895

185

Railroad station in Little Rock, built in 1872. This photograph was made in 1890

The railroads and industrial growth. As the railroads pushed through the great virgin forests of Arkansas the lumber companies were not far behind. Railroad spur lines were built into new timber areas and sawmill towns sprang up along the tracks. Lumbering became the most important Arkansas industry and production was still increasing at

Steamboat loaded with cotton bales

the end of the century. As a rule the lumber companies acted as though the supply of timber would last forever. The magnificent stands of cypress, oak, gum and pine were cut down to make quick profits for a few people. An interesting by-product of the timber boom was the organization in Gurdon in 1892 of a fraternal order for lumbermen called the "Concatenated Order of Hoo-Hoo."

Wood-working plants making shingles, sashes, doors and blinds used some of the lumber output. Other industries grew slowly. Flour mills and grist or corn-meal mills were fairly numerous. Cottonseed products such as oil and cake were produced. About 1880 commercial coal mining began in the valleys of the upper Arkansas River. The coal, most of which was mined in Sebastian County, was of good quality but Arkansas was so far from the big North-

Steamboat landing on the Arkansas River at Little Rock, about the year 1885

ern markets that the mines were not worked heavily.

Railroad transportation helped some industries, but in other ways the railroads hindered industrial growth. Arkansas factories making cotton and woolen cloth went out of business after railroads began bringing in cheaper cloth from Northern and Eastern mills. Railroad freight rates in Arkansas and the South were higher than rates elsewhere. The railroads set their own rates, paid few taxes, and exercised great influence in state and county government.

One reason that Arkansas industry failed to grow was because Northern capitalists wanted the state to remain an economic colony. They wanted raw materials like cotton and lumber from Arkansas but they did not want Arkansas factories to turn out products that would compete with the output of Northern plants.

The struggle to tax the railroads. Many citizens were disturbed by the great power of the railroad companies in Arkansas. A long legal struggle by the state government was necessary to force the railroads to pay taxes.

In 1883 the General Assembly created a board to assess the property of the railroads. The railroad companies claimed that their charters had exempted them from taxation. The case was carried to the United States Supreme Court and the right of Arkansas to tax the railroads was established. The state then won a suit to collect back taxes for the period 1874-1883. The St. Louis, Iron Mountain and Southern Railway Company offered the state $250,000 in settlement of tax claims prior to 1883, and the General Assembly of 1887 accepted the offer.

The railroads and immigration. The railroads were greatly interested in promoting immigration to Arkansas. The Federal government had granted hundreds of thousands of acres of land to the railroads. The railroad companies wanted settlers to buy and cultivate this land so that trade and shipping would increase. Businessmen and farm organizations like the Grange also wanted new settlers.

187

Virgin stand of white oak timber, Grant County

188

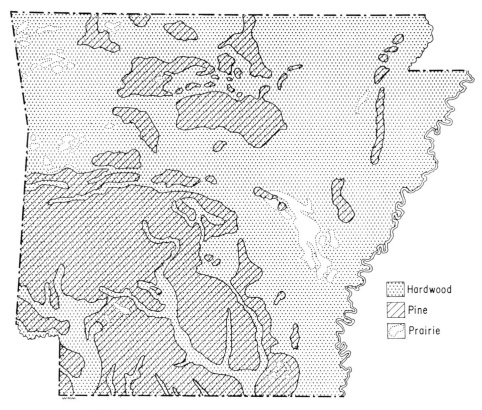

The forests of Arkansas, from a map made in 1881

In 1875 Arkansas railroad and real estate executives promoted a tour of the state by representatives of Northern and Western newspapers. Reactions of the visitors were published in a book called **The New Arkansas Travelers.** Two years later a state association to promote immigration was organized, and the Southern and Western Immigration Convention met at Little Rock. Local immigration societies sprang up all over Arkansas. Encouragement of immigration was one objective of the new State Bureau of Mines, Manufactures and Agriculture which was set up in 1889.

Beginning with the United States Centennial Exposition at Philadelphia in 1876, Arkansas was represented at a series of such displays in New Orleans, Louisville, Chicago, Atlanta, and other places. State fairs in Little Rock, particularly the Arkansas State Exposition of 1887, were designed to advertise products and resources. Also in 1887, a geological survey of the state was begun under the supervision of John C. Branner. Tons of literature praising the riches and advantages of Arkansas were distributed. The promoters not only wished to attract new people and industries, but also to encourage cotton farmers to grow more fruits, grains, and vegetables.

The immigration societies held conventions, heard speeches and passed resolutions, but the railroads brought in the people. The St. Louis, Iron Moun-

Arkansas display at an exposition in St. Louis, 1894

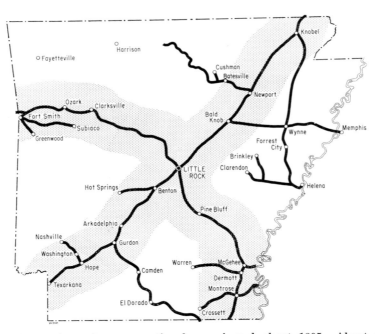

Railroad land grants, as shown by a promotional map issued about 1895. About 2,000,000 acres lying within the shaded area belonged to the St. Louis, Iron Mountain and Southern Railroad and to the Little Rock and Fort Smith Railroad

tain and Southern Railway Company employed 300 immigration agents in the West. No great flood of settlers came to Arkansas, but the state's population increased from 802,000 in 1880 to 1,128,-000 in 1890. At the turn of the century Arkansas had 1,311,000 people, of whom about a fourth were Negroes.

The new immigrants. Before 1875 almost all Arkansas settlers were people of Scottish-Irish, English, and African descent from the Southern states east of the Mississippi River. After 1875 many immigrants came from Northern states such as Iowa, Illinois, Indiana, and Pennsylvania. Numbers of the new immigrants were of continental European descent and some came directly from European countries. This meant the introduction of new customs, traditions and even new languages in some parts of Arkansas.

The Germans were the most numerous of the new groups. They settled in Little Rock, Fort Smith and up and down the Arkansas River Valley between the two cities. Other German families stopped in northeast Arkansas. Towns with German names like Stutt-gart and Ulm appeared on Grand Prairie.

A Polish settlement was established at Marche, near Little Rock. Bohemians from Illinois came to Dardanelle. Slavonians worked in the timber industry of southeast Arkansas. Italians led by the Rev. Pietro Bandini left Chicot County to establish Tontitown and grape culture in the hills of the northwest. A scattering of French, Swiss, Syrians and Greeks appeared in Arkansas. Even a few Chinese laborers were brought in to work on lowland cotton plantations.

The new immigration was not heavy enough to change the general pattern of Arkansas population, for many settlers from the older South continued to come to Arkansas. Most of the new immigrants settled on farms. Arkansas towns grew, but no big cities developed. Little Rock, the largest city, had 13,000 people in 1880, 26,000 in 1890, and 38,000 in 1900. In 1900 fifteen Arkansas towns had more than 2,500 people. Besides Little Rock, only Fort Smith and Pine Bluff numbered more than 10,000 population.

City hall and fire department, Dardanelle, Yell County, 1887

STUDY AIDS

Vocabulary

Be sure that you understand the meaning of the following words and phrases:

Southwest Trail route
Hoo-Hoo
comeback
Wall Street
executives
economic colony
by-product
sashes
spur lines
silt
Grange
Slavonians
invested
golden age

Identification

Tell what part each of the following had in the story:

Jay Gould
Pietro Bandini
John C. Branner
St. Louis, Iron Mountain and Southern
The New Arkansas Travelers

To test your reading

On other paper, list 1-9. Opposite each number write the word or words which complete each sentence.

1. In 1880 there were __ miles of railroad track in Arkansas.

2. The steamboat made a comeback in the years __.

3. In the year __, a geological survey of the state was begun under the supervision of __.

4. In 1900 Arkansas had a population of __.

5. A Polish settlement was established at __ near Little Rock.

6. Bohemians from __ came to __.

7. Italians left __ County and established __ and grape culture in the hills of northwest Arkansas.

8. Arkansas was represented at the United States Centennial Exposition at __ in the year __. It was later represented at similar expositions at __, __, __, __, and __.

9. Towns with German names like __ and __ appeared on __.

Things to do

1. Have a committee find out about the first railroads in your community. Visit the local railway station and ask about rail travel and traffic today in your area.

2. Have a committee investigate the history of the factories in your community. Find out when they were started, by whom, and how they have grown.

3. Arrange a visit to Old Jacksonport State Park, located near Newport. Jacksonport is a river town which declined after the coming of the railroad.

4. If you live in a community which was affected by the "new immigration" after 1875, investigate the history of these settlers and report to the class.

4   Hard Times for the Farmer

During the Conservative period the Arkansas farmer found himself confronted with poverty and hardship and enmeshed in a credit system from which he could not seem to escape. For such conditions many farmers began to blame the railroads and other special interests.

Rise of the sharecrop system. When the Civil War ended the Arkansas Negro found himself legally free but without land or money. Many Negroes were bewildered, for they had thought that the end of slavery would mean no more work or that the Federal government would give each family "forty acres and a mule."

Under the slavery system the Negroes had been used primarily in agricultural work. Few of them knew how to do anything else. Since the Negro could offer nothing but his labor, and the whites had land but little money, the sharecrop or tenant system arose.

Under this system landless Negroes and whites lived and worked as tenant farmers on land which belonged to someone else. Landowners furnished tenant farmers with land, houses, barns, tools, and some supplies. In return the tenant paid a share, often half, of his crop to the landowner.

In the Arkansas lowlands the sharecrop plan continued the old plantation system in a new form. In the hills, where there were few Negroes and landholdings had always been small, the farmer tried to carry on as he had always done.

The farmer's problems. Most of the white farmers of Arkansas were glad to see the end of reconstruction, but they soon discovered that political change did not bring prosperity. The years from the Civil War to the First World War were generally hard ones for the farmers though the period after about 1898 brought some improvement.

For more than half a century after 1860, the size of farms declined as the number of farms increased. During the ten years before 1880 the number of farms in Arkansas almost doubled. The sharecrop system was spreading, and more land was being placed in cultivation by farm families moving to Arkansas from other states.

Cotton was the only cash crop of most Arkansas farmers, and more cotton was produced than world markets could buy. The price of cotton dropped from twenty-five cents a pound in 1868 to eleven cents in 1874. By 1894 the price was down to four or five cents a pound. The farmer had to sell his cotton in the fall in order to get money to live. Year after year he found that the more cotton he grew, the less he got for it.

Prices of manufactured goods and other things which the farmer had to buy did not go down. Railroads charged high freight rates. Taxes on land and personal property were high, at least in proportion to the farmer's income. The average Arkansas farmer was always short of money and in need of credit.

The farm credit system. Since farming was uncertain and often unprofitable, banks would not lend money to farmers except at high rates of interest. Actually Arkansas had too few banks to meet farm credit needs, for in 1882 there were only twenty-three banks in the entire state.

Under the sharecrop system the landowner often provided supplies for his tenant. The crop-lien system was another attempt to meet farm credit

A mule-operated cotton press

Cotton gin operated by Lawrence McCrary near Nashville, Howard County, about 1895

194

Spinning wheels, such as this one at a home in Dover, were used to make yarn and thread from cotton and wool. The implements held by the woman are cards, used to clean and disentangle the cotton and woolen fibers before spinning

needs. Merchants would extend credit to farmers during the crop season, with the understanding that the debt would be paid when crops were gathered in the fall. The farmer who bought under this arrangement often had to pay from twenty-five per cent to forty per cent more than the person who could pay cash for supplies.

Sometimes a written mortgage bound the farmer to surrender his property if he failed to pay his debt. "Anaconda" mortgages, named for a tropical snake which encircles and crushes its prey, ran thirty to seventy per cent higher for the credit price than for cash. The crop-lien system was more widespread than the mortgage system, since most merchants wanted cash crops rather

than property. Land values were generally low after the panic of 1873.

Frequently the cotton did not bring enough when sold in the fall to pay the merchant. The farmer thus came under more or less permanent obligation to the store owner. The merchant, banker or physician who chose to foreclose on his mortgages often found it possible to become a large landowner with numerous tenant families on his holdings.

Poor crops and low prices meant that more and more farm owners lost their lands and became tenants. The one-crop cotton economy was fastened on the state because merchants and landlords insisted that farmers raise a cash crop. Since continuous cotton growing

Hand-operated loom, used to weave cotton and woolen thread into cloth. This photograph was made in Eureka Springs, Carroll County

Placing corn in the hopper to be ground into meal at a water mill near Batesville, Independence County. Notice the kerosene or "coal oil" lamps in the background

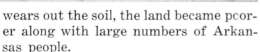

wears out the soil, the land became poorer along with large numbers of Arkansas people.

The farmer's protest. As the emotions aroused by Civil War and reconstruction cooled and the price of cotton dropped, the Arkansas farmer began to think about his economic troubles. His conclusions were not always correct, for he did not understand such complex problems as overproduction, competition in world markets, and the national depression which began in 1873. He did know that something was wrong.

196

The farmer could see that while railroads and manufacturers received many kinds of assistance from state and national governments, he himself got little help in times of flood, drouth, and low prices. His taxes were heavy because railroads and manufacturers did not pay their fair share. His children could not read and write because there were no schools. He found it hard to get to town for the supplies he needed because there were no good roads. The church which he attended was drab and poorly furnished because nobody had the money to improve it.

For these conditions the farmer blamed the merchants, railroads, banks, manufacturers, and the politicians who supported special privileges for these classes. Money was so scarce that he began to believe there must be a conspiracy somewhere to keep the supply inadequate. Many farmers did nothing but try to make the best of a bad situation, but others began to join organizations which claimed to represent their interests.

STUDY AIDS

Vocabulary

Be sure that you understand the meaning of the following words and phrases:

inadequate	mortgage
bewildered	drab
enmeshed	conspiracy
credit	sharecrop
crop-lien	foreclose
	special privileges

To test your reading

On other paper, list 1-8. Opposite each number write the word or words which complete each sentence.

1. In 1882 there were only ___ banks in Arkansas.

2. Under the slavery system the Negroes had been used primarily in ___.

3. For more than a half century after 1860 the size of farms declined as ___.

4. The only cash crop of most Arkansas farmers was ___.

5. The price of cotton dropped from ___ a pound in 1868 to ___ in 1874.

6. The average Arkansas farmer was always short of ___ and in need of ___.

7. The ___ system was more widespread than the ___ system.

8. Land values were generally ___ after the panic of ___.

Things to do

1. If you live in a cotton-growing region, find out what growers receive for their cotton at the present time. How do current prices compare with those of the period described in this chapter?

2. Ask a lawyer to explain how mortgages are drawn. Secure a blank mortgage form and bring it to class.

3. Do you think that life on a farm one hundred years ago would have been more interesting than life on a farm today? Why or why not? Arrange a panel discussion.

5   The Farmer in Politics

For a number of years discontented farmers formed organizations and tried to find ways to improve their economic condition. Militant farmers and workers failed to win political control of Arkansas, but their efforts caused the Democrats to steer the ship of state in new directions.

The farmers' organizations. During the twenty years after 1872 Arkansas farmers formed several organizations in a search for better times. The first one was the National Grange, led in Arkansas by John Thompson Jones. The Granger movement began near Helena in 1872 and in three years had 600 local groups and over 20,000 members. Jones became head of the National Grange, which was active in many states. But after 1875 the Grange declined rapidly and soon ceased to be of any importance in Arkansas.

The Greenback party, active in Arkansas politics in 1880, had been organized by Indiana Grangers and received considerable farmer support. Much more important was the Agricultural Wheel, which originated near Des Arc in 1882. Within five years the Wheel had grown into a national movement active in at least nine states and claiming half a million members.

One of the most prominent leaders of the Wheel in Arkansas was Isaac McCracken, who first headed a group called the Brothers of Freedom. The Wheel merged with the Brothers of Freedom in 1885. Then in 1888 the Agricultural Wheel combined with the Farmers' Alliance, a group which had spread from Texas into Arkansas. These mergers strengthened the farmers' movement and encouraged its leaders to enter Arkansas politics.

The Populist or Peoples' party, organized in 1890-91, was the climax of the farmers' protest movement. In Arkansas the Populists put up candidates, established newspapers, adopted platforms, and elected a few county officials and legislators. In the depression year of 1894 they were able to draw 2,000 supporters to Little Rock for a convention. But like the other farmers' organizations before them, the Populists never succeeded in unseating the Democrats. After 1896 Populism faded from the scene.

Objectives of the farmers' organizations. All of the farmers' organizations had about the same objectives. They wanted the state to regulate the railroads, or even take over and operate them. They wanted to get more money into circulation by issuing greenback paper currency or by the free coinage of silver. They opposed the national banks and distrusted manufacturers. They wanted the state to help the farmers by building good roads and by establishing public schools, an agricultural college and an experimental farm.

Some of the protest groups tried to help the farmer to improve his own condition. Grangers, Wheelers and Alliancemen experimented with cooperative buying and selling associations. They hoped that such associations would free the farmer from the crop-lien system, but little came of the attempt.

Farm leaders hoped to secure the support of the wage earners who labored in the mills and factories. Some of them, notably the Populists, tried to win the support of Negro farmers and workers as well as whites.

At first the farmers hoped to achieve their objectives by working within the Democratic party. The General Assembly of 1887 showed some disposition to regulate railroads and hold down interest rates, but the stronger measures were repealed two years later. The Conservatives made a few concessions, such as the establishment of agricul-

tural experiment stations in 1889, but most of these came after the farmers had turned to independent political action.

Political action by farmers and workers. In 1880 the Greenbackers frightened the Democrats by enlisting the support of the Republicans. Greenback leaders W. P. Parks and Rufus K. Garland waged a vigorous campaign, but Parks polled little more than a fourth of the vote for governor.

The Wheeler candidate for governor did poorly in 1886 because the Wheelers themselves were divided. Two years later the Wheelers, Alliancemen, Republicans and Knights of Labor united behind Charles M. Norwood, the candidate for governor of the Union Labor party. Norwood came within 15,000 votes of beating James P. Eagle, the Democrat. Encouraged, the same

Atkins, Pope County, about the year 1890

Short-lived little newspapers such as these were established in many Arkansas towns by farmers' organizations

groups joined again in 1890, but Union Labor candidate N. B. Fizer did not run as well as had Norwood.

The Alliancemen and Union Laborites drifted into the Populist camp when that party appeared. The Populists never enjoyed the success in Arkansas which they achieved in states such as Kansas. No statewide agreement could be reached with the Republicans, and Populist candidates for governor ran behind Republican as well as Democratic candidates.

Why the farmer - worker movement failed. The parties which claimed to represent the farmers and workers were never able to win the support of a majority of Arkansas voters. Some of their leaders accused Democratic

election officials of dishonesty. The Union Labor candidate for governor in 1888 claimed that he had been cheated out of at least 3,000 votes in eleven counties. In Pulaski County the poll books were stolen and a thousand or more ballots destroyed.

After the election of 1888 a Democratic congressman lost his seat to a Union Labor candidate as the result of a contest. John M. Clayton, a Republican candidate for another congressional seat, was shot and killed at Plumerville while trying to collect evidence of fraud. After his death Clayton was adjudged the winner and the office declared vacant. The Democrats did their best to keep Populists off county election commissions, and sometimes found other ways to hold down the Populist and Republican vote.

Democratic State Ticket.

Election, Monday, Sept. 4, 1882.

For Governor,
JAMES H. BERRY.
For Secretary of State,
JACOB FROLICH.
For Auditor of State,
A. W. FILES.
For Treasurer of State,
W. E. WOODRUFF, Jr.
For Attorney General,
C. B. MOORE.
For Commissioner of State Lands.
WM. P. CAMPBELL.
For Chancellor,
D. W. CARROLL.
For Chancery Court Clerk,
J. W. CALLAWAY.
For Superintendent of Public Instruction,
WOOD E. THOMPSON,
For Associate Justice of the Supreme Court,
W. W. SMITH.
For Judge Sixth Judicial Circuit,
F. T. VAUGHAN.
For Prosecuting Attorney Sixth Judicial Circuit,
THOS. C. TRIMBLE.

THE PEOPLE'S COUNTY TICKET

For Sheriff,
JOHN G. FLETCHER.
For County and Probate Judge,
WM. J. PATTON.
For Circuit Clerk,
J. L. BAY.
For County and Probate Clerk,
R. W. WORTHEN.
For Treasurer,
JOSEPH GRIFFITH.
For Assessor,
H. H. ROTTAKEN.
For Coroner,
ISAAC GILLAM.
For Surveyor,
L. S. DUNSCOMB.

A Democratic ballot of 1882, Pulaski County

The Democrats succeeded in convincing many Arkansas voters that the Wheelers, Populists and their allies were actually Republicans, and that their victory would mean a return to reconstruction and Negro rule. In 1891 the Democratic legislature passed new election laws and proposed that a poll tax amendment be added to the Arkansas constitution. The amendment, which required payment of an annual poll tax as a requirement for voting, was declared adopted by the General Assembly of 1893 even though it had not received a majority of all votes cast in the general election. The poll tax and other measures discouraged voting by Negroes and poorer whites, and helped to reduce the strength of the Republicans and Populists.

The influence of the farmer-worker movement. Conservative leaders realized that the farmer-worker movement indicated widespread dissatisfaction with Democratic rule, and that changes would have to be made. After 1890 the direct primary replaced the party convention in many counties, and Democratic candidates now had to make public campaigns in order to be nominated. Before each election the Democrats endorsed a little more of the farmer-worker platform, such as railroad regulation and the free coinage of silver. In this way much of the reform program was eventually adopted by the Democrats. Farmer-worker principles also influenced later organizations such as the Farmers' Union, the Farm Bureau, and the Arkansas Federation of Labor.

STUDY AIDS

Vocabulary

Be sure that you understand the meaning of the following words and phrases:

militant
mergers
concession
Populist
greenbacks

free coinage
agricultural experiment stations
direct primary
cooperative buying

Identification

Tell what part each of the following had in the story:

James P. Eagle
C. M. Norwood
John T. Jones

Isaac McCracken
N. B. Fizer
John M. Clayton

To test your reading

On other paper, list 1-9. Opposite each number write the word or words which complete each sentence.

1. The first important farm organization in Arkansas was the ___. It was led by ___.

2. The Agricultural Wheel originated near ___ in the year ___.

3. The Populist party was the climax of ___. In the year 1894 they were able to draw ___ supporters to Little Rock for a ___.

4. In 1880 Greenback leaders ___ and ___ waged a vigorous campaign but ___ polled little more than a fourth of the vote for governor.

5. The poll tax amendment was adopted in the year ___.

6. After 1890 the direct primary replaced the ___ system in many counties.

7. In Arkansas much of the farmer-worker program was eventually put into effect by the ___.

8. The Granger movement in Arkansas began near ___ in ___ and in three years had ___ local groups and over ___ members.

9. The Agricultural Wheel merged with the ___ in the year ___. In 1888 it combined with the ___.

Things to do

1. Make a report on the Populist party. You can find material in a good encyclopedia or in a United States history book.

2. Imagine yourself a Union Labor party candidate for statewide office in the election of 1888. Make a speech to your supporters explaining why you lost the election.

3. Have a classroom debate on the following question: "Resolved—That the poll tax should have been adopted as a prerequisite for voting."

6   Education, Religion and Literature

In the midst of poverty, the people of Arkansas struggled to build an educational system, to advance the cause of religion and to develop a better-informed citizenry. Old traditions, prejudices and fears sometimes stood in the way.

The uphill struggle of the schools. The Constitution of 1874 provided that Arkansas should maintain a "general, suitable and efficient system of free schools, whereby all persons in the State between the ages of six and twenty-one years may receive gratuitous instruction." The attempt to build such a public school system was handicapped at the start. From pioneer days many Arkansas people regarded education as a luxury which should be left to tuition-supported private schools. Tax-supported schools were looked down upon as schools for paupers. The fact that the Radicals had talked so much about public schools during reconstruction made many people suspicious of the idea.

Public schools were poorly financed, for taxes did not bring in much money. The state constitution limited school revenues to an annual poll tax and twenty cents on each one hundred dollars of taxable property. School districts could vote an additional annual tax of fifty cents on each one hundred dollars of taxable property, but not all of them did so. Some financial help came from the Peabody Education Fund, which had been set up for the promotion of education in the South.

What the schools were like. Schools then were far different from schools today. The buildings were usually small frame or log structures with one or two teachers and no more than a few dozen students. School districts were small and numerous; in 1896 Arkansas had 4,757 such districts. Since farm children could not attend school during planting and harvesting seasons, school terms were limited to a few weeks in summer and in winter. Country children walked to school through the woods and over bad roads.

Arkansas had no compulsory attendance law and no uniform system of textbooks or grades. Subjects taught included reading, spelling, penmanship, arithmetic, English grammar, geography, and history. Books and supplies were scarce. Pupils wrote on slates and borrowed books from one another.

Teacher training was a problem. Persons wishing to become teachers were supposed to pass a test administered by the county examiner, but school directors sometimes hired unqualified friends and relatives as teachers. The average salary of Arkansas public school teachers in 1892 was $34.59 a month, and few teachers ever received more than $60 a month.

Progress in public education. In spite of all the difficulties and handicaps, the schools made some progress during the period 1874-1898. In 1876 only one child in ten was enrolled in a public school. Twenty years later the proportion had risen to two children in three, white and Negro. Many Arkansans still could not read or write, but the percentage was being reduced. One person in three was illiterate in 1880, one person in four in 1890, and one person in five in 1900.

The State Teachers' Association, which began in 1869, and some of the state superintendents of public instruction tried hard to raise teaching standards. Short training schools for teachers, called "normal schools" or institutes, were established on a county and district basis. While Josiah H. Shinn was state superintendent in 1890-94 the normal school system included three short-lived state schools at Stuttgart, Jonesboro, and Morrilton. Arkansas Industrial University in Fayetteville and Branch Normal College in Pine Bluff had teacher-training departments.

City schools were generally better financed and equipped than those in the country. Private academies and institutes declined in number and enrollments as public schools gained favor. From 1880 to 1885 Arkansas had at least one educational magazine published within its borders, and in 1896 the **Arkansas School Journal** was revived.

The beginnings of higher education. Arkansas Industrial University, later renamed the University of Arkansas, was the only state-supported institution

Classroom of Colored Industrial Institute, a Catholic school in Pine Bluff, 1893

Restored country schoolhouse at Bull Shoals, Marion County

of higher education during the Conservative era. The Branch Normal College for Negroes opened in Pine Bluff in 1875 under the control of the university board.

Small private colleges sprang up in different parts of Arkansas. In 1892 fifteen such schools, plus the university and its Branch Normal, enrolled 3,221 students. Twelve of the fifteen private colleges were supported by religious denominations, particularly the Methodists, Baptists and Presbyterians.

Since Arkansas had no high school system, the university and most of the colleges were little more than secondary schools. Libraries were small, and faculty members were sometimes as poorly prepared as they were paid. A college degree had little real meaning because requirements for admission and graduation varied from school to school.

Some private schools soon closed their doors, merged with other colleges or changed their names. Others developed into fairly strong institutions. Such colleges as Ouachita and Henderson at Arkadelphia, Philander Smith at Little Rock, Hendrix and Central at Conway, and College of the Ozarks at Clarksville began during the Conservative period, though not always with the same names that they bear today.

Religion changes little. Religious life in Arkansas changed little during the last quarter of the nineteenth century. The Baptists and Methodists continued to be most numerous. In 1890 about eighty-five per cent of Arkansas church members were Methodists or Baptists. The Presbyterian and Christian churches also claimed sizable memberships.

Immigration of Germans, Poles, Italians and other people of continental European descent added substantial Catholic and Lutheran populations in some parts of Arkansas. Episcopalians were mostly to be found in the larger towns, as were the few Jews who lived in the state.

The typical Baptist or Methodist church was a log or frame building located on a country road. In many churches services were held on only one weekend a month. Ministers usually lacked formal training, and one man often served several churches located miles apart. Most clergymen had to farm or do some other kind of secular work in order to make a living.

Revivals or "protracted" meetings and camp meetings were held in the heat of summer after crops were laid by. "Brush arbors," made of upright poles with leafy branches for a roof, were sometimes used for outdoor preaching services. Camp meetings and revivals were important social as well as religious occasions, and large numbers of people attended.

The churches considered doctrine very important, and each denomination insisted that its own interpretation of the Bible was the correct one. Religious rivalry was keen. Preachers of different beliefs sometimes engaged in public debates which attracted great crowds and caused feeling to run high.

Central Collegiate Institute at Altus, Franklin County, a Methodist school opened in 1876

Occasionally churches divided over doctrinal questions. Popular preachers enjoyed such great prestige that children were named for them.

Negroes established their own churches during reconstruction, and in the Conservative period the religious separation of the races was complete. Most of the former slaves had accepted the faith of their masters, and this meant that Arkansas Negroes became Baptists and Methodists. The Negroes liked the freedom and informality of Methodist and Baptist worship.

The printed page. In the twenty years after 1870 the number of newspapers and magazines published in Arkansas more than tripled, and circulation figures rose even more. By 1900 the state had 257 newspapers and periodicals, as compared with only fifty-six in 1870. The average newspaper was a small weekly with fewer than a thousand subscribers, though dailies increased in number from six in 1880 to twenty-five at the turn of the century.

Arkansas produced no first-rate writers during the period. Novelists like Ruth McEnery Stuart and Alice French, who called herself "Octave Thanet," enjoyed limited success. Fay Hempstead's verse earned him the honorary title of "poet laureate of Freemasonry," awarded at Chicago in 1908. Opie Read, a newspaperman, added to the growing store of comic tales and jokes about Arkansas.

The first general histories of Arkansas, written by John Hallum and Fay Hempstead, were published in 1887 and 1890. The Goodspeed histories of Arkansas counties and people appeared about the same time. Another sign of growing interest in the past was the formation in Arkansas of such organizations as the United Confederate Veterans, Daughters of the American Revolution, United Daughters of the Confederacy, and Colonial Dames of America.

STUDY AIDS

Vocabulary

Be sure that you understand the meaning of the following words and phrases:

gratuitous	protracted
poet laureate	"laid by"
faculty	handicaps
normal school	secular
paupers	revivals

Identification

Tell what part each of the following had in the story:

Josiah H. Shinn	Alice French
"brush arbors"	Peabody Education
Ruth McEnery	Fund
Stuart	Goodspeed histories

To test your reading

On other paper, list 1-10. Opposite each number write the word or words which complete each sentence.

1. The first general histories of Arkansas were written by __ and __.

2. Fay Hempstead's verse earned for him the title of __ of Freemasonry.

3. By 1900 the state had __ newspapers and periodicals, as compared with __ in 1870.

4. In 1890 about __ per cent of Arkansas church members were __ or __.

5. The Branch Normal College for Negroes opened in __ in __.

6. The Arkansas State Teachers Association began in the year __.

7. The average salary of Arkansas public school teachers in 1892 was __.

8. In 1876 only one child in __ was enrolled in a public school.

9. One person in three was illiterate in __, one in four in __, and one in __ in 1900.

10. In 1896 Arkansas had __ school districts.

Things to do

1. Find out when your local newspaper was established and who the various editors have been. Has the name of the newspaper been changed since it was first established? Does the newspaper keep a file of back issues?

2. If there is a college in your community, make a report on its history. Usually college catalogs contain some historical information.

3. Talk with older people, and with your minister, priest or rabbi, and prepare a report on the history of your own church or congregation. When was it organized?

4. Find out if the Daughters of the American Revolution, the United Daughters of the Confederacy, or the Colonial Dames of America has an active group in your community. If so, find out about its history, principles and activities.

5. Make a list of books written by Arkansas authors.

7 The Persistence of the Frontier

The old frontier lingered long in the interior of Arkansas and along its western border. In some areas violence and lawlessness were as slow to disappear as were the jokes and tall tales which accompanied the name of Arkansas all over the country.

The Arkansas backwoods. Changes seemed to occur more slowly in Arkansas than in many other states. Swamps, mountains and unbridged rivers discouraged travel and made communication difficult. Travelers who passed through the back country, away from the railroads and larger towns, found people living much the same as before the Civil War. Many people outside Arkansas came to believe that the entire state was an isolated backwoods.

Frontier conditions lingered in Arkansas partly because of the existence of the Indian Territory. Bordering western Arkansas, from Fort Smith northward, was the Cherokee Nation. The Choctaw Nation lay to the south, between the Arkansas and Red rivers. Farther westward in what is now Oklahoma were the Creeks, Seminoles and Chickasaws, who together with Choctaws and Cherokees were known as the Five Civilized Tribes. The Plains Indian tribes roamed the vast region toward the Rockies.

Since the Indian Territory was supposed to be reserved for the Indians, white immigrants could not move across Arkansas to settle there. The Indian barrier on the west also held back the settlement and development of Arkansas. The tide of white migration moved around Arkansas into Texas, Kansas and beyond.

The border outlaws. Lawlessness was widespread along the frontier during the decades following the Civil War. The Indian Territory became a refuge for outlaws and renegades of every color and description. This was the era of the Daltons, Bill Doolin, Belle Starr, Ned Christie, Cherokee Bill, and the Cook and Rufus Buck gangs. When hard pressed by the law the border outlaws sometimes took refuge in the mountains of Arkansas. Belle Starr, for example, was seen in the Yell County village of Chickalah more than once.

Occasionally the border outlaws brought their operations into the state. In 1874 the Jesse James gang held up a stage near Hot Springs, and as late as 1893 Henry Starr rode up out of the Indian Territory to rob a bank in Bentonville.

Arkansas produced its own crop of outlaws also. Moonshiners were always a problem for county sheriffs. In 1883 the remote "Three Corners" region of

Fort Smith soon after the close of the Civil War

Yell, Garland and Montgomery counties was ruled for a time by Jack and Bud Daniels and Rial Blocker. In 1877 Governor William R. Miller authorized the formation of two militia companies in Union County to break up a bandit gang which infested the Louisiana state line area. The Hempstead County militia then had to be called out to prevent an armed rescue of prisoners by other bandits.

The Parker court. The name of Fort Smith caused dread among the border outlaws, for it was there that the court of Judge Isaac C. Parker was located. Parker, a native of Ohio, presided over the Federal District Court for Western Arkansas from 1875 until 1896. In spite of its name, the Parker court handled cases from the Indian Territory rather than Arkansas.

In twenty-one years Parker's court hanged eighty-eight criminals and brought in almost 9,500 convictions. Thousands of people witnessed the hangings from the great gallows, on which as many as six criminals were executed at one time. Parker's deputy marshals brought in outlaws from wide reaches of the Indian Territory, and from the judge's sentences there was no appeal.

The methods of the "Hanging Judge" were hard and direct, but they got results. At the end of Parker's career, life and property were much safer in the Indian Territory and the great days of the border bandits were over.

Restored Parker gallows, Fort Smith

210

VOL. 5. NO. 22.   LITTLE ROCK, ARK., U. S. A., SATURDAY, OCTOBER 25. 1884.   PRICE, 5 CENTS.

Masthead of Opie Read's "Arkansaw Traveler"

Tall tales of "Arkansaw". The frontier survived in literary form. From territorial times Arkansas had acquired a reputation for backwardness and peculiarity. Tall tales and jokes about Arkansas were repeated all over the country.

This tradition was continued in plays like "Kit the Arkansas Traveler," which was performed in Northern theaters for thirty years after 1869. **Three Years in Arkansas,** a book by Marion Hughes, introduced the razorback hog to the world. A humorous speech called "Change the Name of Arkansas?" was widely circulated in several different versions. Though never actually delivered in the Arkansas legislature, the speech probably resulted from the General Assembly resolution of 1881 that the name of the state should be pro-

A lynching in Arkansas, as pictured in "Frank Leslie's Illustrated Newspaper," September 30, 1882

211

Main Street in Nashville, Howard County, about 1888

nounced "AR'kan-saw" rather than "Ar KAN' sas."

The name of Opie Read, the most outstanding Arkansas literary figure of the Conservative era, is connected with backwoods humor. Read worked for newspapers in Carlisle, Conway, and Little Rock, and wrote a large number of books. For five years beginning in 1882 he edited **The Arkansaw Traveler,** a humorous weekly, in Little Rock. Partly because many Arkansans resented his tales and funny stories, Read moved his paper to Chicago.

Read was accused of having written **On A Slow Train Through Arkansaw,** a yellow-backed little volume which first appeared in 1903. Actually the author was Thomas W. Jackson of Chicago, a writer of joke-books. **On A Slow Train** made many Arkansas people angry, but it sold so well that the publisher kept reprinting it for thirty years.

Outbreaks of violence. Civil War, reconstruction, and the frontier left a legacy of violence which was slow to disappear from the Arkansas scene. Murders and other violent crimes were frequent. Arkansas gentlemen no longer challenged one another to duels, but instead often tried to settle serious differences by "shooting - on - sight."

Negroes suspected of crimes against white persons were sometimes lynched, or killed by white mobs without a trial.

Racial trouble broke out in Hempstead and Howard counties in the summer of 1883. Near Nashville a large band of armed Negroes killed a white man at work in a field and suffered the loss of one of its own number. Several more Negroes were killed by the arresting posse, and jails at Washington and Center Point were filled. Rumors of a Negro uprising and threats by the whites led to visits to the area by General Robert C. Newton and Governor James H. Berry. In the end the law was allowed to take its course.

Trouble in hill counties occasionally brought militia intervention. A bloody factional war in Scott County, in which Waldron was at one time seized by an

Livery stable and buggies in Nashville, Howard County, about 1888

212

armed band, caused Governor William R. Miller to send in the state guards twice. In 1881 the Quapaw Guards, a Little Rock militia company, spent three weeks in Perryville because of factional strife and murders in Perry County. Such use of the militia was unpopular in Arkansas because it reminded people of reconstruction, and Conservative governors usually confined themselves to sending arms and ammunition to county sheriffs.

The expansion of the railroads brought labor violence to Arkansas. In 1886 strikers on the St. Louis, Iron Mountain and Southern Railway threatened trouble at Texarkana, and Governor Simon P. Hughes called out the Gate City Guards there. The Pullman strike of 1894 led to threats and attempts by workers to stop trains, and again militia companies in Arkansas were mobilized. On both occasions there was more excitement than violence.

Hot Springs had occasional trouble over gambling. Rival gangs fought over control of gambling revenues, as in the "Flynn-Doran War" of 1878. In 1898 a gun battle on Central Avenue between city and county officers left five men dead and several wounded.

Aroused citizens who wanted an end to lawlessness joined such organizations as the Anti-Horse Thief Association, long active in parts of Missouri. Members of the Association organized "pursuing committees" to chase down thieves who stole horses or other property. The Arkansas division of the group began in 1906 and within a few years claimed 2,000 members in western and northwestern Arkansas.

Garland County jail in Hot Springs, 1878. Prisoners were taken up the steps and lowered into the interior by the ladder, after which the ladder was drawn up and the door closed. Food was passed to inmates through the small opening in the front wall

Cover of a printed copy of the constitution of the Anti-Horse Thief Association, 1906

The
Anti-Horse Thief
Association

Arkansas Constitution
1906

STUDY AIDS

Vocabulary

Be sure that you understand the meaning of the following words and phrases:

lingered	moonshiners
revenues	renegades
Five Civilized	gallows
Tribes	razorback hog
barrier	refuge
posse	version
Quapaw Guards	legacy

Identification

Tell what part each of the following had in the story:

Simon P. Hughes	William R. Miller
"Three Corners"	"Change the Name
region	of Arkansas?"
Three Years in	Anti-Horse Thief
Arkansas	Association
James H. Berry	Thomas W. Jackson
Pullman strike	Chickalah
Opie Read	

To test your reading

On other paper, list 1-10. Opposite each number write the word or words which complete each sentence.

1. Many people outside Arkansas came to believe that the entire state was ——.

2. The tide of white immigration moved around Arkansas into ——, —— and ——.

3. The Indian Territory became a refuge for ——.

4. In 1878 the —— gang held up a stage near ——.

5. Moonshiners were always a problem for ——.

6. Judge Isaac Parker presided at Fort Smith from —— to ——.

7. In twenty-one years Parker's court hanged —— criminals.

8. In 1893 —— robbed a bank in Bentonville.

9. The most outstanding Arkansas literary figure of the Conservative era was ——. He worked on newspapers at ——, —— and ——.

10. Governor William R. Miller sent state guards twice to —— County.

Things to do

1. Visit the restored Parker courtroom, jail and gallows in Fort Smith.

2. Try to find a book or pamphlet which contains "tall tales" or jokes about Arkansas. Make a report on its contents. Why do you think such books were written?

3. Consult books in your school or public library for more information about famous border outlaws such as Jesse and Frank James and Belle Starr. Do you think that television programs give a true picture of what these outlaws were really like? Arrange a debate or panel discussion on this question.

4. Visit Arkla Village, located at Emmet between Prescott and Hope.

8 Hints of Change

Change came to Arkansas slowly, but change did come. New inventions and new methods of entertainment brought change to the growing cities and towns. Signs of progress appeared in the fields of medicine, temperance and flood control. And in 1898 Arkansans fought in a foreign war for the first time since the War with Mexico fifty years before.

The changing cities. In the thirty-five years following the Civil War, life for most of the people of Arkansas was an uphill struggle. Poverty, low prices for farm products, poor transportation, lack of schools and other handicaps made it impossible for boys and girls growing up in that time to have the advantages that they deserved. There were few books to read and few people could secure a high school or college education. Everyone had to work hard to make a living. For most people life seemed to go on in the same way year after year.

In spite of the difficulties that confronted the people of the state, here and there the old ways of life were changing. Change was most evident in the cities. In Little Rock, which in 1890 was more than twice the size of any other Arkansas town, mule-drawn street cars appeared and were replaced by steam and electric trolleys. A weather bureau station was set up. Within the decade beginning in 1879 Little Rock saw its first telephones, a waterworks system, and electric street lights replacing hand-lighted gas lamps. Baseball and manufactured ice became a part of the Little Rock scene. The city grew westward and southward away from the river.

Hot Springs, long famous for its healing waters, emerged from its pioneer period. The Chicago capitalist "Diamond Joe" Reynolds built a railroad from Malvern in 1875, and the United States Supreme Court settled a long dispute over ownership of the springs in favor of the Federal government. After the fire of 1878 wiped out the old town, bathhouses, hotels, and stores sprang up. Congress established a hospital in Hot Springs for soldiers and sailors. Several other places in Arkansas where mineral springs happened to be located became popular resorts.

Amusements old and new. Amusements in rural Arkansas continued to be those enjoyed by the pioneers. Hunting, fishing, spelling-bees and debates at the schoolhouse, play-parties and quiltings at home occupied the spare time of the average Arkansan.

In Little Rock the Grand Opera House and the Capital Theater presented traveling companies of actors in plays and musical entertainments. The Hot Springs opera house opened in 1882, and Fort Smith had its own opera establishment five years later. Increasing numbers of minstrel shows and acting companies visited towns along

A group of tourists in Hot Springs, about 1895

railroads, and show boats stopped in river towns. Circuses, now often moving by rail rather than in wagons, pitched their "big top" tents in many Arkansas towns and villages. The state fairs included balloon ascensions and carnival entertainment as well as exhibitions of Arkansas products and resources.

Mardi Gras, a carnival holiday, was first officially celebrated in Little Rock in 1875 and in Pine Bluff seven years later. The holiday became so popular that it appeared even in smaller towns such as Jacksonport. Featuring street parades, masked balls, and merrymaking in general, Mardi Gras was observed in Little Rock until about 1900.

Social progress. The s t a t e government continued to support the schools

for the blind and deaf which had been established during reconstruction. A state insane asylum was opened in 1883. The Ex-Confederate Association persuaded the state government to set up a Confederate Home near Little Rock and begin paying pensions to disabled veterans and their widows.

Standards of public health and sanitation remained low. Public health work was largely confined to epidemics such as the yellow fever scare of 1878. For most people medical care meant taking patent medicines or old herbal remedies and hoping for the best. The death rate was high among children, infants and women in childbirth.

Some signs of progress appeared in the medical field. The medical school of Arkansas Industrial University held its first classes at Little Rock in 1879. Beginnings were made at regulating the practice of medicine, dentistry and pharmacy by setting up state boards of examiners. The Federal government established Fort Logan H. Roots Hospital on Big Rock in Pulaski County and small private hospitals opened in Little Rock and Fort Smith. The State Medical Society, already twenty years old in 1890, began publishing a monthly journal.

The temperance movement. Liquor circulated freely in pioneer Arkansas, and excessive drinking continued to be a problem for a long time. Saloons were located almost everywhere, and drinks were often sold to all purchasers regardless of their age. The temperance movement, which aimed at legal restriction or prohibition of liquor sales, began before the Civil War and continued afterward.

Beginning streetcar service in Little Rock, 1876

Organizations such as the Woman's Christian Temperance Union and some of the Protestant churches led the prohibition forces. A temperance play called **Ten Nights in a Bar Room** was presented before audiences in many places.

The temperance movement gained ground in Arkansas throughout the Conservative era. In 1874 a dealer was not allowed to sell liquor until he presented a petition signed by a majority of the voters in his township. The General Assembly in 1879 passed a local option law, which provided that no liquor license could be issued by a county court without the approval of a majority of voters in a general election. The Three Mile law of 1881 allowed voters to petition the county court that liquor sales be prohibited within three miles of a designated school or church.

Local option, the Three Mile law, and the numerous special prohibition acts

The old opera house in Hot Springs, from a photograph made in 1961

The "Cotton Palace Floating Theater," a showboat, welcomed by crowds at a river landing

218

"That the aged men be sober, grave, temperate."

THE TEMPERANCE VOICE.

"The voice of one crying in the wilderness."

| A TEMPERATE LIFE. | A HEALTHY BODY. | A HOLY SABBATH. |

L. A, CAMPBELL, EDITOR.   QUITMAN, ARKANSAS. APRIL' 1897.   VOL. 1. No 4.

Masthead of a temperance newspaper

passed at each legislative session were drying up the state at a rapid rate by the turn of the century. Under local option each county voted for or against legal sales of liquor at every general election. In 1894 forty-two of the seventy-five counties banned legal sales, and by 1900 dry areas under the Three Mile law covered a fifth of the state.

Progress in flood control. Floods were a frequent problem in the Arkansas lowlands, especially in the eastern counties along the Mississippi River. Major floods causing great losses in property and even lives occurred in 1882, 1883, 1884, 1886, 1890, 1893, and 1897.

For a long time Arkansas people had been aware of the need of a flood con-

Ladies of Arkansas City, Desha County, shopping in boats during the flood of 1882

Governor Dan W. Jones (center) with Arkansas officers during the Spanish-American War

Emergency hospital of the Second Arkansas Infantry Regiment at Anniston, Alabama during the Spanish-American War

trol system, and levees had been built before the Civil War and during the reconstruction p e r i o d. Some levee work was done in eastern Arkansas after 1879, when the Federal government began to provide assistance. In 1893 the General Assembly created the St. Francis Levee District and donated to it all the state lands within its boundaries except the sixteenth section school lands.

The huge new district took in all the area of the St. Francis River basin and subject to overflow by the Mississippi, a total of 1,500 square miles including much of eight counties. Work was soon under way to reclaim a million acres of the richest lands of Arkansas. Effective flood control was still a long way in the future, but Arkansas had finally begun to master the problem.

The Spanish-American War. When in 1898 the United States became involved in war with Spain, Arkansas was asked to provide 2,000 volunteers for the army. Two infantry regiments, the First and the Second, were mustered into service in Little Rock in May and moved to military camps in Georgia and Alabama. The war ended before either regiment got into the fighting, but the men suffered severely from diseases, bad food and poor sanitation. Arkansas men who served with other units saw action in Cuba, Puerto Rico, and the Philippines.

The war affected few Arkansans personally, but Arkansas people shared in the national outburst of patriotic feeling. The short struggle helped to end some of the bitterness between North and South which had lingered since the Civil War. Economically, the war with Spain raised prices and brought better times to many of the people of the state. In 1898 Arkansas stood on the brink of a new century and a new era of its history.

STUDY AIDS

Vocabulary

Be sure that you understand the meaning of the following words and phrases:

weather bureau
play parties
masked ball
asylum
trolley
pharmacy
herbal remedies
spelling-bee
quiltings

resort
minstrel shows
yellow fever
temperance
   movement
saloon
sanitation
carnival
local option law
prohibition acts

To test your reading

On other paper, list 1-7. Opposite each number write the word or words which complete each sentence.

1. The Hot Springs Opera House opened in the year ___.

2. Mardi Gras came to Little Rock in the year ___, and to Pine Bluff in the year ___. It was observed in Little Rock until about the year ___.

3. A state insane asylum was opened in the year ___.

4. A Confederate home was established near ___.

5. A local option law was enacted by the General Assembly in the year ___.

6. The three mile law of the year ___ allowed ___.

7. The St. Francis Levee District was created in the year ___. It took in a total of about ___ square miles.

Things to do

1. Find out if there are any veterans of the Spanish-American War still living in your community. Ask them to write or tell about their experiences.

2. Begin a collection of old pictures of people, places and events in your community and county. Try to identify the subject of each picture and determine when each picture was made.

3. Plan a visit to "Bathhouse Row" in Hot Springs.

4. Think of yourself as living in one of the larger Arkansas towns about 1890. Tell of your recreations and amusements.

5. Were there any popular resorts of this period, such as places where mineral springs were located, in your county? Investigate and report to the class.

Reviewing the Unit

1. How did the railroads affect immigration? Industrial growth?

2. What was the difference between the sharecrop system and the crop-lien system?

3. What was the real significance of the farmer-worker movement?

4. What is meant by "Conservatism" and what were some Conservative policies?

5. What were schools and churches usually like during the Conservative period?

6. Why did frontier conditions continue so long in parts of Arkansas?

7. In what ways were social conditions changing?

Unit Seven

Progressive Arkansas: Political and
Economic Change, 1898-1930

The Chapters

1. Politics and Reform

2. Farm Progress and Poverty

3. Industrial Growth: Lumber, Coal
   and Bauxite

4. Industrial Growth: New Sources
   of Power and Wealth

5. The Industrial Workers

SOON AFTER THE Spanish-American War the people of the United States embarked on a great crusade of reform. Many citizens became concerned about corrupt politics, control of government by big business, and social and economic injustices. Historians call the period from about 1900 to the First World War the "Progressive Era."

The national interest in reform extended to Arkansas. The Populists and other farmers' organizations had already pointed the way to many changes. Attempts were made to clean up elections, regulate trusts and railroads, and give the people a larger share in lawmaking. Women received the right to vote. Liquor and gambling came under determined attack. A new constitution was almost adopted.

During the Progressive years agriculture and industry were changing also. Farmers introduced new crops and began to learn better methods of farming. Bauxite and oil joined lumber and coal as leading Arkansas industries. Electric power lines began to connect Arkansas cities. The working class became more numerous and important. The state had entered a new and different century.

1 Politics and Reform

The Democratic party, which became the only effective party in Arkansas after 1896, moved in progressive directions for more than twenty years thereafter. The tide of reform affected moral as well as political issues, and women emerged as a major political force.

The Democrats in control. When the Negroes no longer could vote and the Populist party had died, Arkansas politics was left to the Democrats. The Democratic primaries became the real elections, for in the general elections the nominees of the Democratic party were nearly always elected. Leadership of the Republican party passed into the hands of a little group of business and professional people in Little Rock. Except in a few Ozark counties, Republican candidates were seldom a threat to the Democrats anywhere in the state.

Candidates for major offices built up temporary factions or groups of supporters within the Democratic party. Campaigns were usually waged on a personal basis, with each candidate attacking his opponent's record or background and trying to prove himself best qualified to hold the office. Since campaigns were expensive, elections were sometimes lost because a candidate could not get enough money. Candidates seldom disagreed on basic issues, and many people did not bother to vote.

The outcome of Democratic primaries in Arkansas depended mainly on influential people in the counties. Local leaders often decided which candidates they would support and then passed the word to their friends. In some counties groups of politicians formed "machines." Machine leaders decided how the county would vote in each primary and election. Leo P. McLaughlin, who became mayor of Hot Springs in 1927, headed one of the most powerful machines. In 1930 at least a dozen Arkansas counties were controlled by political machines.

Political leaders. Dan W. Jones, who was governor from 1897 to 1901, was the last of the former Confederate leaders to occupy that position. He was followed by Jeff Davis, who served three terms as governor and then became United States senator. Davis, a Russellville lawyer, was the only politician of the period who aroused a great factional division in the Democratic party. Using some of the same issues that had been raised by Wheelers and Populists, Davis won the support of many rural voters especially. He died in 1913, but his "Old Guard" faction was active in state politics for another twenty years.

George W. Donaghey, governor from 1909 to 1913, was one of the most able and progressive of later chief executives during the period. Joseph T. Robinson, who became United States senator in 1913, served as Democratic leader in the Senate and in 1928 was the Demo-

A political rally at Harrison, Boone County, 1910. The speaker is William Jennings Bryan, who toured the state with Governor George W. Donaghey on behalf of the proposed initiative and referendum amendment to the Arkansas constitution

cratic candidate for vice-president. William F. McCombs, a native of Arkansas, managed Woodrow Wilson's successful campaign for the presidency in 1912. Arkansas in 1917 and 1921 placed statues of Uriah M. Rose, a Little Rock lawyer, and James P. Clarke, a former governor and United States senator, in the Capitol at Washington, D. C.

Electoral reforms. The Democratic primary had replaced the convention method of making nominations practically everywhere by 1910. Many people regarded the primary system as a step toward better government. With the primary, voters could choose their party candidates directly instead of entrusting the task to convention delegates. Beginning in 1913 a number of laws were passed which attempted to prevent dishonest practices in primaries and general elections.

Until the adoption of the Seventeenth Amendment to the Federal Constitution in 1913, United States senators were elected by state legislatures. As early as 1903 the Arkansas General Assembly went on record as favoring the election of senators by the people. The General Assembly of 1913 ratified the proposed Seventeenth Amendment.

Since 1874 state elections had been held earlier than national elections. The Democrats had been afraid that holding both elections on the same date might lead to heavy Negro voting and Federal interference. In 1915 the General Assembly provided that state elections should be held on the same date as national elections, the Tuesday following the first Monday in

November. Opposition developed in the counties with large Negro populations, and in 1921 the two elections were separated again. An initiated act of 1926 again combined the two on the November date.

Controlling the trusts. Long before 1900, many American business firms became large and powerful. Large business corporations made agreements with one another to control prices and competition. The Populists and other minor parties had opposed the "trusts," as these price-fixing combinations were called, and advocated that trusts be regulated by the government in the interest of the people.

Arkansas was not an industrial state, but trust practices ruled the insurance and cottonseed businesses. In 1897 the

Jeff Davis

Jeff Davis (center, left of tree) opening his first campaign
for governor at Center Point, Howard County, 1900

Interior of a railroad dining car, 1910

General Assembly passed a mild anti-trust law. When it proved ineffective the General Assembly of 1899 enacted the Rector Antitrust Act, which prohibited all trusts and conspiracies to control prices.

The Rector law provoked a legal battle. Attorney-General Jeff Davis began prosecutions at once and tried to drive all trusts from the state. When he was stopped by the Arkansas Supreme Court, Davis ran for governor on an antitrust platform in 1900 and was elected.

The General Assembly of 1905 passed a new antitrust law which the courts upheld. More than two-thirds of the fire insurance companies doing business in Arkansas promptly withdrew from the state. They were soon back after the law was amended in 1907.

Little more was said about antitrust legislation, but the state extended its regulation of business and finance. In 1913 a state bank department was created. The first of a series of "blue sky" laws, intended to protect investors against fraudulent stock and bonds, was passed the same year. Regulation of insurance companies was placed under a separate commissioner in 1917, and two years later a commission was created to regulate public utilities such as electric, telephone, water and gas companies.

Regulating the railroads. To a great extent the economy of Arkansas depended on the railroads. The farmers' parties of the period 1880-1896 had criticized some of the practices of the railroad companies. By 1896 many people were demanding that the state regulate the railroads so they could not charge unfair rates. At the same time businesses wanted to encourage the railway companies to build more lines, and the railroads were very influential in state politics.

In 1897 Governor Dan W. Jones recommended the establishment of a state railroad commission. The General Assembly authorized the state government to build and operate its own railroad and telegraph lines, but this measure was repealed four years later. In 1898 the voters provided for a state railroad commission, and the new agency began its work the following year.

The railroad commission found that railway companies had been managing the commerce of Arkansas by charging different freight rates in different places. Supported by the General Assembly, the commission forced rate reduction and other adjustments by the railroads.

Lawmaking by the people. Many Arkansas citizens believed that the General Assembly was too greatly influenced by the railroads and other special interests. They thought that the legislators stayed in session too long, spent too much money, and wasted too much time passing minor legislation. One proposed remedy was to allow the voters themselves to help make the laws.

In 1896 the Populists advocated the initiative and referendum plans. Under the initiative, voters could file petitions to have new laws or constitutional amendments placed on the general election ballot. Under the referendum, voters could petition to have laws already passed by the General Assembly referred to the people for approval or rejection.

The initiative and referendum were added to the state constitution in 1910,

Governor George W. Donaghey (rear seat, left) and William Jennings Bryan (rear seat, right) at Camden in 1910. On the front seat with the driver is George W. Hays, governor from 1913 to 1917

A moonshine still in operation

but the results disappointed supporters of the plans. The new measures caused legal confusion and a number of lawsuits. General Assemblies began calling some bills "emergency" measures in order to get around the referendum. Many voters did not bother to find out anything about laws they were being asked to approve. On the other hand, some people believed that the initiative and referendum helped make the General Assembly more careful in its lawmaking. In 1926 an initiated amendment to the constitution prohibited the passage of local or special legislation by the General Assembly.

Statewide prohibition. The campaign to stop the sale of liquor in Arkansas, which had been gaining ground for many years, scored a statewide victory in 1915. The Newberry law, which became effective on the first day of 1916, made Arkansas legally dry.

Local option had already closed saloons in all but nine counties. The General Assembly had steadily restricted the liquor business by passing special laws, but local option and special legislation could not make prohibition effective as long as some townships and counties remained "wet". It was too easy to bring liquor from wet areas into dry ones.

The final drive for statewide prohibition was led by the Anti-Saloon League, the Woman's Christian Temperance Union, and some of the churches. The Newberry act was followed by the passage in 1917 of a "bone-dry" law which was intended to banish liquor from the state completely. In 1919 the Eighteenth Amendment to the United States Constitution made prohibition the law all over the country.

Prohibition proved very hard to enforce. Many people believed that such laws were unjust. The illegal manufacture and sale of liquor became a major problem for law enforcement officers. By 1930 many Arkansas citizens who had favored prohibition were convinced that the attempt to outlaw liquor was a failure.

The reform attack on gambling. Hot Springs, long famous as a health resort, became noted also for horse racing and illegal gambling. Racing had been popular in Arkansas long before the Civil War, and races were held in Hot Springs as early as 1894. In 1905 Oaklawn track began operation, but the General Assembly of 1907 made betting on horse races illegal.

Disastrous fires in 1905 and 1913 destroyed much of the town of Hot Springs, and business losses brought an attempt to revive racing. In 1915 the General Assembly passed a bill legal-

Governor Charles H. Brough (center, wearing white suit) with woman suffrage delegation on the steps of the new state capitol

izing race track gambling. Governor George W. Hays vetoed the measure, but races were held anyway until 1919.

Hot Springs reformers launched an attack on illegal gambling beginning about 1898. The Citizens Improvement Union, the reform group, won partial control in 1910 but lost again two years later. In 1914 the reformers were victorious and the big gambling operators were out of business within a year. They returned after Leo P. McLaughlin became mayor of Hot Springs in 1927, and the reform movement disappeared.

Woman suffrage. The movement to give Arkansas women the right to vote began as early as 1884, but not until 1911 did the question come up for debate in the General Assembly. During the next few years the advocates of woman suffrage waged a major campaign. Women's organizations held conventions, distributed literature, sponsored exhibits at fairs, and did their best to win the support of public officials for their cause.

The debate over woman suffrage was heated and sometimes bitter, but the women won their fight when the General Assembly of 1917 gave them the right to vote in Democratic primaries. Some 40,000 Arkansas women voted in 1918. The next year the General Assembly approved an amendment to the state constitution granting full voting rights to women. The amendment was passed by the voters in 1920, but because of a legal problem it was not declared in force for another six years. The Nineteenth Amendment to the United States Constitution gave women the right to vote nationally for the first time in 1920.

Defeat of the new constitution. Widespread talk about the need for a new state constitution had arisen several times since 1874 and in 1917 a convention was chosen to write one. Completed in 1918, the new constitution provided for the initiative and referendum, woman suffrage, statewide prohibition, banned local legislation by the General Assembly, and limited state officials to one four-year term.

Governor Charles H. Brough supported the new constitution, which was submitted to the voters in a special election on December 14, 1918. Much to the surprise of its advocates, the constitution was turned down by 39,000 votes to 24,000. Actually the question attracted little popular interest, even in the cities. The weather on election day was so bad that many precincts did not open. Some voters opposed the entire constitution because they disliked one or more of its parts. The defeat of the Constitution of 1918 proved to be no great loss to the state, for many of its provisions were later enacted into law.

STUDY AIDS

Vocabulary

Be sure that you understand the meaning of the following words and phrases:

professional people

trusts

blue sky laws

bone-dry law

public utilities

initiative and referendum

woman suffrage

Progressive Era

Old Guard

Identification

Tell what part each of the following had in the story:

Rector Antitrust Act

State Railroad Commission

Anti-Saloon League

Oaklawn track

Charles H. Brough

George W. Donaghey

Jeff Davis

William F. McCombs

George W. Hays

Leo P. McLaughlin

Joseph T. Robinson

Dan W. Jones

To test your reading

On other paper, list 1-10. Opposite each number write the word or words which complete each sentence.

1. In 1930 at least a dozen Arkansas counties were controlled by ___.
2. The last of the Confederate leaders to be governor was ___. He was followed by ___.
3. Two Arkansans whose statues are in the United States Capitol are ___ and ___.
4. After 1913 United States senators were elected by ___.
5. In 1900 Jeff Davis was elected governor on an ___ platform.
6. By 1896 many people were demanding that the state regulate the railroads so they could not ___.
7. The initiative and referendum were added to the constitution in the year ___.
8. The Newberry law which became effective on January 1, 1916 made Arkansas ___.
9. In 1917 the General Assembly gave women the right to vote in ___.
10. A proposed new state constitution was rejected in the year ___ by a vote of ___ to ___.

Things to do

1. Make an oral report using information from other books on a topic that interested you in the chapter.
2. Read Amendments 16, 17, 18 and 19 to the Constitution of the United States. How did each of these amendments affect Arkansas and its people?
3. Investigate and make a report on the Arkansas state flag, adopted in 1913. What was the flag design intended to mean?
4. Select a committee to interview older people in the community and find out what they remember about one or more of the following subjects:
   (a) Jeff Davis as governor and public speaker.
   (b) Law enforcement problems during prohibition times.
   (c) The woman suffrage movement; arguments for and against woman suffrage.
5. How is an initiated act or constitutional amendment placed on the ballot? How does the referendum operate?

2 Farm Progress and Poverty

Arkansas farmers enjoyed rising prices and better times until 1920, when the great war boom ended in disaster. During the 1920s many independent farmers slipped into tenancy. But during the Progressive period fruit and grain crops increased in importance, and multitudes of farmers were introduced to better agricultural methods.

The importance of cotton. In 1900 more than ninety per cent of the people of Arkansas lived on farms or in small towns. Though cities grew larger, almost eighty per cent of the population was still rural in 1930. Anything that happened to Arkansas agriculture affected almost everybody in the state.

Cotton production continued to increase. Early in the new century the lumber companies cleared away the great forests of northeastern Arkansas and opened vast areas of rich land. Cotton acreage in Arkansas grew from about 1,650,000 in 1899 to almost 3,450,000 acres in 1929. Over half the total crop acreage of the state was in cotton in 1930, and cotton occupied seventy to eighty per cent of the crop land in the southern and eastern lowlands. Arkansas ranked near the top among the states as a cotton producer.

The number of farms in Arkansas increased between 1900 and 1930, and farms became smaller in size. On the larger farms and orchards tractors and other machinery began to appear, but the use of mules and human labor was still the rule.

The coming of better times. The years 1890-99, sometimes called the "Gay Nineties," were not gay years for the cotton grower. The depression of 1894 plunged cotton prices to an average of less than five cents a pound. Near the end of the decade things took a turn for the better. American and foreign cloth mills were expanding and demanding more cotton. American industry began to use more cottonseed products such as oil, meal, and hulls. Cotton prices rose to eight and even ten cents a pound.

With better times appeared a new source of trouble, the boll weevil. This insect, which eats the developing seed of cotton, spread from Mexico into Texas and was damaging the Arkansas crop before 1910. The worst weevil season came in 1921.

Boom and collapse. When the First World War began in Europe in 1914 cotton prices improved, and after the United States entered the conflict they rose sharply. The government urged farmers to produce more food and fiber for the war effort, and with cotton selling for thirty-five and forty cents a

Picking cotton on an Arkansas plantation

"Weighing up" during cotton picking season

234

pound they responded quickly. Farmers bought more land at high prices, placed worn-out land back in production, and borrowed money to increase output. The year 1919 saw the crest of the boom, with good crops and prices. Many farmers hoarded their cotton and waited for prices to go even higher. Speculators bought cotton on credit, expecting to sell at a profit in a few months.

The bubble burst in 1920 and brought ruin to many farmers, businessmen, and cotton buyers. In a few months the price of cotton dropped from thirty-five to sixteen cents a pound, and kept going down. Wartime demand had encouraged cotton growing in foreign countries, and now American cotton had to compete with the foreign product in world markets. The Arkansas farmer awoke from his dream of permanent prosperity to find his land overplanted and his credit overextended.

The return of hard times to agriculture hurt small-town businesses and banks. Fifty-two Arkansas banks failed in the period 1926-29, almost twice as many as had closed during the preceding five years. For many people the great depression which began in 1929, with its bank failures and farm poverty, was no more than a worsening of trends under way since 1920.

Farm tenancy. In 1920 more than half the farmers of Arkansas were tenants, who cultivated land which belonged to someone else. During the next ten years tenancy increased. Farmers mortgaged their property to get money and then lost it to banks, corporations, insurance companies, and professional men. By 1930 sixty-three per cent of Arkansas farmers had slipped into tenancy. In the plantation counties of the east, eight or nine out of every ten farmers were tenants.

Moving time for a tenant family

235

Tractors and cultivating equipment in the Highland orchard, Pike County

Three out of five families lived in mortgaged homes or were at the mercy of landlords. The greatest tenancy increase during the twenties was among white farmers, since most Negroes were tenants already.

There were several kinds of farm tenancy. Renters paid cash or produce for the use of the land. Share tenants provided their own labor, work mules, and equipment and received at least half the crop. Croppers exchanged their labor for a smaller share of the crop. Wage hands worked by the day, month or year for cash, living quarters, and sometimes board. In 1930 almost a third of Arkansas farmers were croppers.

Tenancy usually meant poor food and housing, disease, and a low standard of living. Since the landlord kept the records, a tenant might be cheated and be able to do nothing but move to another plantation. If the tenant were in debt it might not even be possible for him to move. Many landlords were also in debt, which made the position of the tenant more uncertain. Frequent moves by tenant families interrupted the education of their children, and tenants ordinarily had little interest in improving the land or the community.

Fruits and grains. Apples were shipped by the carload from Benton County as early as 1887. By 1900 the northwestern highlands, where no cotton could be grown, were checkered with orchards. The industry reached its peak in 1919, when the harvest totaled 7,000,000 bushels. Beginning in 1921 drouth, parasites and falling prices caused a rapid decline in production and acreage. Soon most of the great orchards were gone.

Grinding sorghum cane for syrup

Harvesting rice near Stuttgart, Arkansas County

Peaches did well in Johnson County and in parts of the southwest. Bert Johnson developed a huge orchard near Highland in Pike County. Including some 4,500 acres in 1928, the Highland orchard was known for several years as the largest peach orchard in the world.

In White County strawberry acreage increased after 1920 as growers sought a substitute for cotton. Grape production at Tontitown and Altus increased after the coming of prohibition. Hope watermelons became famous for their size and quality. In many parts of Arkansas mule-powered mills made syrup of good quality from sorghum cane.

The cotton farmer grew some corn for his mules and hogs, and in 1929 a fourth of the crop land was planted to corn. Cattle raising was not yet very important, though the average farmer kept a cow or two to provide his family with milk and butter.

Rice. In 1904 William H. Fuller, who learned rice culture in Louisiana, raised his first successful rice crop near Hazen. The Grand Prairie region proved to be ideal rice country. Rice mills appeared in Stuttgart and Lonoke, and acreage jumped from 27,000 in 1909 to 143,000 ten years later. German-American farmers migrated from Illinois and Iowa to help develop the new crop.

Like the cotton farmer, the rice producer profited during wartime and suffered when the postwar slump began. Rice sold for three dollars a bushel in 1919, compared with only one dollar six years before. When hard times came again the rice farmers organized a cooperative marketing association to deal with the milling companies. In 1929 rice ranked fourth in value as an Arkansas crop, exceeded only by cotton, corn and hay.

New farmers' organizations. The old farm organizations such as the Grange and Alliance had disappeared from Ar-

Office of J. B. Paine, secretary-treasurer of the Arkansas Farmers' Union, at Jonesboro in 1910

First District Agricultural School, Jonesboro, 1912

kansas by 1900. The new organizations which took their place were different in many respects. While some of the old groups had fought business and industry, the new organizations tried to secure business cooperation in the struggle for farm prosperity.

The Farmers' Union, which began in Texas, grew rapidly in Arkansas after 1903. Arkansas representatives helped organize the National Farmers' Union in 1905, and Arkansas became one of the strongest Farmers' Union states. At the state convention of the Farmers' Union in Little Rock in 1908, 250 delegates represented over 75,000 members living in all but two counties.

The union worked hard but with little success to raise cotton prices. Farmers were urged to plow up some of their cotton in order to create a scarcity, and to hold their ginned cotton for higher prices. In 1908 between four and eight per cent of the cotton acreage in the state was plowed under. The union established cooperative stores and in 1908 had eighty-eight cotton warehouses in Arkansas.

The Farmers' Union campaigned for agricultural education by the state. In 1905 a college of agriculture was set up at the University of Arkansas, and in 1909 the General Assembly established four district agricultural high schools. Located at Jonesboro, Russellville, Magnolia and Monticello, these schools became junior colleges in 1925. The influence of the Farmers' Union declined when the First World War brought prosperity to agriculture.

The Arkansas Farm Bureau Federation, which appeared soon after the end of the war, grew out of the educational work of the county agents. The new federation hoped to equalize agriculture and business, and its program contained no radical proposals. The Farm Bureau represented the better educated, commercial farmers rather than the small farmers and tenants.

Home canned vegetables and fruit, Newton County

Toward better farming. The Grangers, Wheelers and others had tried to teach farm families to grow food crops and use better farming methods. The fight against the boll weevil led to the beginning of farm demonstration work, and in 1912 there were thirty-six county agents. Farm boys and girls were enlisted in 4-H Clubs, and home demonstration agents worked with farm women.

Beginning in 1914 the Arkansas Profitable Farming Bureau, sponsored by the Little Rock Board of Commerce, enlisted the aid of business in the struggle to improve agriculture. The bureau conducted annual "Profitable Farming Campaigns," and sent speakers into rural areas to urge farmers to raise their food and feed at home. Newspapers, railroads, banks and chambers of commerce joined in the

attack on the one-crop cotton economy.

Encouraged by the Profitable Farming Bureau, the General Assembly of 1915 agreed that Arkansas would cooperate with the United States Department of Agriculture in agricultural extension work. By 1917 Arkansas led all the states except Texas in the number of farm demonstration agents. Aided by Federal funds, the state provided for the teaching of agriculture and home economics in high schools. A state plant board began working to eliminate insect pests and crop diseases. County agricultural fairs were held every fall.

Though much progress was made, most farmers continued to rely on cotton for cash income. Extension workers found that some farmers resented efforts to teach them better farming. In some parts of the state the campaign to stamp out cattle ticks failed because farmers dynamited dipping vats and ran government agents out of communities.

An old-fashioned country kitchen at Nail, Newton County. Wood stoves instead of fireplaces were used for cooking in most Arkansas homes by 1900 or earlier

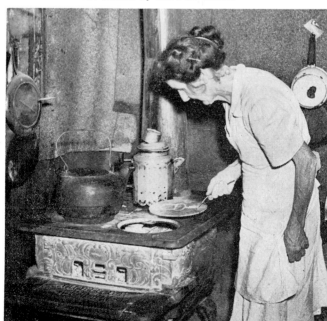

STUDY AIDS

Vocabulary

Be sure that you understand the meaning of the following words and phrases:

hoarded	output
croppers	cooperative
parasites	marketing
extension workers	fiber
dipping vat	corporation
overplanted	chamber of
4-H Clubs	commerce

Identification

Tell what part each of the following had in the story:

Bert Johnson	Profitable Farm-
Farmers' Union	ing Campaigns
district agricul-	Farm Bureau
tural schools	

To test your reading

On other paper, list 1-10. Opposite each number write the word or words which complete each sentence.

1. In 1900 more than __ per cent of the people of Arkansas lived on __ or in __.

2. The years 1890-99, sometimes called the __ were not gay years for the __.

3. With better times for the cotton farmer appeared a new source of trouble, the __.

4. When the First World War began in Europe in __ cotton prices __.

5. In 1920 more than half the farmers in Arkansas were __; in 1930 almost a third were __.

6. Apples were shipped by the __ from __ County as early as the year __. In 1919 the apple harvest totaled __ bushels.

7. In 1904 __ raised his first successful rice crop near __. In 1919 rice sold for __ dollars a bushel. In 1929 it ranked __ in value as an Arkansas crop.

8. The Farmers' Union grew rapidly in Arkansas after the year __.

9. The fight against the __ led to the beginning of __, and in 1912 there were __ agents.

10. By 1917 Arkansas led all the states except __ in the number of farm __.

Things to do

1. Investigate the work of the Farm Bureau and the Farmers' Union, if either organization is active in your community. Perhaps a representative of one of these organizations will tell the class about his work on behalf of the farming people.

2. See if you can locate an old-fashioned sorghum mill which is still in operation. Take some pictures of the mill and show them to the class.

3. Interview your county agent and home demonstration agent to find out what they do to help farm families in your community.

4. Arrange a tour of the Grand Prairie rice-growing region. Include a visit to a rice mill.

3   Industrial Growth: Lumber, Coal and Bauxite

Industrial growth was slow in Arkansas, for several reasons. But Arkansas was rich in forests and minerals, and during the years 1898-1930 bauxite mining joined lumber and coal to become one of the most important of the state's industries.

The slow growth of industry. Industry developed slowly in Arkansas. The state was located a long way from the great cities which provided markets. Railroads charged higher freight rates in Arkansas and the South than in other sections. Arkansas had a poor reputation in Northern financial circles, partly because the state had repudiated a large part of its debt in 1884. Northern capitalists hesitated to invest their money in Arkansas, and interest rates were high.

Such capital as was invested in Arkansas went mostly into industries such as lumber, oil, and bauxite. Products of Arkansas soil and woodlands were shipped out of the state to be processed or manufactured elsewhere. Costs went up and cutbacks were made as the best supplies of timber and crude oil were exhausted.

Arkansas was too poor to provide a good market for its own products. In the prosperous year of 1919 the average income per person in Arkansas was $379, as compared to $627 in the United States as a whole. Arkansas labor was plentiful and cheap, but most workers were unskilled. Corporations hesitated to build plants in Arkansas because of the poor school system, but Arkansas could not do much to improve its school system until such plants brought wealth into the state.

The business class. Arkansas leaders favored industrial growth, and the state tried to encourage business and industry. The Bureau of Mines, Manufactures and Agriculture held meetings and published literature. A constitutional amendment of 1926 exempted new textile mills from taxation. Chambers of commerce and new businessmen's clubs such as Rotary, Kiwanis and Lions worked for industrial progress.

Arkansas business and industry shared the national trend toward concentration. Corporations replaced smaller businesses. Chain stores pushed out the local merchants, newspaper chains swallowed up the local papers, and big power companies absorbed the smaller ones.

Most Arkansas industry was owned by Northerners. Arkansas businessmen were managers of branch plants, branch banks, chain stores, captive mines, and local outlets for national firms. Their job was to handle labor, keep the politicians friendly, and insure good public relations for their companies.

Interior of a sawmill at Kearney, Jefferson County, 1909

The vanishing forests. In 1898 forests of pine, cypress and hardwood covered more than three fourths of Arkansas. Lumbering was already under way, and for another decade production continued to rise. Logs were hauled out of the woods on railroad cars and floated down rivers to sawmills. Until 1919 or later the lumber and timber products industry employed sixty per cent of all Arkansas wage earners.

Larger towns like Little Rock and Pine Bluff, as well as dozens of smaller places, depended on lumber for much of their income and trade. Planing mills turned out doors, sashes, and blinds. Fort Smith factories made furniture, carriages, and wagons. Arkansas lumber went into railroad crossties, roofing shingles, packing crates, boxes, barrel staves, and fence posts.

In 1909, Arkansas ranked fifth in the nation in lumber production. After 1909 production declined, for the best timber had been cut and costs were increasing. Large timber companies such as Crossett, Dierks, and Long Bell built larger mills and installed better machinery. Lumber prices rose, and the sawmills began to use cheaper hardwood timber in addition to pine.

By 1925 the lumber industry was in trouble. Production was only half what it had been in 1909, and timber was being cut four times faster than it was being replaced. Cutover land eroded or grew up in brush thickets. The virgin timber stands were gone. Sawmills closed down and sawmill towns became deserted. Railroad track in Arkansas dropped from a total of 5,306 miles in 1910 to 4,826 miles in 1930 as logging lines were abandoned.

Three trainloads of Arkansas coal starting from Fort Smith to St. Louis

Forest conservation begins. Timber conservation began in Arkansas in 1907 when President Theodore Roosevelt set aside the Arkansas National Forest, later called the Ouachita National Forest, as a Federal reserve. The Ozark National Forest was added the next year. Lumber interests persuaded the General Assembly of 1911 to pass resolutions calling for the abolition of the forest reserves, but in 1917 a state law made possible the enlargement of the national forests.

After 1925 the lumber companies began to turn to conservation. Large tracts of forest land were cut over systematically so that new trees could replace those taken out. Fire protection methods were improved. In 1928 a mill near Camden began producing kraft paper and paper bags. Such mills could use timber once considered almost worthless.

The decline of coal. From 1880 until 1920 coal ranked first in value among Arkansas mineral products. Great coal reserves existed in western Arkansas, especially in Sebastian County. But the coal industry was "sick" and the general trend was downward. In 1925 less than half as much coal was mined as in the peak year of 1907.

The chief trouble was that Arkansas was too far from Northern industrial markets which used coal, and transportation costs were high. Local markets for coal were limited, especially after electricity began to be produced from water power. The price of coal remained low, except briefly about 1920. Arkansas coal deposits were thin, seamed, broken, and deeply buried, all of which made mining expensive. After 1922 oil replaced coal as the state's most valuable mineral product.

The gray earth. Bauxite, the whitish-gray ore used to make aluminum was discovered in Arkansas in 1887 by State Geologist John C. Branner. The gray earth was then being used to surface a new road near Fourche Bayou southeast of Little Rock. Large deposits were later discovered in Saline County.

Mining began in 1899 and Arkansas soon led all other states in production.

244

In 1925 the state produced ninety-four per cent of American bauxite, and total output down to 1926 was over five million tons. Most of the best ore had been mined before the First World War, when the needs of the aircraft industry increased bauxite mining to a peak.

Aluminum Company of America ("Alcoa"), a Pennsylvania corporation, owned most of the bauxite reserves. Bauxite was usually mined by the open-pit and strip methods, and the steam shovels turned great areas of Pulaski and Saline counties into ugly wastelands. Since the power supply was uncertain, Alcoa shipped the ore out of Arkansas to be processed. Except for the laborers who dug and loaded bauxite, the aluminum companies employed few people in the state.

Early bauxite mining, Saline County (above). Below, bauxite mining in the same county in 1965

STUDY AIDS

Vocabulary

Be sure that you understand the meaning of the following words and phrases:

bauxite	concentration
planing mill	kraft paper
eroded	conservation
textile mills	open pit method
virgin timber	captive mines
stands	public relations
chain stores	barrel staves
cutbacks	seamed

Identification

Tell what part each of the following had in the story:

Alcoa   Theodore Roosevelt
Fourche Bayou

To test your reading

On other paper, list 1-9. Opposite each number write the word or words which complete each sentence.

1. A constitutional amendment of __ exempted new __ from taxation.

2. In 1919 the average income in Arkansas was __ as compared to __ in the United States as a whole.

3. In 1898 forests of __, __ and __ covered more than __ of Arkansas.

4. In 1909 Arkansas ranked __ in the nation in __.

5. Railroad track in Arkansas dropped from a total of __ miles in __ to __ miles in __ as logging lines were abandoned.

6. From __ to __ coal ranked first in value among Arkansas __.

7. After __ oil replaced coal as the state's most valuable __.

8. Bauxite was discovered in Arkansas in __ by State Geologist __.

9. In 1925 the state produced __ per cent of American bauxite.

Things to do

1. Determine what civic clubs, such as Rotary, Kiwanis and Lions, are active in your community. Contact officials of each club and find out what their organizations are doing to benefit the community and state.

2. Choose a committee to investigate the activities of your local chamber of commerce and report to the class.

3. If land in your area is owned by a large lumber company, find out what the company is doing to conserve the timber supply. Perhaps you can arrange a class visit to a lumber mill.

4. List as many products made from aluminum as you can.

5. If you live near the headquarters of a national forest, find out all you can about its management and operation.

4 Industrial Growth: New Sources of Power and Wealth

Industrial growth proceeded more rapidly as natural gas and electric power became widely available. The discovery of diamonds in Arkansas attracted wide attention. New industrial operations increased in number during and after the First World War.

Natural gas and electricity. Since industrial machinery requires an abundance of cheap power, Arkansas industries could not grow much until natural gas and electricity became available. Soon after 1900 a gas field was developed in the Fort Smith area. In 1911 a gas transmission line was built from northern Louisiana to Little Rock, and in 1927 it was extended to Conway and Clarksville. Other lines were built across the eastern part of the state in 1928. The discovery of natural gas near El Dorado in 1920 opened the south Arkansas field, and gas deposits near Clarksville were first tapped in 1925.

In 1912 fewer than fifty communities in the state had electric light plants, and only a few miles of power lines connected Arkansas towns. The following year Harvey C. Couch organized the Arkansas Power Company and acquired electric systems in Arkadelphia, Malvern, Magnolia, and Camden. Loans from New York bankers made possible the expansion of Couch's firm into the rice fields of Grand Prairie and other parts of Arkansas.

The First World War and the discovery of oil in south Arkansas increased the need for electricity. In 1924

Remmel Dam on the Ouachita River made hydroelectric power available in Arkansas. Harvey Couch knew that the prosperity of his power firm, which in 1926 became Arkansas Power and Light Company, depended on expanded use of electricity. He and his associates brought parties of Eastern investors to Arkansas in a campaign for new industry and low-interest loans. In 1929 construction began at Carpenter Dam on the Ouachita, and three years later the new installation began producing power.

By 1930 Arkansas Power and Light Company had grown into one of the most important businesses in the state. The Couch interests swallowed up smaller concerns and purchased water companies, ice plants, transportation firms, and other business. A network of transmission lines was built throughout the state. In the six years before 1931, full-time electric service reached 180 communities for the first time.

Black gold. For years some Arkansas people dreamed of finding buried treasure or of "striking it rich" by discovering gold or silver in the hills. In 1885-88 there was a gold and silver

Harvey C. Couch

"silver," changed its name to North Little Rock.

The real Arkansas gold which produced millionaires was "black gold," as petroleum was sometimes called. Oil reserves had long been known to exist in Arkansas, and in 1920 the Hunter Oil Company brought in a small well near Stephens, in Ouachita County. The big strike came on January 10, 1921, when a well near El Dorado blew in a "gusher." Within a few days over 5,000 people poured into El Dorado, and wooden oil derricks began to rise everywhere as new wells were drilled.

The Smackover oil field became the greatest in Arkansas after a new discovery there in 1922. The population of Smackover increased swiftly from about a hundred to more than 10,000. Besides crude oil, many wells produced natural gas, and some of them a kind of natural gas from which gasoline could be made.

In the rush to get the oil vast quantities were wasted, and the boom was quickly over. The El Dorado field began to decline after its first year in

boom in the Ouachita Mountains. A town called Golden City appeared in Logan County and prospectors were everywhere, but the so-called "strikes" amounted to nothing. The town of Argenta, named for the Latin word for

Remmel Dam on the Ouachita River, Hot Spring County

production. The Smackover field reached its peak in 1925, when Arkansas wells produced 77,398,000 barrels of oil. By 1930 production had dropped sharply, but oil had become a permanent part of the economy of south Arkansas. Prospecting continued, and new oil reserves were discovered in a zone reaching from Union County to the Texas border. Severance taxes paid by oil companies helped the state government, and towns like El Dorado and Smackover settled down to a period of solid growth.

Diamonds. In 1906 Arkansas suddenly became famous as the only place in North America where diamonds could be found in the rock where they were formed. John M. Huddleston, a Pike County farmer, discovered the first diamonds near the mouth of Prairie Creek not far from Murfreesboro. Diamond experts from New York and elsewhere praised the quality of the stones.

Several different companies tried to work the mines, but profits were small. At one time Henry Ford wanted to buy and develop the entire field, but the deal fell through. After years of inactivity, in 1952 the diamond area reopened as a tourist attraction.

The diversity of Arkansas industry. Timber, oil, bauxite and coal were the big industries, but other operations were numerous. Arkansas was so rich in natural resources that some boosters were fond of saying that the state could survive even if she were walled off from the rest of the world.

Cottonseed oil mills, railroad repair shops, printing establishments, bakeries, and ice plants employed many workers. Flour and grist milling declined, but rice milling increased in im-

Oil well in the pine woods of southern Arkansas

portance. Vinegar was a by-product of the apple district, and canneries processed vegetables and fruits.

Several industries prospered especially during the First World War. Zinc, lead and manganese mines in north central Arkansas began production. The output of some saddle and harness firms went to the cavalry. The Federal government spent a million dollars on a picric acid plant and an aviation warehouse at Little Rock, but the war ended before either was finished.

Soon after the war the Curtis and Climber automobile companies made brief attempts to produce cars in Little Rock. In 1928 an airplane plant opened there. During the ten years after the war the men's clothing industry more than doubled in importance. A few cotton textile mills and glass factories were established.

Production of pottery, brick and tile from Arkansas clays became more important after 1921. Sixteen firms were bottling and selling mineral water in 1927. Sand and gravel were quarried from hills and dredged up from river bottoms.

Quartz crystals from Garland and Montgomery counties were cut into "Hot Springs diamonds" as well as used in new optical and electrical equipment. Beginning in 1921 a plant at Guion, Izard County, produced glass sand. Batesville marble went into the new state capitol and other public buildings over the nation. Novaculite from Garland County was mined for whetstones.

Limestone production in northern Arkansas was at its peak in 1930. A year earlier a new plant in the southwest began making portland cement. On White River, mussels were searched for pearls and the shells then used for buttons. Occasional attempts were made to exploit resources such as anti-

Advertisement for the Climber automobile

mony, tripoli, phosphate rock, slate, fuller's earth, and a granite-like rock called nephelite syenite.

STUDY AIDS

Vocabulary

Be sure that you understand the meaning of the following words and phrases:

quarried
available
hydroelectric
transmission lines
severance tax
installation
mussels

mineral water
dredged
tapped
gusher
oil derricks
tourist attraction
picric acid
optical

Location

On a map find the following places:

El Dorado
Smackover
Guion
Conway
Camden

Stephens
Clarksville
Murfreesboro
Malvern
Arkadelphia

To test your reading

On other paper, list 1-8. Opposite each number write the word or words which complete each sentence.

1. The discovery of gas near __ in 1920 opened the __ field.

2. In 1913 __ organized the __ Company. In 1926 it became the __.

3. The first oil well in Arkansas was brought in by the __ Company near __ in the year __.

4. The big strike came on __ 1921 when a well near __ blew in a "gusher".

5. The Smackover field reached its peak in __ when Arkansas wells produced __ barrels of oil.

6. Diamonds were discovered near __ in the year __.

7. Batesville marble went into the new __ and other __ over the nation.

8. Novaculite from __ County was mined for __.

Things to do

1. Investigate and make a report on the Murfreesboro diamond mine as it is today. Are diamonds still found there?

2. Draw an outline map of Arkansas and on it indicate the regions where each of the following is produced: oil, bauxite, rice, peaches, apples, cement, coal, cotton.

3. Consult an encyclopedia and list the uses made of the following resources: quartz, marble, novaculite, limestone, antimony, slate, tripoli, phosphate rock, fuller's earth, nephelite syenite, manganese, zinc, lead.

4. Visit your local electric or gas company and try to find answers to the following questions:

   (a) Where does the electricity or gas used in your community come from?

   (b) Where are the transmission lines and pipelines in your area?

   (c) How long has your community had gas and electric service? What was used for heating and lighting before gas and electricity became available?

5　The Industrial Workers

Arkansas people proved to be willing and efficient industrial workers. Labor troubles were generally unpopular, but the working class made many gains during the Progressive period.

From farm to factory. The Arkansas working people who cut the timber, dug the coal and bauxite, and labored in mills and factories made industrial growth possible. Without them no industrial enterprise could have succeeded, no matter how much money corporations invested.

Industrialists found Arkansas people ready and willing to work. Farm people were used to working long hours for little pay. Many of them were glad to leave the farms and take jobs at sawmills and factories. Life in the mill towns seemed better than the struggle to survive on run-down tenant farms.

In some sawmill towns the company owned almost everything. The worker and his family lived in a company house and traded at the company store. The sick were treated by the company doctor. Sometimes the worker had to take his pay in scrip which was good only at the company store.

Most of the workers, in mill towns and elsewhere, accepted control by "the company" without much complaint. On the plantations they had been used to similar control by the landlord. Men, women and children worked in the factories and mills just as they had on plantations and farms.

Organizing the workers. As Arkansas industries grew, labor unions began to try to organize the workers. United the working people could bargain with employers for better pay and other advantages. They could also persuade the state government to help the working class, just as owners of factories, mines and mills used their influence to get the legislation they wanted.

Little organizing was done before 1900, and for a long time the unions found the going hard. Some of the older workers had learned the value of organization during the era of the Knights of Labor and the farmer-labor parties. But new workers fresh from the farms were independent and glad to be as well off as they were. Many of them were suspicious of unions. The general public, including government officials, held similar opinions. Some objected to unions because they were afraid capitalists might be frightened away and industrial growth held back.

About 1898 or earlier the United Mine Workers began organizing the coal miners of western Arkansas. The Arkansas State Federation of Labor held its first convention in Little Rock in 1904. Connected with the American Federation of Labor (A F of L), the new union was interested in organizing the skilled craftsmen rather than the masses of unskilled workers.

The Brotherhood of Timber Workers, which began in 1910, was an "industrial" union which tried to organize all the lumber workers in Louisiana, Texas, and Arkansas. Negroes as well as whites were recruited, and the BTW joined the Industrial Workers of the World or "Wobblies." The union was broken by the lumber companies in a bitter strike and lockout in Louisiana.

At about the same time another movement called the Working Class Union had members in Oklahoma and Arkansas. This group advocated the abolition of profit, rents, and interest, and wanted government ownership of utilities. Neither the "Wobblies" nor the Working Class Union attracted much support among Arkansas workers. The small Socialist party of Arkansas, which attained its largest total vote in 1912, got little encouragement from the working people.

Strikes. Labor trouble was frequent in the coal fields. The miners were on strike at the turn of the century, and strikes continued at intervals. The worst trouble came at Prairie Creek near Hartford, Sebastian County, in 1914. There the United Mine Workers called a strike when the company began following an "open shop" policy of hiring non-union men. A riot and battle between union and non-union employees left two men dead and several mines wrecked. The Federal district court intervened but the strikers drove out the U. S. marshals. Finally President

Lumber workers in a company store at Millersville, Grant County, 1909

Woodrow Wilson sent four units of cavalry into the Prairie Creek area to enforce court rulings and restore order.

Beginning in 1925 the mine operators again shifted to an open shop basis, and there was occasional trouble until the union was recognized once more in 1933. In most Arkansas strikes, company owners could count on the support of the newspapers, state and local government officials, and the general public.

One of the longest and most destructive strikes took place on the Missouri and North Arkansas Railroad. This line ran from Joplin, Missouri, southeast across Arkansas to Helena, and was the only rail outlet for several Ozark counties. In 1921 the railroad workers went on strike after their wages were reduced. At first the company tried to operate with strikebreakers, but for nine months no trains ran at all.

When operations began again in 1922 on an open shop basis, bridges were burned and dynamited and attempts were made to wreck trains. Early in 1923 the public rose against the strikers. Citizens' committees were organized in Harrison and other towns. One worker was lynched and others were whipped or jailed. The strike collapsed and the railroad company was again in control of the situation.

Government helps the workers. Despite public hostility to strikers, laws to help the workers were enacted. General Assemblies of 1901, 1903, and 1905 passed legislation requiring that workers be paid in money rather than scrip, regulating railroad labor practices, fixing a ten-hour day in sawmills and planing mills, recognizing union labels, and prohibiting blacklisting of employees. The General Assembly of 1913 set up the State Bureau of Labor and Statistics.

Some places hired small children who worked twelve hours or more a day for less than five dollars a week. In 1914 an initiated act attempted to prohibit the labor of children under fourteen years old. The General Assembly of 1915 followed with another law regulating the wages and hours of women. These laws were never enforced very well. The Bureau of Labor and Statistics was too small and poorly financed to do much. Not until 1923 did the bureau have authority to help workers collect wages which employers refused to pay.

The position of labor declined after the First World War. Wages went down, unions lost members, and government made few attempts to help the working class. In 1924 Arkansas became the first state to ratify a proposed Federal constitutional amendment against child labor, but the amendment never went into effect. Arkansas in 1928 was one of five states without a workmen's compensation law.

STUDY AIDS

Vocabulary

Be sure that you understand the meaning of the following words and phrases:

industrialist   blacklisting
craftsman   industrial union
lockout   union labels
craft union   workmen's
open shop   compensation
strikebreaker   "Wobblies"

To test your reading

On other paper, list 1-8. Opposite each number write the word or words which complete each sentence.

1. As Arkansas industries grew, ___ began to try to ___ the workers.

2. Little organizing was done before ___ and for a long time the unions found the going ___.

3. The Arkansas State Federation of Labor held its first convention in ___ in ___.

4. One of the longest and most destructive strikes took place on the ___ Railroad in ___. Operation began again in ___ on an ___ basis.

5. The General Assembly of ___ set up the State Bureau of ___.

6. In 1914 an initiated act attempted to prohibit ___ of children under ___ years old.

7. Some objected to unions because they feared that ___ might be frightened away and ___ held back.

8. The worst coal strike came at ___ near ___, Sebastian County in ___.

Things to do

1. Dramatize a discussion between a farmer and a sawmill worker during this period. Let each tell what he likes about his job and what his troubles are.

2. Make a report on the history and current activities of labor unions in your community. Perhaps a local union representative will visit your class and explain the purpose and work of unions.

3. Write a series of newspaper headlines as they might have appeared during the Prairie Creek labor troubles and the Missouri and North Arkansas Railroad strike.

Reviewing the Unit

1. In what ways did the state government extend its control over business?

2. How did the First World War affect agriculture?

3. What were the different kinds of farm tenancy? What were the usual effects of such tenancy?

4. What did the Farmers' Union do to help the farm people?

5. Why did Arkansas industry develop so slowly?

6. What was the general attitude toward labor unions and strikes?

7. What changes occurred in the lumber industry during this period?

Unit Eight

Progressive Arkansas: Social Patterns
and Problems, 1898-1930

The Chapters

THE NEW CENTURY brought new problems and tensions to Arkansas life. Primitive roads could no longer serve in the new age of the automobile. The state government grew so large that a new capitol had to be built and new sources of revenue found. Following the First World War a secret society called the Ku Klux Klan arose with the announced aim of defending white, Protestant supremacy. Modernism invaded the realm of religion to challenge traditional beliefs. Race relations between white and Negro Arkansans hardened into harsh new patterns, with occasional flareups of violence.

Yet Arkansas was maturing during this first third of the twentieth century. Public education improved steadily if slowly. A state-supported system of higher education evolved. Effective work in public health became a reality at last. Public libraries were no longer unknown. A growing public sense of pride in Arkansas led to the adoption of a state flag and other symbols. Old ways of life continued in the rural districts, but soon new influences such as good roads, radios, movies, and organized sports added new dimensions to Arkansas living.

1   Problems of Change and Growth

Difficult problems confronted Arkansas early in the twentieth century. Among these were completing the new capitol, building new roads, financing an expanding government, and improving the penal system and the public health.

The new capitol. Before 1900 the government of Arkansas had outgrown the Old State House, located at Markham and Center Streets in Little Rock. The General Assembly of 1899 levied a special property tax to build a million-dollar capitol. The site chosen was the penitentiary grounds, on a hill west of downtown Little Rock.

Building the new capitol proved to be troublesome as well as expensive. Governor Jeff Davis opposed the project and stopped the work for a time. Construction was resumed in 1903, but for several years little progress was made. Many people were dissatisfied with the way the work was carried on, and the situation was soon badly confused.

George W. Donaghey, who was elected governor in 1908, promised to complete the capitol. Under his leadership the General Assembly of 1909 made a new start. Donaghey appointed a new commission to manage the project, and hired Cass Gilbert of New York as the architect.

The Donaghey commission rebuilt the upper part of the capitol, including the inside walls and dome. The General Assembly moved into the new building on January 9, 1911. The rest of the state government followed by 1914, and three years later the project was formally ended. The new capitol had cost more than $2,200,000 but no bonds were issued and it was paid for when it was finished.

The road problem. Automobiles began to appear on Arkansas roads in the early years of the century. The number of automobiles in the state increased from fewer than a hundred in 1907 to 4,800 in 1914. In the year 1913 Little Rock dealers sold more than 300 cars.

The coming of the automobile brought the road problem to the forefront. Horse-drawn buggies and wagons could get through the mud or dust of the old dirt roads, but when people began to use automobiles they found that better roads were a necessity.

At first road building was the responsibility of the counties. Able-bodied men were supposed to work on the roads for a certain number of days each year. Road taxes, when levied, were light. There was no statewide road system.

The General Assembly of 1907 authorized the formation of local road improvement districts. Landowners who formed districts could issue bonds and tax themselves to build roads. In 1911 the General Assembly began requiring automobile owners to buy licenses

The new state capitol under construction

for their cars, and in 1913 a State Highway Commission was established.

The Alexander road law of 1915 gave a new boost to the creation of road improvement districts, and two years later the state began to receive Federal aid for roads. During the prosperous period of the First World War, automobiles became more numerous and landowners formed hundreds of improvement districts. The state government created many more. The regular session of the General Assembly of 1919 passed 689 road laws.

The road district method did not work well. Roads were often poorly planned and built, and dishonesty sometimes entered the picture. After farm prices began to go down in 1920, many landowners were unable to pay the taxes levied by road improvement districts. Soon the districts were bankrupt and $60,000,000 in debt.

Called into special session late in 1923 by Governor Thomas C. McRae, the General Assembly adopted a new approach to the road problem. The Harrelson road act shifted the cost of building roads from the landowner to the person who used the roads. The law raised the gasoline tax, set up a new system of auto license fees, taxed motor oil, and provided for a state highway system.

In 1927 a new road law sponsored by Governor John E. Martineau provided that the state would assume the debts of the road improvement districts. New bonds would be issued by the state to finance a four-year construction pro-

Wagons crossing a river by ferry. The ferryboat was kept on course by an arrangement of ropes and pulleys attached to an overhead cable

The first traffic on Broadway bridge, across the Arkansas River at Little Rock, 1922

A section of "Dollarway," one of the earliest hard-surfaced roads in Arkansas, built between Little Rock and Pine Bluff in 1912-13. Dollarway got its name from the building contract rate of one dollar a square yard

gram. Proceeds of the gasoline tax, which was raised again, and auto license fees were to be used to pay off the debt. New bridges on state roads would be financed by charging tolls. The Martineau program of 1927 marked the real beginning of the Arkansas highway system, and roads became one of the biggest responsibilities of state government.

The financial problem. In the early days the state government was not expected to do much. Communities and families provided for their own needs. But as the population increased and cities grew, the government also grew. People began to expect the government to provide many services for them. This meant that the government had to increase taxes or borrow money.

The main trouble with the Arkansas tax system was the assessment of property. County officials almost always valued land and personal property at much less than its true worth. Assessments were uneven from county to county as well as within counties. Large businesses such as lumber companies sometimes paid very low taxes.

Governor Jeff Davis claimed that the state was out of debt and led the General Assembly to reduce taxes. Each session of the General Assembly found itself under pressure to do more for the schools, roads or some other public need. Instead of setting up a budgetary plan, the legislators usually appropriated money freely and left the governor to wrestle with deficits.

Governors George W. Donaghey and George W. Hays tried to persuade the General Assembly to reform the assessment system and the revenue laws, but nothing was done. Hays practiced strict economy, but when Charles H.

Brough succeeded him in 1917 the deficit had grown until state warrants were being sold at a discount. New York banks refused to handle Arkansas securities.

Brough secured a loan of $750,000 to put the state on a cash basis, but a budget system was still lacking. During the war period of 1917-19 several new state boards and bureaus were created, and the cost of government continued to increase. After 1920 the state began to tax gasoline, cigars, cigarettes, insurance, incomes, minerals, and other sources. When Arkansas entered the road-building business in 1927 a huge bonded indebtedness piled up. A bond issue for paying Confederate pensions was authorized. During the same period many counties, cities, school districts, drainage and improvement districts were also going deeply into debt.

The penitentiary problem. The Arkansas penitentiary system was not well-managed. Politicians and t h e i r friends often made money by leasing or hiring out convicts to contractors, railroads, and planters. G o v e r n o r Jeff Davis tried to bring reforms but did not succeed.

The purchase of Cummins prison farm in 1901 failed to stop the leasing of convicts. Late in 1912 Governor George W. Donaghey pardoned 361 convicts at one time in a blow at the lease system. The governor's action aroused so much support that the General Assembly of 1913 put an end to prisoner leasing.

Trouble continued after the abolition of the lease system. The penitentiary went into debt and had to issue bonds. In 1916 the Tucker Farm was purchased. Attempts were made to revive leasing. Prisoners were sometimes mistreated, and there was no rehabilitation work. Questions about the management of the penitentiary led to several legislative investigations.

Convicts building a road near Eureka Springs, Carroll County, 1918

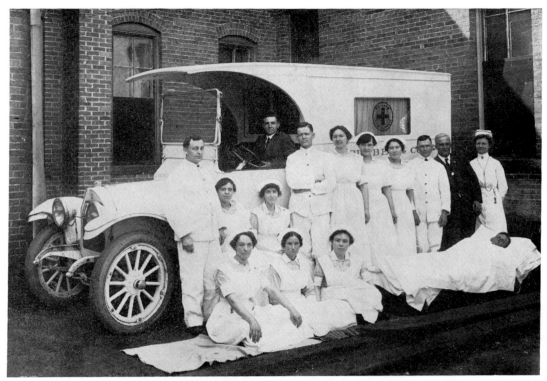

One of the first motor ambulances in Little Rock, about the year 1915

Some progress was made in the correctional field. A juvenile court system was begun in 1911, and by 1925 three "industrial schools" or "training schools" had been set up for young offenders. In 1920 a state farm for women was established. Arkansas was the first Southern state to adopt a parole system. Public executions were prohibited, and the electric chair replaced hanging as a means of execution.

The health problem. In 1910 the Rockefeller Sanitary Commission, a New York organization, began anti-hookworm work in Arkansas. Examinations showed that a fourth of Arkansas school children had hookworm, and up to sixty-five per cent in some counties. The Commission campaigned for better sanitation and treated 12,000 children in free clinics.

The General Assembly of 1913 created the State Board of Health. A system of county and city health offices was set up. The state board was empowered to institute quarantines and take other action to protect the health of the people.

In 1916 the State Board of Health required that school children, teachers, and school employees be vaccinated against smallpox. Arkansas became the first state to have compulsory statewide school vaccination, and smallpox was practically stamped out. An experiment at Crossett in malaria control in 1916 became a model for new campaigns against mosquitoes. Water supplies were purified and typhoid practically disappeared. Improved diet checked pellagra. Fewer mothers and babies died, especially after a health campaign started in 1921.

A state tuberculosis sanatorium opened near Booneville in 1910, and a similar institution for Negroes began near Little Rock in 1931. The state began regulating doctors, nurses, dentists, pharmacists, and others who practiced the healing arts. Starting in 1914 the Bureau of Vital Statistics kept records of Arkansas births and deaths, and marriage records after 1917.

The health picture was not everywhere one of progress. Arkansas in 1930 had few good orphanages and few homes for older people. The State Hospital for Nervous Diseases suffered from overcrowding and a number of other problems. The General Assembly of 1929 authorized the expansion of the State Hospital system, and a new hospital unit was begun near Benton.

The State Hospital, Little Rock, as it appeared before the construction of the present buildings

STUDY AIDS

Vocabulary

Be sure that you understand the meaning of the following words and phrases:

rehabilitation   discount
parole   securities
deficit   tolls
resumed   budgetary
project   assessment
improvement   pellagra
  districts

Identification

Tell what part each of the following had in the story:

George W. Donaghey
industrial school
George W. Hays
Alexander road law
Thomas C. McRae
Harrelson road act
John E. Martineau
Cummins and Tucker farms
Charles H. Brough
Bureau of Vital Statistics
Jeff Davis
Cass Gilbert

To test your reading

On other paper, list 1-10. Opposite each number, write the word or words which complete each sentence.

1. In the year 1913 Little Rock dealers sold more than __ cars.

2. The governor elected in 1908 was __.

3. The new capitol cost more than __ dollars.

4. In 1927 the __ program marked the real beginning of the Arkansas highway system.

5. Governor Brough secured a loan of __ to put the state on a cash basis.

6. Late in the year __ Governor George W. Donaghey pardoned __ convicts at one time as a blow to the __ system.

7. A juvenile court system was set up in the year __, and in 1920 a __ for women was established.

8. In 1910 the Rockefeller Sanitary Commission began __ work in Arkansas.

9. In 1916 the State Board of Health began requiring __ __ and __ to be vaccinated against smallpox.

10. A state tuberculosis sanatorium for whites opened near __ in __.

Things to do

1. Visit the state capitol.

2. Begin a collection of pictures of early automobiles. A visit to the Museum of Automobiles on Petit Jean Mountain might be interesting.

3. Go to your county courthouse and ask the tax assessor to explain how he assesses property.

4. Write to the Bureau of Vital Statistics in Little Rock for a copy of your birth certificate. (The bureau charges a fee for supplying such copies.)

5. Report on current public health work in your community.

2   Tensions of War and Peace

The First World War took the lives of some Arkansas men and affected the lives of all Arkansas people. The Ku Klux Klan and the fundamentalist movement expressed some of the tensions of the postwar period. In 1927 Arkansas experienced one of the greatest natural disasters in its history, when the rivers overflowed their banks.

The First World War. The European war which broke out in 1914 went on for nearly three years before the United States became involved. In 1916 Arkansas National Guardsmen got a taste of military service against Mexican revolutionaries along the Rio Grande, but they saw practically no fighting. The United States declared war on Germany on April 6, 1917.

Arkansas men entered the armed forces with National Guard units and as volunteers, but most of them were drafted by Selective Service boards. About 72,000 Arkansas men saw military service and over 2,000 of them died, mostly of disease rather than enemy bullets. Fewer than 500 Arkansans were killed in action and died of wounds.

As in every war, a few Arkansas men were recognized officially as heroes. The name of Private Herman Davis, an infantryman from Mississippi County, stood fourth from the top in General John J. Pershing's list of the hundred greatest heroes of the war. Captain Field E. Kindley, a Gravette aviator, shot down twelve German planes to become America's fourth ranking ace of the First World War.

At home, the State Council of Defense headed a network of county and community councils engaged in promoting the war effort. Arkansans were urged to save food and coal, buy Liberty bonds, and give to the Red Cross and Young Men's Christian Association. Thousands of soldiers were trained at Camp Pike, near North Little Rock. Eberts Camp, an aviation training field at Lonoke, was still under construction when the war ended on November 11, 1918.

The worst hardship endured by people at home was the influenza epidemic which swept the entire country in late 1918. Hospitals and doctors could not care for the crowds of sick, and nobody knew how to cure the disease. Over 7,000 Arkansans died of the "flu" before the epidemic ran its course.

The American Legion, organized by returning veterans of the First World War, became an important influence in the life of the state. By 1922, in Arkansas, the Legion had 150 local groups called "posts."

The new Ku Klux Klan. Following the end of the First World War there was a marked increase in crime and

Scenes of the First World War, 1917-18. Above is a view of Camp Pike

FOR GOD AND HOME AND NATIVE LAND

KU KLUX KLAN

KOMMEMORATION

AT LITTLE ROCK

Under Auspices of the
Realm of Arkansas, Little Rock Klan No. 1, Rose
City Klan No. 1 and Junior Klan

SEE
GREATEST ROBED PARADE IN HISTORY OF STATE
LARGEST CLASS EVER NATURALIZED IN ARKANSAS
STATE'S MOST STUPENDOUS FIREWORKS DISPLAY
GREATEST AGGREGATION OF NATIVE AMERICANS

Part of a Ku Klux Klan advertisement in the "Arkansas Gazette," July 1, 1924

lawlessness in Arkansas. In some areas law enforcement officers seemed unable or unwilling to halt crime. Statewide prohibition had apparently opened the door to the "moonshiner" who made illegal whiskey and to the "bootlegger" who sold it. Early in 1921 Governor Thomas C. McRae proclaimed "Law and Order Sunday" in an attempt to discourage lawbreaking.

Many Arkansas people worried about other new problems. Cities like Fort Smith and Little Rock were growing rapidly. Some people were suspicious of Catholics, Jews, Negroes, radicals, and the foreign-born. To many Arkansans it seemed that the world was changing too fast and going in the wrong direction.

The new Ku Klux Klan, a secret organization which began in Georgia in 1915, advocated government by native-born, white, Protestant Americans and the enforcement of a strict moral code. After the war the KKK became a national organization. Klan members wore peaked hoods and white robes, and burned crosses at outdoor night meetings.

The Ku Klux Klan appeared in Arkansas in 1921 and grew rapidly. The Grand Dragon, or state leader, was a Little Rock attorney named James A. Comer. At first Klansmen concerned themselves with moral problems. During 1922 there were widespread reports of floggings and other violence

directed at bootleggers, loafers, wife-beaters, and the immoral.

As Arkansas became one of the strongest Klan states, with the order claiming 50,000 members in 1924, KKK leaders moved into politics. Arkansas politicians had to line up either for the Klan or against it, and the Klan became an issue in many campaigns.

The Ku Kluxers took control of Little Rock, Fort Smith, and several counties and towns, but their candidate for governor in 1924 lost to Tom J. Terral. Following this defeat the KKK declined rapidly. In 1928 Klansmen opposed the presidential candidacy of Alfred E. Smith, a Catholic, but Smith carried Arkansas.

The flood of 1927. In the spring of 1927 the Mississippi, Arkansas, and other rivers overflowed their banks and flooded vast areas of lowlands. Heavy rains had set in almost a year earlier, and flood waters eventually covered more than 4,000,000 acres of land in eastern and central Arkansas. Property losses ran into millions of dollars, thousands of families were made homeless, and 127 Arkansans lost their lives.

The Federal government and the American Red Cross came to the aid of Arkansas, but human suffering was still very great. Agriculture and industry received serious setbacks. The flood of 1927 convinced most Americans that flood control was a national as well as a state problem, and Congress began a Federal program in 1928 to try to prevent future disasters.

The c h u r c h e s face new challenges. Arkansas churches increased in num-

A Sunday congregation at County Line Baptist Church, in Howard County, about the year 1911

ber, wealth and membership during the first thirty years of the twentieth century. In 1906 about a third of the people of the state were church members, and by 1926 the percentage had risen slightly. Most church people were Baptists or Methodists, with Negro Baptists reporting more churches than any other denomination in 1926.

Some churches were disturbed by the modernist - fundamentalist controversy. The modernists believed that the Bible should be studied scientifically, that man had evolved from lower forms of life, and that the churches should teach a "social gospel" aimed at improving the world. The fundamentalists insisted on the literal truth of the Bible and its doctrines.

Fundamentalists became greatly excited about the theory of evolution during the ten years following the First World War. They objected especially to any teaching in public schools that "man descended from the monkey." An anti-evolution law failed narrowly in the General Assembly of 1927, but was then passed as an initiated act at the general election of the following year. The law prohibited the teaching in tax-supported schools of any theory that man ascended or descended from a lower order of animals.

Soon after the turn of the century new religious movements began to appear on the Arkansas scene. Pentecostal revivals featured speaking in tongues, divine healing, and the doctrine of sanctification or entire holiness of life. As Baptist and Methodist churches became wealthier and more formal, Pentecostal and Holiness churches won more of their members. The Assemblies of God, organized at Hot Springs in 1914, grew rapidly.

The Churches of Christ were first reported separately from the Christian Churches or Disciples of Christ in the Federal census of 1906. At about the same time the Landmark or Missionary Baptists withdrew from the Southern Baptist Convention. The Churches of Christ and Landmark Baptists were especially strong in rural areas.

Organized religion played a large part in the life of many Arkansas Negroes. Negro churches were social and recreational as well as religious centers, and preachers were the leaders of the Negro community. A new Negro denomination, the Free Christian Zion Church of Christ, had its beginning in Arkansas in 1905.

STUDY AIDS

Vocabulary

Be sure that you understand the meaning of the following words and phrases:

initiated act
speaking in
  tongues
bootlegger
involved
divine healing
posts
tensions

revolutionaries
National Guard
American Red
  Cross
Liberty bonds
modernist
fundamentalist
social gospel
theory of evolution

Identification

Tell what part each of the following had in the story:

Tom J. Terral
American Legion
Alfred E. Smith

Anti-evolution law
James A. Comer
State Council of
  Defense

To test your reading

On other paper, list 1-7. Opposite each number, write the word or words which complete each sentence.

1. The United States declared war on Germany on ___.

2. About ___ Arkansas men saw military service and over ___ died, mostly of disease. Fewer than ___ were killed in action.

3. Two servicemen who were honored as heroes were ___ and ___.

4. Thousands of soldiers were trained at ___ near Little Rock.

5. In the winter of 1918 over ___ Arkansans died of ___.

6. The Ku Klux Klan appeared in Arkansas in ___ and grew rapidly.

7. Arkansas suffered one of its worst floods in the spring of ___.

Things to do

1. Make a report on the part which your community or county played in the First World War. See if you can find out how many local men served in the armed forces; how many lost their lives; whether any local men had outstanding war records; and how the influenza epidemic affected your community.

2. Ask a veteran of the First World War to tell the class of his experiences.

3. Visit the Herman Davis Memorial near Manila. Is there a World War One monument in your town or city?

4. If there is an American Legion post in your community, investigate and report on its activities.

5. Did the flood of 1927 affect your community? Interview older residents and look for pictures of flood scenes.

6. Draw a cartoon illustrating an outdoor night meeting of the Ku Klux Klan. How did Klan members dress for such meetings? Why?

7. Ask your minister, priest or rabbi how the fundamentalist-modernist controversy affected your own church or religious denomination.

3   Segregation and the Negro

The new segregation system which arose after 1890 was intended to keep the white and Negro races apart politically, socially, and economically. Occasional lynchings and one major race riot marred the generally good relations between white and Negro Arkansans.

Political segregation. Racial segregation, or some form of separation of the white and Negro races, had been the custom in Arkansas since the period of early settlement. After the Civil War the Negro was given political responsibilities for which he was generally unprepared, and this action caused many difficulties during reconstruction. The political situation in Arkansas about the year 1890 convinced many of the white people that another period like reconstruction might be at hand unless steps were taken to remove the Negro from politics.

Arkansas used the poll tax, adopted as a voting requirement in 1892, as one way to discourage Negro voting. The poll tax was not large, but many Negroes either could not or would not pay it. The courts voided the first poll tax amendment to the Arkansas constitution, but another was passed in 1908.

Even more effecive in keeping Negroes from voting was the "white" primary. Democratic party officials adopted rules limiting voting in primaries to whites only. In some communities Negroes were allowed to vote, but such voters were few. Arkansas Republicans also were careful to keep Negroes out of positions of party leadership, and few Federal jobs went to Negroes when Republicans were in power in Washington. In 1920 Negro Republicans ran their own "black and tan" candidate for governor of Arkansas in opposition to the "lily white" Republican candidate.

Social and economic segregation. A series of measures called "Jim Crow" laws attempted to separate whites and Negroes socially. In 1891 segregation on railway trains was made compulsory, and in 1899 the system was extended to waiting rooms in railway stations. Later measures included laws requiring separate seating on street cars, and separating white and Negro prisoners in jails and in the penitentiary.

The segregation system became much more extensive and complete than state laws indicated. City ordinances, local customs, and public sentiment enforced the pattern. Whites and Negroes were separated practically everywhere except in stores and on the streets, and sometimes even this was attempted. Negroes could not serve on juries, and Negro lawbreakers were sometimes punished more severely than whites who had committed similar offenses.

Like the whites, most Arkansas Negroes made their livings in agriculture, but fewer Negroes owned farms.

Houses occupied by Negro sharecroppers, southern Arkansas

Negro farmers were usually tenants or day laborers. Sawmills and factories employed many Negro workers. Occasionally Negroes overcame their disadvantages and became wealthy. Scott Bond, an uneducated ex-slave who lived at Madison in St. Francis County, became one of the leading farmers and businessmen of eastern Arkansas. In 1917 Bond turned down an offer of $2,000,000 for his assets.

Lynching. When a Negro committed a serious crime, especially when a white man or woman was involved, white mobs sometimes took the law into their own hands. In Arkansas during the period 1882-1937, a total of 285 persons were lynched, or put to death without trial. Negroes accounted for 226 cases, or about eighty per cent of the lynchings. Law enforcement officers avoided some lynchings by hiding prisoners, but in many instances the sheriff or police force made no move to interfere.

The General Assembly of 1909 tried to check lynching by giving county sheriffs authority to speed up trials of accused persons when mob violence threatened. In 1917 Arkansas ranked third in the nation in the number of lynchings, and in 1921 Governor Thomas C. McRae deplored the practice as a disgrace to the state. Prominent white citizens and leading newspapers agreed with him, and lynchings gradually became less frequent.

The Elaine race riot. In October 1919 racial trouble broke out near Elaine, in Phillips County, Arkansas. Some Negro sharecroppers were discontented and feared that plantation owners were trying to cheat them. Led by Robert L. Hill, a number of Negroes organized the "Progressive Farmers and Household Union of America" to secure what they regarded as their rights.

Rumors and increasing fear among both Negroes and whites led to armed clashes and then to violent fighting at Hoop Spur and in the woods around Elaine. The whites believed that the Negroes planned to murder several planters and then stage a general revolt. Governor Charles H. Brough placed Elaine under martial law and sent in troops armed with machine guns. Negroes were rounded up and placed in stockades.

Five whites and eleven Negroes were reported killed in the fighting, but according to some accounts a much larger number of Negroes lost their lives. Governor Brough appointed a secret committee of seven whites to find out the causes of the trouble, and they reported that the Negroes had been planning a rebellion. Negroes claimed that they had sought economic justice and nothing else.

The trouble at Elaine made headlines all over the United States. Twelve Negroes were sentenced to death and several dozen others to terms in the penitentiary. The death sentences were appealed to the United States Supreme Court and none of the twelve was ever executed.

Segregated education. Negro schools were generally inferior to schools for whites. Negroes had many children to be educated and owned little property, so the burden of Negro education fell on the white taxpayers. Some whites were reluctant to spend much tax money for Negro schools, and some Negroes would not send their children to school even when schools were available. In 1930 Arkansas spent less than half as

Branch Normal College for Negroes, Pine Bluff. The building was completed in 1881

much to educate a Negro child as it did to educate a white.

Northern charity took up a part of the slack. The Rosenwald Fund built schools for Negroes. The Slater Fund established county training schools. The Jeanes Fund and the General Education Board trained and paid teachers, conducted research and helped in other ways. Negro high schools, practically ignored until 1924, numbered twenty-six accredited institutions four years later.

Signposts of the future. During the First World War, Negroes began leaving Arkansas to find better jobs in the North and West. The postwar farm depression and the decline of sawmilling caused others to move away. This migration to the North, along with poor sanitation, a high death rate among infants, and susceptibility to tuberculosis caused the percentage of Negroes in the population to decline. In 1910 Negroes made up 28.1 per cent of the people of Arkansas; in 1930, 25.8 per cent.

Educationally, the Negro people began to make greater progress after the First World War. More Negro children attended school and more young people enrolled in college. The rate of illiteracy went down. Negro business and professional men began to replace the uneducated preachers as leaders in the Negro community.

In 1928 some Arkansas Negro leaders worked for Alfred E. Smith, the Democratic presidential candidate, claiming that they had been promised that Negroes could begin to vote in Democratic primaries. Afterward more Negroes began voting regularly in primaries, especially in the cities. By 1930 the growing Negro interest in politics, education and better jobs warned that greater changes in race relations might be expected in the future.

STUDY AIDS

Vocabulary

Be sure that you understand the meaning of the following words and phrases:

lily white   stockades
black and tan   white primary
Jim Crow laws   lynching

Identification

Tell what part each of the following had in the story:

Robert L. Hill   Charles H. Brough
Scott Bond

To test your reading

On other paper, list 1-10. Opposite each number write the word or words which complete each sentence.

1. In 1920 Negro Republicans ran their own ___ candidate for governor.

2. In 1899 segregation on ___ was made compulsory.

3. Most Arkansas Negroes made their living in ___.

4. An uneducated ex-slave named ___ who lived at ___ in ___ County became quite wealthy.

5. In October 1919 occurred the ___ riots in ___ County.

6. The troubles at ___ made headlines all over ___.

7. In 1930 Arkansas spent less than ___ as much to educate a Negro child as it did to educate a white child.

8. The Rosenwald Fund built ___ for Negroes.

9. The Slater Fund established ___.

10. In 1928 there were ___ accredited Negro high schools in Arkansas.

Things to do

1. Write newspaper stories about the Elaine race riot of 1919 (a) from the white point of view and (b) from the Negro viewpoint.

2. Using information from other books in your library, make an oral report on one of the following:

   (a) the poll tax in the South

   (b) Jim Crow laws in other states

   (c) lynching

   (d) the presidential election of 1928

4 Education Moves Ahead

During the Progressive period Arkansas began to overcome its backwardness in public education. Teacher training improved, high schools were organized, and a number of state-supported colleges appeared.

Higher standards and longer terms. In 1898 a third of the children of Arkansas were not enrolled in school. The average school term was only sixty-nine days, and many rural terms were shorter. Attendance was poor, there were no regular courses or grading methods, and school libraries were few. Some counties spent as much on the jail as on the public schools. Many country schools still had split terms so pupils could help with farm work.

The General Assembly of 1899 gave counties permission to require uniformity in textbooks, and in 1917 a state commission began selecting textbooks for use in all the public schools. After 1903 the state provided a graded course of study. The General Assembly of 1927 authorized county boards of education to require a minimum school term of 120 days, and by 1930 the average school term had been lengthened to 148 days. The first compulsory attendance law was passed in 1909, but such measures were usually poorly enforced.

The consolidation movement. Most Arkansas schools were small. In 1902 over 500 districts enrolled fewer than twenty pupils to the school. School districts became more numerous as the population increased. In 1912 Arkansas

had 5,143 districts, and the number did not begin to decline until after 1920.

Educational leaders advocated consolidation of small districts into larger ones, but many rural people did not want to give up their neighborhood schools. Actually little consolidation could take place until the age of good roads and motor buses. In the ten years after 1920 the number of districts declined from 5,112 to 3,703 as a result of consolidation.

Better financing. The educational problems of Arkansas were not due to lack of interest. Arkansas spent a larger part of its income on education than did many other states. The trouble was that Arkansas people had many children and little money to spend on education. A one-crop agricultural economy provided little taxable wealth.

Many rural schoolhouses were so dilapidated that classes could meet only in summer. As late as 1930 over half of the schools in Arkansas were one-room structures in which one teacher tried to teach all subjects. Arkansas spent less money on each school child than any state except Mississippi.

School taxes remained low, but the trend was upward. The poll tax went to the schools. In 1907 the state school tax was raised from twenty cents to

Interior, Smyrna schoolhouse near Huntsville, Madison County. The log building was used as a church before it was deeded to the school district in 1880. This photograph was made in 1950

thirty cents on each hundred dollars of taxable property. School district taxes were raised steadily. After 1926 local districts could levy an eighteen-mill tax, or $1.80 on each hundred dollars of taxable property. Cigar and cigarette taxes and a part of the state income tax were devoted to education.

Several charitable organizations aided Arkansas education. Peabody institutes were held and Peabody scholarships awarded. The Southern Education Board and the General Education Board contributed money, professional advice, and advertising. Between 1914 and 1928 the Julius Rosenwald Fund built more than 300 schools for Arkansas Negroes.

Organized effort. The growing interest in better schools was due partly to the activities of school improvement associations and parent-teacher associations. The General Education Board and the State Teachers Association (renamed the Arkansas Education Association) encouraged the state government to better organize its educational efforts.

Creation of a State Board of Education was followed by formation of county boards. County superintendents were charged with local responsibilities. The state schools for the blind and deaf located at Little Rock were removed from the list of "charities" and placed under the education department. Dedicated educators like William E. Halbrook, who supervised Ozark mountain schools, worked hard for the cause of learning. In 1926 A. B. Hill, state superintendent of public instruction, published a series of bulletins which for the first time showed Arkansas people exactly where their state stood in education.

High schools. Arkansas had no standardized high schools until after 1909. In that year there were seventy-six schools c l a i m i n g secondary rank, but only a few in the larger cities were real high schools. The state was responsible for elementary schools and colleges but had no system of secondary schools.

The General Education Board of New York backed the first attempt to establish a high school system. Real progress followed after the General Assembly of 1911 set up a State Board of Education and provided state aid for high schools. Opponents of the aid plan secured a court decision invalidating it in 1915, but the General Education Board continued to help.

By 1930 the number of high schools had increased to 417, but most of them lacked the highest accreditation. The best high schools were located in the cities and wealthier counties. A secondary education was still beyond the reach of many rural young people.

Teacher training. One of the greatest drawbacks to educational progress was the poorly trained teacher. In 1899 the state government stopped aid to the normal institutes which had been held for several years. Because of the attitude of the state government, the Peabody Fund withdrew its support also. The teachers were left without training facilities of any kind.

A country school near Patmos, Hempstead County, conducted by J. H. Atkinson (left) in 1908. There were no grades and one teacher taught all pupils and all subjects

DeWitt High School, built in 1910 at a cost of $19,000

The institute program was revived by teachers at their own expense. The General Assembly of 1903 tightened requirements for examining and licensing teachers. Then in 1907 teachers were required to attend summer normal institutes sponsored by the state superintendent of public instruction. Only about half of the teachers had attended institutes in 1904, but within a few years the percentage in attendance rose to ninety.

The county normal system was helpful, but short summer institutes could not provide the training that teachers needed. In 1907 the State Teachers Association and the Farmers' Union persuaded the General Assembly to establish a State Normal School at Conway. It became Arkansas State Teachers College in 1925.

Summer terms for teachers began at State Normal and the University of Arkansas in 1910. The General Assembly of 1927 required that teachers attend summer terms rather than institutes to secure renewal of their licenses. In 1917 the University of Arkansas added a college of education, and Henderson State Teachers College was established at Arkadelphia in 1929.

Arkansas was moving toward better teacher education, but in 1929 only about 800 of the 10,000 teachers of the state were college graduates. More than 1,600 teachers had no training higher than the eighth grade. Many teachers found college and even high school education too expensive for their small salaries, which in 1930 averaged $753 a year for whites and $434 annually for Negroes.

The expanding college system. Genuine higher education began to emerge in Arkansas after 1900. Arkansas Industrial University, renamed the University of Arkansas in 1899, increased its course offerings and raised its standards. Enrollment on the Fayetteville campus tripled in the period 1912-30.

The University of Arkansas had trouble securing buildings. The General Assembly of 1905 made appropriations for several new buildings, but twenty years passed before other buildings were authorized. Not only was the state short of money, but there was frequent talk of moving the university to Little Rock.

Unfortunately the state government took on more colleges than it could support properly. Teachers' colleges were established at Conway and Arkadelphia. The district agricultural high schools at Jonesboro, Russellville, Monticello, and Magnolia became junior colleges in 1925. Then a junior agricultural college was set up at Beebe. Branch Normal College for Negroes at Pine Bluff became Arkansas Agricultural, Mechanical and Normal College with its own board of trustees.

Church-related colleges such as Hendrix, Ouachita, Philander Smith, Central, Galloway, and College of the Ozarks contributed much to higher education. Municipal junior colleges, a new idea in education, opened in El Dorado, Little Rock, and Fort Smith.

Professional education made some progress before 1930. The University School of Medicine in Little Rock received help from the General Assembly beginning in 1913. The university set up a law school in 1926 and a graduate school the following year.

The first public libraries. By 1900 interest in public libraries was increasing. Women's clubs and literary societies established libraries in Helena, Van Buren, Arkadelphia, and Mena.

State Normal School at Conway, built in 1908 at a cost of $75,000. The president was J. J. Doyne

Campus of Ouachita College in Arkadelphia, 1910

The earliest libraries operated by means of subscriptions or fees. General Assemblies of 1903 and 1911 provided that cities could levy taxes to support libraries.

Fort Smith established the first free public library in Arkansas in 1908. The building was donated by Andrew Carnegie, the steel manufacturer. Later other Arkansas libraries received Carnegie grants. In 1930 there were twenty-seven public libraries in the state. The General Assembly of 1927 allowed counties to establish free libraries.

After the First World War the Arkansas Federation of Women's Clubs began collecting books to send to different counties where no libraries existed. A free library service bureau was set up in the State Department of Education, but it was ended during the depression.

STUDY AIDS

Vocabulary

Be sure that you understand the meaning of the following words and phrases:

consolidation
one-crop economy
dilapidated
standardized
invalidating
accreditation
professional
    education

literary societies
subscriptions
uniformity
split terms
eighteen-mill tax
junior college
graduate school

Identification

Tell what part each of the following had in the story:

General Education
    Board
William E.
    Halbrook
county normal
    system

State Normal
    School
consolidation
    movement
A. B. Hill

To test your reading

On other paper, list 1-10. Opposite each number write the word or words which complete each sentence.

1. The first free public library in Arkansas was established in __ in the year __. The building was donated by __.

2. In 1929 only about __ of the __ of the state were college graduates.

3. Arkansas had no standard high schools until after __.

4. The first compulsory attendance law was passed in __.

5. In 1912 Arkansas had __ school districts. In 1930 it had __ such districts.

6. As late as 1930 over half the schools in Arkansas were __ structures in which one teacher tried to teach __.

7. In 1902 over __ districts enrolled fewer than __ pupils to the school.

8. In 1898 the average school term was only __ days.

9. After 1903 the state provided a __.

10. The earliest municipal junior colleges were at __, __ and __.

Things to do

1. It is not too soon for you to be thinking about going to college. Choose an Arkansas college in which you might be interested and make a report on it. Tell something about its history, its enrollment, its courses of study, and its entrance requirements.

2. From information available in the office of your county supervisor, try to determine the number and location of schools in your county which have been eliminated by consolidation since 1920. Indicate the location of each school on a large outline map of the county.

3. Think of yourself as a visitor to an early school in your community. Compare conditions with those of the present day. Review Unit 3, Chapter 5 and Unit 6, Chapter 6. Interview older persons about schools that they attended.

5 Social Life and Amusements

During the 1898-1930 era most of the people of Arkansas lived in the country or in small towns, and the average Arkansan still enjoyed many of the amusements and followed many of the customs of his rural ancestors. Yet the Arkansas way of life was changing under the influence of many new factors ranging from the Model T to game and fish regulations.

Fun at home and at school. The average Arkansan lived in the country or in a small town, and he seldom ventured far away. His amusements, like his entire life, centered in the home, the school, and the church. Young people gathered in homes for play-parties, and square dances except where religious objections to dancing were strong. The local "fiddler" was a man of importance at dances as well as at "musicals" where he was joined by guitar and banjo players. Many people, especially in the highlands, remembered the old folk ballads of English and Scottish origin.

At the neighborhood schoolhouse there were plays and programs by the pupils at Thanksgiving, Christmas, and the end of the school term. Spelling bees and "ciphering matches" were still held in some places. As a result of such contests some person might acquire the reputation of being able to "spell down" or "figger down" anybody in the neighborhood. Occasionally wandering companies of actors, usually comedians, performed in the schoolhouse. Pie suppers, cakewalks, and debates enlivened the rural scene.

Holidays. Christmas was an important holiday in Arkansas, though it was festive rather than religious for most people. The customary greeting was "Christmas Gift!" and fireworks were exploded on Christmas Eve. Before firecrackers and skyrockets became available, sometimes merrymakers fired anvils as a noise-making device. A blacksmith's anvil was placed upside down atop another anvil, with a charge of black powder between the two. People "shot anvils" to celebrate political victories as well as to observe holidays.

Country people usually could not afford expensive gifts, but the women baked pies and cakes, and there was chicken or ham for Christmas Day. For the children there was a pine or cedar Christmas tree, some fruit and peppermint stick candy, and perhaps a toy made by the father or an older brother.

The Fourth of July was the most important summer holiday. In pioneer Arkansas the Fourth had been observed with banquets, toasts, and speeches. In the early twentieth century picnics, barbecues, watermelon feasts, and political speakings were the order of the

A farmhouse in Columbia County, 1905

day. The Negroes observed June 19 as "Emancipation Day" in much the same fashion but without the political rallies. Swimming in creeks and rivers was popular during the hot summer months after crops were laid by, and marble games and horseshoe pitching had wide appeal.

All-day singings and summer revivals. Church buildings were usually the scene of the "all-day singings with dinner on the ground" which were the special delight of the rural people. Annual "singing conventions," attended by the best quartets and song leaders, attracted even larger crowds. Experts

A baptismal service or "baptizing" in Howard County, 1924

Interior of a grocery in Morrilton, 1912

Butchering a hog near Scott, Pulaski County

taught summer "singing schools" lasting one or two weeks. Publishers brought out new song books every few months. The songs were hymns, at least as far as the words were concerned, but the "singings" were basically entertainment and not religious services. Concession stands sold ice cream, lemonade, and soft drinks on the church grounds. Sometimes such all-day affairs were held in honor of the "old soldiers" or the "old folks," or combined with cemetery "decorations" in memory of the dead.

Summer church revivals and camp meetings attracted large crowds who came to visit and talk as well as to hear the preaching. Such meetings usually closed with solemn "baptizings" on a Sunday afternoon in a nearby creek or river.

Rural self - sufficiency. Many rural families needed little money. Food was simple but plentiful, with most of it produced on the farm. The farmer had his vegetable garden, fruit orchard, tobacco patch, cow, and hogs. He carried his corn to the gristmill to be ground into meal. In some parts of Arkansas as late as 1920 clothing and shoes were still made at home. Farm families bought little except coffee, and perhaps sugar and flour.

Of course tenant farmers were less self-sufficient than were farmers who owned their land. In the plantation lowlands, sharecroppers were sometimes allowed little or no land for garden plots or animals of their own. This served to keep them dependent on the plantation store.

The Arkansas farmer had few contacts with the world beyond his community. After 1896 Rural Free Delivery (RFD) routes began bringing his mail to his home. Peddlers stopped at farmhouses selling groceries, vanilla flavoring, books, or magazine subscriptions, and often took chickens and eggs in trade. On Saturdays the farm family went to town, visited the stores, and perhaps attended a tent show or listened to a street medicine salesman.

In the fall of the year, when crops had been gathered and the farmer might have a little extra money, he took his family to the county fair. A circus or carnival was usually in town. Soon afterward it was time for school to start again, and with the first cold weather hogs had to be killed and the meat hung in the smokehouse to cure. Sorghum-makers with portable mule-drawn mills ground the cane in the fall, and made the syrup by cooking out impurities in shallow pans.

The practice of visiting relatives and friends was popular. Families would travel several miles by wagon, buggy or Model T to visit and "stay all night" at another home. Small-town neighbors sat and talked on wide front porches during the warm months. Most Arkansas people always found time to visit, or at least to stop and talk.

Except in the coal-producing regions, wood was the customary fuel, and the farmer provided his own. Cooking on open fireplaces gradually gave way to the iron cookstoves which burned short lengths of "stovewood." Later came the kerosene or "coal oil" burner, and fi-

A country peddler in Lonoke County, 1910

A country store at Wattensaw, Lonoke County, 1912

A carnival on Main Street in Russellville, Pope County, about 1910

nally bottled or natural gas. Occasionally the farmer used a broadax to hew out railroad crossties which he sold.

Broadening horizons. In Little Rock and the larger towns, people could attend theaters where actors presented plays and operas. After 1903 the Chautauqua Movement sent performers and lecturers into the smaller towns for one or two-week stands. The lecturers usually spoke on patriotic and inspirational subjects. Charles H. Brough, Arkansas governor in 1917-21, was a successful Chautauqua lecturer. The Chautauqua Movement reached its peak during the period 1910-24.

After the First World War the radio, automobile and motion pictures gradually put the stage shows out of business. The first radio station in Arkansas, WOK at Pine Bluff, went on the air in 1921. It was followed in 1923 by station KFMQ at Fayetteville, and by KTHS at Hot Springs the next year.

Movie theaters appeared in almost every town, and after sound was added in 1928 the "talkies" became one of the most popular forms of entertainment in Arkansas. During the same period the automobile brought better roads and helped end rural isolation.

Orders, clubs and societies. Arkansas people joined and supported a large number of clubs and societies. Freemasonry came to Arkansas with the pioneers, and Masonic lodges were to be found in almost every village in the state. Other fraternal orders included Knights of Pythias, Odd Fellows, Elks, Moose, Knights of Columbus, and Woodmen of the World. The Mosaic Templars, a Negro order which began in Little Rock in 1883, had members in more than half the states of the Union in 1930.

Service clubs for business and professional men appeared in Arkansas after 1911, and soon almost every town

Parade at the national reunion of United Confederate Veterans, Little Rock, 1911

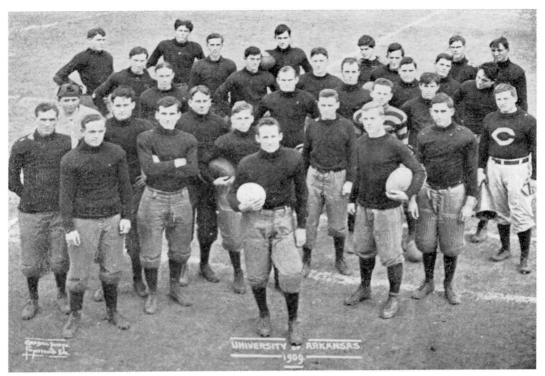

Football team of the University of Arkansas, 1909. Coach Hugo Bezdek is on the right

had its Rotary, Lions or Kiwanis group. By 1930 many towns also had chambers of commerce or similar organizations.

Until the American Legion was organized following the First World War, the most important ex-soldiers' organization in Arkansas was the United Confederate Veterans. In 1911 Little Rock was host to 110,000 visitors who attended the national reunion of the UCV. Arkansas Union veterans joined the Grand Army of the Republic, and by 1912 "blue and gray" reunions were being held in some north Arkansas towns.

The Arkansas Federation of Women's Clubs, organized in 1897, became one of the strongest of the women's organizations. The Arkansas Federation of Business and Professional Women's Clubs began in 1919. The years from 1893 to 1906 saw the appearance of several patriotic societies for women. Confederate monuments were erected on courthouse lawns in many Arkansas towns as a result of the efforts of the United Daughters of the Confederacy.

Sports. Baseball, w h i c h had been played by Little Rock and Fort Smith teams as early as 1867, increased in popularity after 1900. Football gained favor more slowly. The University of Arkansas, then called Arkansas Industrial University, started an athletic program about 1894. Coach Hugo Bezdek is credited with naming the university football team in 1909 when he referred to his men as "a wild band of Razorback hogs." After 1915 the high schools took up football, and basketball and track soon followed. Country clubs and the establishment of parks brought swimming pools, golf courses, and tennis courts to Arkansas cities and towns.

As early as 1885 the General Assembly began passing laws intended to protect fish and game. The complete extermination of the passenger pigeon, which once darkened Arkansas skies, warned that a similar fate might overtake other wildlife. Bear, once so plentiful that Arkansas was called the "Bear State," had nearly disappeared by the turn of the century. Deer and turkey were becoming scarce.

The General Assembly of 1915 enacted a statewide game and fish law and set up a Game and Fish Commission. Later the state government began a system of game refuges, and the Federal government established refuges in national forests. By 1930 it seemed that Arkansas fish and game would be saved from extinction.

Shooting passenger pigeons on a plantation near the Ouachita River, 1875. The last known passenger pigeon died in a zoo in 1914

☆　　☆　　☆　　☆

STUDY AIDS

Vocabulary

Be sure that you understand the meaning of the following words and phrases:

folk ballads
cipher
anvil
singing convention

Model T
stovewood
coal oil
Freemasonry

RFD
passenger pigeon

Grand Army of the
　Republic
game refuges

Identification

Tell what part each of the following had in the story:

Hugo Bezdek
Chautauqua
　Movement

fish and game laws

To test your reading

On other paper, list 1-10. Opposite each number write the word or words which complete each sentence.

1. Many people remembered the old folk ballads of __ and __ origin.

2. People "shot anvils" to celebrate __ as well as __.

3. The Negroes observed __ as Emancipation Day.

4. In some parts of Arkansas as late as __, __ and __ were still made at home.

5. Occasionally the farmer used a __ to hew out __ which he sold.

6. The Chautauqua Movement reached its height in the period of __.

7. The first radio station in Arkansas went on the air at __ in __.

8. In 1911 Arkansas was host to __ visitors who attended the national reunion of the __.

9. The Arkansas Federation of Women's Clubs was organized in __.

10. The Arkansas Game and Fish Commission was set up in __.

Things to do

1. Have a committee make a report on your community as it was in some year between 1898 and 1930. Ask older people what they remember. Make a bulletin-board display of drawings and old pictures. On a map of your community today, show the boundaries of your community as they were in the earlier year which you have chosen.

2. Make a report on the fraternal orders now active in your community.

3. Investigate and report on the game and fish laws and regulations now in effect in Arkansas.

4. Try to find a "crystal set" or other early type of radio and bring it to class.

5. Try to find rural cemeteries in your county where annual "decorations" are still held.

6. Collect words and music to folk songs remembered by older persons in your community. Perhaps you can secure the use of a tape recorder for this purpose and donate the tapes to your library after playing them for the class.

7. Visit the Ozark Folk Culture Center in Mountain View.

Reviewing the Unit

1. Why did it take so long to build the new state capitol?

2. Why did Arkansas have a financial problem?

3. What were the major new questions which disturbed many churches?

4. What were the effects of racial segregation in the fields of education and politics?

5. In what ways did Arkansas move toward better teacher education in the years from 1899 to 1929?

6. Why did many rural families need little money?

7. What sports became popular during this period?

Unit Nine

Contemporary Arkansas:
Economic and Social Crisis, 1930-1965

The Chapters

1. Arkansas in Depression and War
2. Leaving the Land
3. Industrial Revolution in Arkansas
4. The Changing Face of Arkansas
5. Race Relations and the Little Rock Crisis

THE YEARS SINCE 1930 have been years of crisis for Arkansas. First came the depression, and for a decade Arkansas and the rest of the country struggled to find a way out of hard times. Then the Second World War exploded on the global horizon, and soon tens of thousands of Arkansas men were on their way to battlefields beyond the seas.

The war started new trends in economic and social life. People left the farms to find better jobs in cities. After the war the movement away from the land continued, and Arkansas began losing population. After 1955 a determined drive to build Arkansas industry reversed the population decline. Arkansas emerged from its long rural past into the unfamiliar terrain of the industrial age.

Race relations became a problem of first importance after the Second World War. In 1957 a crisis over school integration at Little Rock made international headlines. The Negro demand for equality rocked Arkansas society to its foundations, but by 1965 there were many signs that peaceful adjustments would in time be made.

1　Arkansas in Depression and War

The great depression which began in 1929 brought the worst economic conditions that most Arkansans had ever seen. For a decade the state and nation struggled to recover. Then a new world war ended the depression but also brought tragedy and heartbreak to thousands of American homes.

The great depression. The First World War dislocated the economy of the United States and the entire world. After the war, American farms produced too much and farm prices went down. Industry was also overexpanded, and world trade declined. Credit was easy, and people borrowed too much. A great deal of borrowed money was invested in the stocks and bonds of business corporations. The investors expected the value of these stocks and bonds to increase. In October 1929 the New York stock market broke, and the United States slid into a major depression.

Arkansas people had known hard times before, but the depression years brought the worst conditions that most of the people of that day had ever experienced. Between 1929 and 1933 more than half of the manufacturing establishments in Arkansas shut down. Businessmen went bankrupt. Wages and salaries were reduced again and again. In the fall and winter of 1930-31 over a hundred banks failed, and dozens more followed. Many people lost their life savings in bank failures and in the failure of building and loan companies.

Surplus farm products piled up as prices dropped. The drouth of 1930, one of the worst in history, completed the ruin of the farmers. Farmers mortgaged their lands to get money and then lost them when they could not pay the debt. Other farmers, as well as property owners in the cities, lost their lands and homes because they could not pay their taxes. In 1933 taxes were delinquent on almost a third of all rural land in Arkansas.

As the depression deepened, more and more people lost their jobs. In 1933 Arkansas had 245,000 unemployed, as compared with only 24,000 four years earlier. Unemployed men and boys hitched rides on freight trains or walked from place to place looking for work. Homeless families camped by the roadsides. Bread lines and soup kitchens were set up in the cities. Thousands of Arkansas people experienced hunger, cold, and despair.

First attempts at recovery. Depression conditions were so bad that private charitable organizations and local governments soon ran out of money. The state tried to help in some ways. The General Assembly of 1931 set up a State Agricultural Credit Board to lend money to farmers. The plan failed because farmers could not repay loans. In late

1931 a special session of the General Assembly tried to reduce cotton acreage for the following year, hoping that cotton prices would go up. The attempt had little effect.

Arkansas people began to look to the Federal government for help. President Herbert Hoover, who happened to be in office when the depression struck, became very unpopular. In 1932 Arkansas voters helped elect Franklin D. Roosevelt, the Democratic candidate for president, who promised the people a "new deal."

Federal relief in Arkansas. Relief for the jobless and hungry was the first task of the government. Relief work began under the Hoover administration. The Reconstruction Finance Corporation (RFC), set up in 1932 to enable states to borrow money for relief, distributed $7,000,000 in Arkansas. Before the end of 1936 Arkansas had received $59,000,000 in Federal grants for relief purposes.

Farmers seeking "relief" help at Red Cross headquarters in Conway, 1930

Unemployed men and boys at a crossroads store during the depression

Workers' houses in a coal mining town in Arkansas during the depression

NYA workers building concrete sidewalks in Greenwood, Sebastian County, 1938

The New Deal provided direct relief grants, and set up agencies to conduct work relief programs. The Civil Works Administration (CWA) and the Public Works Administration (PWA) built roads, airports, water plants, schools, sewers, hospitals, public buildings, levees, and light plants.

The most important New Deal relief agency was the Works Progress Administration (WPA), set up in 1935 to provide useful jobs for those on the relief rolls. Arkansas WPA workers built roads, streets, public buildings, recreational facilities, canning plants, utility systems, libraries, and many other projects.

Young people employed by the National Youth Administration (NYA) built almost 500 new school buildings in Arkansas. The NYA helped many students to finish high school and go to college. Young men who joined the

Civilian Conservation Corps (CCC) lived in camps and worked in national forests and state parks. CCC workers set out trees, built roads and dams, and learned to read, write and make a living.

Crop control and conservation. In 1933 Congress set up the Agricultural Adjustment Administration (AAA) to help the farmers. Under the AAA program, farmers were paid to reduce crop acreages. By decreasing the supply, the government hoped to raise prices. In 1933 farmers had to plow up a part of the cotton crop or suffer a penalty at market time. A drouth in 1934 also helped reduce farm production.

Later Congress provided for a soil conservation program, under which farmers were paid for planting crops that would build up the soil rather

The soil conservation program taught Arkansas farmers to use contour cultivation on sloping land

than wear it out. Arkansas farmers accepted the soil conservation program with enthusiasm in 1937. Millions of acres of Arkansas land were badly eroded, and Arkansas led the nation in the percentage of farm land voluntarily included in soil conservation districts. By 1939 such districts had been formed in sixty counties.

Arkansas took steps to conserve other natural resources. The General Assembly of 1933 set up a control board which undertook a conservation program in the oil and gas industry. The same General Assembly strengthened the State Forestry Commission which had been created in 1931. Sawmill companies, especially the larger ones like Crossett, showed increased interest in fire protection, reforestation and selective cutting.

The proposed "Coin" Harvey pyramid at Monte Ne (right) was to have been sixty feet square at the base and 140 feet high. The amphitheater (below), intended as a preliminary to the pyramid, is now (1966) beneath the waters of Beaver Reservoir

Lake Dick, a Federal cooperative colony for landless
farmers near Altheimer, Jefferson County, 1940

In 1930 not one Arkansas farm home out of ten had running water and electricity. The Rural Electrification Administration (REA), which began its work in Arkansas in 1937, made loans to farmers' cooperatives for building electric lines into rural areas. Many Arkansas farm families had to wait for telephone service until after the Second World War.

Radical protest movements. The depression caused some Arkansas people to seek radical solutions to their problems. In 1932 about 1,000 Arkansas voters supported William H. "Coin" H a r v e y, the presidential candidate of the Liberty party, who advocated drastic reforms in the American money system. Harvey believed that civilization was doomed, and tried unsuccessfully to build a great concrete pyramid at Monte Ne, in Benton County, to preserve the records of his own time.

Other Arkansas people admired Senator Huey P. Long of Louisiana, who proposed to take money from the rich and give it to the common people. Commonwealth College, a private school near Mena, closed in 1940 after being accused of teaching atheism, Russian Communism, and racial equality.

When government control programs reduced crop acreage, many tenant farmers could no longer find work. In 1934 unemployed tenant farmers organized the Southern Tenant Farmers Union in Poinsett County. Strikes against landlords were attempted, and violence broke out in some places in eastern Arkansas. By 1936 the union had 23,000 members in the state, but decline set in after the union joined the CIO, a national labor organization, the following year.

To help the tenant farmers, the Federal government began several resettlement projects in eastern Arkansas. Dyess Colony in Mississippi County, an agricultural cooperative founded in 1934, included 16,000 acres divided into 500 farms. Such cooperatives helped many farmers become independent landowners. The government made loans to farmers and others to help them keep their homes, and bought unproductive lands for forests and grazing areas.

A new war ends the depression. Roosevelt's New Deal program helped the economic situation, at least temporarily. Government aid to Arkansas amounted to over $80,000,000 by the close of 1936. Then in 1937 a new business slump came, and the WPA rolls began to grow again. Arkansas had 90,000 unemployed, 67,000 employed only part time, and 30,000 emergency relief workers. Farm income was still low, though better than in 1933, and crop surpluses continued to pile up.

In the fall of 1939 European nations plunged into the Second World War, less than twenty-one years after the First World War had ended. The United States entered the conflict in 1941, after the Japanese attacked Hawaii and the Philippines on December 7. The war used up farm surpluses, put the unemployed to work, expanded production, stopped relief programs and ended the great depression.

The war years in Arkansas. The Second World War resembled the First World War in its effects on Arkansas people. Camp Pike, renamed Camp Joseph T. Robinson, again became an army training center. Another large training center, Camp Chaffee, was established near Fort Smith. Five air bases were located in the state. Men in uniform could be seen on the streets of every Arkansas town and village. Two hundred thousand Arkansans entered military service. Again Arkansas produced its heroes, including nine men who won the Congressional Medal of Honor. Arkansas natives like Generals Douglas MacArthur and Brehon B. Somervell were among the top military leaders.

The war of 1941-45 was longer than the struggle of 1917-18, with longer casualty lists. The Federal government imposed a system of rationing and price controls. Ration stamps or coupons were required to buy sugar, meats, butter, other fats, canned goods, coffee, shoes, gasoline, and fuel oil. Arkansans worked hard, worried about their men on the fighting fronts, cultivated "victory gardens," served in civilian defense units, bought war bonds and stamps, saved scrap metal and paper, and donated blood to Red Cross "blood banks." A few people grumbled about shortages of consumer goods and the 35-miles-an-hour speed limit on the highways, but most Arkansans were better off financially than ever before.

The Federal government established two concentration camps for Japanese-Americans in southeast Arkansas in 1942. One was located at Rohwer, the other at Jerome. Most of the inmates were brought from the west coast of the United States because Federal authorities were suspicious of their loyalty in the war against Japan. Many Arkansas people disliked these "relocation centers," as they were called, but the Japanese gave little trouble. As the war drew to an end the camps were gradually closed.

The Second World War brought increased industry to Arkansas. New plants were built to manufacture war materials. Thousands of Arkansans learned industrial skills and were ready to work at something besides farming after the war. Wartime needs led to the construction of two aluminum plants in Arkansas, each costing many millions of dollars, one located at Hurricane Creek, the other at Jones Mill. At these plants bauxite mined in Arkansas began to be processed in the state for the first time.

President Franklin D. Roosevelt (in front seat of automobile) at Camp Robinson, 1943

STUDY AIDS

Vocabulary

Be sure that you understand the meaning of these words and phrases:

relief
delinquent
contemporary
slump
concentration
  camp
stock market
selective cutting

bankrupt
rationing
utility system
farm surpluses
price control
drastic
cooperatives
New Deal

Identification

Tell what part each of the following had in the story:

William H.
  "Coin" Harvey
Huey P. Long
WPA
Southern Tenant
  Farmers Union
REA
Douglas
  MacArthur

Brehon B.
  Somervell
Franklin D.
  Roosevelt
Herbert Hoover
AAA
CCC

Location

Find these places on a map.

Monte Ne
Mena
Jones Mill
Camp Chaffee

Poinsett County
Camp Robinson
Rohwer
Jerome

To test your reading

On other paper, list 1-10. Opposite each number, write the word or words which complete each sentence.

1. The date of the coming of the depression was ___.

2. In Arkansas in the fall and winter of 1930-31 over ___ banks failed.

3. In 1933 taxes were delinquent on ___ of all rural land in Arkansas.

4. In 1933 Arkansas had ___ unemployed.

5. The RFC distributed $___ in Arkansas.

6. The most important New Deal relief agency was the ___.

7. Members of the CCC lived in camps and worked in ___.

8. Arkansas led the nation in the percentage of ___.

9. In 1934 unemployed tenant farmers organized the ___.

10. Camp Pike was renamed ___.

Things to do

1. Interview a local businessman or farmer about the great depression which began in 1929. Find out how he was affected and how he felt about the New Deal measures which affected him.

2. Ask someone who served overseas during the Second World War to tell the class about his experiences.

3. If you live on a farm, tell the class about conservation practices with which you are familiar.

4. Try to organize a temporary "World War Two Museum." See if you can find newspapers and magazines published during the war, ration books, service ribbons and medals, German and Japanese flags, V-Mail letters, photographs, souvenirs brought or sent home from foreign countries, and anything else connected with the war.

5. See if you can find out what the NYA and CCC did in your community.

2 Leaving the Land

Conditions are never the same after a great war, and the Second World War was no exception. As the machine age reached Arkansas farms, people abandoned the land and moved to the cities. Large numbers of Arkansans left their native state, never to return.

The agricultural revolution. The Second World War increased the speed of a number of trends in Arkansas agriculture that had been under way since the worst part of the depression. During the war farmers expanded crop acreage in order to supply wartime needs. High prices for farm products made it possible for farmers to buy tractors and other machinery. Since labor was scarce, farmers learned to get along with less hired help.

The number of farms in Arkansas had been decreasing since 1935, when there were 253,000. After the war farms became fewer and fewer. From 1949 to 1959 the number declined from 182,000 to 95,000, with a very rapid decrease after 1954. Arkansas had about the same number of farms in 1959 as in 1880.

As the number of farms declined, remaining farms grew larger. The average size of Arkansas farms increased from 103 acres in 1949 to 173 acres ten years later. Larger farms and increased use of machinery meant that farming became more expensive. The small farmer could not keep up and had to sell or lease his farm to a larger operator. Machinery took the place of hired hands and tenants. In 1959 only twenty-four per cent of Arkansas farm-ers were tenants, compared with forty-five per cent in 1944 and sixty-three per cent in 1930. Almost half of the cotton crop was harvested mechanically in 1960, while only ten years earlier human hands were still doing almost all such work.

The large new commercial farms steadily became more productive, with the result that fewer farms and farmers were needed. The New Deal era brought tight Federal controls over agriculture. As the government reduced crop acreages, farmers used fertilizers, soil-enriching crops, and other scientific methods to increase the yield. Cotton acreage in Arkansas in 1959 was only a third of the 1929 acreage, but more bales were produced.

Arkansas remained a leading cotton state, but most of the cotton was grown in the eastern counties. Federal crop subsidies and soil conservation payments encouraged upland farmers to replace worn-out cotton "patches" with pine trees, pastures and stock ponds. Cotton gins disappeared from the highland counties and livestock sale barns took their place. The state government began encouraging livestock raising through subsidizing shows and fairs as early as 1938.

Plowing cotton with mule-drawn cultivators

Rice fields continued to spread over Grand Prairie and parts of the northeast. Soybeans became increasingly important to lowland farmers after about 1950. The depression had encouraged broiler raising in northwestern Arkansas and after the war the poultry business spread over the western counties. In broiler production Arkansas advanced to second rank in the nation by 1960. Feed mills and poultry processing plants became important industries, and feed dealers began financing chicken raisers by a new form of the old farm credit system.

End of the family farm. The coming of large-scale, mechanized commercial agriculture spelled the end of the family farm. Rising costs that outran farm prices made it hard for the small farmer to make ends meet. He could not afford to buy costly tractors and other equipment. Drouth in the early 1950s encouraged many small farmers to give up the struggle and leave.

The movement of population away from the farms left abandoned farmhouses and crumbling mule barns all over the state. Old fields grew up in thickets of pine and sedge. Rural families scattered, and the old "homeplace" was sold or deserted. In many rural areas almost the only people left were elderly pensioners.

Some small farmers stayed on the land and got jobs in town. Prosperous farm families enjoyed modern conveniences such as well pumps, washing machines and refrigerators, and most of the drudgery once connected with rural life disappeared. But some farmers continued trying to make a living on acreages too small to provide an adequate income, and the low income small farmer remained a problem for Arkansas. In 1964 the Federal government began an experimental rural renewal program in Little River County.

304

The growing cities. Since the depression masses of farm people have moved to Arkansas cities and towns. In 1940 four out of five Arkansans still lived on farms. Almost half of the people of the state lived in towns and cities by 1960. In the same twenty-year period the number of Arkansas cities with over 10,000 population increased from nine to nineteen.

Little Rock remained the largest Arkansas city, but it grew less than others. Between 1940 and 1960 North Little Rock tripled its population, and Pine Bluff doubled in size. Cities like Blytheville, El Dorado, Jonesboro, Fayetteville, West Memphis, Jacksonville, Conway and Benton grew rapidly.

The growing cities were centers of transportation as well as population. In 1960 three major airlines provided service to the state, and almost a hundred cities and towns had airports. Highways radiated from the larger cities like spokes on a wheel.

Rapid urban growth created many new problems. Cities had to find money for streets, fire and police protection, and many other services. Slums had to be cleared and good housing made available. In 1962 Little Rock secured a Federal loan to begin a huge urban renewal project, intended to remake the entire downtown section of the city. Other cities also began planning urban renewal projects, but the idea was rejected in some places. Beginning in 1957 several Arkansas cities, including Little Rock, adopted the city manager plan of government under which the city's affairs are handled by a professional administrator.

Arkansas loses population. During the depression years Arkansas people generally stayed at home because times were hard all over the country. When the Second World War brought an economic boom, people began leaving the farms and small towns of Arkansas in order to find good jobs in the war plants of other states. Not many of these people came back when the war ended, and others continued to leave.

When the Korean War broke out in 1950, another large migration began.

Farmers' market during strawberry season at Bald Knob, White County, 1941

High-paying jobs were again easy to find in Texas, California and other states. In the period 1950-54 the population of Arkansas again declined as it had in 1942-45. Many of the people who moved away from Arkansas would have preferred to stay, but Arkansas agriculture and industry could not provide them with a good living.

Most of the migrants were farm people, many of them uneducated and unskilled. But Arkansas was also losing too many of her best educated young adult workers. Many of those left behind were school-age youths and older workers or retired people. This situation meant that fewer workers had to support more dependents and pay more taxes.

The Federal censuses of 1950 and 1960 reflected this population loss. The 1960 total was 1,786,272 people. This was six and one-half per cent lower than the 1950 total, and nine per cent less than the population in 1940. Negroes moved away in especially large numbers.

A declining population meant an Arkansas on the downhill road. Arkansas would have to provide jobs for her people by developing industries. Even before the end of the Second World War, some Arkansas leaders recognized the problem and began looking for solutions.

Saturday afternoon at the wagon yard in Arkadelphia, 1940

Preparing spinach for canning, Van Buren, 1939

Opening the levees to control water flow in a newly seeded rice field, Arkansas County

STUDY AIDS

Vocabulary

Be sure that you understand the meaning of these words and phrases:

trends	drudgery
migrants	"cotton patches"
city manager plan	pensioners
urban renewal	commercial farms
spelled	broiler raising
subsidies	soybeans

Location

Find these places on a map:

Jonesboro	Blytheville
Fayetteville	Arkansas City
West Memphis	Jacksonville
	Benton (city)

To test your reading

On other paper, list 1-8. Opposite each number, write the word or words which complete each sentence.

1. Arkansas had about the same number of farms in 1959 as in ___.

2. Almost half of the cotton crop was harvested mechanically in the year ___.

3. In many rural areas almost the only people left were ___.

4. In 1960 almost a hundred cities and towns had ___.

5. In 1957 Arkansas cities began to adopt the ___ plan of government.

6. In 1960 the total population of the state was ___.

7. In 1959 only ___ per cent of Arkansas farmers were tenants compared with ___ per cent in 1944 and ___ per cent in ___.

8. Cotton acreage in Arkansas in 1959 was only ___ of the 1929 acreage but more bales were produced.

Things to do

1. If you live in a farming area, look for evidences of the "agricultural revolution" described in this chapter. In what ways has farming changed in the last ten or twenty years? Select a committee to interview local farmers and businessmen and make a report.

2. Plan a visit to Winrock Farm on Petit Jean Mountain, or to the agricultural experiment station nearest your school.

3. What is the average size of farms in your county? What percentage of the farmers in your county are tenants? Ask your county agent for information.

4. Find out how the present population of your city or town compares with its population in 1960, 1950, 1940 and 1930.

3 Industrial Revolution in Arkansas

As the old rural Arkansas dwindled and disappeared, a new industrial state arose. Arkansas leaders and people united their efforts to restore the state's prosperity and population. The ten years after 1955 saw Arkansas move ahead economically as never before in its history.

The Arkansas Plan. Though the Second World War brought prosperity to Arkansas, farsighted business leaders realized that postwar jobs would be a problem. Tractors and other machinery were reducing the demand for farm labor. The war increased the number of skilled workers. Many of the 200,000 Arkansas servicemen would not be satisfied to return to their old low-income jobs.

In 1943 C. Hamilton Moses of Arkansas Power and Light Company called a meeting of business leaders to organize the Arkansas Economic Council. The Council, later merged with the State Chamber of Commerce, began planning for postwar industrial growth. The General Assembly of 1945 created the Arkansas Resources and Development Commission and set up a Bureau of Research at the University of Arkansas.

The "Arkansas Plan" which these agencies worked out was an effort to balance agriculture with new industry. Business leaders made speeches all over Arkansas to arouse interest in the plan. New c h a m b e r s of commerce were formed in many cities, and counties set up development committees.

Leaders of the program encouraged local communities to plan their own growth. More than 300 community clinics were conducted, where people had a chance to study and discuss their problems. In 1950 the Arkansas Community Development Contest was begun in an attempt to encourage cities to improve themselves, and the following year the Rural Community Improvement Contest was launched.

The AIDC and industrial financing.
The Arkansas Plan interested the people in industrial development, but there was little money to help new industries get started. Industrialists expected financial assistance from the cities and towns where new plants would be located, but Arkansas towns usually could not raise enough money. As a result new industries continued to bypass Arkansas and go to other states.

The General Assembly of 1955 created the Arkansas Industrial Development Commission (AIDC), which proved to be one of the most important new state agencies in twenty years. Governor Orval E. Faubus appointed Winthrop Rockefeller, a Republican, as chairman. The AIDC set out to bring new industry to Arkansas and help existing plants to expand.

At the same time the legislators began to search for new ways of financing industry. The act establishing

Blocks and poles of pure aluminum at a plant storage yard near Arkadelphia

AIDC provided also for the organization of local non-profit industrial development corporations. Such corporations could own property, raise money, and aid new industries. A state board was set up to lend money to local corporations.

The First Arkansas Development Finance Corporation (FADFC) was established by the General Assembly of 1957. This statewide institution could make loans of a type not usually offered by banks and other investors, and thereby help local businesses.

In 1958 the voters adopted Amendment 49 to the state constitution. This amendment allowed cities, towns and counties to issue bonds for industrial development and repay the money by a local tax. Act 9 of 1960, passed by a special session of the General Assembly, permitted counties and municipalities to issue bonds, buy and equip industrial properties, and pay off the bonds by revenue such as rent from the property owned. Each step in the industrial

financing program was an attempt to meet new needs and correct shortcomings.

The drive for industry. The ten years after 1955 witnessed a drive in Arkansas for industrial development. The AIDC advertised the "Land of Opportunity" all over the United States. A statewide "Committee of 100" business and professional people helped the AIDC campaign with donations and volunteer work. Industrial development corporations were formed in many communities, and planning programs got under way in Arkansas towns and cities.

A Graduate Institute of Technology, connected with the University of Arkansas, was established at Little Rock in 1957. Its purpose was to provide scientific and technical training for industrial growth. The Industrial Research and Extension Center of the University of Arkansas worked closely with the AIDC. Newspapers, television, and radio stations gave time and space to industrial development. Public utilities, railroads, insurance companies, banks, and the State Chamber of Commerce joined in the industrial drive.

The results were encouraging. By 1965 Arkansas had gained several hundred new industrial plants and thousands of new jobs. Wages and income were going up. As the industrial program caught on, the state began to gain rather than lose population. By the summer of 1964, Arkansas had an estimated 1,933,000 people, an increase of almost 147,000 in four years and a larger population than in 1950.

Industrial trends since 1939. More than sixty per cent of the land of Arkansas is still covered with forests, and timber has remained the most important single industry. In 1964 hardwood timber was still being cut faster than it could grow, but better forest management had resulted in more pine timber being grown each year than was being removed. Before 1939 paper mills began operation in Camden and Crossett, and new mills were built later in Pine Bluff. Though lumber production continued to rise, many workers lost their jobs as companies turned to machinery in an attempt to keep down costs.

In 1962 the food processing industry stood second to lumber as the largest employer of manufacturing workers in Arkansas. New fruit and vegetable canneries and poultry processing plants accounted for most of the growth of the food industry after 1939. Next to food processing, the production of cloth-

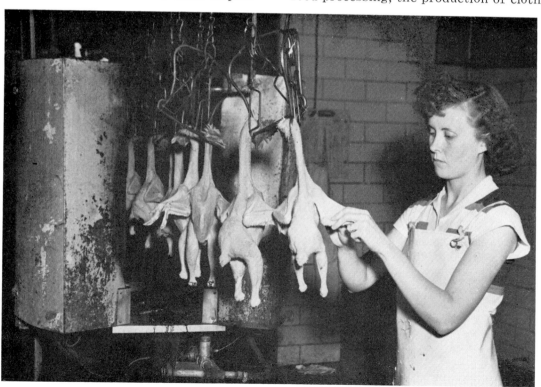

Processing line in a broiler plant

The antenna of the Caddo Gap research station for communications satellites, Montgomery County. The station began operating in 1966

ing has provided Arkansas people with more new jobs since 1939 than any other industry. Furniture-making became more important after about 1950, and a number of shoe factories have located in Arkansas since the Second World War.

Other industries which provide many jobs for Arkansas workers include glass, brick and concrete products; chemicals; electrical machinery; printing; aluminum; fabricated metals; petroleum; instruments; machinery; transportation; rubber; toys; and sporting goods. Most of these industries either came to the state for the first time after the Second World War, or expanded during the postwar years.

By 1964 Arkansas, more and more dependent on its factories for a living,

was a closely related part of the nation and the world. Symbolic of this closeness was the dedication of the new Little Rock Air Force Base near Jacksonville in 1955, the same year that the first jet bombers landed at another new base at Blytheville. In 1961-62 the Federal government built eighteen underground launching sites for Titan missiles in an arc across north central Arkansas from Morrilton toward Newport. If another world war should come, Arkansas might become one of the first targets of enemy action.

Industrial labor since the depression. The New Deal period brought an increase of union organization in Arkansas, especially in the timber industry which employed half of the state's industrial workers. Though labor unions made progress after the Second World War, in 1960 more than half the work force in manufacturing was still unorganized.

Two labor measures passed during the Second World War were disliked by the unions. The General Assembly of 1943 enacted an anti-violence law directed at strikers. Then in 1944 the voters approved a constitutional amendment called the "Freedom to Work" or "Right to Work" law. This amendment provided that workers did not have to belong to labor unions in order to secure and hold jobs.

Arkansas has not passed many laws regulating conditions of employment. A workmen's compensation act, requiring payment by employers in case of injury or death of employees, became effective in 1940. Repeated attempts to pass a general minimum wage law ended in failure. The Federal and state governments help unemployed workers with cash payments and assistance in finding jobs.

The world's largest rice driers at Stuttgart, Arkansas County

Since the Second World War, Arkansas has had a labor surplus because industry has not been able to employ all the workers leaving the farms. The unemployment rate has helped keep Arkansas wages lower than the national average. The trend in industry is to automation, or the use of machinery to perform work formerly done by men.

STUDY AIDS

Vocabulary

Be sure that you understand the meaning of these words and phrases:

industrial revolution	merged
	labor surplus

bypass
rural community
symbolic
automation
hardwood
Right to Work law
clinic

local tax
Institute of Technology
food processing industry
State Chamber of Commerce
minimum wage

313

Location

Find these places on a map:

Camden   Pine Bluff
Crossett   Morrilton
                Newport

Identification

Tell what part each of the following had in the story:

C. Hamilton Moses Committee of 100
Amendment 49   Orval E. Faubus
Winthrop
  Rockefeller

To test your reading

On other paper, list 1-10. Opposite each number, write the word or words which complete each sentence.

1. The "Arkansas Plan" was an effort to ___.

2. The AIDC proved to be ___.

3. The first chairman of the AIDC was ___.

4. Act 9 of 1960 permitted counties and cities to ___.

5. The ten years after 1955 witnessed a drive in Arkansas for ___.

6. The Graduate Institute of Technology was established in the year ___.

7. By 1965 Arkansas had gained several hundred new ___ and thousands of new ___.

8. In 1960 the largest employer of manufacturing workers was the ___ industry; the second largest was the ___ industry.

9. Arkansas in 1962 had ___ launching sites for ___.

10. More than ___ per cent of the land of Arkansas is covered with ___, and ___ has remained the most important single industry.

Things to do

1. Make a report on an Arkansas industry in which you might be interested in working when you get older. Find out something about the history of the industry, the raw materials used, where the manufactured goods are sent, the number of people who work there, and the services provided for the employees.

2. From newspapers and magazines, collect advertisements of products made in Arkansas.

3. Has your community participated in either the Arkansas Community Development Contest or the Rural Community Improvement Contest? Interview civic leaders and report to the class. What are the standards used in judging communities in these contests?

4. If there is a new factory in your community or town, has the town or county helped to finance it through one of the plans described in this chapter? Ask your mayor or city manager, or someone designated by him, to explain local industrial financing to the class or to a committee representing the class.

4 The Changing Face of Arkansas

In recent years the appearance of many parts of Arkansas has been changing. Great dams have created lakes where none existed before. A plan to control and develop the Arkansas River is under way. An improved system of state parks attracts thousands of visitors. In many places new building projects can be seen.

President John F. Kennedy dedicating Greers Ferry Dam, Cleburne County, 1963. Congressman Wilbur D. Mills is standing directly behind the President. Congressmen Oren Harris, E. C. Gathings, and J. W. Trimble are in the front row, right

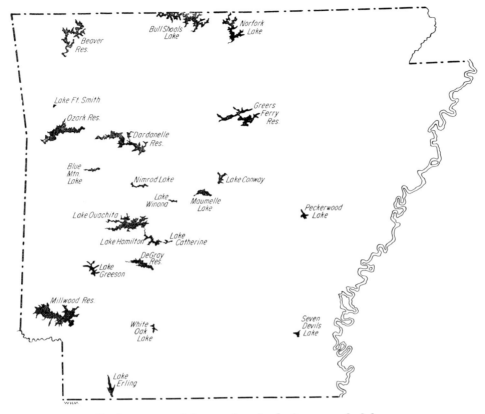

Contemporary Arkansas is a land of man-made lakes

The new lakes. As a result of the great flood of 1927, the Federal government took over flood control work on the Mississippi River. An important part of flood control was the building of dams, which could also provide hydroelectric power. Arkansas Power and Light Company built two such dams, forming Lake Hamilton and Lake Catherine, on the Ouachita River before the depression.

In 1937 floods on the Ohio River caused new interest in dam construction. The Federal program which had begun in 1928 kept the Mississippi within its banks, but backwater floods on the Arkansas, White, and St. Francis rivers caused great damage.

The Federal government began to plan a system of dams on Arkansas streams, but the Second World War interrupted the program. Nimrod and Norfork dams were completed during the war, but other construction had to wait until the conflict was over.

After the war the Federal program, conducted by the Army Corps of Engineers, moved into high gear. By 1965 huge concrete dams had formed Blue Mountain, Greeson, Bull Shoals, Ouachita, Table Rock, Greers Ferry, Dardanelle, and Beaver reservoirs. According to plans, in a few years Gillham, Millwood, Ozark, DeGray and perhaps other lakes would be created by more dams. The Arkansas Game and Fish

Commission built a number of smaller lakes for fishing. Big Maumelle Lake provided a new water supply for Little Rock. Besides the dams the Federal government spent money in Arkansas on levees, bank stabilization, and drainage projects.

The new lakes provided flood control, water, electric power, and outdoor recreation, but there was another side to the story. Dams put an end to many of the free-flowing natural streams of Arkansas. And as great areas of Arkansas land disappeared under the lake waters, old communities vanished and many people had to give up their homes and farms.

The Arkansas River Project. Throughout history the Arkansas River has been an unruly, destructive stream. Plans to control and develop the river in Arkansas and Oklahoma were discussed for many years. Advocates of river development agreed that a series of dams and locks on the Arkansas River would provide flood control, navigation, electric power, and recreation. The valley of the Arkansas, poor economically, could become one of the great industrial valleys of the world, comparable to the Ohio, the Tennessee and the Rhine.

Only the Federal government had the resources necessary to undertake such

Transformers behind Bull Shoals Dam. Electricity generated by water power has become one of Arkansas' great resources

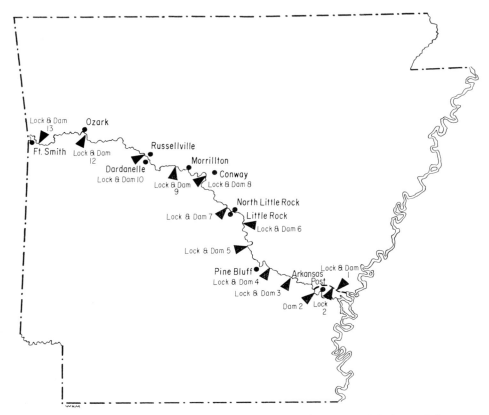

The Arkansas River Project, showing the proposed system of locks and dams
(There is no Lock and Dam 11)

a project. In 1943 a destructive flood caused Arkansas and Oklahoma leaders to join in an effort to persuade Congress to act. Congress approved a plan in 1946, but another ten years passed before enough money was appropriated to get the Arkansas River Project started.

The development project, supposed to be completed in 1970, involved spending over a billion dollars on a 450-mile stretch of the Arkansas River in Arkansas and Oklahoma. Twelve of the eighteen dams, with locks to make boat traffic possible, were to be built in Arkansas. Of the two largest Arkansas dams, in 1965 Dardanelle had been completed and work on Ozark

Dam was under way. The Army Corps of Engineers, which was supervising the Arkansas River Project, planned a navigation channel nine feet deep and 250 feet wide.

As the project moved forward, cities along the river began planning to establish ports to handle shipments of timber, bauxite, oil and other products. Deepening of the Ouachita River channel up to Camden began in 1960, and there was discussion of similar improvement of White River. In 1965 it appeared that the rivers of Arkansas, which had carried the pioneers and their goods, might again come into their own.

The tourists. Since the Second World War, automobiles and good highways have made it possible for Americans to travel as never before. The state government has advertised widely in an attempt to attract tourists to Arkansas. In 1962 an estimated 20,000,000 persons visited the state, more than three times the number in 1950. Since 1941 governors have awarded "Arkansas Traveler" certificates to distinguished visitors as well as citizens.

Many people came to Arkansas to fish and hunt. Conservation and new game refuges increased the number of deer, turkeys, and other game. The new lakes drew fishermen, boaters, and campers. Natural beauties and historic places attracted other visitors. The state park system, which began with Petit Jean near Morrilton in 1923, expanded rapidly after 1955. Motels, lodges and tourist courts multiplied.

To attract visitors and promote their products, Arkansas towns sponsored fairs, festivals and celebrations. Few such events were complete without a "beauty queen" or princess, who then traveled to advertise the project or activity she represented. "Miss Arkansas" pageants were held every year beginning in 1944, and Donna Axum of El Dorado became "Miss America" of 1964. The state fair and livestock show was attended by thousands in Little Rock every fall. Football games, especially those at the new War Memorial Stadium in Little Rock, drew visitors from all over Arkansas and from neighboring states.

New construction. A construction boom was under way in Arkansas in 1965, as new building projects took shape in many places. River navigation and flood control projects were proceeding at a steady rate. The state was spending millions of dollars for new buildings to house government departments, and construction was also under way on new state college buildings. Private colleges, generally more prosperous than ever before, were carrying out large construction projects of their own.

Urban renewal continued to change the appearance and composition of several Arkansas cities. Millions were being spent for private homes, apartment buildings, and commercial and industrial plants. Public utility companies were expanding, in order to keep up with increasing needs for gas, electricity, and other services. Public works projects under way in 1965 included highways, streets, waterworks, sewers, hospitals, levees, post offices, airports, and many others. Altogether more than one billion dollars would be spent on new construction in Arkansas in the year 1965.

STUDY AIDS

Vocabulary

Be sure that you understand the meaning of the following words and phrases:

dams and locks
ports
Arkansas Traveler
  certificate
public utility
  plants

free flowing
  streams
building projects
pageant
bank stabilization

Location

Find these places on a map:

Petit Jean
Lake Ouachita
Greer's Ferry
  Lake

Big Maumelle
  Lake
Lake Hamilton
Lake Greeson

Identification

Tell what part each of the following had in the story:

Corps of
  Engineers
Arkansas River
  Project

War Memorial
  Stadium

To test your reading

On other paper, list 1-9. Opposite each number write the word or words which complete each sentence.

1. An important part of flood control was the ___ which could also provide ___ power.

2. By 1965 huge concrete dams had formed ___, ___, ___, ___, ___, ___, ___, and ___ reservoirs.

3. Lake Hamilton and Lake Catherine were built by ___ Company on the ___ River near ___.

4. Advocates of river development for the Arkansas River agreed that a series of ___ would provide ___, ___, ___, and ___.

5. The navigation channel planned for the Arkansas River is to be ___ feet deep and ___ feet wide.

6. In 1962 an estimated ___ persons visited Arkansas, more than ___ times the number in ___.

7. The state park system began with Petit Jean near ___ in the year ___.

8. In 1964 Donna Axum of El Dorado became ___.

9. Public works projects under way in 1965 included ___.

Things to do

1. Visit one of the large dams constructed by the Army Corps of Engineers in Arkansas.

2. Prepare a sketch map of Arkansas showing state parks and the larger lakes.

3. Does your community have an annual fair, festival or other celebration? If so, plan a parade float or exhibit about Arkansas history.

4. Draw a large map of Arkansas for your bulletin board and title it "Arkansas Today." Let each class member choose two places of interest. Include colleges, state and national parks, cities and towns, historic sites, and vacation spots. Each member will find information on his places and report to the class.

5   Race Relations and the Little Rock Crisis

Since the Second World War, Negro Arkansans have become increasingly insistent on political, social and economic rights denied them under the old segregation system. The question of voting rights caused little trouble, but school integration resulted in a crisis that placed Little Rock at the center of the world stage.

The Negro and politics. The changing relations between the white and Negro races became one of Arkansas' greatest problems after the Second World War. During the depression and war period, many Negroes left the plantations and farms and moved into the cities. As Negroes secured better jobs and came into contact with the outside world, they became more interested in education, voting, and other opportunities equal to those enjoyed by white people.

In Arkansas the Democratic party did not usually allow Negroes to vote in primaries, run as candidates or hold party offices. Other Southern states also had "white" primaries. In 1944 the Supreme Court of the United States declared the white primary illegal. The Arkansas General Assembly of 1945 tried to get around this ruling by setting up four different primaries instead of two. Negroes could vote in the two primaries in which candidates for Federal offices were nominated, but they were not to be allowed to vote in the primaries for state and local officials.

This four-primary scheme was tried in 1946. It proved expensive and in 1947 the General Assembly abandoned the plan. Over 20,000 Negroes voted in Democratic primaries in 1948. Two years later the State Democratic Convention did away with the white primary entirely. At the recommendation of Orval E. Faubus, Democratic nominee for governor in 1954, the party convention of that year admitted Negroes as party officials for the first time.

School integration begins. In the field of education, Arkansas Negroes were making progress before 1954. In 1948 the University of Arkansas began admitting Negroes to some classes. Philander Smith College, a Negro school in Little Rock, secured full accreditation. New Negro schools were built in many districts, and attempts were made to equalize the salaries of Negro and white teachers. The state opened a training school for delinquent Negro girls at Fargo in 1949, and improved the facilities for Negroes at other state institutions.

On May 17, 1954 the United States Supreme Court ruled that racial segregation in public schools must be ended. A year later the Court said that school districts should make a "prompt and reasonable start" to end segregation "with all deliberate speed." Few white

Negro students barred from entering Central High School in Little Rock by an officer of the Arkansas National Guard, September 1957

Arkansans liked the desegregation ruling, but many of them thought the state would have to accept it. Whites who believed strongly that integration was wrong began to join organizations like the White Citizens' Councils. Negro and white integrationists supported the National Association for the Advancement of Colored People (NAACP).

School districts in Charleston and Fayetteville desegregated quietly in the fall of 1954. The next year eight more school districts announced plans for gradual integration. Besides the university, five of the six white state-supported colleges admitted Negroes in 1955. The other college received no applications from Negro students.

The first integration trouble. The first trouble over integration came at Hoxie, in Lawrence County. Hoxie admitted twenty Negro students to white schools in the fall of 1955. After three weeks a strong protest movement developed. The Hoxie school board had to go to Federal court to restrain the troublemakers and have its rights upheld.

In October 1955 Negroes brought suit against the Van Buren school board and forced the board to submit a desegregation plan. Mrs. L. C. (Daisy) Bates, state president of the NAACP, brought suit in 1956 to force immediate integration in Little Rock. The Federal courts upheld the gradual integration plan which had been announced by the Little Rock school board.

Political resistance to integration was beginning to appear by 1956. In November the voters approved a constitutional amendment and a pupil assignment act, both directed against integration. The General Assembly of 1957 passed four segregation laws which Governor Orval E. Faubus would use in the Little Rock crisis later.

Crisis at Little Rock. Little Rock planned to integrate its schools over a period of six years. The first Negroes were to be admitted to Central High School in September 1957. On the second day of September, Governor Faubus sent armed National Guardsmen to Central High School and announced that he was doing this to keep the peace. When the nine Negro children attempted to enter the school two days later, the Guardsmen would not let them in. This action was widely taken to mean that the governor was defying the authority of the Federal government.

For three weeks the Arkansas National Guard kept the nine Negro students out of Central High School. A conference at Newport, Rhode Island, between Governor Faubus and President Dwight D. Eisenhower was a failure. Under a new Federal court order issued September 20, the governor withdrew the National Guard. For two days Little Rock police tried and failed

Little Rock police attempting to restrain crowd in front of Central High School during the integration crisis of 1957

323

Federal troops escorting Negro students into Central High School, 1957

to control the crowds that gathered at the school each morning.

President Eisenhower then placed the Arkansas National Guard under Federal control. Troops of the 101st Airborne Division of the United States Army entered Little Rock on September 24, and the next day the nine Negroes re-entered Central High School. Troops continued to patrol the school until the academic year ended in 1958.

Closing of the schools. Before school opened again in the fall of 1958, Governor Faubus called a special session of the General Assembly. Laws were passed giving the governor authority to close schools that were being integrated by force. When the United States Supreme Court refused to allow integration to be delayed at Little Rock, Governor Faubus closed all four of the city's

high schools. In a special election, Little Rock voters endorsed the governor's action. The schools remained closed throughout the 1958-59 academic year. Several private schools for whites were opened, but many white and Negro students did not have a chance to go to school at all.

The schools reopen. After the closing of the schools the Little Rock school board resigned and a new board was elected. Three members of the board were extreme segregationists and three were moderates who wanted to reopen the schools. In 1959 opposition to the policies of some of the board members led to a recall election. In the election Little Rock voters removed the three segregationists and kept the three moderates on the board. In June 1959 a special Federal court declared the

Arkansas school closing law unconstitutional. The Little Rock school board, now made up of six moderates, announced that schools would reopen in the fall.

A segregationist mob tried to prevent the opening of the integrated high schools on August 12. Little Rock police and firemen stopped the marchers a block away from Central High School. On a stormy night three weeks later dynamite explosions went off at three different places in Little Rock, one of them the school board office. The five offenders were rounded up and convicted. Eight Negro students attended Central and Hall high schools in 1959-60.

Effects of the Little Rock crisis. The school integration trouble in Little Rock gave Arkansas worldwide publicity. The capital city swarmed with

newsmen. Many news stories were highly unfavorable to Arkansas, and made the situation appear much worse than it really was. Troublemakers from outside Arkansas added to the confusion.

The Little Rock trouble aroused the emotions of many Arkansas people. There were protest rallies, threats, ugly telephone calls, and the like. The **Arkansas Gazette,** a Little Rock daily which advocated moderation, suffered losses of circulation and income. Congressman Brooks Hays of Little Rock was defeated in the general election of 1958 after an eight-day write-in campaign by Dr. Dale Alford, an outspoken segregationist. Governor Faubus was widely admired by segregationists and opponents of a strong Federal government, and disliked by integrationists and many moderates. In 1960 the National States Rights party nominated

Little Rock police stopping a segregationist march on Central High School, 1959

him for president, but the governor supported Democratic candidate John F. Kennedy.

The crisis caused hard feelings between many white and Negro Arkansans. The sending of troops to Little Rock aroused great resentment in Arkansas against the Eisenhower administration. Some people were afraid that the bad publicity would keep new industries from coming to the state. Most Arkansans agreed that the school troubles of 1957-59 should never have occurred, but they disagreed over who had been at fault.

Racial integration since 1957. Integration in public schools advanced very slowly in Arkansas for several years. Some districts ended segregation voluntarily, others under Federal pressure or court orders. More than ten years after the Supreme Court decision of 1954, ninety per cent of the public school districts having both white and Negro students were still segregated. At the rate that integration was moving it would be more than a century before Arkansas schools were completely desegregated.

In 1964 Congress passed a strong civil rights law which required that school districts begin to integrate or face loss of Federal aid. By the time schools opened in the fall of 1965 almost all the districts in Arkansas had agreed to comply with the law. In many places Negro organizations staged public demonstrations to force restaurants, theaters, drive-ins and other businesses to desegregate. They were to a considerable degree successful.

Governor Orval E. Faubus holding a press conference in the state capitol, 1957

STUDY AIDS

Vocabulary

Be sure that you understand the meaning of these words and phrases:

primaries	defy
nominee	patrol
nominated	moderates
desegregation	recall election
pupil assignment	academic year
integration	write-in campaign
restrain	civil rights law

Identification

Tell what part each of the following had in the story:

Dwight D. Eisenhower	Brooks Hays
101st Airborne Division	Daisy Bates
	Dale Alford
Arkansas National Guard	Orval E. Faubus

To test your reading

On other paper, list 1-10. Opposite each number, write the word or words which complete the sentence.

1. In Arkansas before 1944 the Democratic party did not usually allow Negroes to __, __ or __.
2. The University of Arkansas began admitting Negroes in the year __.
3. On May 17, 1954 the United States Supreme Court ruled that __.
4. The letters NAACP stand for __.
5. The first trouble over integration came at __ in the fall of __.
6. Troops of the 101st Airborne Division entered __ on __.
7. In 1958 Governor Faubus closed __ in the city of __.
8. The school trouble in Little Rock gave Arkansas worldwide __.
9. The *Arkansas Gazette* was an outspoken advocate of __.
10. In 1964 Congress passed a __ law which required that schools begin to __ or lose Federal aid.

Things to do

1. In what ways, if any, have race relations changed in your community since 1945? Organize a panel discussion.
2. Do both whites and Negroes attend your school? If so, make a report on how and when integration first occurred.
3. Pretend that you were an eyewitness to some of the events in the Little Rock integration crisis of 1957-59. Write a brief account of what you saw.

Reviewing the Unit

1. What were the causes of the great depression? What were some of its effects?
2. How did the Second World War affect the lives of Arkansas people?
3. What is meant by the "end of the family farm"?
4. Why did Arkansas lose population in the years following 1950?
5. How has Arkansas attempted to attract new industries?
6. What is the purpose of the Arkansas River Project?
7. What were the causes of the Little Rock school integration crisis of 1957? What have been some of its effects?

Unit Ten

Contemporary Arkansas: The Government
and the People, 1930-1965

The Chapters

1. Recent Politics
2. Some Problems of Recent Government
3. The Highway System
4. Education Enters a New Era
5. Contemporary Life and Culture

THE POLITICS OF contemporary Arkansas followed old and familiar patterns until 1957, when the crisis in race relations cast Governor Orval E. Faubus in the role of defender of states' rights against excessive Federal authority. Faubus dominated the politics of Arkansas as had no other governor in the state's history. In 1964 he was elected to a sixth term. Only one other governor, Jeff Davis, had ever been elected to as much as a third term.

Other Arkansas leaders achieved national and world prominence also. In Washington, contemporary Arkansas has been represented by such men as Joseph T. Robinson, J. William Fulbright, John L. McClellan, and Wilbur Mills. At home, state government assumed more and more responsibilities. Immense strides were made in public education, highways, health and welfare. Increasing public services resulted in a constant search for new sources of revenue to finance them.

By 1965 the backwoods era was in the past. Contemporary Arkansas was a modern state, with face toward a future which though always uncertain seemed bright with promise. Arkansas still had many problems, and would continue to have them, but there were none which could not be solved by an intelligent and enlightened people.

1 Recent Politics

Since 1930 Arkansas has remained Democratic in politics, and some of the governors and other state officials have been persons of exceptional ability. Several Arkansas political leaders have exercised great influence in national politics and government.

Old patterns in politics. Arkansas politics until 1957 exhibited few changes from the period before 1930. Every governor except Francis Cherry served two terms. No important political factions developed, except the Bailey and Adkins groups which competed for control of state government for ten years beginning about 1934. Following the Little Rock school integration crisis of 1957, voters divided into factions supporting or opposing Governor Faubus.

Three adult Arkansans out of every four continued to show little interest in voting, though public interest in poli-tics seemed to increase after the Second World War. In order to attract attention candidates used television and radio programs, helicopters, parachute jumps, gospel singers, hillbilly bands, fireworks displays, motor caravans, highway billboards, and huge newspaper advertisements. Such devices were expensive, and a candidate for governor could not hope to make a serious race without plenty of money.

Special interest groups had great influence in politics and government. The Farm Bureau, Arkansas Education Association, Arkansas Free Enterprise Association, County Judges Association,

Homer M. Adkins opening his first campaign for governor in Russellville, 1940

liquor and gambling interests, highway contractors, public utility companies, and trucking lines were among the most powerful special interests. The political influence of the railroads declined as rail traffic decreased and track was abandoned.

A few changes entered the traditional political picture. The double primary, which insures that winning candidates receive a majority vote, was used in 1934, dropped, and then adopted again beginning in 1940. A constitutional amendment passed in 1962 made voting machines legal, but three years later none were in operation. The poll tax as a requirement for voting lasted until 1964, when an amendment to the state constitution provided for a voter registration system administered by the county clerks.

As Arkansans moved away from the rural areas and into the cities, there were complaints that more state senators and representatives in the General Assembly should be elected from city districts. In 1956 a constitutional amendment "froze" state senatorial districts as they were at the time, but urban counties gained a few representatives following the census of 1960. In 1965 a Federal court ordered that both houses of the General Assembly be reapportioned on the basis of population.

Depression politics. The second term of Governor Harvey Parnell ended in 1933 during the darkest period of the depression. Parnell's successor, J. Marion Futrell, struggled for four years with the problems of hard times and a depleted state treasury.

During the New Deal years before the Second World War, Federal influence was a powerful factor in Arkansas politics. The state government looked to Washington for financial aid. Thousands of Arkansas voters depended on the Federal government for relief and temporary jobs such as the WPA provided. Farmers received Federal subsidy checks. Senator Joseph T. Robinson, a New Deal leader in Congress, and Homer M. Adkins, Federal Collector of Internal Revenue for Arkansas, became powerful figures in state politics and government.

Robinson died in 1937, soon after Carl E. Bailey began his first term as governor. The Democratic state central committee nominated Bailey to succeed Robinson. Adkins and others persuaded Congressman John E. Miller to run as an independent, and in the special senatorial election Miller defeated Bailey by a large margin.

Bailey won a second term as governor in 1938, but two years later lost to Homer M. Adkins. When in 1944 Governor Adkins tried for a Senate seat,

Governor Sid McMath with bust of John R. Steelman, state capitol, 1951. Steelman, who served as assistant to President Harry S. Truman, was a native of Thornton in Calhoun County

Bailey supported Congressman J. William Fulbright for the office. Fulbright, whom Adkins had removed as president of the University of Arkansas, defeated the governor. The rivalry between Bailey and Adkins, which some considered a power struggle between state and Federal factions, ended with the Second World War.

Ben Laney and the Dixiecrats. In 1947 President Harry S. Truman proposed a strong civil rights program designed to secure equality for Negroes. As a result some Southern Democrats refused to support Truman in 1948 and organized the States Rights Democrats, or "Dixiecrat" party.

Governor Ben T. Laney of Arkansas, who was nearing the close of his second term, helped organize the Dixiecrat party and became its leader in the state. For awhile there was talk that the Dixiecrats might nominate Laney for president, but instead they named J. Strom Thurmond of South Carolina as their candidate.

Because of the influence of Sid McMath, Senator J. William Fulbright and others, the Democratic party of Arkansas remained loyal to the Truman ticket. In the general election of 1948 Truman carried the state. The Dixiecrats ran well in some counties of eastern Arkansas where Negroes were numerous, but statewide their ticket received less than seventeen per cent of the votes.

The GI revolt and Sid McMath. The GI revolt of 1946 was a protest movement against the political machines that controlled some counties in Arkansas. Young veterans, home from military service in the Second World War,

Governor Francis Cherry

tried to overthrow some of these machines in the Democratic primaries or in the general election.

In Hot Springs and Garland County the GIs swept the old Leo P. McLaughlin machine out of office, but GI tickets lost in Crittenden and Yell counties. GIs were active also in Cleveland, Montgomery, and Pope counties, and in Pine Bluff. Sid McMath, who led the GI revolt in Hot Springs, was elected governor in 1948 and re-elected two years later.

The Faubus era. In 1954 Orval E. Faubus, a former official of the McMath administration, defeated Governor Francis Cherry in the Democratic primary. Cherry had defeated McMath two years before. The campaign of 1954 was one of the most bitter of the century, with Cherry supporters trying to link Faubus with the radicalism of old Commonwealth College near Mena.

Faubus won a second term in 1956 over an opponent who charged him with being too "moderate" in opposing the integration of whites and Negroes in the public schools. Then in 1957 Faubus won the support of most segregationists by trying to stop integration of the Little Rock schools.

Riding the high tide of the crisis in race relations, Faubus ran for a third term in 1958 and carried every county. In 1960 he had little difficulty in defeating another field of weak opponents. Two years later the governor first announced that he would not run again and then changed his mind. In the first primary in 1962 he defeated former Governor Sid McMath and former Congressman Dale Alford, the strongest candidates he had faced since his first race.

The election of Faubus to a fifth term ended all effective opposition to the governor within the Democratic party of the state. When he ran for a sixth term in 1964 his only Democratic opponents were ineffective minor candidates. Those who opposed Faubus then rallied around Winthrop Rockefeller, the Republican candidate, who made a strong but unsuccessful race in the fall of 1964.

The Republican party stirs to life.
After the national Democratic party became committed to civil rights for the Negro and more Federal control over the economy, the number of "presidential" Republicans in Arkansas increased. "Presidential" Republicans were Democrats who voted Republican in presidential elections. In every general election from 1952 to 1964 Republican candidates for president polled more than forty per cent of the Arkansas vote. "Presidential" Republi-

Senator J. W. Fulbright (left) and Governor Orval E. Faubus, 1961

cans were especially numerous in the cities.

On the state and local levels, the Republican party was still weak. One or two mountain counties usually sent Republican representatives to the General Assembly. Little Rock elected a Republican mayor twice after 1950. Republican candidates for governor polled respectable votes in 1954 and 1960, but offered no real challenge to Orval E. Faubus.

Winthrop Rockefeller, a New York millionaire who moved to Arkansas in 1953, began trying to build a strong Republican party in the state. In 1964 the Republicans nominated Rockefeller for governor and put up numerous candidates for state, district, and county of-

Senator John L. McClellan filing for re-election in the office of Secretary of State C. G. "Crip" Hall, 1960

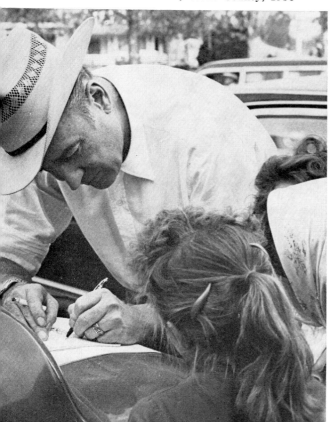

Winthrop Rockefeller signing autographs at Mountain View, Stone County, 1964

fices. Though Rockefeller himself polled forty-three per cent of the votes, only a few Republican candidates for county offices were elected.

Arkansans in Washington. Arkansas senators and representatives in Congress, like elected state officials other than governors, customarily serve for many years. Only one United States senator, Mrs. Hattie W. Caraway, has been defeated for re-election since 1930. Senator John L. McClellan, first elected in 1942, and Senator J. William Fulbright, elected in 1944, were still in office after more than twenty years. Every one of the state's four representatives (usually called "congressmen") in 1964 had held office twenty years or longer.

Long service, as well as personal ability, has placed Arkansas senators and representatives at the head of im-

333

portant Congressional committees. The Congressional "seniority rule" gives the most important committee chairmanships to those members with the longest service. Because of declining population Arkansas lost three seats in the national House of Representatives after 1950, but remaining Arkansans such as Wilbur D. Mills and Oren Harris continued to exercise great influence there.

Senators Robinson, Fulbright and McClellan became figures of national and even international importance. Joseph T. Robinson was Democratic majority leader in the Senate and a leading New Dealer. While a congressman in 1943, Fulbright secured passage of a resolution committing the United States to support a United Nations organization after the war. As senator he sponsored a program of international exchange scholarships for students, and became a prominent spokesman on foreign affairs. McClellan directed investigations of corruption and racketeering in American life.

During the Truman administration (1945-53) natives of Arkansas held several high government positions. John R. Steelman was assistant to the president, John W. Snyder was Secretary of the Treasury, Frank Pace Jr. became Secretary of the Army, and Leslie Biffle served as secretary of the Senate.

Senators Joseph T. Robinson and Hattie W. Caraway

STUDY AIDS

Vocabulary

Be sure that you understand the meaning of each of these words and phrases:

states' rights	special interests
depleted	exchange
racketeering	scholarships
voting machines	exhibited
froze	seniority rule
enlightened	customarily

Identification

Tell what part each of the following had in the story:

Homer M. Adkins	Orval E. Faubus
Sid McMath	Dixiecrats
Francis Cherry	Commonwealth
GI revolt	College
Carl E. Bailey	"presidential"
Winthrop	Republicans
Rockefeller	

To test your reading

On other paper, list 1-9. Opposite each number, write the word or words which complete each sentence.

1. The double primary insures that the winning candidates receive a ___ of the votes cast.

2. In 1965 a Federal court ordered that both houses of the General Assembly be ___ on the basis of ___.

3. Senator Joseph T. Robinson died in the year ___. He was succeeded by ___.

4. In 1948 ___ was elected as governor.

5. In 1944 ___ was elected United States senator.

6. Governor Orval E. Faubus has been elected governor in each of the following years: ___ ___ ___ ___ ___ ___.

7. In 1964 Winthrop Rockefeller, the Republican candidate for governor, polled ___ per cent of the votes.

8. U. S. Senator John L. McClellan has been elected in each of the following years: ___ ___ ___ ___.

9. In 1965 the four congressmen from Arkansas were: ___ ___ ___ ___.

Things to do

1. Arrange a bulletin board exhibit on "Famous Living Arkansans." Emphasize anyone from your own community. Include people who have won fame in all fields, as well as famous political figures.

2. Make a directory of elected officials in your county, city or town.

3. Pretend that you are a candidate for governor of Arkansas. Choose another member of the class as your "campaign manager." The two of you should then tell the class how you plan to advertise and conduct your campaign.

4. From the *World Almanac, Arkansas Almanac* or similar source, copy the number of votes received by candidates for president in your county and in the entire state in the three latest presidential elections.

2 Some Problems of Recent Government

Since the depression, state government has been called upon to provide increased services for the people. Taxes have become generally higher, and the state has received Federal aid for many new purposes. The state government conducts health, welfare and correctional programs which affect the lives of thousands of citizens. Legal control of liquor and gambling has continued to be a problem.

The repeal of prohibition. By 1933 a national movement to repeal the Eighteenth Amendment to the United States Constitution was gaining ground. Most Americans seemed to believe that prohibition had failed.

Arkansans voted in favor of repeal in a special election held July 18, 1933. After a state convention had ratified repeal, Governor J. Marion Futrell called the General Assembly into special session to legalize the sale of beer and wine. The General Assembly of 1935 passed a general liquor law providing for regulation and taxation.

With the end of statewide prohibition, Arkansas returned to the local option system. By 1964 more than half the counties in the state had voted themselves dry. Cities and townships could also vote wet or dry under the local option laws.

The gambling problem. Race t r a c k gambling returned to Arkansas along with legal liquor. Oaklawn track in Hot Springs opened in 1934, and the General Assembly of 1935 made racing legal and set up a regulatory commission. A greyhound track operated in West Memphis from 1934 until 1941,

and reopened in 1956. The voters adopted a constitutional amendment in 1956 which legalized horse racing and betting at Hot Springs, thus making the practice more secure against the attacks of reformers.

Illegal forms of gambling continued to flourish in Hot Springs, protected and controlled by the Leo P. McLaughlin machine. Occasionally state officials conducted raids on gambling houses and destroyed equipment, but the gamblers were soon back in business.

The GI revolt of 1946, led by Sid McMath, kept gambling down for awhile. Governors Francis Cherry and Orval E. Faubus held that control of illegal gambling was the responsibility of Hot Springs officials. Early in 1964 the Arkansas House of Representatives passed a resolution calling for an end to illegal gambling, and Governor Faubus closed the Hot Springs casinos. Within a year there were reports that some of them had reopened, and in 1965 the House of Representatives again urged that anti-gambling laws be enforced.

Our g r o w i n g government. The depression cut tax revenues in half and drained the state treasury. Salaries

Finish of a horse race at Oaklawn Park, Hot Springs, 1939

could not be paid and services had to be cut back. In 1933 Governor J. Marion Futrell and the General Assembly consolidated agencies, eliminated jobs, and reduced the cost of state government by more than half.

Since the depression, Arkansas government has grown again. New Deal measures required new boards and bureaus, and more employees. The Second World War increased the trend to bigger government and this did not halt with the return of peace.

Government continues to grow because the people constantly demand increased services. The state supports schools and colleges, builds highways, and plays a major part in health, safety, welfare, and recreation. The government also regulates utility companies, transportation lines, banks, insurance firms, liquor outlets, and many other businesses and activities. As cities grow and industries develop, there are more and more things to regulate, more people have to be employed, and more money must be spent.

Every new state responsibility has meant the creation of a new government agency or the expansion of an older one. Since 1930 the General Assembly has created, abolished and reorganized a large number of boards and commissions. After the Second World War new buildings to house expanding state agencies began to go up on the state capitol grounds and in other parts of Little Rock. In 1963 the capitol grounds

The state seal is based on a design originated by Samuel C. Roane in 1820, and revised in 1836, 1864, and 1907. The Latin motto "Regnat Populus" means "The People Rule"

were expanded to provide space for more buildings.

Arkansas has no general civil service system, though some agencies hire employees on the basis of merit alone. Governor Carl E. Bailey secured passage of a law in 1937 setting up a civil service system, but the General Assembly of 1939 did away with the plan.

The search for revenue. Since the depression Arkansas taxes have become higher. The people have demanded that government do more and more for them, and at the same time inflation has driven prices up and money has declined in value. State and local governments have had to look constantly for new sources of revenue.

In 1935 the General Assembly levied a sales tax of two cents on every dollar purchase. Most of the sales tax revenue went to the schools, and the Arkansas Education Association and its allies have pressed constantly for more money for education. A constitutional amendment adopted in 1948 removed the millage tax restriction and allowed school districts to set their own taxes. The General Assembly of 1957 increased the sales tax rate to three per cent and raised state income and severance taxes.

Property assessments in the counties had been unequal as well as too low for many years. In 1955 the General Assembly required that all real and personal property be reassessed so that more tax revenue could be collected. Two years later all counties were required to raise assessments to at least eighteen per cent of market value or suffer penalties.

The Federal government has borne much of the financial load of Arkansas government. Federal grants, made for dozens of purposes, have risen from less than $9,000,000 in 1939-40 to over $96,-000,000 in 1961-62. Industrial expan-

The new state revenue building on the capitol grounds in Little Rock, 1965

Free chest X-rays are an important part of the Arkansas public health program

sion since 1955 has helped solve many of the state's financial problems. Revenues have increased, the state highway debt has been whittled down, and new building programs have been undertaken at state colleges and other institutions.

Since 1945, state funds have been handled in more businesslike fashion than ever before. Better auditing methods have removed most of the uncertainty and confusion from the financial affairs of the state. By 1957 most state employees were covered by retirement plans.

Health and security. The people of contemporary Arkansas are healthier than in the past and enjoy a higher standard of living. Inproved diet and better sanitation have almost eliminated some diseases.

Hospital care has become available to people all over the state. For most Arkansans a trip to a hospital once meant a long train ride to one of the larger cities. Since 1942 counties and cities have been allowed to levy taxes to build and support hospitals, and Federal aid has helped. In 1963 Arkansas had almost 150 hospitals and infirmaries. A great new University of Arkansas Medical Center was dedicated in Little Rock in 1957.

Since the depression, Federal and state governments have assumed more and more responsibility for the welfare of the people. The Arkansas Department of Public Welfare, set up in 1935, became one of the largest and most important of state agencies. Welfare expenditures increased from $3,000,000 in 1937-38 to about $58,000,000 in 1963-64. In the latter year the state helped the aged, the blind, the disabled, crippled and dependent children, and those needing food and medical care. The Federal government provided more than three-fourths of the money for the state welfare program.

Public welfare increased in importance as the average life span lengthened and the number of old people multiplied. Since the aged could seldom live with relatives in crowded cities as they once had done on the farms, retirement homes and nursing homes increased rapidly in number. In 1964 there were 150 nursing homes in Arkansas capable of caring for a total of more than 7,500 people.

The Arkansas Children's Colony, established for the "care, custody, treatment and training" of mentally defective children, opened at Conway in 1959. Two years after the Federal government closed the Army-Navy Hospital at Hot Springs, the state government reopened it as a rehabilitation center for training the handicapped.

The state mental hospital continued to be a problem. Completion of the Benton unit, planned since 1929, was delayed until 1936 by the depression. The Benton and Little Rock units were plagued by overcrowding, small budgets, shortage of doctors, outdated buildings, and political disputes. A huge new construction program finally got under way at the Little Rock unit in 1963, and during the same period improved treatment reduced overcrowding. By 1965 the state hospital, with one of the finest facilities to be found in the nation, had at last entered a new and brighter era.

The depression brought financial ruin to the state penitentiary. In 1933 the Futrell administration moved the prisoners to the state farms and placed the penitentiary on a cash basis. After the Second World War there were further improvements in the correctional system of the state. New institutions included reformatories for women and delinquent Negro girls, and "training

Governor Ben T. Laney breaking ground for a new building at Cummins prison farm, Lincoln County, 1948

schools" were declared to be educational rather than penal in purpose. Construction programs at the penitentiary emphasized better housing for prisoners. The state penitentiary was operated as a self-supporting institution, expected to produce and sell farm products to pay the upkeep, and the system usually showed a profit. The State Police force, created in 1935, doubled in size between 1955 and 1964.

STUDY AIDS

Vocabulary

Be sure that you understand the meaning of each of these words and phrases:

casinos

millage tax

mentally defective

bureaus

wet or dry

dedicated

greyhound track

auditing

civil service system

market value

retirement plan

correctional system

Identification

Tell what part each of the following had in the story:

J. Marion Futrell

Public Welfare Department

Children's Colony

nursing homes

To test your reading

On other paper, list 1-10. Opposite each number, write the word or words which complete the sentence.

1. The General Assembly of 1935 passed a general liquor law providing for __ and __.

2. The GI revolt of __, led by __, kept __ down for a while.

3. In 1935 the General Assembly levied a __ tax of __ cents on every dollar purchase. In 1957 it was raised to __ cents.

4. Federal grants to Arkansas have risen from less than __ in 1939-1940 to over __ in 1961-62.

5. By 1957 most state employees were covered by __ plans.

6. In 1963 Arkansas had almost __ hospitals and infirmaries.

7. Welfare expenditures increased from __ in 1937-38 to __ in 1963-64.

8. In 1964 there were in the state __ nursing homes capable of caring for a total of more than __ people.

9. The Arkansas Children's Colony was opened at __ in the year __.

10. By 1965 the state hospital was one of the __ to be found in the __.

Things to do

1. Ask your state senator or representative to visit the class and answer questions about current Arkansas government. You may wish to arrange a television-style interview for this purpose.

2. Make a list of all types of Federal expenditures in your county.

3. Investigate and report to the class on the number of hospitals, infirmaries, nursing homes and clinics now maintained in your town, city or county. How many patients can be cared for at one time? When was the first hospital established in your area?

4. Visit the Children's Colony in Conway or the State Hospital in Little Rock.

3 The Highway System

New and improved roads, and how to pay for them, has been a chief concern of Arkansas government for half a century. In 1965 Arkansas had a highway system that ranked well up with those of other states.

The Martineau-Parnell road program. Under the Martineau road law of 1927 the state government assumed the debts of the road improvement districts and embarked on a vast road-building program. The new program was financed by bond issues. This meant that the state would borrow money to build and maintain highways, and hope that revenue from gasoline taxes and license fees would pay the debt and interest as they came due.

The next four years, while Harvey Parnell was governor, were boom years in highway construction. Every year more bonds were sold, roads and bridges were built, and the state went deeper into debt. By the middle of 1931 the highway debt was over $90,000,000.

Depression and dishonesty. The depression that began in 1929 ended the road program. Within two years no more bonds could be sold. Tax revenues dropped. By the end of 1931 almost all road building had stopped.

The General Assembly of 1931 set up an audit commission to check on the affairs of the state highway department. According to a resolution passed by the General Assembly of 1933, the audit revealed a conspiracy by certain highway commissioners to use the people's money for private gain. Mil-

lions of dollars had been wasted or stolen. The resolution described the situation as "a state of moral turpitude and official corruption unparalleled in our history." The audit investigation was followed by a number of lawsuits by the state to recover money from contractors, and lawsuits by contractors against the Highway Commission.

For the next ten years and longer nearly all highway revenues had to be spent to pay debts. Small amounts were spent to keep up the roads, and toll bridges were eliminated, but the only construction work was done with Federal funds. During the Second World War little highway work could be done because labor and materials were being used in the war effort.

Refunding the highway debt. The highway debt was so large that Arkansas would have had trouble paying it if times had been good. When the depression came, something had to be done to reduce the financial burden. One proposed solution was the refunding of the highway bonded indebtedness. Refunding meant that the state would borrow more money and pay off the old debt. Of course the new debt would have to be paid too, but the interest rate would be lower and the state would have longer to pay.

Governor Homer M. Adkins (center) signing the highway refunding act, 1941

For almost a decade, refunding was a troublesome problem. The first refunding attempt was made in 1932, but the old bonds could not be exchanged for new ones in time to prevent default. As early as August 1932 Arkansas was defaulting, or failing to pay its debts as bonds came due.

The General Assembly of 1933 took the position that road maintenance had to go on even if the debt remained unpaid. A second attempt at refunding was made. The bondholders refused to accept the proposed plan and won their case in Federal court. The state still could not pay.

At a special session in 1934 the General Assembly passed another refunding measure. Old highway and toll bridge bonds were exchanged into refunding bonds. The gasoline tax was raised to six and one-half cents a gallon. The General Assembly again required that highway maintenance must come before debt payment.

The refunding act of 1934 aroused opposition because it provided for no new highway construction and left open the door to another default. The General Assembly of 1937 passed a new refunding law, but no bonds could be sold because of a business recession. A proposed refunding amendment to the state constitution was defeated in the general election of 1938. A refunding act passed by the General Assembly of 1939 was ruled unconstitutional by the Supreme Court.

In the summer of 1939, Governor Carl E. Bailey at a special session of the General Assembly secured passage of a new highway program, including refunding. At that time the state owed more than $140,500,000 on its highways. The Bailey plan was delayed by the courts and defeated when referred to the voters in the general election of 1940.

A new refunding plan sponsored by Governor Homer M. Adkins was passed by the General Assembly of 1941 and approved by the voters in a special election. The refunding bonds were purchased by the Reconstruction Finance Corporation, a Federal agency. Arkansas was given until 1972 to pay its highway debt.

The McMath highway program. In 1945, after sixteen years of depression and war, the Arkansas highway system was in poor condition. Most of the roads were old and worn out. They were too crooked and narrow for modern high-speed traffic, and too weak to carry the heavy traffic load which began to move over them after the Second World War ended.

Led by Governor Sid McMath, the General Assembly of 1949 authorized a four-year road program. Under this plan $7,000,000 in bonds would be issued each year and matched by Federal grants. At a special election Arkansas voters approved the program.

The McMath program checked the deterioration of the road system and gave Arkansas a new start in highway and bridge construction. Then in 1951 the General Assembly created an audit commission which began an investigation of highway affairs. The audit resulted in charges of waste, fraud, and favoritism in highway contracts. No new bonds were issued in 1952, and McMath was defeated when he ran for a third term.

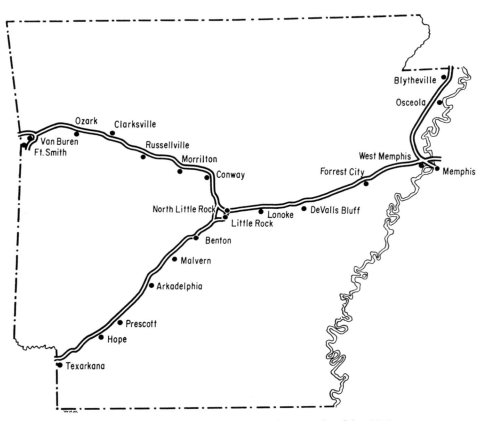

The interstate highway system, to be completed by 1972

344

In 1952 Arkansas voters added Amendment 42, called the Mack-Blackwell Amendment, to the state constitution. The amendment set up a new Highway Commission of five members and provided that the first commissioners would be appointed for terms of different lengths. Succeeding commissioners would each be appointed for ten-year periods, and it was assumed that no one future governor would be able to dominate the commission. Governor Francis Cherry appointed all five of the members of the new Highway Commission in 1953.

Progress and expansion. In recent years Arkansas has made real progress with its highway program. In 1965 eighty-three per cent of the state roads were hard-surfaced, as compared with only twenty-five per cent in 1936, and the Highway Commission was spending more than $67,000,000 a year on construction alone. The highway debt, which had been greatly reduced, was to be refunded again in order to release more money for current needs.

The state highway system grew from less than 7,000 miles of road in 1923 to more than 12,000 miles in 1964.

The General Assembly of 1957 required the addition to the state system of ten to twelve miles of road in every county. At the recommendation of Governor Orval E. Faubus, the General Assembly of 1965 increased gasoline taxes and raised most vehicle license fees in order to finance an expanded highway program.

Since 1917 the Federal government has helped the states build highways. Over the years, and especially since the Second World War, Federal grants for Arkansas roads have increased enormously. From 1917 to 1964 such aid totaled over $450,000,000.

In 1956 Congress provided for completion of a huge interstate system of highways by 1972, with the Federal government paying ninety per cent of the costs. At the same time Federal aid for other roads was increased. From 1957 to 1963 the Federal government provided an average of $35,400,000 a year for Arkansas roads. By 1965 the new multiple-lane interstate highways were reaching across Arkansas in several directions, bypassing cities, spanning rivers and bringing a new era in rapid transportation.

STUDY AIDS

Vocabulary

Be sure that you understand the meaning of each of these words and phrases:

sponsored   interstate
deterioration   highways
bypassing   refunding
spanning   default
business recession   audit commission
turpitude   favoritism
    multiple-lane

Identification

Tell what part each of the following had in the story:

Harvey Parnell   Mack-Blackwell
McMath road   Amendment
    program   Bailey refunding
         plan

To test your reading

On other paper, list 1-8. Opposite each number, write the word or words which complete each sentence.

1. From 1917 to 1964 Federal aid to Arkansas roads totaled over __.

2. Under the __ road law of 1927 the state government assumed the debts of the __ and embarked on a vast __. The new program was financed by __.

3. By the middle of 1931 the highway debt was over __.

4. In 1939 Arkansas owed more than __ on its highways. In 1941 Governor __ secured the adoption of a __ plan that gave the state until __ to pay its debt.

5. Governor Sid McMath secured the adoption of a __ road program by which __ in bonds would be issued each year and matched by __ grants.

6. In 1965 __ per cent of the state roads were __ as compared with only __ per cent in 1936.

7. The state highway system grew from less than __ miles of road in 1923 to more than __ in 1964.

8. From 1957 to 1963 the Federal government provided an average of __ a year for Arkansas roads.

Things to do

1. Make a transportation map of Arkansas. Put on it the routes of the major airlines, the principal railroads, and the new interstate highways.

2. Have a committee to find out when the first paved road was built in your area, and report on improvements to the roads or streets in your community since 1945.

3. Plan a trip to a distant part of the state. Determine the destination, distance, and the kind of transportation that you prefer. Chart the route to be traveled.

4   Education Enters a New Era

The Arkansas school system, hurt badly by hard times, has shown great improvement since the depression era. Public concern for better education continues.

Education in the depression. The depression dealt education a heavy blow at a time when great progress was being made. School revenues dropped off. Terms had to be shortened. Building programs stopped. The average annual salary of teachers decreased from $730 in 1931 to $489 in 1934. The State Department of Education was reduced in size and budget, and some state services had to be abandoned. Many school districts wrestled with a heavy load of debt incurred in better times. In 1933-34 Arkansas spent less than $10,500,-000 on the public schools.

In an effort to raise money for the schools the General Assembly of 1935 levied a two per cent sales tax. Under the law sixty-five per cent of the money collected was to go to the schools. At first the sales tax was regarded as a temporary measure. In 1936 Arkansas voters adopted an initiated act providing textbooks for children in the first eight grades. The General Assembly extended the sales tax so the state could buy the books. A teacher retirement system began in 1937.

New concern for education. After the Second World War, Arkansans heard a great deal about the educational backwardness of the state. Statistics placed Arkansas near the bottom of the national educational ladder. The Arkansas Education Association and the Arkansas Teachers Association kept up a constant campaign to get more money for schools. Inflation made the need of increased revenue more urgent.

In 1948 a constitutional amendment removed the eighteen-mill tax limit on school districts. Each district could now set its own tax rate, and taxes went up in most districts. The General Assembly of 1957 increased the sales tax rate from two or three per cent and raised other taxes. Counties were required to raise assessments of personal and real property so the property tax would bring in more revenue.

These new tax measures, especially the 1957 increases, improved the school financial situation. Total funds spent on public schools climbed from $24,-000,000 in 1945-46 to $125,000,000 in 1963-64. In the latter year the state government was spending half its general revenues on schools. The amount spent per pupil increased from $129 in 1953-54 to $302 in 1963-64. The level of state support of public education was higher in Arkansas than was true for the United States as a whole.

Better qualified teachers. After the war Arkansas schools faced the old

A. L. Whitten Elementary School at Marianna, Lee County, completed in 1965

problem of unqualified teachers, now complicated by a teacher shortage as teachers left the state for better pay or went into other occupations. Salaries of teachers remained low. In 1955 the average was only $2,280 a year. The General Assembly of 1957 enacted a minimum salary law, and by 1964 increased revenues had pushed the average annual salary above $4,000.

In 1950 only about half the schoolteachers of Arkansas had college degrees. Beginning in 1952 the Ford Foundation poured several million dollars into the state in an attempt to improve teacher training. Fifteen colleges participated in this "Arkansas Experiment in Teacher Education."

Such efforts to improve teacher quality bore fruit. By 1964 more than 12,000 of the 17,000 teachers in the Arkansas public school system had bachelor's degrees, and over 3,000 had master's degrees. In 1963 the State Department of Education began requiring that all new teachers have college degrees.

Other trends in public education. Before the Second World War Arkansas had 3,000 school districts. In 1948 an initiated act dissolved all districts with fewer than 350 enumerated pupils, and hundreds of rural schools closed. Actually country schools were already disappearing rapidly as people moved to cities and towns. In 1963 there were 417 school districts in the state, with prospects that the number would be reduced further. The old one-room school had practically vanished.

Bus transportation to consolidated schools has improved since 1930. The "dinner bucket" of earlier days has been replaced by hot lunches at most schools. Art, music, physical education, commercial subjects, and other new courses have been added to the school curriculum. Counseling service is now emphasized. Athletics plays a large role in the program of the modern school.

Since the Second World War Arkansans have spent millions of dollars on new school buildings. The average school term lengthened from 140 days in 1932 to 173 days in 1960. Ninety-eight per cent of school age children were enrolled in school in 1960 as compared with only three out of four in 1932-39. In 1965 the state government began building an educational television station with studios in Conway.

The college boom. The end of the Second World War brought a flood of veterans to college campuses to complete their education. After the veterans left the colleges, enrollments continued to rise. Since 1950 enrollments at the University of Arkansas and the s e v e n state - supported colleges have been doubling about every ten years. In 1963-64 the state schools had 21,000 students, and students also crowded the campuses of private colleges.

Increased enrollments created problems for all Arkansas colleges. Course offerings were expanded. All the state schools moved up to senior college rank, and some began offering graduate degrees. In 1961 the state began a four-year construction program for the university and colleges, to cost $17,000,000. Though faculty salaries rose, some colleges had trouble keeping teachers of top quality in the state.

The need of trained workers for new industries led the state government to begin a system of vocational-technical schools. Two such schools, located at Pine Bluff and Morrilton, were opened after 1959, and plans called for at least eight others. In 1964 a new constitutional amendment authorized the establishment of community junior colleges.

New buildings such as this one at Little Rock University were under construction at several colleges in Arkansas during 1965-66

STUDY AIDS

Vocabulary

Be sure that you understand the meaning of each of these words and phrases:

senior college	statistics
minimum salary	wrestled
graduate degrees	teacher retirement
private college	real property
bachelor's degree	master's degree
curriculum	State Department
counseling service	of Education
	enumerated pupils

Identification

Tell what part each of the following had in the story:

Ford Foundation	vocational-techni-
Arkansas Educa-	cal schools
tion Association	

To test your reading

On other paper, list 1-11. Opposite each number, write the word or words which complete the sentence.

1. A teacher retirement system began in the year ___.

2. In 1935 to raise money for the schools the General Assembly levied a ___ per cent ___ tax.

3. In 1948 a constitutional amendment removed the ___ mill tax limit on ___.

4. In 1936 voters adopted an ___ act providing free ___ for school children in the first eight grades.

5. The amount spent per pupil annually increased from ___ in 1953-54 to ___ in 1963-64.

6. By 1964 more than ___ of the ___ teachers in the Arkansas public school system had ___ degrees.

7. Before 1941 Arkansas had ___ school districts. In 1963 it had only ___ districts.

8. The average school term lengthened from ___ days in 1932 to ___ in 1960.

9. In 1965 the state government began building an ___ station with studios in ___.

10. After 1959 vocational - technical schools were opened at ___ and ___.

11. In 1964 a new constitutional amendment authorized the establishment of ___.

Things to do

1. Compare your own school today with any year in a previous ten-year period for which records are available. Compare as to (a) total enrollment, (b) total annual budget, and (c) number of graduates. Report your findings to the class.

2. Write a brief history of your school for your local newspaper. Try to get the names of the different principals.

3. Secure information about one of the following topics and write a summary report:

   (a) The work of the Arkansas Education Association or the Arkansas Teachers Association.

   (b) Teacher training in Arkansas colleges.

   (c) New courses added to our school curriculum since 1945.

   (d) The history of athletics in our school.

   (e) Educational TV in Arkansas.

5 Contemporary Life and Culture

Since 1930 organized religion has continued to influence the lives of many Arkansas people, and many churches have grown and prospered. Increased public interest in libraries, literature, history, archeology and the fine arts indicates still greater cultural progress in the future.

Architecture. Arkansas has developed no distinctive type of architecture. Pioneer log houses were replaced by plain frame structures with porches at front and rear. Ornate Victorian houses graced the streets of some cities and towns, and a few stately white-columned mansions survived to remind travelers of the vanished days of the Old Southwest. Before the Second World War native stone began to be used in homes and public buildings, especially in the highlands. After the war the low ranch-style house became popular, and split-level homes appeared in new suburban areas.

Arkansas courthouses and other public buildings were usually commonplace, and even the new state capitol represented little more than an attempt to copy the appearance of the national capitol. Main streets were lined with rectangular business buildings that looked much alike. After 1920 a few structures of eight, eleven, and even sixteen stories rose above the skylines of the larger cities. Little Rock's Tower Building, eighteen stories high, was completed in 1960. Modern architectural forms were appearing in many places in 1965. The modern influence could be seen in new government buildings, in new structures on college campuses, new banks, new shopping centers and apartment houses, and even in the architecture of the new highways, highway exchanges, and bridges.

Reading and the arts. Arkansas has produced numerous poets, novelists, and other writers, but none of national reputation. John Gould Fletcher of Little Rock, who lived for many years in England, was closest to being a first-rank poet. The General Assembly designated Charles T. Davis as Poet Laureate of Arkansas in 1923, and Rosa Zagnoni Marinoni was similarly honored in 1953.

The number of Arkansas newspapers declined after about 1909. In 1964 only half as many weeklies were published as in 1909, and fewer dailies than in 1922. The average Arkansan continued to rely heavily on his newspaper for information, even after the coming of radio and television.

The Works Progress Administration, set up in the depression year 1935, included a relief program for intellectuals. The WPA conducted projects for writers, artists, actors, and the like. In Arkansas the program helped preserve historical records, directed plays, and published a "guide" to the state in 1941.

The Tower Building, Little Rock

from the University of Arkansas, won high honors on a European tour. The Community Concert movement reached several Arkansas cities and towns.

Painters and sculptors of distinctive ability continued to be scarce, as in earlier periods of Arkansas history. Eureka Springs became an artists' colony, and soon after the Second World War a fine arts center went up on the University of Arkansas campus. Arkansas claimed movie actors Dick Powell and Alan Ladd as native sons. In 1964 the seventh annual Arkansas State Festival of Arts was held in Little Rock, and at least a dozen other art shows were held at various places during the year.

The Arkansas Arts Center. The Little Rock Museum of Fine Arts, built in what is now MacArthur Park in 1937, housed the most important collection of art objects and paintings in Arkansas. In 1957 a public drive was launched to expand the small museum into a state arts center.

The Arkansas Arts Center, which cost over a million dollars, opened in MacArthur Park in 1962. It included

The religious music of "gospel quartets" continued to be popular with many Arkansas people, and the old folk songs tended to degenerate into the "hillbilly music" of the juke boxes. The Arkansas Federation of Music Clubs tried to encourage appreciation of good music, and Little Rock had a symphony orchestra as early as 1933. Arkansas produced a few composers, and occasional opera singers like Mary McCormic and Mary Lewis. In 1962 the Schola Cantorum, a choral group

Bookmobiles bring library service to many parts of Arkansas

Files of Arkansas newspapers at the Arkansas
History Commission, Little Rock

installed on a large highway trailer, carried exhibits to the people. Schools were encouraged to offer courses in art. By 1964, local chapters of the Arkansas Arts Center had been organized in more than twenty communities.

Libraries. The WPA established small libraries in some Arkansas communities, but the state's first comprehensive library program began in 1935 when the General Assembly created the Arkansas Library Commission. Constitutional amendments adopted in 1940 and 1946 authorized cities and counties to levy library taxes. In 1948 over a third of the counties levied the tax, and by 1963 the number had increased to all but twelve of the seventy-five counties.

exhibition galleries, a theater, classrooms, and offices. Courses of instruction were offered in painting, sculpture, and other fine arts.

The Arts Center extension program represented the first real attempt in the history of the state to interest Arkansas people in the fine arts. An "Artmobile," or traveling art gallery

The Library Commission helped establish county and regional libraries and assembled a book collection for loan. Bookmobiles made regular trips into rural areas. In 1962 there were twenty-three libraries in towns and cities, a dozen of them tax-supported. School library service remained generally poor, and most college libraries were below standard.

The Roberta Fulbright Memorial Library, Fayetteville, opened in 1962

Microfilming newspapers at the Arkansas History Commission

State history and archeology. Dallas T. Herndon, who became secretary of the new Arkansas History Commission in 1911, pioneered in the collection of source materials for the study of Arkansas history. Herndon, David Y. Thomas and a few others wrote books on the subject, but for many years there was little popular interest.

The centennial of statehood in 1936, observed with pageants and special newspaper editions, caused new interest in Arkansas history. In 1941 the Arkansas Historical Association was organized, and its journal began publication the next year. The files of this m a g a z i n e, the **Arkansas Historical Quarterly,** have become one of the best references on Arkansas history. The state government sponsored the Territorial Restoration and restored the Old State House in Little Rock.

After 1950 more than thirty local historical societies were organized. The Civil War centennial of 1961-65 was observed with special programs and activities in several places over the state. Successive G e n e r a l Assemblies set

The restored Greathouse home in Conway, a project of the Faulkner County Historical Society, 1966

Arkansas centennial half dollar, a special coin which was issued by the U. S. Treasury in 1935-39

aside historic places as state parks. The National Park Service began developing Pea Ridge battlefield, old Fort Smith, and Arkansas Post.

The University of Arkansas Museum conducted archeological research work and helped begin a state archeological society in 1960. The building of new lakes and highways lent special urgency to the task of salvaging as much as possible of the remains of the prehistoric cultures of Arkansas.

Decline of the backwoods tradition. Bob Burns, a native of Van Buren, became a popular radio entertainer of the 1930s by telling tall tales about his Arkansas relatives. During the same period Chester Lauck and Norris Goff won radio fame as "Lum and Abner," of the little town of Pine Ridge in Montgomery County.

No later Arkansas humorists of the traditional type have appeared. Television, which came to Arkansas with station KRTV in Little Rock in 1953, and travel have helped Americans learn more about one another. Serious scholars like Otto Ernest Rayburn and Vance Randolph collected and studied the rich folklore of the Ozarks, and mountain towns welcomed outsiders to folklore festivals and handicrafts shows. Since the Second World War, Hollywood film companies have made movies at Piggott and Scotland.

Religion since 1930. Religion in Arkansas has remained generally conservative and fundamentalist. Though still opposed to the theory of evolution, many fundamentalists have turned their major attention to the end of the world rather than its beginning. Depression, war and the atomic threat led some churches to emphasize Bible prophecy. Fundamentalist churchmen tended to be strongly anti-Communist, segregationist in race relations, opposed to such unity efforts as the National Council of Churches, and suspicious of modern editions of the Bible such as the Revised Standard Version.

Arkansas Methodism moved toward liberalism, especially after the merger of Northern and Southern Methodists in 1939. In 1955 Methodists joined with Presbyterians, Disciples of Christ, Episcopalians and others to form the Arkansas Council of Churches, a racially integrated cooperative organization. In the Little Rock crisis of 1957 liberal Protestant leaders advocated moderation.

A country church, 1939

Many country churches disappeared as rural people moved to the cities. Those that remained usually had smaller congregations, but fewer financial problems than ever before. Camp meetings and religious debates were almost things of the past, but tent revivalists still visited Arkansas cities and almost a third of the people claimed membership in some church.

In the growing cities of Arkansas the churches tried hard to keep up with changing times. Congregations went into debt to erect costly buildings, or groups of buildings that sometimes resembled small college campuses. Downtown churches moved to the suburbs as population patterns changed. Many city churches became social and recreational centers as well as places of worship, with kitchens, baseball teams, and activities of some kind almost every night of the week.

New buildings at Arkansas College, a Presbyterian institution in Batesville, include this chapel and fine arts center

☆   ☆   ☆   ☆

STUDY AIDS

Vocabulary

Be sure that you understand the meaning of each of these words and phrases:

culture	handicrafts
commonplace	distinctive
fine arts	architecture
centennial	salvaging
Artmobile	bookmobile
ornate	suburban
Bible prophecy	Victorian
sculptor	intellectuals

Identification

Tell what part each of the following had in the story:

John Gould Fletcher	Arkansas Council of Churches
Mary McCormic	Bob Burns
Dick Powell	Otto Ernest Rayburn
Schola Cantorum	
KRTV	Arkansas Library Commission
Dallas T. Herndon	

To test your reading

On other paper, list 1-10. Opposite each number, write the word or words which complete the sentence.

1. Little Rock's Tower Building, ___ stories high, was completed in the year ___.

2. The General Assembly designated ___ as Poet Laureate of Arkansas in ___, and ___ was similarly honored in 1953.

3. In 1964 the Seventh Annual ___ was held in Little Rock.

4. The Arkansas Arts Center, which cost over a ___ dollars, opened in ___ in 1962.

5. By 1964 local chapters of the Arkansas Arts Center had been organized in more than ___.

6. By 1963 library taxes were levied by all but ___ of the seventy-five counties.

7. After 1950 more than ___ local historical societies were organized.

8. *The Arkansas Historical Quarterly* began publication in ___. By the end of 1965 it had published ninety-six issues or twenty-four volumes.

9. The University of Arkansas Museum helped to begin a ___ society in 1960.

10. Chester Lauck and Norris Goff won radio fame as ___ and ___, of the little town of ___ in ___ County.

Things to do

1. Arrange a class visit to the Arkansas Arts Center.

2. Have a classroom discussion of the ways that Arkansas has made progress since 1930. What are some of the things that still need to be done?

3. Do you think that there is a site in your community which should be marked with a historical marker? Tell the class why you think it should be marked.

4. Take pictures of houses, buildings, bridges and other structures in your area which represent the "modern" influence on architecture.

5. Write a short report on the history and current status of your local public library.

Reviewing the Unit

1. Why does the year 1957 mark a major change in the pattern of Arkansas politics?

2. What was the significance of the long political rivalry between Carl E. Bailey and Homer M. Adkins?

3. Of what importance have Arkansans been in the Federal government in recent years? Give examples.

4. Why has government become steadily larger and more expensive?

5. In what ways has Arkansas made progress with its highway program?

6. What are some recent trends in public education?

7. How has contemporary Arkansas improved with respect to the fine arts, libraries, and state history?

BOOKS ABOUT ARKANSAS

The books listed here are not the only good books about Arkansas. There are others, but many of them are out of print and hard to find. All of the books listed here are to be found in one or more of the following libraries: University of Arkansas; Little Rock Public Library; Arkansas History Commission; Arkansas Library Commission. For a more complete list of books about Arkansas, see *Arkansiana for High Schools*, compiled by Anne Jackson and published by the Arkansas Library Commission.

Alexander, Henry M. *Government in Arkansas*. Little Rock, 1963.
A reference book on state and local government.

Allsopp, Fred W. *Folklore of romantic Arkansas*. Grolier Society, 1931.

Arkansas almanac. Little Rock, 1966.
A general reference book on the state. New editions are issued frequently.

Arkansas encyclopedia. Little Rock, 1957-62. 4 v.
Includes an industrial history of Arkansas and an economic atlas of the state. Published by Arkansas Industrial Development Commission.

Blossom, Virgil T. *It HAS happened here*. New York, 1959.
An account of the Little Rock school integration crisis.

Brooks, Juanita. *The Mountain Meadows Massacre*. Norman, Okla., 1962.

Chamberlain, Samuel E. *My confession*. New York, 1956.
A personal account of the author's adventures in the Mexican War. Includes many references to Arkansas soldiers and officers.

Constitution of the state of Arkansas with all amendments.
Published by Secretary of State, Little Rock.

Croy, Homer. *He hanged them high*. New York & Boston, 1952.
A biography of Judge Isaac C. Parker.

Davis, Clyde Brion. *The Arkansas*. New York & Toronto, 1940.
One of the volumes in "The Rivers of America" series.

Duncan, Robert L. *Reluctant general: the life and times of Albert Pike*. New York, 1961.

Ferguson, John L., ed. *Arkansas and the Civil War*. Little Rock, 1965.
A general reference book on the war in Arkansas.

Fletcher, John Gould. *Arkansas*. Chapel Hill, N. C., 1947.
A history written by a poet.

Foreman, Grant. *Indian removal; the emigration of the five civilized tribes of Indians*. Norman, Okla., 1956.

Gammage, W. L. *The camp, the bivouac, and the battle field*. Little Rock, 1958.
A history of the Fourth Arkansas Infantry Regiment, CSA, written by the brigade surgeon and first published in 1864.

Halbrook, William E. *A school man of the Ozarks*. Van Buren, Ark., 1959.
An autobiography which provides much information about the struggle for better schools in Arkansas.

Hall, C. G. "Crip." *Historical report of the Secretary of State 1958*.
Contains extensive lists of Arkansas state, district and county officials since the beginning of our history.

Harrington, Fred H. *Hanging judge.* Caldwell, Ida., 1951.
Another biography of Judge Isaac C. Parker.

Hays, Brooks. *A Southern moderate speaks.* Chapel Hill, N. C., 1959.
Deals principally with race relations and the school integration crisis of 1957-58.

Higgins, Earl L. *Source readings in Arkansas history.* Little Rock, 1964.

Johnson, Boyd W. *The Arkansas frontier.* Privately printed, 1957.

Johnson, Ludwell H. *Red River campaign: politics and cotton in the Civil War.* Baltimore, 1958.

Lavender, John W. *They never came back; the war memoirs of Captain John W. Lavender, CSA.* Edited by Ted R. Worley. Pine Bluff, Ark., 1956.

Mapes, Ruth B. *Old Fort Smith: cultural center on the Southwestern frontier.* Little Rock, 1965.

Morris, Robert L. *Opie Read, American humorist.* New York, 1965.

Noland, Charles F. M. *Pete Whetstone of Devil's Fork. Letters to the "Spirit of the Times."* Edited by Ted R. Worley and Eugene A. Nolte. Van Buren, Ark., 1957.

Rayburn, Otto Ernest. *Ozark country.* New York, 1941.

Schoolcraft, Henry R. *Schoolcraft in the Ozarks: reprint of Journal of a Tour into the Interior of Missouri and Arkansas in 1818 and 1819.* Edited by Hugh Park. Van Buren, Ark., 1955.

Staples, Thomas S. *Reconstruction in Arkansas 1862-1874.* New York, 1923.

Taylor, Orville W. *Negro slavery in Arkansas.* Durham, N. C., 1958.

Thomas, David Y. *Arkansas in war and reconstruction 1861 - 1874.* Little Rock, 1926.

Washburn, Cephas. *Reminiscences of the Indians.* Edited by Hugh Park. Van Buren, Ark., 1955.

White, Lonnie J. *Politics on the Southwestern frontier: Arkansas Territory 1819-1836.* Memphis, 1964.

Woodruff, William E. *Wilderness to statehood with William E. Woodruff.* Edited by Thomas Rothrock. Eureka Springs, Ark., 1961.
News items taken from early editions of the *Arkansas Gazette.*

Writers' Program, Arkansas. *Arkansas; a guide to the state.*
Compiled by workers of the Writers' Program of the Works Projects Administration in the State of Arkansas. New York, 1941.
Contains a wealth of historical information, and an excellent bibliography of material organized according to subject.

INDEX

Arkansas Game and Fish Commission: 291, 316-317

Arkansas Gazette. See Newspapers

Arkansas Historical Association: 354

Arkansas Historical Quarterly: 354

Arkansas History Commission: 354

Arkansas Industrial Development Commission (AIDC): 309-310

Arkansas Industrial University. See University of Arkansas

Arkansas Library Commission: 353

Arkansas Military Institute. See Tulip

Arkansas National Forest. See Ouachita National Forest

Arkansas National Guard: 265, 323-324. See also Militia, state; State guards

Arkansas penitentiary. See State penitentiary

Arkansas Plan: 309

Arkansas Post: 10, 14-16, 26, 33-34, 36-38, 40-43, 48, 56, 72, 97, 122, 126; attacks on, 18, 21; battle of, 123-124; capital of Arkansas Territory, 27, 45; description, 35; French government, 17; Indian trade, 45; land office, 55; National Park at, 355; population in 1768, 20; priests at, 18; Spanish government, 20; town destroyed, 124

Arkansas Power and Light Company: 247, 309, 316

Arkansas Resources and Development Commission: 309

Arkansas River: 2, 4, 6, 10, 14, 16, 20, 22, 33, 35-42, 45, 47, 50, 53, 56-58, 60, 76, 105, 123, 129, 134, 144, 186, 209, 269; development, 315-319; Project, 317-318

Arkansas River Valley: 191

Arkansas school closing law: 324-325

Arkansas School for the Deaf: 97, 158, 216

Arkansas School Journal: 204

Arkansas State Exposition of 1887: 189

Arkansas State Federation of Labor: 201, 252

Arkansas State Festival of Arts: 352

Arkansas State Teachers College: 280

Arkansas Supreme Court. See Courts

Arkansas Teachers Association: 347

Arkansas Territory: 26-27, 34, 48, 60

Arkansas-Texas: boundary line, 60, 79

Arkansas Trading House: 45

Arkansas Traveler, The: 109; certificates, 319; painting, 110

Arkansas Union veterans: 290

Arkansas, village of: 14

Arkansaw Traveler, The. See Newspapers

Arkopolis. See Little Rock: attempt to rename

Army of Arkansas: 116

Army Corps of Engineers: 316, 318

Army-Navy Hospital: 340. See also Hospital(s)

Army of Northern Virginia: 119

Army posts: 29, 60

Army of Tennessee: 132

Arpent, arpen: 22

Arrington, Alfred W.: 106, 108-109

Arsenals, United States: 114. See also Fort Smith; Little Rock

Art: artists, 110, 351-352; pioneer, 110; in schools, 348

Artmobile. See Arts Center

Arts Center: 352-353

Ashley County: 89, 119

Asia: 2

Assemblies of God: 270

Assembly, General: state, 31, 64, 67, 70, 74, 88, 91, 93-94, 97, 99, 102, 114, 131, 145-146, 150, 154, 156, 162, 168-169, 176, 187, 199, 211, 218, 225-227, 230-231, 244, 254, 257-258, 262-263, 274, 277, 279-280, 282, 291, 294, 298, 309-310, 312, 321, 323-324; territorial, 27-31, 47, 57

Asylum, state insane. See Hospital(s): State

Atlanta (Georgia): 129

Atlantic Ocean: 8

Attorney general: of Arkansas, 227; of the United States, 176

Austin: 138

Authors, Arkansas: 207, 211-212, 351, 354

Automobiles: 257, 289

Aviation: air bases, 265, 301, 312; airlines, 305; airplane plant, 249; airports, 305, 319

Axum, Donna: 319

Bailey, Carl E.: 329-331, 338, 343

Bandini, Pietro: 191

Bank(s): 197, 209, 337, 351; department, state, 227; failure of, 73-74, 235, 294; and farm credit, 194; first in Arkansas, 70; First and Second, of the United States, 71; forbidden by law, 74; and industrial development, 310-311; number in 1882, 194; Real Estate, 70-74, 102, 160, 178; State, 70-74, 102, 160

Banks, Nathaniel P.: 127

Baptist churches: 97-99, 205-207, 270; Landmark or Missionary, 270

Barkman, Jacob: 33, 89

Base line. See Land: surveying

Baseball. See Sports

Bates, James Woodson: 27

Bates, Mrs. L. C. (Daisy): 323

Batesville: 27, 34, 41, 49, 58, 76, 84, 90, 105, 123; early bank, 72; first academy at, 95; land office, 55; marble, 250

Capital, state: at Hot Springs, 123; at Washington (Hempstead County), 126
Capital, territorial: moved to Little Rock, 27, 45, 48
Capital Theater (Little Rock): 215
Capitol, state: grounds, 337-338; new, 257, 351; old, see Old State House
Capitol, territorial: 28
Caraway, Mrs. Hattie W.: 333
Carlisle: 212
Carnahan, John P.: 97-98
Carnegie, Andrew: 282
Carolinas (North and South): 8, 57
Carpenter Dam: 247
Carpetbaggers: 146, 148-150, 162, 169
Carroll County: 82, 84
Cassidy, Henry: 26
Catholic Church: 14, 17-18, 21, 68, 96-99, 206, 267, 269; Diocese of Little Rock, 99. See also Church(es); Missionaries; Religion
Catterson, Robert F.: 167
Cattle drives: 82
Cattle raising. See Farming: livestock
Caves: 2
Census. See Arkansas: census of population
Centennials: Civil War, 354; statehood, 354
Center Point: 157, 212
Central America: 80
Central College: 205, 281
Central High School (Little Rock): 323-325
Chambers of commerce: 240, 242, 290, 309
"Change the Name of Arkansas?" (speech): 211-212
Charleston: 322
Chautauqua Movement: 289
Cherokee Bill: 209
Cherokee Indians. See Indian(s)
Cherokee Nation: 209; boundary, 60; West, 58. See also Indian(s)
Cherokee-Osage wars: 59-60
Cherry, Francis: 329, 331, 336, 345
Chicago: 212, 215
Chickalah. See Yell County
Chickasaws. See Indian(s)
Chicot County: 72, 158, 191
Chihuahua (Mexico): 78
Chinese immigration: 159, 191
Choctaw Indians. See Indian(s)
Choctaw Nation: 41, 76, 209. See also Indian(s)
Choctaw reservation: 57
Christ Church Parish. See Little Rock: churches
Christian Church (Disciples of Christ): 96-99, 206, 355
Christie, Ned: 209

Church of Jesus Christ of Latter Day Saints. See Mormons
Church(es): 35, 70; at Arkansas Post, 17-18, 21; buildings, 93, 98-99, 206, 356; colleges supported by, 96-97, 205, 281; during Civil War, 135-136; during Conservative period, 205-207; on the frontier, 97-98; growth and influence of, 98-99, 229, 269-270; and modernist-fundamentalist controversy, 270; new, after 1900, 270; and prohibition, 218, 229; revivals and camp meetings, 98, 206, 286, 356; since 1930, 355-356; and slavery, 99. See also Missionaries; Negro(es); Religion; and Baptist, Catholic, Methodist, etc.
Churches of Christ: 270
Churchill, Thomas J.: 124, 180
CIO (national labor organization): 299
Cities and towns: 345; discriminatory ordinances, 272; government of, 305; growth of, 48-49, 84, 191, 215, 260, 305; problems of, 305; urban renewal in, 305, 319. See also Fort Smith, Little Rock, Pine Bluff, etc.
Citizens Improvement Union: 231
City manager plan. See Cities and towns: government of
Civilian Conservation Corps (CCC): 297
Civil rights: 169, 332; law, 326; program, 331
Civil service system: 338
Civil War: 45, 64, 68, 74, 78, 89, 91, 93-94, 97, 99, 103-104, 109-110, 113-145, 154, 156, 158, 174, 184, 193, 196, 209, 212, 215, 217, 221, 230, 272; Arkansas organizing for, 116, 118; beginning of, 115; causes of, 113; end of, 131-132, 145; fighting, 119-130; importance of Arkansas in, 118-119; lawmaking, 130-131; life in Arkansas during, 134-139; politics, 124; record of Arkansas in, 132; Union sentiment in Arkansas during, 142-145. See also Confederate(s); Union
Civil War centennial. See Centennials
Civil Works Administration (CWA): 297
Clarendon: 76, 138, 156
Clark County: 27, 89; formed, 26
Clarke, James P.: 225
Clarksville: 184; blind and deaf schools, 97; college at, 205; natural gas deposits, 247
Clayton, John M.: 200
Clayton, Powell: 126, 150, 156-157, 160, 162, 165, 168, 178
Clayton regime: 159
Cleburne, Patrick R.: 132
Cleveland County: 331
Cleveland, Grover: 176
Climate. See Arkansas: climate of

English: agents influence Indians, 20; settlements in North America, 18; traveler in Arkansas, 36-37; wars with French, 18
Episcopal Church: 98-99, 206, 355
Eureka Springs: 352
Europe: 12, 15, 23, 85, 301
Everetts, The: 66
Evolution, theory of: 270, 355
Ex-Confederate Association: 216
Executions (of criminals): 47, 210, 262
Experiment stations. See Farming

Factories. See Industry; Manufacturing; Mills and factories
Fairs: county, 240, 287; state, 216, 303, 319
Fancher, Alexander: 82
Fancher c a r a v a n. See Mountain Meadows massacre
Fargo school (for Negroes): 321
Farm Bureau: 201, 239, 329
Farm, farms. See Farming
Farmer-labor parties. See Farming; Populist party; Union Labor party, etc.
Farmers' Alliance: 198-200, 238
Farmers' Union: 201, 239, 280
Farming: after Second World War, 303-304; agricultural experiment stations, 198-199; corn, 36, 76, 85-86, 131, 134, 238; cotton, 33, 35, 37, 85-86, 89, 131, 152, 154, 184, 193, 233, 235, 238-240, 295, 297, 303; credit system, 194-196, 304; drouth and, 197, 294, 297, 304; during the great depression, 235, 294-301; extension and demonstration work, 240; flax, 86; on the frontier, 84-86; fruits and grains, 35-36, 85, 236, 238; labor engaged in, 86, 88, 152-154, 182, 193, 235-236, 303, 309; livestock, 33, 36, 58, 76, 82, 85-86, 238, 240, 303; methods, improvement of, 240; New Deal and, 297-301, 303; number and size of farms, 193, 233, 303; organizations, 198-201, 238-239; poultry, 304; prehistoric and Indian, 6, 10-12, 58; problems, 193-197, 235-236, 240, 294-301, 303-306; rice, 35, 86, 238, 247, 304; rural life, 85-86, 286-289; sharecrop system, 154, 193-195, 287, 236; soybeans, 304; tenant, 235-236, 274, 287, 299, 303; tobacco, 86; under France and Spain, 22; use of machinery in, 233, 303-304, 309
Faubus, Orval E.: 309, 321, 323-325, 329, 331-332, 336, 345
Faulkner, Sanford C. (Sandy): 109
Fayetteville: 41, 49, 84, 91, 123, 139, 281, 289, 305, 322; early academy, 95; early bank, 72; college at, 96-97; land office, 55; state school at, 204; university established at, 158. See also University of Arkansas

Featherstonhaugh, George William: 36-37, 46
Federal control: 324
Federal government. See Government: Federal; and United States: government
Federal grants: 295, 301, 338. See also Government: F e d e r a l; Land; United States: government
Federal Homestead Act: 104
Federal land grants. See Land: grants
Federal(s). See Civil War; Union
Ferriday (Louisiana): 11
Finney, Alfred: 59
First Amendment: 179
First Arkansas Development Finance Corporation (FADFC): 310
First Arkansas Infantry: 119
First Regiment of Arkansas Cavalry: 80
First white settlement. See Arkansas
First World War: 193, 233, 239, 247, 249, 254, 265, 275, 282, 289-290, 294, 301
Fishback, William M.: 144, 179, 182
Five Civilized Tribes. See Indian(s)
Fizer, N. B.: 200
Flanagin, Harris: 124, 131
Fletcher, John Gould: 351
Flint, Timothy: 45
Flood control: 101-103, 159-160, 219, 221, 269, 297, 316-319
Floods: of 1858 and 1859, 103; of 1927, 269, 316; of 1943, 318
Floods, major: dates of, 219
Florida: 8, 10, 21; secession, 113
Flu epidemic: 265. See also Health, public
"Flynn-Doran War" of 1878: 213
Folk ballads, songs: 284, 352. See also Music
Folklore: 355
Folsom (New Mexico): 3
Folsom people. See Indian(s)
Food: of early settlers, 35-36, 46-47, 85; on farm, 286-287; of Indians, 6, 11-12; problem during war, 134; processing industry, 311; of slaves, 86
Football. See Sports
Ford Foundation: 348
Ford, Henry: 249
Forests. See Conservation; Industry: lumber
Fort Charles III: 20
Fort Esperanza: called Hopefield, 21
Fort Gibson: 80; established, 60
Fort Hindman: 124
Fort Logan H. Roots (hospital): 217
Fort St. Louis: 15
Fort Smith: 36, 38, 41, 49, 57, 76, 80, 91, 95, 98-99, 118, 123, 128-129, 139, 145, 191, 209, 267, 269, 281-282, 290, 301, 355; arsenal, 115; College of St. Andrew opened, 96;

established at Belle Point, 60; factories, 243; naming of, 60; natural gas field, 247; opera establishment, 215; population in 1860, 84

Fort Sumter (South Carolina): 115

Fort Towson: 76, 80

Fourche Bayou: 126, 244

Fourche la Fave River: 108

Fourteenth Amendment: 146, 150

Fowler, Absalom: 68

France: 14-15, 18, 22-23, 50. See also French

Franklin, battle of: 132

Fraternal orders. See Elks; Masonic; Moose, etc.

Free Christian Zion Church of Christ: 270

Free library service bureau: 282

"Freedom to Work" law. See Constitution, state: amendments; Labor

Freedmen's Bureau: 148, 150; established, 153-154

Freeman, Thomas: 33

Freemasonry. See Masonic

Freemasonry, poet laureate of: 207

French: amusements, 45; explorers, 14-16, 33, 46; flag, 26; government and laws, 14, 17; houses, 22; hunters, 19, 33; land grants, measurement, 22; maps, 19; names in Arkansas, 19; Revolution, 23; Rock, 17; settlements and settlers, 15, 18, 20, 22, 45, 98, 191; wars with Indians, English, 18, 57

French, Alice: 207

French and Indian War: 18

"French Rock." See Big Rock

Fruit growing. See Farming

Fry, Joseph: 132

Fulbright, J. William: 331, 333-334

Fuller, William H.: 238

Fulton: 36, 41, 57, 137

Fulton, William S.: 28-30, 64, 79

Fusion tickets: 178

Futrell administration: 340

Futrell, J. Marion: 330, 336-337

Galloway College: 281

Gambling: 45, 48, 213, 336; attack on, 230-231

Game and Fish Commission. See Arkansas Game and Fish Commission

Game refuges: 291, 319

Gantt, Edward W.: 144

Garland, Augustus H.: 131, 150, 169, 171, 176

Garland County: 90, 250, 331; outlaws, 210

Garland, Rufus K.: 199

Gas, natural. See Mining and minerals

Gate City Guards: 213

Gates, Noah P.: 158

"Gay Nineties" (1890-1899): 233

General Assembly. See Assembly, General

General Education Board: 275, 278-279

General Land Office: 55

Georgia: 8, 57, 84, 118, 221; secession, 113

German(s): airplanes, 265; at Arkansas Post, 16; immigration, 99, 191, 206, 238; as settlers, 84, 159

Germany: 265

Gerstaecker, Frederick: 108-109

Gettysburg (Pennsylvania), battle of: 126

Gila River: 80

Gilbert, Cass: 257

Gillham (lake): 316

Gins, cotton: 35, 303. See also Farming

GI revolt: 331, 336

Goff, Norris: 355

Gold. See Mining and minerals

Golden City: 248

Gold rush. See California

Goodspeed histories (of Arkansas): 207

Gould, Jay: 182, 184

Government: city, 161, 305; Confederate, 122, 131-132; county, 29, 64, 145, 161, 187, 224, 331, 338; Federal, 29, 60, 76, 93, 102-103, 115, 131, 167, 171, 176, 180, 187, 193, 197, 217, 221, 249, 269, 295, 299, 301, 304, 312, 316-317, 323, 330, 338-340, 345; French, 14, 17; Indian, 12; military, 144, 148; Spanish, 20; state, 64, 93, 101, 126, 128, 148, 154, 156, 171, 174, 180, 187, 197, 216, 249, 257, 260, 278-279, 281, 291, 303, 313, 319, 329-330, 337-339, 342, 349; territorial, 27, 29, 48; Unionist state, 131, 144-145

Government, United States. See United States: government

Governors of Arkansas: first two, 27; former Confederate leaders as, 224

Governors of Arkansas: (state) Homer M. Adkins, 329-331, 343; Carl E. Bailey, 329-331, 338, 343; Elisha Baxter, 164-165, 167-169; James H. Berry, 212; Charles H. Brough, 231, 260-261, 274, 289; Francis Cherry, 329, 331, 336, 345; Thomas J. Churchill, 124, 180; James P. Clarke, 225; Powell Clayton, 126, 150, 156-157, 160, 162, 165, 168, 178; Elias N. Conway, 68, 91; James S. Conway, 31, 68, 74; Jeff Davis, 224, 227, 257, 260-261; George W. Donaghey, 224, 257, 260-261; Thomas S. Drew, 68, 80; James P. Eagle, 199; Orval E. Faubus, 309, 321, 323-325, 329, 331-332, 336, 345; William M. Fishback, 144, 179, 182; Harris Flanagin, 124, 131; J. Marion Futrell, 330, 336-337; Augustus H. Garland, 131, 150, 169, 171,

176; Ozra A. Hadley, 164; George W. Hays, 231, 260; Simon P. Hughes, 182, 213; Dan W. Jones, 224, 228; Ben T. Laney, 331; Sid McMath, 331-332, 336, 344; Thomas C. McRae, 258, 267, 274; John E. Martineau, 258, 342; William R. Miller, 210, 213; Isaac Murphy, 115, 131, 145-146, 148, 154, 160; Harvey Parnell, 330, 342; Henry M. Rector, 68, 114-116, 121-124; John S. Roane, 66; Joseph T. Robinson, 224, 330, 334; Tom J. Terral, 269; Archibald Yell, 74, 80, 94; (territorial) William S. Fulton, 28-30, 64, 79; George Izard, 27, 46; James Miller, 27, 45-46, 60; John Pope, 28-29, 42, 64

Graduate Institute of Technology. See University of Arkansas

Grand Army of the Republic: 290

Grand Dragon. See Ku Klux Klan

Grand Opera House (Little Rock): 215

Grand Prairie: 6, 42, 48, 247, 304; region, 238

Grand River: 60

Grange: 187, 238, 240

Grant, Ulysses S.: 120, 126, 156, 164, 167-168, 171

Gravette: 265

Great depression. See Depression: of 1929-1941

Great Raft: 16, 33, 38

Greeks, immigration: 191

Greeley, Horace: 164

Greenback party: 198-199

Greers Ferry (lake): 316

Greeson (lake): 316

Gregg, Josiah: 78

Grey, William H.: 149, 159

Greyhound race track: 336

Gristmills: 35-36, 70, 134, 186, 249, 287

Guerrillas: 135

Guion: 250

Gurdon: 186

Hadley, Ozra A.: 164

Halbrook, William E.: 279

Hall, Benjamin F.: 98

Hallie (steamboat): 167

Hallum, John: 207

"Hanging Judge." See Parker, Isaac C.

Harrelson road act. See Roads and road improvement

Harris, Oren: 334

Harrison: 82, 142, 254

Harrison, M. LaRue: 142

Harrison, William Henry: 65-66

Hartford: 253

Harvey, William H. ("Coin"): 299

Hawaii: 301

Hays, Brooks: 325

Hays, George W.: 231, 260

Hazen: 238

Health, p u b l i c: anti-hookworm work, 262; dentistry, 46, 217, 263; during Civil War, 138, 154; during Conservative period, 216-217; in early Arkansas, 46; epidemics, 76, 138, 154, 216, 265; medicine, practice of, 46, 88, 216-217, 263; since 1930, 339-340; State Board of Health, 262; tuberculosis sanatoriums, 263; vaccination, 262. See also Hospital(s); University of Arkansas

Helena: 9, 14, 22, 33, 49-50, 72, 95, 97, 102, 114, 122, 126, 143-145, 198, 254, 281; Negro regiments enlisted at, 152

Hemphill, John: 89

Hempstead County: 26, 33, 36, 76, 126, 169; militia, 210; racial trouble, 212

Hempstead, Fay: 207

Henderson State Teachers College: 205, 280

Hendrix College: 205, 281

Henry, John: 97

Henry's Chapel: 97

Herndon, Dallas T.: 354

Hesper (steamer): 156

Highland peach orchard: 238

Highways. See Roads and road improvement; State Highway(s)

Hill, A. B.: 279

Hill, Robert L.: 274

Hindman, Thomas C.: 68, 122-123, 150, 156

Hinds, James: 149, 156

Historical societies: 354

Holford banking house: 74

Holford debt: 160, 178-179. See also State debt

Holford, James & Company: 160

Holidays. See Amusements

Holiness churches: 270

Hollywood (California): 355

Holmes, Theophilus H.: 122, 126

Hoo-Hoo, Concatenated Order of: 186

Hoop Spur: 274

Hoover administration: 295

Hoover, Herbert: 295

Hope: 238

Hopefield: 41, 91, 137-138; called Fort Esperanza, 21

Horse racing. See Racing

Hospital(s): 46, 265, 319; military, 136, 138, 215, 217, 340; nursing homes, 340; private, 217; State, 216, 263, 340; State and Federal aid for, 339

Hot Spring County: 86, 119

Joliet, Louis: 14
Jones, Dan W.: 224, 228
Jones, James K.: 176
Jones, John Thompson: 198
Jonesboro: 239, 305; college at, 281; state schools at, 204, 239, 281
Jones Mill: 301
Joplin (Missouri): 254
Joutel, Henri: 14-15
Julius Rosenwald Fund: 275, 278

Kansas: 129, 156, 200, 209
Kennedy, John F.: 326
Kentuckians: 33
Kentucky: 20, 22, 27, 84
Kindley, Field E.: 265
Kit the Arkansas Traveler (play): 211
Kiwanis clubs: 242, 290
Knights of Columbus: 289
Knights of Labor: 182, 199, 252
Knights of Pythias: 289
Know-Nothing party. See American party
Korean War: 305
Kraft paper: 244
Ku Klux Klan: 150, 156, 158, 265, 267, 269

Labor: child, 252, 254; constitutional amendments affecting, 254, 312; importance of, 252; legislation, 182, 254, 312-313; Negro, 146, 182, 199, 274; number of workers, 89, 181-182; organization of, 182, 199-201, 252-253, 299, 312; and Second World War, 301, 309; strikes, 181, 213, 253-254, 299, 312; wages, 182, 294, 311, 313; of women, 252, 254. See also Farming; Industry; Manufacturing
Ladd, Alan: 352
Lafayette County: 79
La Harpe, Benard de: 16-17, 33, 105
Lake Catherine: 316
Lake Hamilton: 316
Lakes, new: 52, 355; listed, 316-317. See also Dams and lakes; and Beaver, Millwood, Norfork, etc.
Land: claims, 50; districts, 55; grants, 15-18, 22, 28, 50, 93-94, 97, 101-104, 187; to guarantee Real Estate bank, 71; laws, 52, 101, 103-104; sales by government, 51-52, 55, 93-94, 101-104; s p e c u l a t o r s, 52-53; surveying, 29, 50-55; values, 55, 195, 235; warrants or patents, 51, 53. See also Conservation; Farming; Indian(s); Swamp land(s)
Landmark Baptists. See Baptist churches
"Land of Opportunity": 310

Laney, Ben T.: 331
L'Anguille River: 9
La Salle: assassinated, 14; claims Arkansas for France, 14-15
Lauck, Chester: 355
Law, John: 22; colony, 15-17
"Law and Order Sunday": 267
Lawrence County: 43, 84, 322; established, 26
Lead Hill: 90
Lee, John D.: 82
Lee, Robert E.: 119, 126
Legislative Council: of Arkansas Territory, 27
Legislature. See Assembly, General
Levees. See Flood control; Floods
Lewis, James M.: 159
Lewis, Mary: 352
Lewisburg: academies, 95; location of, 157
Liberal Republican party: 162, 164-165
Liberty bonds: 265
Liberty party: 299
Libraries: Carnegie grants for, 282; established by WPA, 297, 353; first circulating one, 42; public, 281-282; school and college, 205, 277, 353; state program for, 353; tax support for, 282, 353
"Lily white" candidate. See Republican party
Lincoln, Abraham: 113, 115, 143-145, 148, 153
Lindsey, Eli: 97
Lions clubs: 242, 290
Little Missouri River: 6, 11, 89
Little Red River: 22
Little River County: 304
Little Rock: 2, 17, 31, 36-39, 41-42, 53, 79-80, 91, 99, 105-106, 110, 123-124, 127-129, 131, 138, 142, 144-145, 212, 215, 224, 243-244, 247, 267, 269, 281, 289-290, 310, 319, 321, 337, 339-340, 351-352, 354-355; academies and High School for Young Ladies, 95; Air Force Base, 312; arsenal, 76, 114, 116, 137, 167; attempt to rename, 48; Board of Commerce, 240; capital moved to, 27, 45, 48; churches, 48, 98; early manufacturing, 90; early merchants, 46; first banks, 71-72; first criminal hanged, 47; first school, 93; first telephones, 215; government, 305; hotels, 48, 136, 167; industries, 249; integration crisis, 323-326, 329, 332; land office, 55; Mardi Gras, 216; Museum of Fine Arts, 352; occupied by Union forces, 126; in pioneer days, 48; population, 48, 84, 191; school board, 324-325; schools before Civil War, 94; streets, 48, 72, 257; symphony orchestra, 352; Town Branch, 48; urban renewal in, 305; Whig parade, 66
Livestock production. See Farming

Missionaries: Catholic, 17-18, 98; Protestant, 45, 59
Missionary Baptists. See Baptist churches
Missionary Ridge, battle of: 132
Mississippi: 8, 84, 89, 114, 277; Choctaw Indians, 57; secession, 113
Mississippi Company: 16-17
Mississippi County: 265, 299
Mississippi River: 2, 5-6, 8-10, 14-15, 18, 21, 23, 33, 36-37, 41, 52, 56, 76, 84, 86, 91, 97, 102-103, 118, 121-123, 126, 129, 138, 144, 156, 184, 219, 221, 269, 316
Mississippi Valley: 4, 12, 14, 18, 21, 52
Missouri: 20, 34, 36, 40-41, 47, 52, 60, 68, 76, 84, 91, 121-122, 129, 134, 144, 157, 213, 254; Civil War in, 119; legislature, 26
Missouri River: 53
Missouri Territory: 26, 33
Missourians: 82
Mobile (Alabama): c a p t u r e d by Spanish forces, 21
Model T (automobile): 287
Money: 28, 54, 71-72, 89, 101, 160-161, 180, 194, 224, 228, 235, 254, 260-261, 274, 277, 281, 286, 295, 305, 318-319, 329, 337-338, 342, 347; circulation of, 198; Confederate, 131, 137-138; Conservative attitude toward, 175; free coinage of silver, 198, 201; gold and silver, 73, 79; greenback, 198; issued by first banks, 70, 73-74; scarcity of, 46, 70, 93, 131, 174, 193, 197, 242, 294, 309; scrip, 102, 161, 178, 252, 254; theories of "Coin" Harvey, 299
Monks, William: 157
Monroe (Louisiana): 41, 43
Monroe, James: 26-27
Monte Ne pyramid: 299
Montgomery (Alabama): 114
Montgomery County: 118, 250, 331, 355; outlaws, 210
Montgomery, William: 37
Montgomery's Point: 22, 37, 42
Monticello: 130-131, 239, 281
Moonshining, moonshiners: 209-210, 267
Moore, James Wilson: 98
Moose (fraternal order): 289
Mormons: 82
Morrilton: 57-58, 312, 319, 349; state school at, 204
Mosaic Templars: 289
Moses, C. Hamilton: 309
Motion pictures: 289, 352, 355
Mound City (gunboat): 123
Mound people. See Indian(s)
Mounds, Knapp or Toltec: 2

Mount Ida: 118
Mount (or Mound) Prairie: 33, 36, 41, 97
Mountain Meadows massacre: 82
Movies. See Motion pictures
Murfreesboro: 89, 137, 249
Murphy, Isaac: 115, 131, 145-146, 148, 154, 160
Murrell, John A.: 48, 88
Music: 109, 136-137, 164, 215-216, 284-286, 329, 352
Musick, David: 33-34
Mussels: 250

Napoleon, academies at: 95
Napoleon (French dictator): 23, 26
Nashville: 212
N a t c h e z (Mississippi): 15; captured by Spanish forces, 21
Natchitoches (Louisiana): 41
National Association for the Advancement of Colored People (NAACP): 322-323
National Council of Churches: 355
National F a r m e r s' Union. See Farmers' Union
National Grange: 198-199. See also Grange
National Guard. See Arkansas National Guard
National Park Service: 355
National Road. See Roads
National States Rights party: 325
National Youth Administration (NYA): 297
Natural resources: 247-250. See also Conservation; Industry; Manufacturing; Mining and minerals
Negro(es): B l a c k Code, 17; churches and religious life, 99, 207, 270; discrimination against, 146, 267, 272; during Civil War, 132, 138, 142-143, 152-153; fraternal orders, 289; free, before Civil War, 88; as freedmen, 152-154, 193; holidays, 285; immigration, 159, 191, 275, 306; integration, 321-326, 329, 332, 355; lynching, 212, 274; as militiamen, 157, 167; and politics, 143, 145-146, 148-150, 159, 162, 169, 171, 174, 176, 178, 199, 201, 224-225, 272, 275, 321, 331; population, 20, 22, 86, 150, 191, 226, 275; race riots, 212, 274; schools and colleges, 154, 158, 204-205, 274-275, 278, 321; segregation, 158, 272, 274-275, 321-326, 332, 355; as slaves, 17, 31, 42, 58, 84, 86, 88-89, 99, 113, 132, 142-144, 152, 193; state institutions for, 263, 321, 340; in Union army, 142-143, 152. See also Farming; L a b o r; Slavery
Nettie Jones (steamer): 156
New Arkansas Travelers, The (book): 189
Newberry law: 229

New Deal: 295, 297, 301, 303, 312, 330, 334, 337
New England: 59, 127
New Gascony: 167
New Hampshire: 27
New Madrid (Missouri): 52; certificates, 52-53; earthquake, 52
New Orleans (Louisiana): 15, 18, 20, 22, 35-36, 38, 43, 50, 80, 85-86, 89-90, 119, 184
New World: 8, 23
Newport: 312
Newport (Rhode Island): 323
Newspapers: 42-43, 47-48, 65, 108-110, 139, 162, 198, 207, 240, 242, 254, 274, 310-311, 325, 329, 351, 354; *Arkansas Advocate*, 28, 42; *Arkansas Gazette*, 28, 42, 105-106, 149, 165, 325; *Arkansaw Traveler*, 212; *Daily Republican*, 162; *Spirit of the Times*, 105-106; *Times and Herald*, 110; *True Democrat*, 110, 124; *Washington Telegraph*, 139
Newton County: 137, 142, 145
Newton, Robert C.: 180, 212
Newton, Thomas W.: 64
New York: 42, 149, 247, 249, 257, 262, 294, 332
Nimrod dam: 316
Nineteenth Amendment: 231
Noland, Charles Fenton Mercer ("Fent"): 105-106, 108
Norfork dam: 316
Norristown: 110, 137
North America: 2, 18, 249
North Carolina: 84, 115
North Little Rock: 10, 265, 305; name changed from Argenta, 248
Norwood, Charles M.: 199
Notrebe, Frederick: 37; house of, 42
Nuttall, Thomas: 36, 47; trip on the Arkansas River, 35

Oak Hills, battle of: 116, 119-120
Oaklawn race track: 230, 336
Odd Fellows (fraternal order): 289
Ohio: 149, 210
Ohio River: 316-317
Oil production. See Mining and minerals
Oklahoma: 20, 60, 209, 253, 317-318; Indians, 56-57, 59-60, 76
Old Guard: 224
Old South: 174
Old Southwest: 351
Old Southwest Trail: 184
Old State House: 110, 167, 257; construction, 28, 101; restoration, 354; secession convention in, 114-115
On a Slow Train Through Arkansaw (book): 212

"Open shop" policy. See Labor: strikes
Ord, Edward O. C.: 148
Orphanages: 263
Osage Indians. See Indian(s)
Ouachita: College, 205, 281; County, 248; lake, 316; Mountains, 5-6, 10, 142, 248; National Forest, 244; River, 2, 10-11, 33, 38, 76, 89, 127, 247, 316, 318
Outlaws: 18, 20, 39-40, 45, 47-48, 78, 80, 108, 135, 156, 209-210, 213
Owen, David Dale: 90
Ozan (settlement): 33
Ozark(s): counties, 135, 224, 254; dam, 316, 318; mountain schools, 279; Mountains, 3-4, 6, 34-35, 47, 66, 90, 122, 134, 142, 178, 355
Ozarks, College of the. See College of the Ozarks

Pace, Frank Jr.: 334
Pacific (ocean): 80
Painters. See Art
Palarm Creek: 167
Panic of 1873: 158, 174
Parent-teacher associations: 278
Parker, Isaac C.: 210
Parker, William: 33-34
Parks, state. See State park system
Parks, W. P.: 199
Parnell, Harvey: 330, 342
Parole system: 262
Passenger pigeon: 34, 291
Patterson, William: 22, 97
Pawnee Indians. See Indian(s)
Peabody: Education Fund, 203, 279; institutes, 278; scholarships, 278
Peace and Constitutional Society: 142
Peace of Paris: 18
Pea Ridge: 122; battle of, 120-121; battlefield park, 355
Penitentiary. See State penitentiary
Pennsylvania: 191
Pensacola (Florida): captured by Spanish forces, 21
Pentecostal churches: 270
People's party. See Populist party
Perry County: 213
Perryville: 108, 213
Pershing, John J.: 265
Peru: 8
Petit Jean State Park: 319
Phelps, John S.: 144
Philander Smith College: 205, 281, 321
Philippines: 221, 301
Phillips County: 9, 274

Phillips, Sylvanus: 22, 33
Piggott: 355
Pike, Albert: 68, 105, 109, 121, 150
Pike County: 238, 249
Pine Bluff: 36, 49, 56, 98, 127-129, 176, 216, 243, 289, 305, 311, 331, 349; Branch Normal College at, 158, 204-205, 281; Jefferson High School of, 95
Pine Ridge: 355
Pioneers: American, 51; laws, 47-48; society and life, 45-48. See also Settlements, settlers: early
Pittsburgh (Pennsylvania): 35
Plains, Western: 5
Plantations: during depression days, 235-236; early, 84-89; freedmen on, 152-154; Negro tenants, 236. See also Farming
Plumerville: 200
Pocahontas: 119; academies, 95
Poet Laureate of Arkansas: 351
Poets: 207, 351
Poinsett County: 299
Point Chicot: 36
Point Remove Creek: 57
Poison Spring, battle of: 128; Negro troops in, 143
Poke Bayou: 34
Poland committee: 171
Poland, Luke P.: 171
Polish: immigration, 206; settlements, 191
Politics. See Government; Elections; Primaries; Voting
Polk, Leonidas: 98
Poll tax. See Taxation, taxes
Pope County: 82, 331; under military rule, 158
Pope, John: 28-29, 42, 64
Pope, William F.: 42
Populist party: 181-182, 198-201, 226, 228; after 1896, 224
Postal routes: 29, 43. See also Mail service
Post of Arkansas. See Arkansas Post
Post offices: 29, 43. See also Mail service
Poteau River: 60
Potosi (Missouri): 34
Pottery: 2, 250
Poultry: processing plants, 304, 311; raising, 304. See also Farming
Powell, Dick: 352
Prairie Creek (Pike County): 249
Prairie Creek (Sebastian County): 253-254
Prairie De Ann, battle of: 128
Prairie Grove, battle of: 123
Pratt, Parley P.: 82
Preemption: 52. See also Land

Presbyterian Church: 98-99, 206, 355; Cumberland, 96-99
Prescott: 128
"Presidential" Republicans: 332
Price, Sterling: 121, 126, 129
Primaries: 201, 224-225, 275, 332; double, 330; white, 272, 321. See also Elections; Voting
Princeton: 95
Prisons: 261-262; camps, 301. See also State penitentiary
Profitable Farming Bureau: 240
"Profitable Farming Campaigns": 240
Progressive Farmers and Household Union of America: 274
Prohibition of sale of liquor: 99, 217-219, 229-231, 238, 267, 336
Public health work. See Health, public
Public utilities: 311, 319, 330; regulation of, 227, 337
Public Works Administration (PWA): 297
Public works projects: 319. See also New Deal
Puerto Rico: 221
Pulaski County: 26, 200, 245
Pullman strike of 1894: 213
Pyeatt, Jacob: 36
Pyeatt, James: 36

Quakers: 154
Quapaw Guards: 213
Quapaw Indians. See Indian(s)
Quesenbury, William (Bill Cush): 109

Race relations. See Negro(es)
Racial trouble: in 1883, 212; in 1919, 274; in 1957, 321-326. See also Negro(es)
Racing: greyhound, 336; horse, 48, 106, 230-231, 336
Radical party: 143, 145-146, 148-150, 154, 156, 158, 160-162, 165, 167, 169, 171, 174, 178, 203. See also Reconstruction, period of; Republican party
Radio: 289, 311, 329
Railroad(s): 89, 209, 216, 249, 261, 294; Cairo and Fulton, 91, 103, 160; crossties, 289; "Diamond Joe" line, 215; Federal land grants to, 103, 187; first, 90-91, to cross state, 184; high freight rates, 193-194, 242; and immigration, 187, 189, 191; and industrial growth, 186-187, 311; Jim Crow laws affecting, 272; Little Rock and Fort Smith, 103, 160, 184; Little Rock and Memphis, 91, 103, 122, 160, 184; miles of track, 91, 138, 184, 243, 330; Missouri and North Arkan-

Rural renewal program: 304
Russellville: 59, 110, 239, 281
Russia: 176
Rust, Albert: 68

St. Charles: 10, 122, 132; captured, 123
St. Francis: County, 274; Levee District, 221;
    River, 9-10, 17, 22, 33, 38, 47, 52-53, 58, 91,
    103, 138, 221, 316
St. John's College: 97, 136, 167
St. Louis (Missouri): 20, 34, 36, 41, 91, 139;
    Indian council at, 60
St. Mary's mission: 98
Salem Church (Randolph County): 97
Saline County: 94, 244-245
Saline River: 10
Salt Lake City (Utah): 82
San Antonio (Texas): 80
San Francisco (California): 139
Santa Fe (New Mexico): 78, 80
Scalawags: 146, 156, 158, 169
Schola Cantorum: 352
School improvement associations: 278
Schoolcraft, Henry Rowe: 34-35, 47
Schools: academies, 94-96, 136, 204; agricul-
    tural, 239, 281; blind and deaf, 97, 158, 216,
    279; Freedmen's Bureau, 154; high, 95-96;
    industrial or training, 262, 340; medical,
    216; mission, 58; normal, 204, 279-280;
    private, 93-94, 204-205; singing, 285-286;
    vocational-technical, 349. See also Colleges
    and universities; Negro(es); S c h o o l s,
    public; Taxation; University of Arkansas
Schools, public: after Civil War, 146; before
    Civil War, 89, 93-94; in Conservative period,
    203-204; considered poor, 242, 347; con-
    solidation of, 277, 348; desegregation of,
    321-326; during reconstruction, 150, 158;
    financing, 93-94, 101, 158, 203, 261, 277-278,
    338, 347; in Progressive period, 277-281;
    since 1930, 337, 347-349; teacher training,
    203-205, 279-281, 347-348; teachers' salaries,
    93, 203, 280, 321, 347-348; teaching of evo-
    lution in, 270. See also Libraries; Negro-
    (es); Schools; Taxation
Scotland: 355
Scott County: 212
Scottish: financier, 15. See also Scottish-
    Irish
Scottish-Irish: 191
Searcy: 84, 123, 156
Searcy County: 142
Sebastian County: 186, 244, 253
Sebastian, William K.: 143-144
Secession. See Arkansas; Civil War
Secession convention. See Conventions

Second World War: 299, 301, 303, 305-306, 309,
    312, 316, 319, 321, 329-331, 337, 340, 342,
    344-345, 347-349, 351-352, 355
Selective Service: 265
Seminole Indians. See Indian(s)
Segregation. See Negro(es)
Senate: of Arkansas, 64-65, 162, 330; of the
    United States, 68, 80, 143, 145-146, 162, 164,
    176, 224-225, 330, 334. See also Assembly,
    General; Congress of the United States
Senators, United States, from Arkansas: 64,
    145, 176, 333-334. See also Congress of the
    United States: Arkansans in
Sequoya: 58
Settlements, settlers (early): 23, 33-37, 39, 41,
    43, 45, 48-49, 51-52, 55-58, 84, 98, 103-104;
    first American, 22; first white, 15; Indian,
    5, 36, 58. See also French; German(s);
    Immigration; Pioneers; Spanish
Seventeenth Amendment: 225
Seven Years' War: 18
Sevier, Ambrose H.: 28, 30, 64, 68, 80
Sevier County: 137, 157
Sharecrop system. See Farming
Sharp County: 90
Shawnee Indians. See Indian(s)
Sherman, William T.: 129
Shinn, Josiah H.: 204
Shreve, Henry M.: 38-39
Shreveport (Louisiana): 80, 127
Slater Fund: 275
Slavery: 12, 17; abolished, 144-145, 154; and
    admission of Arkansas, 30-31; attempt to
    eliminate or restrict, 26; divides churches,
    99; effects, 89; importance, 86, 89; issue,
    68, 113. See also Civil War; Farming;
    Negro(es)
Slavonians: 191
Slow Train Through Arkansaw, On a (book):
    212
Smackover: 248-249
Smith, Alfred E.: 269, 275
Smith, Edmund Kirby: 127, 129-130
Smith, Thomas: 158
Smith, Thomas A.: 60
Smith, Volney V.: 169, 171
Snagboats: 38-39
Snyder, John W.: 334
Socialist party: 253
Soil conservation program: 297-298. See also
    Conservation
"Solid South": 174
Somervell, Brehon B.: 301
Soulesbury College: 97
South America: 2, 80
South Carolina: 84, 331; secession, 113

158; planned, 94, 97, 101, 146, 150; school of medicine, 216, 281. See also Colleges and universities

Urban renewal: 305, 319

Utah: 82

Van Buren: 41, 72, 78, 82, 84, 91, 123, 137, 281, 323, 355

Van Buren County: 142

Van Buren, Martin: 66

Van Dorn, Earl: 120-121

Vicksburg (Mississippi): 126

Victorian houses: 351

"Victory gardens": 301

Villemont: 41

Virginia: 84, 115, 118-119

Vocational-technical schools. See Schools

Voting: interest in, 329; machines, 330; methods, 67; registration system, 67, 148, 164, 169, 330; requirements for, 67, 148, 150, 162, 164-165, 169, 178, 201, 231, 272, 330. See also Elections; Negro(es); Primaries

Wages and salaries, during depression: 294. See also Labor

Waldron: 145, 212

Walker, David: 115

Wall Street (New York City): 184

War Memorial Stadium (Little Rock): 319

War of 1812: 53

War, Revolutionary. See Revolution, American

Wars. See First World War, Korean War, Mexican War, etc.

Washburn, Cephas: 110; established Dwight Mission, 59

Washburn, Edward Payson: 110

Washington (Arkansas): 36, 41, 49, 76, 79-80, 128, 137, 212; bank, 72; land office, 55

Washington (D.C.): 31, 144, 146, 150, 167-168, 171, 176, 225, 272, 330, 333

Washington County: 78, 84, 86, 89, 94, 119; Osage claims eliminated, 56

Washington Telegraph. See Newspapers

"Washita". See Ouachita

Waterworks systems: 215, 297, 319

Weather bureau station: 215

Welfare, public: 339-340

West Indies: 8

West Memphis: 21, 305, 336

Western Company. See Mississippi Company

Wheel, Wheelers. See Agricultural Wheel

Whig party: 28, 31, 64-66, 68, 162, 174

Whiskey: 35, 78

White Citizens' Councils: 322

White County: 238

White, King: 167

White River: 3, 6, 10, 22, 34-35, 37-38, 42, 47, 58, 76, 88, 108, 122-123, 132, 137-138, 250, 316, 318

Wildlife: 291. See also Animals; Conservation

Wilkinson, James B.: 33

Wilshire, William W.: 167

Wilson's Creek, battle of. See Oak Hills, battle of

Wilson, Woodrow: 225, 253-254

Witchcraft: 35

Witness trees. See Land: surveying

"Wobblies". See Industrial Workers of the World

Wolf Creek (settlement): 33

Woman's Christian Temperance Union: 218, 229

Woman suffrage: 231

Woodmen of the World: 289

Woodruff, William E.: 42

Woodruff, William E. Jr.: 180

Workers, working class. See Farming; Labor

Working Class Union: 253

Workmen's compensation: 254, 312-313

Works Progress Administration (WPA): 297, 301, 330, 351, 353

World War, First. See First World War

World War, Second. See Second World War

Writers: 105-106, 108-109. See also Authors, Arkansas

Yankees: 118, 144

Yell, Archibald: 74, 80, 94

Yell County: 331; outlaws, 210; village of Chickalah, 209

Young Men's Christian Association: 265